UNDERSTANDING THE
COMMUNIST PARTY
OF CHINA

www.royalcollins.com

Edited by
XIE CHUNTAO

UNDERSTANDING THE

COMMUNIST

PARTY OF

CHINA

RC

Books Beyond Boundaries

ROYAL COLLINS

Understanding the Communist Party of China

Edited by Xie Chuntao
Translated by Feng Lei and Mark Law

First published in 2024 by Royal Collins Publishing Group Inc.
Groupe Publication Royal Collins Inc.
BKM Royalcollins Publishers Private Limited

Headquarters: 550-555 boul. René-Lévesque O Montréal (Québec) H2Z1B1 Canada
India office: 805 Hemkunt House, 8th Floor, Rajendra Place, New Delhi 110008

ISBN: 978-1-4878-1235-5

To find out more about our publications, please visit www.royalcollins.com.

Contents

— Part III —

— Part IV —

— PART I —

NEW DEMOCRATIC
REVOLUTION

CHAPTER I

In the Vast Land of China, Where Does the Path Lie?

China has a history and civilization that spans over 5,000 years, occupying a leading position in human history for a long time. Regrettably, the rulers of the Qing Dynasty grew arrogant and complacent during their golden age, turning China into an older man clinging to the past. At the same time, the West underwent the bourgeois revolution and the Industrial Revolution, with rapid technological advancements and thriving markets. Capitalism magically summoned unprecedented productive forces, which erupted and surged. A nation left behind is inevitably beaten, and a declining civilization leads to the demise of its people. While the Qing Dynasty's rulers indulged in dreams of the "Celestial Empire," expecting tribute from "all nations," they were instead met with the Western powers' ironclad ships and artillery, bringing disaster and the risk of national extinction.

The Crisis of National Extinction

As early as the 15th century, Western countries eager to find overseas resources and markets expanded outward, seeing China as a vast market. After a long probe, they finally found a breakthrough in the opium trade. The sinister opium trade caused a massive outflow of Chinese silver and severely damaged the Chinese people's physical and mental health. Thus, representatives of the anti-opium faction, led by Lin Zexu, submitted a petition to Emperor Daoguang, warning that if opium imports were not banned, "in a few decades, the Central Plains will have no soldiers to defend against enemies and no silver to replenish the treasury." In June 1839, Lin Zexu, as the Imperial Commissioner, confiscated and destroyed over 20,000 chests of opium from Britain, America, and other countries on the beaches of Humen.

However, Britain was unwilling to lose this rare opportunity for wealth. In 1840, Britain used the Qing government's opium ban as an excuse to launch the Opium War against China. Once the war broke out, China quickly suffered defeat and was forced to sign the first unequal treaty in modern history—*Sino-British Treaty of Nanjing*. This was followed by a dark period where foreign powers flocked to China, mounting one invasion after another and forcing the Qing government to sign unequal treaties. Through these treaties, Western powers extorted vast amounts of territory, indemnities, and special privileges from China, bringing deep disaster to the Chinese nation. From then on, China plunged into the abyss of a semi-colonial and semi-feudal society and entered a humiliating era where it was "butchered by others."

In modern times, nearly all capitalist powers participated in the invasion and plundering of China, with the Qing government suffering devastating defeats in each war. Every invasion resulted in the forcible occupation of Chinese territory. According to statistics, from 1840 to 1919, China signed over 900 unequal treaties, leading to the loss of rights and national humiliation. Through these treaties, foreign powers annexed vast tracts of Chinese territory, occupied concessions in China, forced the leasing of Chinese ports, and divided their respective spheres of influence within China. Under the oppression of these powers, China lost significant territory and sovereignty.

Through aggressive wars, foreign powers also exerted political control over China. An essential provision of the *Treaty of Tianjin*, signed after the Second Opium War, allowed foreign diplomats to live permanently in Beijing. At the time, Western diplomats were not ordinary diplomats but rather the "Grand Emperors" of the Qing government, issuing orders directly to the government. Furthermore, foreign powers manipulated China's domestic and foreign affairs and trampled on its sovereignty by exercising consular jurisdiction, customs administration, and diplomatic privileges.

Each invasion by Western powers involved economic extortion and the plundering of China. Eight unequal treaties, including the *Sino-British Treaty of Nanjing*, the *Treaty of Shimonoseki*, and the *Boxer Protocol*, demanded war indemnities totaling

1.953 billion taels of silver, equivalent to 16 times the Qing government's revenue in 1901. Japan alone extorted 230 million taels of silver through the *Treaty of Shimonoseki*, besides the massive amounts of ships, weapons, and materials looted. This amounted to 510 million yen, equivalent to Japan's fiscal revenue for four and a half years, quickly enabling Japan to become a world power.

Foreign powers exploited various privileges granted by unequal treaties, turning China into a market for their goods and a base for obtaining inexpensive raw materials. China's foreign trade experienced deficits in 1865, with the debt growing more extensive over time. Under the impact of foreign goods, China's handicraft textile industry, especially in the five treaty ports, suffered severe setbacks. After the signing of the *Treaty of Shimonoseki*, foreign powers accelerated the establishment of banks, construction of railways, mining, and factory investments in China, plundering the country through capital exports and gradually controlling China's economic lifeline. Under the invasion of foreign powers, an independent and sovereign China with the whole territory was shattered and scarred. At the same time, a vast and resource-rich China was left weak and impoverished, with the people struggling to survive.

While waging aggressive wars, Western powers also wantonly destroyed China's cultural relics and monuments, causing incalculable losses. During the Second Opium War, the British and French forces occupied Beijing, looting and burning the essence of China's imperial garden architecture—the Old Summer Palace (Yuanmingyuan). This palace and garden complex, which had been in operation for over a hundred years, combined Chinese and Western architectural styles and housed a collection of ancient and modern art masterpieces; it was reduced to ruins after burning for three days and nights. In 1900, during the invasion of the Eight-Nation Alliance, the invaders occupied Beijing again, causing another catastrophe for China and the destruction or looting of many precious historical relics.

In the eyes of Western colonizers, China was a land of ignorance that had not yet been enlightened. As a result, they conducted cultural infiltration activities under the guise of "charitable" religious activities and missionary work. Some used deceit, coercion, forced donations, low-price purchases, and land grabbing to occupy land, build churches, exploit tenants, and rent out properties. Some even monopolized lawsuits and harbored criminals among their converts, forced Chinese converts to abandon traditional customs and even openly interfered in China's internal affairs.

In addition, some Western scholars came to China for geological surveys under the guise of scientific investigations, intending to seize China's natural resources. Others visited historical sites in the name of archaeology, smuggling Chinese cultural relics abroad. The famous Dunhuang manuscripts were taken to the United Kingdom and France by Western sinologists Marc Aurel Stein and Paul Pelliot using deceptive means. Today, numerous Chinese cultural relics are housed in famous museums such as the British Museum in London, the Metropolitan Museum of Art in New York, and the Louvre Museum in France.

In summary, since the Opium Wars, China, a nation with a brilliant history and a long-standing position at the forefront of world civilization, was quickly plunged into a perilous situation of being preyed upon and carved up by both old and emerging powers.

However, along with the invasion of Western powers, the national consciousness and spirit of the Chinese people were awakened. Faced with the unprecedented upheaval of thousands of years, countless patriotic people devoted themselves to seeking solutions, launching a series of arduous explorations and struggles, and proposing various plans to save the nation.

Learn Advanced Western Technology to Resist the Invasion of Western Powers

During the Opium War, the most profound impression the Chinese had of the strangers appearing at their door was their advanced ships and powerful artillery. Faced with this gap, a group of thinkers advocating for learning Western advanced technology emerged among the ruling group of the Qing government, such as Lin Zexu, Wei Yuan, Gong Zizhen, and Xu Jishe. Lin Zexu was an early advocate of resisting alien invasion and learning from their advanced technologies. Before the Opium War, he had already focused on foreign affairs, sent people to investigate Western matters, translated Western books, and purchased Western newspapers. He compiled works such as *Sizhouzhi* (*The Encyclopedia of Geography*), *Huashi Yiyan* (*China: A General Description of That Empire and Its Inhabitants*), and *The Law of Nations*, providing people with much knowledge about politics, economics, military affairs, and the history of Western countries.

Like Lin Zexu, Wei Yuan was committed to exploring ways to save China. Based on *Sizhouzhi*, he collected and added both Chinese and foreign materials to create *Haiguotuzhi* (*Atlas and Description of the Countries beyond the Seas*). This was the first comprehensive work in modern China to introduce the West, covering various aspects such as geography, history, politics, military affairs, science and technology, religion, culture, education, and local customs. In this book, Wei Yuan summarized the lessons from the Opium War and proposed, "Learn advanced Western technology to resist the invasion of Western powers." This reflected the author's significant breakthrough in understanding the world's situation and updating his ideas, marking the beginning of a new trend in modern China to learn from the West.

Unfortunately, *Haiguotuzhi*, which carried Wei Yuan's dream of national rejuvenation, received little attention in Chinese society, with only around a thousand copies printed. Some people could not accept the "praise" for the "foreigners" in the book and even advocated burning it. In stark contrast, *Haiguotuzhi* became very popular in Japan, which also had its doors opened by foreign powers. The book significantly impacted the Meiji Restoration and became popular among many Japanese people. This contrast undoubtedly determined the differences in national strength and fate between China and Japan in the years to come.

After the Second Opium War, the Qing government suffered another devastating blow, and the Taiping Heavenly Kingdom Movement emerged. To maintain the crumbling order, some open-minded officials within the Qing government advocated learning advanced Western technologies within the "Chinese learning as the essence, Western learning for practical use." Representatives of this group included Yixin, Guiliang, and Wenxiang at the central level and Zeng Guofan, Li Hongzhang, Zuo Zongtang, Zhang Zhidong, and Sheng Xuanhuai at the local level. From the 1860s to the 1890s, they launched the Self-Strengthening Movement, which introduced advanced Western technologies, established modern military and civilian industries, trained a new-style army and navy, and developed modern education.

In 1861, Zeng Guofan founded the Anqing Arsenal, the earliest modern arms factory of the late Qing Dynasty and the first modern enterprise established by the Self-Strengthening Movement. In 1865, Zeng Guofan supported Li Hongzhang in establishing the Jiangnan Manufacturing Bureau in Shanghai. In the same year, Li Hongzhang also built the Jinling Machinery Manufacturing Bureau in Nanjing. In 1866, Zuo Zongtang founded the Mawei Shipbuilding Bureau in Fuzhou. In 1867, Wanyan Chonghou established the Tianjin Machinery Bureau. With military industries' development, civilian enterprises also appeared. In 1873, the China Merchants Steam Navigation Company was established in Shanghai. In 1878, the Kaiping Mining Bureau was established in Tangshan, and the same year, the Shanghai Mechanical Weaving Bureau was established. This gradually formed the four major

Western-style civilian industrial systems: coal and iron mining and smelting, textile industry, telegraphy, and steamship shipping.

At the same time, the Qing government established the Zongli Yamen in Beijing in 1861 as the central agency for managing Western affairs. The Tongwen Guan was established in 1862 to train translators, and the Guangfangyan Guan in Shanghai in 1863. To address the growing demands of the Self-Strengthening Movement and nurture fresh talent, the Qing government dispatched the inaugural group of young students to the United States for studies in 1872. In 1876, the Fujian Naval Academy also sent students to study in England and France. In 1875, the Qing government began planning for the Nanyang and Beiyang navies.

These measures for strengthening the nation and pursuing wealth objectively promoted the development of capitalism in China, increased national strength, and led to the so-called "Tongzhi Restoration." However, because the Self-Strengthening Movement adhered to the idea of "Chinese learning as the essence, Western learning for practical use," the goal was to achieve self-strengthening and wealth without changing the feudal system by transplanting Western modern production technology. As a result, the Self-Strengthening Movement inevitably carried strong feudal, decaying, and dependent characteristics of Western powers, which fundamentally restricted its further development.

Corruption in the Qing Dynasty's bureaucracy also severely eroded the Self-Strengthening Movement. In 1894, the total value of assets in the country's industrial, mining, transportation, and shipping industries reached 67.49 million taels, of which 70% were state-owned enterprises. State-owned enterprises brought bureaucratic practices into their operations, leading to low efficiency. More seriously, the Beiyang Navy was not immune, with large amounts of funding being diverted to construct the Summer Palace for Empress Dowager Cixi. On the other hand, Japan aimed to surpass the Beiyang Navy and vigorously expanded its military preparations. For this purpose, Emperor Meiji even allocated special funds from the imperial budget for coastal defense and personally initiated fundraising to construct warships.

The defeat in the Sino-Japanese War in 1894 marked the bankruptcy of the Self-Strengthening Movement. The collapse of this dream showed that in semi-colonial and semi-feudal China, it was impossible to achieve self-strengthening and wealth solely by introducing Western science and technology without fundamentally reforming the social system.

The Taiping Heavenly Kingdom and the Boxers

China has long been an agricultural country, with most of the population comprising peasants. In modern China, peasants are at the bottom of society, enduring heavy oppression. Therefore, their anti-imperialist and anti-feudal consciousness are sensitive, their attitudes resolute, and their actions direct.

In 1851, Hong Xiuquan launched the Taiping Heavenly Kingdom uprising in Jintian, Guangxi. This peasant uprising lasted for over a decade, sweeping across half of China and establishing a regime with Nanjing as its capital, forming a confrontation with the Qing government. The Taiping Heavenly Kingdom Movement was a response to China's social and political situation after the Opium War and a result of the intensifying social contradictions caused by foreign aggression and rotten feudal rule. After the Opium War, capitalist powers used their privileges to intensify their economic plunder, causing a great disaster for the Chinese people. The Qing government, to pay for the indemnity, intensified the exploitation of peasants, making their burden unbearable and class contradictions increasingly acute. The Taiping Heavenly Kingdom uprising brewed and broke out in such a background.

After the Taiping Heavenly Kingdom Movement rose, it defeated the Qing army and the "foreign gun teams" of Britain, the United States, and other countries several times. However, since the Taiping Heavenly Kingdom refused to recognize the *Treaty of Nanjing* and explicitly banned the opium trade, the disappointed Western aggressors turned to help the Qing Dynasty. A joint effort of domestic and foreign reactionary forces eventually suppressed the Taiping Heavenly Kingdom Movement.

The failure of the Taiping Heavenly Kingdom Movement was not only because of the strength of its enemies but also closely related to the limitations of the peasant class itself. The peasant class does not represent advanced productive forces and production relations, so they could not implement a correct revolutionary program or establish an advanced social system. Hong Xiuquan once combined Western Christian ideas with the traditional dreams of Chinese peasants and formulated and promulgated *The Land System of the Heavenly Kingdom*. He tried to establish an ideal society where "everyone has fields to cultivate, food to eat, clothes to wear, and money to spend, with no place uneven and no one cold or hungry." This reflected the peasants' strong desires for centuries. Still, under the production conditions at that time, such a beautiful wish could only be a fantasy that could only stay on paper and not be implemented. Later, Hong Rengan formulated the *A New Treatise on Political Counsel*, trying to develop capitalism and save the fate of the Chinese nation, but it also failed to materialize.

The failure of the Taiping Heavenly Kingdom Movement showed that in semi-colonial and semi-feudal China, the peasant class had a solid anti-imperialist and anti-feudal revolutionary nature and was the main force of the Chinese Revolution, however, a pure peasant war could not complete the dual historical tasks of anti-imperialism and anti-feudalism without the leadership of an advanced class and the guidance of scientific theories.

Around 1900, another large-scale peasant movement, the Boxer Movement, swept across North China. This movement was a spontaneous anti-imperialist patriotic movement with peasants as the main body, triggered by imperialist powers forcibly invading China's coastal ports, plundering resources and rights in the inland, and launching a frenzy of carving up China, resulting in an unprecedented crisis for the Chinese nation. The Boxer Movement was the climax of the nationwide struggle against foreign religions and aggression.

The Boxers initially advocated "anti-Qing and pro-Ming." Later, as national contradictions deepened, they turned to support the Qing government against the West, changing their slogan to "support the Qing and eliminate the foreigners." The Boxers bravely fought against the Eight-Nation Alliance, dealing a heavy blow to the imperialist ambitions to carve up China. However, the Boxer Movement failed under the joint suppression of the Eight-Nation Alliance and the Qing government.

The failure of the Boxer Movement was related to its loss of vigilance against the ruling Qing Dynasty. In particular, when the Qing government's policy toward the Boxers changed from "extermination" to "appeasement," they fell into the trap of being used and controlled, leading to their destruction by the joint efforts of domestic and foreign reactionary forces. Of course, the failure can also be attributed to the dual nature of the Boxer Movement, which possessed both progressive anti-aggression aspects and backward elements of defending feudal traditions. They harbored hostility toward Western while blindly worshipping tradition. They believed they could summon the gods, immortals, heroes, and other figures from Chinese mythology to protect them, rendering them invulnerable to foreign guns and cannons.

The failure of the Boxer Movement teaches us that in the semi-colonial and semi-feudal era, relying solely on the revolutionary struggle of the peasant class was not enough to achieve victory in the anti-imperialist and anti-feudal fight. The peasant class must form alliances with other classes, especially the working class, to create a united force for the Chinese nation to overthrow imperialist and feudal oppression.

From the Hundred Days' Reform to the Revolution of 1911

In the mid-19th century, China gradually became a semi-colonial and semi-feudal state. As foreign investment and modern industrial enterprises grew in the country, the national bourgeoisie began to rise. By the end of the 19th century and the beginning of the 20th century, the Chinese bourgeoisie emerged as a new force in history. They faced the dual oppression and exploitation of foreign imperialism and domestic feudalism, showing a revolutionary nature. However, their growth in the context of feudal society and the capitalist-dominated world system connected them to both feudalism and Western capitalism. This environment made them revolutionary but weak, ultimately unable to bear and complete the historical mission of the national democratic revolution.

After the Sino-Japanese War, China's international status declined sharply. The bourgeoisie and progressive intellectuals who grew up during the Self-Strengthening Movement made political demands. In April 1895, news of Japan's forced signing of the *Treaty of Shimonoseki* reached Beijing. Kang Youwei immediately mobilized over 1,300 provincial graduates taking exams in the capital to jointly submit a memorial to Emperor Guangxu, solemnly presenting the dire situation of the nation's crisis and proposing measures such as refusing the treaty, moving the capital, military training, and reforms. This marked the beginning of the Hundred Days' Reform. Subsequently, public opinion gradually formed to support the Hundred Days' Reform by establishing a series of newspapers, societies, schools, and political organizations and disseminating new ideas and concepts.

How could China change its fate of being carved up by foreign powers? The reformists believed that merely "learning advanced Western technology to resist the invasion of Western powers" was far from enough. China needed comprehensive reforms in politics, economics, culture, and education, particularly following the example of Japan's Meiji Restoration and implementing a constitutional monarchy. This was a bold attempt by the bourgeoisie to reform the feudal system, demonstrating that the reformists had a broader understanding of "reform" and "opening-up" than the Westernization School, displaying a more open-minded perspective.

Under the promotion of Kang Youwei and others, on June 11, 1898, Emperor Guangxu issued an imperial edict announcing the start of the reforms. Over 103 days, Guangxu issued over 110 edicts, covering fields such as the imperial examination system, industry, commerce, military, culture, and education, to perform comprehensive reforms. However, these new measures touched upon the vested interests of feudal conservatives and thus encountered strong opposition and obstruction from conservative factions. Moreover, Guangxu held little power in his hands. Eventually, the conservative coalition led by Empress Dowager Cixi staged a coup, placing Guangxu under house arrest at the Yingtai and executing reformists Tan Sitong, Lin Xu, Liu Guangdi, Yang Shenxiu, Kang Guangren, and Yang Rui, known as the "Six Gentlemen of the Hundred Days' Reform." The Hundred Days' Reform failed.

The failure of the Hundred Days' Reform demonstrated that trying to achieve a constitutional monarchy through reforms was akin to asking a tiger for its skin and was fundamentally impossible. Tan Sitong's poem before his execution, "Having the heart to kill the thieves, but no power to turn back the tide," became an accurate portrayal of the tragic fate of this reform movement that lacked a solid mass foundation.

Almost simultaneously with the formation of the bourgeois reformists, the bourgeois revolutionary faction, represented by Sun Yat-sen, also emerged on the historical stage. Sun Yat-sen once harbored reformist illusions and submitted reform proposals to Li Hongzhang in 1894, but they were not adopted. Harsh reality soon awakened him, and he firmly embarked on revolution. In November 1894, Sun Yat-sen founded the Revive China Society in Honolulu, setting its oath as "expel the Tartars, restore China, and establish a federal government." In 1905, the Revolutionary Alliance's program incorporated "expel the Tartars, restore China, establish a republic, and equalize land rights," thereby constructing the theoretical system of the Three Principles of the People. This allowed him to focus on national independence, democratic politics, and people's well-being as the purpose of the revolutionary struggle amidst the complex issues of modern Chinese society.

To achieve this goal, Sun Yat-sen tirelessly traveled among Chinese people at home and abroad, actively engaging in revolutionary publicity and organizing one uprising after another. Although these uprisings failed, the revolutionaries did not become disheartened or retreat. Instead, they became more resolute in their conviction and more inspired by their willingness to make sacrifices. Under the inspiration of these revolutionary martyrs' spirit of self-sacrifice, the Wuchang Uprising succeeded on October 10, 1911.

The Revolution of 1911 was the first bourgeois-democratic revolution against imperialism and feudalism in Chinese history. It overthrew the decaying rule of the Qing Dynasty, abolished the thousands-year-old autocratic monarchy, and established a bourgeois-democratic republic that had never existed in China. It ingrained the concept of democracy and republicanism in people's minds, struck against imperialist colonial rule, initiated a modern national democratic revolution in a broader sense, opened the gate of social progress, promoted people's intellectual liberation, and explored a path for the development and improvement of the Chinese nation.

However, due to the weakness of the Chinese bourgeoisie, who dared not propose a thorough patriotic movement against imperialism and feudalism revolutionary program, failed to mobilize the vast masses of peasants, and lacked a scientific revolutionary theory as guidance, the Nanjing Provisional Government existed for only three months before it collapsed. The Revolution of 1911 ended in a compromise with the old reactionary forces, and the fruits of the revolution fell into the hands of the Beiyang Warlords led by Yuan Shikai, who was supported by imperialism. China's semi-colonial and semi-feudal social nature did not change, and neither of the two major revolutionary tasks of anti-imperialism and anti-feudalism facing the Chinese nation was resolved. The Chinese still lived in the abyss of suffering marked by poverty, backwardness, division, turmoil, and chaos.

The failure of the Revolution of 1911 showed that in semi-colonial and semi-feudal China, victory against imperialism and feudalism could not be achieved solely by the bourgeois revolutionary faction. China's democratic revolution had to be led by a more advanced and thoroughgoing revolutionary class. In the vast land of China, where did the path lie?

CHAPTER 2

Saving the Nation and the People from Crisis

After the Opium War, China faced a crisis of national extinction. Various social classes sought a way out for the nation and its people. However, whether it was the Confucian scholars, the Self-Strengthening Movement, the Hundred Days' Reform, or the revolutionary faction, their proposals for saving the nation were about seeking the path to wealth and power from the West. These efforts ultimately failed to change the Chinese nation's humiliating status and people's miserable conditions. As Mao Zedong emphasized, "From the time of China's defeat in the Opium War of 1840, Chinese progressive went through untold hardships in their quest for truth from the Western countries … For quite a long time, those who had acquired the new learning felt confident that it would save China, but they could not make it work and were never able to realize their ideals. Their repeated struggles, including such a country-wide movement as the Revolution of 1911, all ended in failure. Day by day, conditions in the country got worse, and life was made impossible. Doubts arose, increased and deepened."

A Revolutionary Change

The Revolution of 1911 was the first time the monarchy was overthrown in Chinese history, and the Republic of China was established. However, it did not completely eradicate the deeply rooted feudal consciousness in people's minds. The restoration of Yuan Shikai and Zhang Xun exposed this. During this chaotic era, a group of progressive intellectuals realized that China's problems could not be solved merely by a political revolution; a more profound ideological revolution was needed to liberate the people from the shackles of feudal thought. The New Culture Movement emerged, focusing on deeper ideological enlightenment.

In 1915, Chen Duxiu founded the *Youth Magazine* (renamed *New Youth* the following year) in Shanghai, marking the beginning of the New Culture Movement. The movement advocated science over superstition, democracy over autocracy, and vernacular literature over classical literature. With the participation of well-known scholars like Li Dazhao, Hu Shi, Lu Xun, Liu Bannong, and Qian Xuantong, the movement formed a powerful momentum, impacting the old traditions with unprecedented intellectual strength and opening a new path for national salvation. However, Chen Duxiu and others soon discovered that Western bourgeois thought could not save China.

From 1914 to 1918, the First World War broke out in Europe. This unprecedented catastrophe in human history sharply exposed the inherent contradictions of the capitalist world. After the war, both victorious and defeated countries faced severe economic crises and serious unemployment, and class conflicts intensified, leading to revolutionary movements. The severe consequences of the First World War shocked more and more Chinese people and Western capitalist civilization's dazzling brilliance gradually faded in their eyes.

On May 4, 1919, due to the Paris Peace Conference's rejection of China's legitimate demands and the unconditional transfer of Germany's special rights in Shandong to Japan, outraged students from Beijing universities gathered near the Jinshui Bridge at Tiananmen Square, staging a protest and sparking the May Fourth Movement. The movement quickly spread nationwide, with various social forces taking action, including worker strikes, student boycotts, and merchant shutdowns. The whole of China was boiling, and the Chinese people were awakened.

As a victorious nation in the First World War, China suffered a humiliating diplomatic failure at the Paris Peace Conference. This event made people recognize the aggressive nature of imperialism and abandon their illusions about it. As the dream of capitalist civilization shattered, Chinese people became increasingly interested in socialism, greatly promoting its spread in China. Of course, the spread of socialism in China was not smooth. Numerous ideologies flooded into China around the May Fourth Movement, including Marxism and Experimentalism, Anarchism, the New Village Movement, Mutualism, Bernsteinism, Pan-laborism, Guild socialism, and National Socialism, creating a diverse and complex intellectual landscape.

As Chinese people stood at the crossroads of history, the October Revolution in Russia brought Marxism-Leninism to China. Li Dazhao was a pioneer in the spread of Marxism in China. In 1918, he published articles such as "A Comparative View of the French and Russian Revolutions," "The Victory of the Common People," and "The Victory of Bolshevism," enthusiastically praising the October Revolution and pointing out that the proletarian socialist revolution was the trend of world history. In 1919, Li Dazhao published "My Views on Marxism," systematically introducing the basic principles of Marxist historical materialism, political economy, and scientific socialism. Influenced by him and Chen Duxiu, a group of radical democrats, including Mao Zedong, Deng Zhongxia, Cai Hesen, and Zhou Enlai, gradually transformed into Marxists with preliminary Communist ideas.

As Marxism spread widely in China, progressive associations sprung up like bamboo shoots after the rain. These included Peking University's Marxist Studies Society, Shanghai's Marxist Research Association, Changsha's New People's Association, Tianjin's Awakening Society, Wuhan's Coexistence Society, and Jinan's Marxist Studies Society. They translated and published many Marxist works, creating conditions for progressive intellectuals to study and research Marxism, promoting its spread in China, and laying a solid ideological foundation for establishing the Communist Party of China (CPC).

At the same time, the class basis for the founding of the CPC gradually formed. After the Revolution of 1911, especially during the First World War, Western powers were preoccupied and temporarily relaxed their plundering of China. This alleviated the pressure on Chinese national capitalism and led to a rapid "golden age" of development. As the national capitalist economy developed rapidly, the ranks of the Chinese working class grew tremendously, gradually becoming a significant social force. Due to the imbalanced layout and structure of the modern industry, the Chinese working class was highly concentrated. Most were located in a few coastal provinces, large cities, and enterprises along water and land transportation routes. This high concentration made it easier for the working class to unite and organize, forming a powerful fighting force.

During this period, because of the increasing exploitation, the Chinese working class experienced continuous strikes that grew larger in scale. Strikes occurred in various locations, from northern cities such as Beijing, Tianjin, Dalian, and Harbin to southern cities like Shanghai, Suzhou, Wuxi, Hangzhou, Wuchang, and Anyuan. At the same time, the political nature of the strikes became increasingly pronounced, transforming from purely economic struggles to a patriotic movement against imperialism and feudalism. For example, the 1915 resistance against the *Twenty-One Demands* and the 1916 Tianjin workers' struggle against the French occupation of Old Xikai showed a significant increase in the political awareness of the working class.

Due to the vigorous development of the labor movement, some progressive intellectuals increasingly felt the immense power within it and began to embrace the idea of mobilizing workers to transform society. They started to leave their studies and propagate Marxism among the workers. Publications such as *Labor World*, *Labor Sound*, *Workers Weekly*, and *Labor and Women* were successively founded in various places. Using accessible language, they exposed the cruel nature of capitalist exploitation of workers, introduced the working class's living conditions and struggle experiences in different countries and regions, and promoted Marxism to the workers, promoting the integration of Marxism with the Chinese labor movement.

It was against this backdrop that the CPC was born. In July 1921, the First CPC National Congress was held in Shanghai, marking the official birth of the Party. The birth of the CPC was a historical inevitability in the development of modern Chinese society and an objective necessity for the development of the Chinese Revolution. It was the product of the combination of Marxism-Leninism with the Chinese labor movement. After a long period of exploration in the dark, the Chinese people finally found the path to save their country and nation from crisis—the path of socialism. History pushed the CPC to the center of the revolutionary stage, becoming the guide on this path. This was an earth-shaking event in Chinese history, and the face of the Chinese Revolution was transformed from then on.

Exploring a New Revolutionary Path

From its inception, the CPC shouldered the heavy responsibility of saving the nation and its people, leading them in a thorough anti-imperialist and anti-feudal democratic revolution. In this unprecedented revolution, the CPC quickly grew from its infancy, undergoing trial by fire repeatedly, constantly overcoming difficulties, and breaking through obstacles. The CPC carved out a revolutionary path with Chinese characteristics.

In July 1922, the Second CPC National Congress was held in Shanghai. Based on Lenin's theory on the question of nations and colonies and the exploration of the basic problems of the Chinese Revolution after the founding of the Party, the congress analyzed the international situation and the semi-colonial and semi-feudal nature of Chinese society, clarifying the nature, driving force, and target of the Chinese Revolution. It formulated the Party's minimum and maximum programs. The Party's minimum program, or the main tasks during the democratic revolution stage, were eliminating internal strife, overthrowing warlords, establishing domestic peace, overthrowing the oppression of international imperialism, achieving complete independence for the Chinese nation, and unifying China as a truly democratic republic. After creating the conditions, the Party would strive to achieve its maximum program: establishing a dictatorship of the proletariat and the peasantry, abolishing the private property system, and gradually achieving a Communist society. This congress was the first in modern Chinese history to clearly put forth a comprehensive anti-imperialist and anti-feudal democratic revolutionary program, pointing out the tasks and direction of the revolutionary struggle in the current stage for the Chinese people.

Although the CPC was still in its infancy at this time, this emerging Party possessed tremendous vitality and organizational strength. Its members had already immersed themselves in the grassroots labor masses, carrying out arduous mass work, organizing workers' night schools, establishing workers' clubs, and successively leading major strikes such as the Hong Kong Seamen's Strike, the Beijing–Hankou Railway Workers' Strike, and the Anyuan Coal Miners' Strike, ushering in the first climax of the labor movement. The rapid development of the labor movement alarmed the ruling class. On February 7, 1923, the warlord Wu Peifu brutally suppressed the strike along the Beijing–Hankou Railway. Communist Party members Lin Xiangqian and Shi Yang sacrificed their lives heroically. This bloody lesson taught the Chinese Communists that the power of the working class alone could not achieve revolutionary victory; it was necessary to unite all possible revolutionary classes and strata and organize a united revolutionary front.

At this time, Sun Yat-sen was also awakened by the sound of Chen Jiongming's betrayal and began to entertain the idea of uniting with the Soviet Union and the Communist Party. In January 1924, Sun Yat-sen presided over the First National Congress of the Kuomintang (KMT), reinterpreting the Three Principles of the People, highlighting the anti-imperialist content, advocating that democratic rights should be shared by ordinary people and not be privately owned by "a few," emphasizing that the essence of the people's livelihood principle was "equal distribution of land" and "regulation of capital," and improving people's lives. At the same time, the First Congress of the KMT decided to absorb many Communist Party members, even allowing them to hold important positions within the KMT. This laid a solid ideological and organizational foundation for the First United Front between the KMT and the CPC.

After the KMT and the CPC joined forces, the Nationalist Revolution achieved rapid development. In July 1926, the National Revolutionary Army set out on the Northern Expedition. Within less than a year, they defeated the main forces of Wu Peifu and Sun Chuanfang of the Beiyang Warlords, achieving initial success in the Great Revolution. With the successive victories of the Northern Expedition Army, the labor movement surged, and the peasant movement unfolded on an unprecedented scale.

Of course, during this period, the CPC was still in its infancy, lacking sufficient political and struggle experience. This led to the emergence of right-leaning mistakes represented by Chen Duxiu. Coupled with the erroneous judgments and remote commands of the Communist International, the CPC failed to seize the revolution's leadership and armed forces, and the fruits of the Great Revolution were usurped by the right-wing of the KMT represented by Chiang Kai-shek. On April 12, 1927, Chiang Kai-shek launched the April 12 Counterrevolutionary Coup in Shanghai, massively slaughtering CPC members, left-wing KMT members, and revolutionary masses. Under the bloody massacre of the enemy, countless CPC members and revolutionaries sacrificed their lives generously. The once-thriving worker-peasant movement was also suppressed, marking the first major setback encountered by the CPC since its establishment.

"However, the CPC and the Chinese people were not frightened, conquered, or annihilated. They got up from the ground, wiped the blood off their bodies, and buried the corpses of their comrades. Then, they continued to fight." On August 1, 1927, the Nanchang Uprising marked the birth of the People's Army and fired the first shot in the armed resistance against the reactionary forces of the KMT. At the August 7 Meeting, Mao Zedong asserted, "Political power comes from the barrel of a gun." The meeting eventually established the general policy of implementing land revolution and armed uprisings, pointing out a new path for the Party to move from defeat to a recent victory. Since then, many Chinese Communists represented by Mao Zedong, through the practice of establishing and developing the Red Army and rural revolutionary bases, broke away from the constraint of the "urban-centric theory" of the Communist International and gradually found a path to lead the Chinese Revolution to victory, namely, the path of armed domination of workers and peasants, the countryside surrounding the cities, and the armed seizure of power. Under the guidance of this revolutionary path with Chinese characteristics, the CPC established dozens of bases such as the Central, E-Yu-Wan, and Xiang-E-Xi, turning the sparks of the Chinese Revolution into a prairie fire and achieving a historical turning point from the failure of the Great Revolution to the rise of the Land Revolution War.

As the establishment and development of the bases and the continuous growth of the Red Army, the enemy panicked, leading to large-scale encirclement campaigns. From October 1930 to March 1933, under the command of Mao Zedong and Zhu De, the Central Base successively crushed the enemy's four encirclement campaigns. However, due to the enemy's exceptionally strong forces and a change in strategy and tactics, coupled with Wang Ming's "leftist" mistakes in the Central Soviet area, the fifth counter encirclement campaign ended in a tragic failure, forcing the main force of the Central Red Army to transfer strategically. The Central Soviet area fell, and other bases and revolutionary forces in the white areas suffered significant losses. The direction of the revolution and how to maximize the preservation of the vital revolutionary forces became a severe test facing the entire Party.

In January 1935, the Zunyi Conference, held at the most critical moment of the Chinese Revolution, independently resolved the organizational and military issues of the Party's central leadership, ended the rule of leftist errors, and began to establish the leadership position of the correct line represented by Mao Zedong in the Party's central leadership and the Red Army, saving the Party, the Red Army, and the Chinese Revolution under extremely critical circumstances. This was a life-and-death turning point in the history of the CPC. Afterward, under the command of Mao Zedong, the Red Army crossed the Chishui River four times, ingeniously crossed the Jinsha River, forcibly crossed the Dadu River, captured Luding Bridge, climbed over snowy mountains, and crossed grasslands. They broke through the encirclement, pursuit, and interception of hundreds of thousands of KMT troops and shattered Zhang Guotao's plot to split the central leadership. They successfully arrived in northern Shaanxi, ultimately completing an unprecedented strategic transfer in world military history and preserving the elite team of the CPC, which would lead to future success.

The Backbone of the National Resistance War

During the KMT's encirclement of the revolutionary bases, Japan intensified its aggression against China. On September 18, 1931, Japan staged the "September 18 Incident" in Shenyang. Under the influence of the KMT's "non-resistance" policy, the entire Northeast quickly fell. Within a month after the "September 18 Incident," the Central Committee of CPC issued four declarations, resolutions, and letters to the people, strongly condemning Japan's aggression and calling on the people of the whole country to rise urgently against Japan's barbaric invasion. On April 15, 1932, Mao Zedong, the Chairman of the Provisional Central Government of the Soviet Republic of China, issued a "Declaration of War against Japan," officially announcing the Soviet government's declaration of war on Japan and calling on the workers, peasants, soldiers, and all working masses to unite in a national revolutionary war to expel Japanese imperialism from China and strive for the independence and liberation of the Chinese nation.

Following the "September 18 Incident," the Central Committee of CPC immediately instructed the Manchuria Provincial Committee to mobilize and organize the masses, establish guerrilla units, open up guerrilla zones, and resist Japanese aggressors through armed struggle. Numerous cadres were also sent to the Northeast to join local anti-Japanese armed forces and form the Northeast Anti-Japanese United Army, persisting in a difficult 14-year resistance. A group of Communists, including Yang Jingyu, Zhao Shangzhi, and Zhao Yiman, shed their blood for China.

As Japan accelerated its aggression, how to save the nation from peril and unite as many forces as possible to wage a national war became the most critical issue for the CPC. The CPC, in line with the demands of the times and the deepening national crisis since the North China Incident and the spirit of the Seventh Congress of the Communist International, proposed the establishment of an Chinese united front against Japanese aggression. On August 1, 1935, the CPC drafted the "Letter to All Compatriots on the War of Resistance and National Salvation by the Chinese Soviet Government and the Central Committee of CPC" (the "August 1 Declaration"). The "August 1 Declaration" pointed out that the Chinese nation was at a critical juncture of life-and-death and resisting Japan and saving the country was the primary task for all Chinese people. The declaration called on all parties, armies, and people of all walks of life, regardless of past and present political views and interests or any hostile actions, to stop the civil war and concentrate all national strength on the struggle against

Japan. The declaration resonated strongly among all strata of society and effectively promoted the upsurge of the national salvation movement.

From December 17 to 25, 1935, the Central Committee of CPC held a Political Bureau meeting in Wayaobu. The meeting focused on the new changes in the national political situation, the Party's strategic line, and military strategy under the circumstances where the conflict between China and Japan gradually became the main contradiction. It formulated a comprehensive political line and strategic guidelines adapted to the new situation, established a new strategy for establishing the Chinese united front against Japanese aggression, and adjusted various specific policies accordingly.

Faced with Japan's increasing aggression, Chiang Kai-shek's attitude toward Japan also changed. Starting from the winter of 1935, the KMT secretly contacted the Central Committee of CPC in Shanghai, Nanjing, and Moscow. However, these negotiations did not yield results as Chiang Kai-shek lacked sincerity in uniting with the Communists against Japan. On December 12, 1936, patriotic KMT generals Zhang Xueliang and Yang Hucheng launched the Xi'an Incident, which shocked both China and the world, demanding Chiang Kai-shek stop the civil war and join forces against Japan. After the incident, the CPC, based on the greater good of the nation, put aside past grievances and determined to resolve the Xi'an Incident peacefully. When Chiang Kai-shek accepted the six conditions, including reorganizing the KMT and the National Government, releasing all political prisoners, stopping the "suppressing Communists" campaign, and uniting with the Red Army to resist against Japan, the Xi'an Incident was peacefully resolved. The peaceful resolution of the Xi'an Incident marked a turning point in the situation, and internal peace in China began to take shape.

In February 1937, the Central Committee of CPC sent a telegram to the KMT's third plenary session of the fifth Central Committee, offering four major concessions, including stopping armed uprisings against the National Government, halting land confiscation from landlords, changing the workers' and peasants' government into a special government of the Republic of China under the guidance of the Nanjing Central Government, and transforming the Red Army into the National Revolutionary Army under the guidance of the National Government's Military Commission. This helped the KMT's third plenary session of the fifth Central Committee pass a resolution accepting the Central Committee of CPC's proposal to "stop the civil war and unite against Japan." With this, the Chinese united front against Japanese aggression, based on the second cooperation between the KMT and the CPC, was initially established, leading to the climax of the resistance against Japanese aggression by the whole nation.

On July 7, 1937, the Lugou Bridge (Marco Polo Bridge) Incident occurred, marking the beginning of Japan's full-scale invasion of China. During this national crisis, the Central Committee of CPC reorganized the Red Army into the Eighth Route Army and the southern guerrilla forces into the New Fourth Army, which fought bravely against the Japanese forces behind enemy lines. In September 1937, the 115th Division of the Eighth Route Army achieved a major victory at the Battle of Pingxingguan, annihilating over 1,000 elite Japanese troops, destroying over 100 vehicles, and capturing numerous weapons, ammunition, and military supplies. This victory, the first major success for Chinese forces since the beginning of the national resistance, shattered the myth of Japanese invincibility and greatly boosted the confidence of the Chinese military and civilians. Subsequently, the 120th and 129th Divisions of the Eighth Route Army launched guerrilla attacks on transportation lines in the northern sections of the Tongpu and Zhengtai roads, cutting off enemy supply lines, capturing the Yanmenguan, and attacking the Japanese airfield at Yangmingbu, destroying 24 enemy aircrafts and assisting the KMT forces in the Battle of Xinkou.

After the fall of Taiyuan in November 1937, most of the KMT forces retreated to the areas south and west of the Yellow River. From then on, the regular war in North China, mainly led by the KMT forces, ended, and guerrilla warfare led by the CPC took center stage. The Eighth Route Army, following the instructions of the Central Committee of CPC and Mao Zedong, adhered to the strategic principle of protracted warfare, mobilized the masses extensively in the enemy's rear areas, and performed guerrilla warfare, successively establishing anti-Japanese bases in North China, such as Jin-Cha-Ji, Jin-Sui, Jin-Ji-Yu, and Shandong. The establishment of anti-Japanese bases and the opening of battlefields behind enemy lines effectively supported the resistance of the KMT forces on the frontlines during this stage, putting the Japanese forces in a difficult position on both fronts. This forced the Japanese to halt their strategic offensive, focusing their main forces on defending the occupied areas, which was an important condition for the transition of the War of Resistance against Japanese Aggression from strategic defense to strategic stalemate.

After entering the stalemate phase, the CPC led the anti-Japanese military and civilians behind enemy lines to continuously crush the enemy's encirclement and suppression while vigorously developing the people's army and liberated areas. From August to December 1940, the Eighth Route Army headquarters launched a large-scale offensive against Japan in North China, with more than 100 regiments and over 200,000 participants involved in the fighting. The Hundred-Regiments Campaign lasted for over three months, with 1,824 battles fought, more than 2,900 strongholds captured, over 2,000 kilometers of transportation lines destroyed, and over 25,000 Japanese soldiers killed or injured. This offensive severely damaged the Japanese forces' arrogance, greatly enhanced the prestige of the CPC and the Eighth Route Army, dispelled skepticism toward the CPC, and boosted national morale during the stagnant anti-Japanese resistance. By the end of 1940, the Eighth Route Army and the New Fourth Army had grown to about 500,000 soldiers, supported by numerous militias and local armed forces. Sixteen bases had been established in North China, Central China, and South China, in addition to the Shaan-Gan-Ning Border Region. The anti-Japanese bases led by the CPC had expanded to more than 100 million people, gradually becoming the main force in sustaining the resistance and striving for victory.

The Hundred-Regiments Campaign greatly alarmed the Japanese invaders, who believed that the crux of the security issue in North China lay with the CPC. Between 1941 and 1942, the Japanese army launched a frenzied "mop-up" campaign against the North China bases, implementing a "Three Alls" policy of "burn all, kill all, loot all," and even resorting to the use of poison gas and bacteriological warfare to create depopulated zones. Under the brutal onslaught of the Japanese forces, the casualties among the anti-Japanese military and civilians were significant, with many troops lost. By 1942, the Eighth Route Army and the New Fourth Army had been reduced from 500,000 to 400,000 soldiers, the area of the bases had shrunk, and the total population had dropped from over 100 million to below 50 million, marking the most difficult period of the War of Resistance against Japanese Aggression.

At this time, Chiang Kai-shek took advantage of the situation to provoke anti-Communist friction and cut off material supplies to the CPC. Despite the extremely difficult conditions, the military and civilians in the liberated areas persisted in their resistance, overcame numerous hardships, launched a large-scale production movement, and carried out counter-clearing, counter-mopping-up, and counter-harassment campaigns, consolidating the liberated areas and enduring the most challenging stage of the War of Resistance. In the battles against the Japanese and puppet forces, various bases developed diverse methods of annihilating the enemy, such as mine warfare, tunnel warfare, sparrow warfare, and raid warfare, compensating for the deficiencies in weapons and equipment and drowning the Japanese invaders in the vast ocean of people's war.

In early 1945, the military and civilians in the base areas launched extensive offensives against the Japanese and puppet forces. The people's army shifted from a highly dispersed state to a concentrated one, transforming from scattered guerrilla units to regular army corps. By April 1945, the Eighth Route Army, the New Fourth Army, and the South China Anti-Japanese Guerrilla Columns had grown to 910,000 soldiers, with around 2 million militias, establishing 19 large liberated areas. The area of the liberated zones had reached 950,000 square kilometers, with a population of 95.5 million. The army and base areas led by the CPC had become important for a major counteroffensive.

On August 9, 1945, Mao Zedong issued a statement on the "The Last Round with the Japanese Invaders." From August 11 to September 2, the various major forces in the base areas broke through the Ping-Han, Zhengtai, Tongpu, and Beining railway lines, essentially connecting the base areas and achieving a major victory in the full-scale counteroffensive.

During the War of Resistance against Japanese Aggression, the Eighth Route Army, the New Fourth Army, and the South China Anti-Japanese Guerrilla Columns fought guerrilla warfare with inferior weapons under extremely scarce material conditions. They fought more than 125,000 battles, annihilating over 527,000 Japanese soldiers. Along with the 170,000 enemy soldiers eliminated by the Northeast Anti-Japanese United Army, the total reached 700,000. Additionally, they wiped out 1.186 million puppet troops. The military and civilians behind enemy lines paid a huge price for this, with over 600,000 military casualties and more than 8.9 million civilian casualties. The heroic resistance of the military and civilians led by the CPC won widespread respect from people at home and abroad. At the same time, the battlefield behind enemy lines tied up many enemy forces, relieving the pressure on the frontlines and becoming an important factor in urging the KMT to fight to the end. This played a critical role in the persistence and ultimate victory of the War of Resistance against Japanese Aggression.

"Chinese People Have Since Stood Up"

In August 1945, Japan announced its unconditional surrender. After 14 years of bloody struggle, the Chinese people finally achieved victory in the War of Resistance against Japanese Aggression, ending a century of humiliation for the Chinese nation that began with the Opium Wars. However, after the victory, Chiang Kai-shek's KMT insisted on a dictatorship and civil war policy, while the CPC made every effort to strive for peace and democracy. Regardless of his personal safety, Mao Zedong resolutely went to Chongqing to negotiate with the KMT, eventually signing the *Summary of Conversations between the Representatives of the KMT and the CPC* (also known as the *October 10 Agreement*), winning the sympathy and support of the people across the country. In January 1946, the Political Consultative Conference opened. The CPC delegation closely cooperated with democratic parties to promote the conference to reach five agreements conducive to achieving peaceful nation-building.

Not long after, the KMT tore up the *October 10 Agreement* and the *Political Consultative Conference Agreement*, blatantly launching a civil war. At the beginning of the war, the KMT, relying on its abundant military strength and excellent equipment, launched a full-scale attack on the liberated areas. At that time, the KMT's total military strength reached 4.3 million, while the CPC's army was 1.27 million, with a ratio of 3.37 to 1 in terms of military strength. The gap in weapons and equipment between the two sides was even more pronounced. However, the CPC was not intimidated but was full of fighting spirit and confidence. In August 1946, Mao Zedong cheerfully told American journalist Anna Louise Strong, "All reactionaries are paper tigers. In appearance, the reactionaries are terrifying, but in reality, they are not so powerful. From a long-term point of view, it is not reactionaries but the people who are really powerful."

Under the strike of the flexible strategy and tactics of the People's Liberation Army (PLA), the KMT was forced to abandon its comprehensive attack plan and change to a focus on key attacks. Soon after, the key attacks were also crushed. In May 1947, the KMT's ace force, the Reorganized 74th Division, was wiped out in Menglianggu, Shandong, severely demoralizing the KMT army. Meanwhile, the PLA began to break through the enemy's blockade and switch to peripheral operations. In June 1947, Liu Bocheng and Deng Xiaoping led more than 100,000 troops from the main force of the Jin-Ji-Lu-Yu Field Army to force the Yellow River and leap into the Dabie Mountains, opening the prelude to the strategic offensive of the PLA; in August, Chen Geng and Xie Fuzhi led a part of the Jin-Ji-Lu-Yu Field Army with 80,000 troops to force the Yellow River and expand operations in the border regions of Henan and Shaanxi; in September, Chen Yi and Su Yu led the main force of 180,000 troops from the East China Field Army to cross the Yellow River, and by late November completed the strategic deployment in the border regions of Henan, Anhui, and Jiangsu. The three major forces plunged deep into the KMT-controlled areas, transferring the strategic initiative to the hands of the CPC. By the fall of 1948, although the KMT army still outnumbered the PLA, it had far surpassed its opponent in terms of morale and quality.

Mao Zedong and the Central Military Commission decisively implemented strategic battles after significantly changing the military power balance between the KMT and the CPC. From the end of 1948 to early 1949, the PLA successively launched the unprecedented scale of the Liaoshen, Huaihai, and Pingjin campaigns, achieving decisive victories. The three major campaigns lasted for more than four months, annihilating a total of 1.54 million enemy troops, and the KMT's main military forces that sustained their rule were basically destroyed. On April 20, 1949, the PLA launched the Yangtze River Crossing Campaign, and on the 23rd, they occupied Nanjing, declaring the collapse of the KMT's 22 years of reactionary rule.

As Chiang Kai-shek's rule teetered on the brink of collapse, the CPC began preparations to establish a new people's democratic government. After several months of careful preparation, on September 21, 1949, the first plenary session of the Chinese People's Political Consultative Conference (CPPCC) was inaugurated. In his opening speech, Mao Zedong boldly said, "The Chinese people, comprising one-quarter of humanity, have now stood up." On the 29th, the *Common Program of the Chinese People's Political Consultative Conference* (hereafter *Common Program*) was adopted. On the 30th, Mao Zedong was elected Chairman of the Central People's Government. On October 1, Mao Zedong stood on the Tiananmen Gate tower and announced to the world: "The Central People's Government of the People's Republic of China is established today!" This loud and clear voice was the first cry of the New China to the world. At that moment, the rising five-starred red flag symbolized the rejuvenation of ancient China with renewed vitality.

The founding of the People's Republic of China fulfilled the dreams of countless patriots since modern times to save the nation, achieved the leap from thousands of years of feudal autocracy to people's democracy, and completely ended the semi-colonial and semi-feudal society's history. It also put an end to the disunity of Old China. The Chinese people have since stood up, and the history of humiliation and being at the mercy of others is gone forever. The great rejuvenation of the Chinese nation has since entered a new historical era.

Chapter 3

Sincerely Solving People's Livelihood Issues

The CPC, to serve the people wholeheartedly, has taken solving people's livelihood issues as its mission since its birth. China is a major agricultural country, with peasants making up most of the population. However, for a long time, a large amount of land had been owned by feudal landlords. The existing feudal land system subjected most peasants to brutal exploitation and oppression by the landlord class, leaving them in extreme poverty. This was not only the economic foundation of the feudal autocracy but also the institutional obstacle to China's independence and prosperity. In leading the New Democratic Revolution against imperialism and feudalism, the CPC, through continuous efforts in different periods, finally solved this problem. Hundreds of millions of peasants were thus filled with immense revolutionary enthusiasm, becoming the strongest and most solid main force and ally. At the same time, the CPC implemented policies to protect national industry and commerce, united the national bourgeoisie, expanded the united front, and made them reliable allies in the revolution.

"The Chinese Revolution Is Essentially a Peasant Revolution"

Even before the founding of the CPC and at its early stage, the founders paid great attention to the peasant issue and began to explore ways to solve it. In 1919, Li Dazhao pointed out, "Our China is an agricultural country, and most of the working class are those peasants. If they are not liberated, it means that our entire nation is not liberated." In 1922, the Second CPC National Congress formulated the program of democratic revolution against imperialism and feudalism, emphasizing that "China's 300 million peasants are the most significant element in the revolutionary movement."

During the period of the Great Revolution, with the vigorous rise of the peasant movement, the CPC's understanding of the peasant issue developed further. In 1925, the Fourth CPC National Congress initially formed the idea that peasants were the allies of the working class. During this period, Mao Zedong gradually realized the importance of the peasant issue. In May and June 1926, he taught "The Chinese Peasant Issue" at the Sixth Peasant Movement Training Institute in Guangzhou, saying that "No one had studied the Chinese peasant issue before, from the times of King Wen, King Wu, and Duke of Zhou to the present schools. The failure of the Revolution of 1911 and the power falling into the hands of warlords were entirely due to the lack of support and endorsement from 320 million peasants. Only by mobilizing the peasants to participate in the revolution can the National Revolution succeed." Therefore, "China's National Revolution is a peasant revolution," and "the central issue of China's revolution is the peasant issue." In September of the same year, he further elaborated on this issue in his article "The National Revolution and the Peasant Movement," pointing out, "The peasant issue is the central issue of the National Revolution. Without the rise and support of the peasants in the National Revolution, the revolution would not succeed." In December of the same year, he emphasized at the First Workers and Peasants Representative Conference of Hunan Province, "The central issue of the National Revolution is the peasant issue. Everything depends on the solution to the peasant issue."

After the failure of the Great Revolution, the CPC shifted its revolutionary focus to rural areas, deeply mobilized farmers, and launched a vigorous land revolution, gaining the support of the vast majority of farmers. In 1936, Mao Zedong succinctly stated when answering a question from American journalist Edgar Snow, "Whoever wins the farmers will win China; whoever solves the land problem will win the farmers." During the War of Resistance against Japanese Aggression, he further elaborated on the importance of the peasant issue in articles such as "Chinese Revolution and

Chinese Communist Party" and "On New Democracy." He said, "The peasantry constitutes approximately 80 percent of China's total population and is the main force in her national economy today. The poor peasants are the biggest motive force of the Chinese Revolution, the natural and most reliable ally of the proletariat and the main contingent of China's revolutionary forces." Therefore, "the Chinese revolution is essentially a peasant revolution."

At the Seventh CPC National Congress in 1945, Mao Zedong made a more comprehensive exposition of the role of farmers. He emphasized that of the so-called masses, the most important part was the farmers, and the main force of the Chinese Democratic Revolution was the farmers. If we forget the farmers, there would be no Chinese Democratic Revolution; without the Chinese Democratic Revolution, there would be no Chinese Socialist Revolution and no other revolutions. We have read many Marxist books, but we must pay attention not to forget the term "farmers"; if we forget this, it is useless to read a million volumes of Marxist books because you have no strength.

It is precisely because of the profound understanding that the essence of China's revolution is the peasant revolution that the CPC has attached unprecedented importance to farmers' land issues, far more than any other political party in the past. They led a difficult, tortuous, and magnificent struggle to abolish the feudal land system in China's vast rural areas, acquiring active support from the farmers. In stark contrast, the KMT never managed to put Sun Yat-sen's "equal land rights" into practice and was eventually abandoned by most farmers. On the eve of the KMT government's retreat to Taiwan, the *New York Herald Tribune* commented, "The KMT ruled for 20 years without implementing Sun Yat-sen's principles. ... The CPC did indeed practice land reform to liberate China's oppressed farmers. They didn't just talk about rent and tax rates, but actually did something about it."

Overthrow Landlords, Distribute Land, and Reduce Rent and Interest

Under different historical conditions, the CPC led farmers in a great attempt at land revolution and formulated land policies that suited the actual situation of the Chinese Revolution, consolidating and developing the worker-peasant alliance.

First, during the period of the Land Revolution War, they fought against landlords and distributed land. After the failure of the Great Revolution in 1927, the August

7 Meeting of the CPC determined the general guideline of the land revolution and armed resistance against the reactionary KMT, proposing to "confiscate the land of large and middle landlords and distribute it to tenant farmers and landless peasants." However, by November, under the influence of left-wing impetuousness, the expanded meeting of the Central Committee of CPC's Temporary Political Bureau decided to confiscate all land to be publicly owned by the laboring people of the Soviet state. This essentially advocated for "state ownership of land," with farmers only enjoying the right to use it.

The Sixth CPC National Congress in July 1928 was a turning point in the Party's land policy. The meeting decided to change the confiscation of all land to the confiscation of all land belonging to the landlord class. It emphasized the correct treatment of rich peasants, believing that the "main enemy is the gentry and landlords" and that "deliberately intensifying the struggle against rich peasants is wrong." These policies were more in line with China's actual situation and greatly promoted the land revolution, with various places quickly experiencing the scene of "busy dividing land and fields." However, the Sixth CPC National Congress still stipulated "state ownership of land," and farmers only had usage rights, which clearly could not satisfy the peasants' desire for land.

In response to this issue, the Soviet Central Bureau issued a notice on February 8, 1931, stating that peasants "enthusiastically participated in the land revolution not only to obtain the right to use the land but mainly to obtain land ownership." Therefore, "the vast number of peasants must obtain the land ownership they long for in the revolution to enhance their enthusiasm for the land revolution and the victory of the Soviet regime nationwide." On February 27, Mao Zedong also wrote a letter to the Jiangxi Soviet Government in the name of the Director of the General Political Department of the Central Revolutionary Military Commission, explicitly stating, "In the past, the atmosphere was strong that the land belonged to the Soviet and the peasants only had the right to use it. The land was divided four or five times, making the peasants feel that it was not their own and that they had no right to control it. Therefore, they did not feel secure in farming, which was not good. The Provincial Committee should order governments at all levels to urge farmers to cultivate the land, and the order should make it clear that the previously divided land (implemented by taking more from the rich and giving to the poor, taking from the fertile and giving to the thin) is considered stable. The person who gets the land will manage the newly divided land, which will be privately owned by him and not violated by others." Under the guidance of these ideas, the Jiangxi Soviet Government issued a statement on March 15, officially announcing that "once the land is divided, the right to use and ownership of the land belongs entirely to the peasants." This corrected the unrealistic slogan of "state ownership of land" in the past and was conducive to the implementation of the land revolution.

After more than three years of land revolution practice, the CPC basically formed a set of feasible land revolution lines, guidelines, and policies, which relied on poor peasants, united middle peasants, restricted rich peasants, and eliminated the landlord class, changing feudal land ownership to peasant land ownership. Land was distributed per capita at the township level, and adjustments were made based on original cultivated land, with excess land being taken from the rich and given to the poor and fertile land being taken from the rich and given to the less fertile. This greatly inspired the revolutionary enthusiasm of the vast number of peasants and provided strong support for the construction and development of base areas. Liu Shaoqi later said, "In the past, the Central Soviet Area had only more than two million people, but a few counties thoroughly implemented land reform, which supported many years of war and resisted Chiang Kai-shek."

However, the land revolution policy soon encountered setbacks due to the rise of the left-leaning Wang Ming line in the fourth plenary session of the sixth Central Committee. In November 1931, the Central Committee of CPC wrote to the Soviet Central Bureau, proposing that "the landlord class must be completely eliminated, and they and their families must not be allowed to distribute land or rent land. All rich peasant land must be confiscated, and only when they cultivate it themselves can they be given poor land." This so-called "no land distribution for landlords, bad land distribution for rich peasants" and the attempt to physically eliminate landlords and not give rich peasants an economical way out forced many of them to take desperate measures or join the enemy. At the same time, the land revolution during this period also infringed upon the interests of middle peasants, seriously endangering the social stability and production development of the base areas. In October 1934, the failure of the fifth counter-encirclement campaign led to the complete loss of the land revolution achievements in the Central Soviet Area, providing lessons for the later formulation of land policies that peasants widely welcomed.

The second stage was the rent and interest reduction during the War of Resistance period. After the "July 7 Incident," the contradiction between China and Japan took precedence over class contradictions. To unite more people against Japan, the CPC changed its policy of confiscating landlord land and distributing it to peasants and instead implemented a land policy that met the needs of the Chinese united front against Japanese aggression, namely rent and interest reduction. On the one hand, it required landlords to reduce rent and interest, improve the lives of peasants, and mobilize their enthusiasm for anti-Japanese and production; on the other hand, it required peasants to pay rent and interest after the reduction, taking care of the interests of landlords, and striving to unite them on the anti-Japanese side.

During the War of Resistance, various base areas generally implemented extensive and in-depth rent and interest reduction policies, achieving remarkable results. First, it achieved an initial land system reform, changing the rural land occupation situation and class structure. The feudal land system in the resistance base was weakened, and the individual peasant economy developed. Second, it mobilized the enthusiasm for production of people from all walks of life, promoting the recovery and development of the base area economy. Third, it mobilized and organized peasants, breaking the autocratic rule of landlords, establishing the political dominance of the basic masses of poor, hired, and middle peasants, fundamentally changing the relationship between the ruler and the ruled among landlords and peasants, and cultivating many grassroots cadres rooted in the masses in rural areas. Fourth, it consolidated and developed the Chinese united front against Japanese aggression, supporting a protracted War of Resistance. Fifth, implementing rent and interest reduction policies laid the foundation for erasing the feudal land system and resolving the peasant land issue in the future. It provided rich experience and created favorable historical prerequisites and conditions.

During this period, in addition to rent and interest reduction, various resistance base also launched large-scale production movements to address livelihood issues. After 1940, the resistance base fell into severe economic difficulties due to the frenzied sweeps of the Japanese invaders and the KMT's suspension of supplies and economic blockades. As Mao Zedong said, "The greatest difficulty was in 1940 and 1941, during the two anti-Communist frictions of the KMT, both of which occurred during this period. We once had almost no clothes, no oil to eat, no paper, no vegetables, soldiers without socks, and workers without blankets in winter. The KMT tried to starve us to death with the suspension of funding and economic blockade, and our difficulties were extreme." To overcome these difficulties, ease the burden on the peasants in the border regions, and ride out the crisis, various resistance base launched a vigorous large-scale production movement.

The large-scale production movement played an extremely important role in helping the various resistance base overcome severe economic difficulties and persist in the War of Resistance. It not only greatly improved the living conditions of institutions and troops, but more importantly, it eased the burden on the people in the base areas and strengthened our engagement with the people. On this, Mao Zedong once said, "Since the institutions, troops, and schools have resolved all or most of their material problems on their own, the portion taken from the people through taxation is reduced, and the portion of the results of the people's production that they can enjoy for themselves has increased."

The Fierce Land Reform

After winning the War of Resistance, Chiang Kai-shek of the KMT soon launched a full-scale civil war. Under these circumstances, where class contradictions were sharply intensified, the previous rent and interest reduction boundaries were constantly broken by the strong land demands of the peasants and the changes in the domestic political situation. To adapt to the new situation and the needs of the war, in May 1946, Mao Zedong proposed at the Yan'an Land Conference, "If the land issue can be resolved among hundreds of millions of people, the struggle can be supported for a long time without fatigue." Therefore, "solving the land issue is a fundamental issue, the basic link of all work, and the whole Party must realize this point." In October of the same year, he pointed out that since the promulgation of the "May 4 Directive," "wherever the land issue has been deeply and thoroughly resolved, the peasants have joined our Party and our army in opposing the attack of the Chiang army."

Under the new circumstances, the CPC timely changed the content and method of solving the land issue step by step. It gradually formed a set of policies to abolish the feudal land system completely and eventually formed a general land reform route, that is, to rely on poor and hired farmers, unite middle farmers, be neutral toward rich farmers, and, step by step, eliminate the feudal exploitation system and develop agricultural production. Under the guidance of this route, the Land Reform Movement in the liberated areas achieved in-depth development. By the second half of 1948, about 100 million peasants in the liberated areas had received land. With the force of a thousand thunderbolts, the fierce land Reform Movement fiercely attacked the feudal land system that had lasted for thousands of years. Especially in the old and semi-old areas with a population of 100 million, the feudal land system was basically eliminated, shattering the feudal shackles that had been on the peasants for thousands of years, changing the old production relations in the countryside, and enabling poor and employed peasants to basically obtain land and other production and living materials at an average level.

In 1948, an American named Harrison Forman, who taught at North China University in the Jin-Ji-Lu-Yu liberated area, participated in the land reform in Lucheng County, Shanxi Province, as an observer. Based on this experience, he later wrote *China's Turnabout: A Revolutionary Chronicle of a Village*. In the book's opening, he wrote, "The Chinese Revolution created a whole new vocabulary, and one important word is 'turnabout' ... For hundreds of millions of landless and small landholding peasants across the country, this meant standing up, breaking the shackles of landlords, and obtaining land, livestock, farm tools, and houses. But its significance goes far beyond that. It also means breaking superstition and learning science; eliminating illiteracy and becoming literate; no longer treating women as property of men but establishing equal relations between men and women; abolishing the appointment of village officials and replacing them with elected rural government institutions. In short, it means entering a new world."

Undoubtedly, the land reform brought about these earth-shaking changes, liberating hundreds of millions of peasants politically and economically and thereby unleashing immeasurable revolutionary enthusiasm, providing continuous human and material support for the War of Liberation. On this point, even the KMT side realized, "The CPC's promotion of rent reduction and land redistribution movement deeply meets the peasants' demands ... Hence, they can widely mobilize peasants to be driven by them and serve them."

In the land reform, hundreds of millions of peasants obtained land, food, and houses. To defend the fruits of their emancipation, they launched a massive wave of enlistment under the slogan "defend the land and join the army." The People's Army, composed of emancipated peasants, was numerous and of high quality, as they were clear about the purpose of fighting. These new soldiers cared about politics and the construction of the troops, had high-class consciousness, had great sympathy for the unemancipated peasants in the newly liberated areas, and were determined to help them achieve complete liberation, thus fighting bravely and often sacrificing themselves without hesitation.

To protect their homes and fields, the emancipated peasants eagerly supported the frontlines under extremely difficult conditions, undertaking a huge amount of war-time service and providing their fellow soldiers with supplies such as grain, forage, and clothing, fully ensuring the material supply and various needs of the People's Liberation Army. During the Huaihai Campaign, five provinces of Jiangsu, Shandong, Henan, Anhui, and Hebei mobilized 220,000 accompanying civilian workers, 1.31 million second-line transport civilian workers, and 3.91 million rear temporary civilian workers, transporting a total of 110,000 wounded, 570 million *jin* (1 *jin* = 0.5 kg) of grain, and 3.3 million tons of ammunition and materials. These civilian workers' wartime services also included digging trenches, erecting wires, repairing transportation lines, clearing battlefields, and transporting captured materials. As a result, Chen Yi once said, "The people's hand carts pushed out the victory of the Huaihai Campaign." Mao Zedong also explicitly pointed out, "These 160 million people mainly won Our War of Liberation. Only with the victory of land reform could we achieve the victory of overthrowing Chiang Kai-shek."

Protecting National Industry and Commerce

In modern Chinese capitalist enterprises, domestic capital is divided into two parts, bureaucratic comprador capital, and national capital, which are differentiated into two classes: the bureaucratic comprador bourgeoisie and the national bourgeoisie. These two classes often infiltrate and transform into each other, but their nature is different. Their attitudes toward the revolution also differ because of the different production relations they represent.

Bureaucratic comprador capital exists as a vassal of imperialist monopoly capital. After the Revolution of 1911, the development of bureaucratic capitalism accelerated. After the KMT took control of the whole country, the bureaucratic comprador bourgeoisie gained control of the national government. They monopolized the economic lifelines of the country and further expanded bureaucratic capital through a series of illegal activities, such as issuing legal currency and domestic debts for speculation, severely hindering the development of productive social forces.

National capital refers to small and medium-scale capital in the Chinese capitalist economy, which has less connection with imperialist forces. After the Revolution of 1911, the provisional government of Nanjing issued decrees to encourage the development of industries. Due to the First World War, the capitalist powers were preoccupied. Along with the rising status of the national bourgeoisie, national capitalism experienced a brief period of prosperity, with an unprecedented boom in the establishment of industries. However, after the end of the First World War, imperialism returned, and due to the dual oppression of imperialism and bureaucratic capitalism, the development of national capitalism encountered great obstacles. This determined that the national bourgeoisie had significant weaknesses, often compromising with imperialism and the big bourgeoisie, but also had a certain revolutionary potential. After being won over, they could become allies of the revolution.

However, on this issue, the CPC's understanding went through a tortuous process. During the Great Revolution, Chen Duxiu overestimated the revolutionary nature of the national bourgeoisie and overlooked its weakness, resulting in the "two-stage revolution theory." This theory believed the Nationalist Revolution should be led by the national bourgeoisie, establishing a bourgeois dictatorship. Only when production developed, and the contradiction between the proletariat and the bourgeoisie sharpened would a socialist revolution be carried out. Under this theoretical guidance, the Party only united with the bourgeoisie without struggle, compromising and conceding everywhere, even voluntarily giving up the leadership of arms, political power, and land revolution, making rightist mistakes and eventually leading to the failure of the Great Revolution.

In the early period of the Land Revolution War, the CPC accepted Stalin and the Communist International's judgment, as the national bourgeoisie had echoed Chiang Kai-shek's regime's betrayal of the revolution. The Party indiscriminately treated the entire bourgeoisie as a revolutionary target, even seeing the national bourgeoisie as the most dangerous enemy, without recognizing the changes in the political attitude of the national bourgeoisie after the "September 18 Incident." This "leftist" closed-door policy led to serious deviations in the Party's general line and eventually hindered the progress of the Land Revolution War. However, during this period, Mao Zedong and others also explored the economic composition of the revolutionary base, suggesting that "for the private economy, as long as it does not go beyond the scope of government laws, it should not only be unobstructed but also encouraged and rewarded. Because the development of the private economy is needed for the interests of the country and the people, the private economy, undoubtedly, currently holds an absolute advantage and will continue to do so for a considerable time." This new understanding, which emerged in practice, laid the foundation for the later formation of the New Democracy theory.

During the War of Resistance, as Mao Zedong's New Democracy theory took shape, the CPC's understanding of the national bourgeoisie gradually matured. In 1940, Mao Zedong outlined the blueprint for a New Democratic Society in "On

New Democracy." He pointed out that the basic program of New Democracy was, politically, to establish a democratic republic under the joint dictatorship of all anti-imperialist and anti-feudal people led by the proletariat, that is, a new-democratic republic. Economically, "the republic will neither confiscate capitalist private property in general nor forbid the development of such capitalist production as does not 'dominate the livelihood of the people.'"

In 1945, Mao Zedong further elaborated on the theory of New Democratic society at the Seventh CPC National Congress. In his report "On Coalition Government," he repeatedly emphasized the development of capitalism. He stated, "Some people suspect that the Chinese Communists are opposed to the development of individual initiative, the growth of private capital and the protection of private property, but they are mistaken. It is foreign oppression and feudal oppression that cruelly fetter the development of the individual initiative of the Chinese people, hamper the growth of private capital and destroy the property of the people. It is the very task of the New Democracy we advocate to remove these fetters and stop this destruction, to guarantee that the people can freely develop their individuality within the framework of society and freely develop such private capitalist economy as will benefit and not 'dominate the livelihood of the people,' and to protect all appropriate forms of private property." He also stated, "Some people fail to understand why, so far from fearing capitalism, Communists should advocate its development in certain given conditions. Our answer is simple. The substitution of a certain degree of capitalist development for the oppression of foreign imperialism and domestic feudalism is not only an advance but an unavoidable process. It benefits the proletariat as well as the bourgeoisie and the former perhaps more. It is not domestic capitalism but foreign imperialism and domestic feudalism which are superfluous in China today; indeed, we have too little of capitalism." Mao also proposed, "From our knowledge of the Marxist laws of social development, we Communists clearly understand that under the state system of New Democracy in China, it will be necessary in the interests of social progress to facilitate the development of the private capitalist sector of the economy (provided it does not dominate the livelihood of the people) besides the development of the state sector and of the individual and co-operative sectors run by the labouring people." In his *Explanation of "On Coalition Government"* at the Seventh Congress, Mao specifically emphasized that this report, unlike "On New Democracy," confirmed the need for the extensive development of capitalism and that "the extensive development of capitalism under the New Democratic government is harmless and beneficial."

The significant proposal to protect national industry and commerce caused a strong societal reaction. Tang Zong, the head of Chiang Kai-shek's attendant office, once recorded in his diary: "At the Seventh Congress, Mao Zedong's political report advocated maintaining private property system and developing capitalism, which was a significant change for the CPC. This change had a substantial impact in China, as many industrial and commercial circles in the rear and disenchanted members within the KMT, who previously feared the CPC, completely changed their views." This demonstrates the immense influence of this policy.

Chapter 4

Implementing True People's Democracy

In 1940, Xie Juezai, one of the "Five Elders" of the CPC, Secretary-General of the Shaan-Gan-Ning Border Region Government, and Vice-Chairman of the Border Region Council, proudly wrote in an article: "Why do progressive people from all over the country flood into the border region like a tide? Because the border region has democracy. Why do progressive people around the world praise the border region, saying that if they haven't been to Yan'an, they haven't been to China? Because the border region has democracy. Why has the border region's progress in culture, economy, and military mobilization since the beginning of the War of Resistance surpassed the rest of the country? Because the border region has democracy." His words aptly unraveled the mystery of the continuous growth and development of the CPC. It was precisely because of the implementation of true people's democracy that the appeal of the CPC was greatly enhanced, gaining more support.

"Democracy Is the Guarantee of Resistance against Japan"

Opposing imperialism and feudalism were the two main tasks of the New Democratic Revolution, and the CPC had long regarded them as its sacred mission. Especially during the War of Resistance, the CPC combined the two, finding a path to drive out the Japanese invaders from China and end the dictatorial rule of the KMT, with democracy being the key link.

In May 1937, Mao Zedong explicitly proposed at the National Representatives Conference of CPC: "To establish a truly solid Chinese united front against Japanese aggression, not only is domestic peace necessary, but so is domestic democracy. Therefore, striving for democracy is the central link in the revolutionary tasks of the current development stage." "For the task of resistance against Japan, democracy is also the essential element in the new stage, and fighting for democracy is resisting against Japan. Resistance against Japan and democracy are interdependent, just as resistance against Japan and peace, and democracy and peace are interdependent. Democracy is the guarantee of resistance against Japan."

Shortly after the outbreak of the Lugou Bridge Incident, Mao Zedong made it clear in the draft outline for publicity and mobilization on the situation and tasks for the Central Publicity Department of the CPC: "Without democracy, the War of Resistance cannot be won." "The struggle for victory in the War of Resistance and the realization of democratic rights are not separate, but rather interconnected and interdependent." Based on this principle, the Central Committee of CPC formulated the *Ten-Point Program for Anti-Japanese National Salvation*, calling for a comprehensive War of Resistance, which was adopted at the Luochuan Conference and became the programmatic document guiding the War of Resistance by the CPC.

In addition to emphasizing the importance of democracy in the War of Resistance within the Party, Mao Zedong repeatedly clarified this point to the outside world. In February 1938, he told United Press correspondent Robert Martin that China needed democracy to persist in the resistance war. In July of the same year, a World Students' Federation delegation visited Yan'an. They asked, "What is the significance and role of the Shaanxi-Gansu-Ningxia Border Region in China?" Mao Zedong first answered, "Understanding the nature of the border region is essential to understanding its significance and role in China. What kind of place is the border region? In a word, it is a democratic resistance base."

In September 1939, Mao Zedong told visiting American journalist Edgar Snow again, "There is no doubt that resistance against Japan without democracy cannot be victorious. Resistance against Japan and democracy are two aspects of the same issue. Some people support resistance against Japan but oppose democracy; such people, in fact, are unwilling to see victory in the War of Resistance and are leading it to failure." This was obviously a criticism of the undemocratic KMT. In February of the following year, a constitution promotion meeting was held in Yan'an, and Mao Zedong said at the meeting, "Resistance against Japan is something everyone agrees on, and it has already been done. The question is persistence. However, there is another thing called democracy that has not yet been done. These two things are the most important issues in China at present. China is short of many things, but the main shortage is two things: one is independence, and the other is democracy. Suppose one of these two things is lacking. In that case, China's affairs cannot be handled well." Therefore, it is necessary to "combine independence and democracy, which means democratic resistance against Japan, or anti-Japanese democracy. Without democracy, resistance against Japan is bound to fail. Without democracy, resistance against Japan cannot be sustained."

In June 1944, a group of Chinese and foreign journalists broke through the KMT blockade to visit Yan'an. Mao Zedong also elaborated on the relationship between resistance and democracy. He emphasized, "China has shortcomings, and they are significant ones. In a word, these shortcomings are the lack of democracy. The Chinese people desperately need democracy because only with democracy can the War of Resistance be powerful. Only then can China's internal relations be put on the right track, achieve victory in the War of Resistance, and build a good country." In July of the following year, six National People's Political Consultative Conference representatives, including Huang Yanpei, visited Yan'an. In a conversation, he said to Mao Zedong, "I have lived for over sixty years, and I have seen it with my own eyes: the rise and fall of individuals, families, organizations, regions, and even countries, many units cannot escape the control of this cyclical rate ... I have a rough understanding of the CPC from the past to the present. I hope to find a new path to break free from this cyclical control." Mao Zedong confidently replied, "We have already found a new path and can break free from this cycle. This new path is democracy. Only by allowing the people to supervise the government can the government avoid slackening. Only when everyone takes responsibility can the government avoid collapse when people pass away."

It is evident that during the War of Resistance against Japanese Aggression, Mao Zedong attached great importance to democracy. He repeatedly emphasized it within the Party and declared it to the outside world, linking democracy with anti-Japanese resistance and integrating them as one, emphasizing that "democracy is the guarantee of anti-Japanese resistance." He also regarded it as the institutional guarantee for establishing New China after the war and breaking free from the historical cycle. This understanding reflects the CPC's strong aspiration for democratic politics.

In contrast, the KMT repeatedly used the War of Resistance as an excuse to oppose democracy during this period. In January 1938, KMT theorist Ye Qing emphasized in his article "On Democratic Politics" that the most urgent requirements of the War of Resistance were "unifying the army" and "unifying the will." Even European democratic countries were under control during the First World War, so he thought it was absurd for Chinese people to demand democracy during the War of Resistance. In May of the same year, he proposed the slogan of "seven ones" in the article "The Fundamental Belief in the Era of Resistance": one country, one government, one party, one doctrine, one policy, one program, and one leader, blatantly advocating authoritarianism.

From the perspective of public reaction, the CPC's passionate appeal for democracy undoubtedly met the needs of the War of Resistance and the trend of the times. Especially in September 1944, at the third session of the third National Political Council, the CPC formally proposed ending the one-party dictatorship of the KMT and establishing a coalition government. This caused a strong response and received widespread domestic and international public opinion support. Mao Zedong later said, "The coalition government is a concrete program, the specific form of the united front government. It took a long time to develop this slogan, which shows the difficulty of finding a slogan and a form … When this slogan was proposed, our comrades in Chongqing felt like they had found a treasure. I didn't expect the people to support it so widely." However, Tang Zong, a senior staff member close to Chiang Kai-shek, realized that the CPC "wants to use this slogan to call on various dissatisfied parties to seize power from the KMT jointly. The coalition government is a means to disintegrate the National Government."

The "Bean Election" in the Liberated Areas

The CPC not only called for democracy in words but also actively put it into practice, especially in the widespread implementation of democratic elections. In January 1941, the Shaanxi-Gansu-Ningxia Border Region Government issued a directive emphasizing that "democratic politics is the first priority in elections." In February 1939, the First Session of the Shaanxi-Gansu-Ningxia Border Region Council passed the "Shaanxi-Gansu-Ningxia Border Region Election Regulations," stipulating that "all people living in the border region who are at least 18 years old, regardless of class, occupation, gender, religion, nationality, property, or educational level, have the right to vote and be elected after being registered by the Election Committee." This undoubtedly expanded the scope of the electorate to an unprecedented extent, truly achieving "universal suffrage."

The Shaanxi-Gansu-Ningxia Border Region was economically backward, with a vast territory, sparse population, inconvenient transportation, and a generally low cultural level of the masses. More than 80% of the electorate was illiterate and could not read. To adapt to this situation and ensure that the masses could express their political will and exercise their right to vote, the border region government drew on the collective wisdom of the masses and created many distinctive and easy-to-implement voting methods tailored to local conditions. For example, there was the "backpack method." With the expansion of the scope of universal suffrage, the elections of the district and county councils in the Shaanxi-Gansu-Ningxia Border Region adopted a decentralized voting method. The backpack method was essentially a mobile ballot box suitable for decentralized voting. Before the start of the election, the Election Committee prepared several locked and sealed ballot boxes, distributed the ballots to the voters in advance, and selected reliable ballot clerks to carry the boxes to various locations to collect the votes. After the votes were collected, a residents' assembly was convened to count the votes in public. The border region created this voting method to adapt to the rural environment. Its advantage was that it ensured the participation of the majority of voters in the election.

There was also the "bean election" method. Before the election, the Election Committee prepared a bowl for each candidate and placed it behind them. Then, they distributed a corresponding number of beans to the voters as a substitute for ballots, each representing one vote. Voters would place the beans in the bowl behind the candidate they supported, and the candidate with the most beans would be elected. Similar methods included the circle-drawing method, the dot-drawing method, the bar-drawing method, and the branding method. The branding method, also known as the burning hole method or the scorching hole method, involved the Election Committee printing ballots with the candidates' names before the official start of voting. Voters would burn a hole in the name of the candidate they supported with incense.

From May 1937 to March 1946, the Shaanxi-Gansu-Ningxia Border Region conducted three democratic elections. The people of the border region, with the serious attitude of "one bean should be worth one bean," elected officials and governments they trusted. A popular song at the time reflected the voice of the masses: "Gold beans, silver beans, beans cannot be cast casually; elect good people, do good deeds, and vote in the bowl of good people." It was through such universally equal democratic elections that the border region established various levels of government that were truly representative of the people's will and closely connected to them, turning the political concept of people being the masters of their own affairs into a living reality.

American journalist Jack Belden recorded the elections he witnessed firsthand in his book *China Shakes the World*: "What a strange thing this 'new democracy' is! The backward peasant is ill equipped to cope with this instrument that has suddenly been thrust into his hands. Formal, stilted, sometimes even farcical are his village elections. Yet they are going on everywhere in rural areas under Communist control. … When the day of election came, the people gathered in the voting place, usually in the schoolhouse or the local temple. The methods of casting votes, due to the inability of many voters to write, were varied and numerous. One method was to use bowls of different colors, each bowl representing a candidate. Into the bowl representing his choice, the voter put a bean given him by the election committee." From this, he concluded: "But no matter how distant they may be from a perfect democracy, no matter how exaggerated have been the claims of their misguided friends, the Communists have taken a gigantic step forward awakening millions of Chinese peasants to their rights to elect the men who shall govern them." He also compared the differences between the KMT and CPC in promoting democracy: "Despite all the rumors that were circulated about their society, certainly, as far as I saw, the villages in the Liberated Areas had achieved a form of government so far superior to that practiced in KMT areas that there was no comparison." "The KMT and Chiang Kai-shek always insisted that the people of China were not ready for democracy and that they must undergo a period of tutelage. Leaders in the Liberated Areas scoffed at that theory."

At that time, the KMT was still unconvinced, which led to a debate. An official newspaper in the KMT-ruled area asserted that the CPC's "universal suffrage" was a show—"Who doesn't know that 80% of the Chinese people can't even write their own names, and they can't remember the names of the officials appointed by the CPC. This kind of government can only be called a 'magic government,' not a 'democratic government.' The Communists, however, are deceiving themselves, insisting that the 'magic government' is a 'democratic' government, which is simply an insult to the people of the whole country." This angered the *Xinhua Daily*, which immediately retaliated by introducing the changes in the border region's electoral system, especially the bean voting method, to prove that "as long as there is a determination to implement democracy, the people's low cultural level and illiteracy will not become insurmountable obstacles." It particularly emphasized: "In any case, whether elections can be conducted and conducted well mainly depends on whether the people have the right to express their opinions and oppose others' opinions; on whether the people can truly support and oppose certain individuals without restraint. As for the technical issues of elections, they are not insoluble."

Implementing the "Three-Thirds System"

Another prominent feature of the border region's democratic politics was the implementation of the "Three-Thirds System." This reflected the CPC's policy of the Chinese united front against Japanese aggression in constructing base area governments. In March 1940, Mao Zedong pointed out in his article "On the Issue of Government in Resistance Base": "The political power we are establishing during the anti-Japanese war is of a united front character. It is the political power of all those who support both resistance and democracy; it is the joint democratic dictatorship of several revolutionary classes over the traitors and reactionaries … In accordance with the united front principle concerning the organs of political power, the allocation of places should be one-third for Communists, one-third for non-Party left progressives, and one-third for the intermediate sections who are neither left nor right." This was the first time the CPC proposed the concept of the "Three-Thirds System."

In May 1941, the *Shaanxi-Gansu-Ningxia Border Region Administrative Program* was passed, which established this policy in the form of law. It stipulated: The Party is willing to form an election alliance with all parties, factions, and mass organizations, and in the determination of candidates, CPC members shall only account for one-third so that members of all parties, factions, and non-partisans can participate in the activities of the border region's democratic institutions and the administration of the border region. When CPC members are elected as heads of a certain administrative agency, it should be ensured that two-thirds of the agency's staff are non-Party members.

From 1941 to 1942, the Shaanxi-Gansu-Ningxia Border Region carried out large-scale re-election of the township (city), county, and border region level councils and governments in accordance with the "Three-Thirds System" principle. According to statistics, CPC members accounted for about one-third of the township council members; in some places, it was even less than one-third. In the election of the Border Region Council, some Party cadres had insufficient understanding of the "Three-Thirds System," and the masses were dissatisfied with some non-Party candidates, resulting in a majority of the 242 elected Border Region Council members being CPC members. Given that the Border Region Council members were elected and could not be replaced at will, the Northwest Bureau and the Border Region Government jointly studied and decided to use the method of appointment as a supplement to the democratic election, appointing 46 non-Party members as formal members of the Border Region Council. Through efforts, the proportion of members in the border region's councils and government committees at all levels basically conformed to the "Three-Thirds System" principle. Some enlightened gentry and centrists entered the border region government, such as Li Dingming, Vice-Chairman of the Border Region Government, An Wenqin, Vice-Chairman of the Border Region Council, and He Liancheng, Deputy Director of the Border Region Education Department, who were all famous gentry from Suide.

In November 1941, the Second Session of the Shaanxi-Gansu-Ningxia Border Region Council was held. The biggest highlight of this meeting was implementing the "Three-Thirds System" principle. In the election of 51 permanent members, since the number of CPC members was six more than the stipulated amount, six CPC members, including Xiao Jingguang and Wang Shitai, withdrew automatically. Among the 39 Border Region Government Committee candidates, CPC members exceeded one-third, and Xie Juezai, Ma Xiwu, and 12 other Party members also voluntarily applied to withdraw. Later, through a secret ballot, 18 government committee members were elected, of which seven were CPC members, exceeding one-third. Xu Teli immediately requested to withdraw, with non-Party member Bai Wenhuan filling the vacancy according to the number of votes received.

The successful experiment in the Shaanxi-Gansu-Ningxia Border Region soon became a model for constructing resistance base governments. In July 1941, the first meeting of the temporary council in the Jin-Ji-Lu-Yu Border Region was held, with 133 council members attending, including 46 CPC members, accounting for one-third. At that time, Deng Xiaoping highly praised it: "We believe that the 'Three-Thirds System' is not only the best form of anti-Japanese democratic government, but also conforms to the government form of the Chinese united front against Japanese aggression, and it is the best form for the future New Democratic Republic. We, Communists, have always opposed one-party dictatorship, neither supported the

KMT's one-party dictatorship nor advocated the CPC's monopolization of power because the result of anyone-party dictatorship can only take care of the interests of one party and cannot take care of the will of all the people, which is contrary to democratic politics." This very clearly affirmed the "Three-Thirds System."

It is worth mentioning that the "Three-Thirds System" was reflected in the election process and the exercise of governing power. In particular, compared with the National Consultative Council and provincial and municipal councils established in the KMT-ruled areas, which were composed of council members selected through a "selection" process, they were called "democratic institutions" but were actually just a decorative facade of advisory bodies. Proposals in the Consultative Council were either "discussed but not decided" or "decided but not implemented," with no power to ensure the government's fulfillment. In contrast, the Shaanxi-Gansu-Ningxia Border Region Council was democratically elected and was a truly supreme authority. It could reflect the demands of people from all walks of life in the border region, turn these demands into resolutions, and implement them through the government.

At that time, some places had encountered phenomena of rejecting the "Three-Thirds System," which dampened the enthusiasm of non-Party members. In response, Mao Zedong advocated a democratic atmosphere of "speaking without reservation and expressing oneself completely," requiring CPC members to respect non-Party members and give them equal opportunities to speak. In March 1940, in his article "On the Issue of Government in Resistance Base," he reminded Party members to overcome their "narrow-mindedness of not wanting and not being used to working with non-Party members, promote a democratic style, consult with non-Party members before acting on matters, obtain the majority's agreement, and then act. At the same time, encourage non-Party members to express their opinions on various issues and listen to their opinions as much as possible."

In November 1941, at the Opening of the First Session of the Second Shaanxi-Gansu-Ningxia Border Region Council, Mao Zedong pointed out that at present, "a portion of CPC members are still not good at implementing democratic cooperation with non-Party members and still maintain a narrow-minded or sectarian style." In light of this, he proposed: "CPC members must listen to the opinions of non-Party members, allow others to speak, and welcome and learn from the correct opinions of others. If someone says something incorrectly, we should let them finish speaking and then explain it slowly. CPC members must not be self-righteous or arrogant, thinking that they are good at everything and that others are not good at anything; they must not lock themselves in a small room, boast about themselves, and claim to be kings." He also said: "National affairs are public affairs of the country, not private affairs of a single Party or faction. Therefore, CPC members are only obligated to implement democratic cooperation with non-Party members and have no right to exclude others or monopolize everything."

Under Mao Zedong's requirements, the governments of the resistance base tried to correct their deviations. For a period, Li Dingming, the Deputy Chairman of the Shaanxi-Gansu-Ningxia Border Region Government, rarely spoke at meetings. Lin Boqu, the Chairman of the Border Region Government, noticed this situation and entrusted Secretary-General Li Weihan to have a sincere conversation with him. In response to his questions about "having a position without power" and "being treated as a guest by peers, and as a puppet by subordinates; the Party makes decisions, the government cannot decide policies," the border region took serious improvement measures to ensure that he truly had both "position and power." Later, Li Dingming's proposal for "streamlining government and creating an elite military force" was adopted by the Central Committee of CPC, promoting the development of the border region and other base areas. As a result, he often used his own experience to publicize: "All these situations are what I have personally seen and what everyone has personally seen. Therefore, it is ridiculous for a few individuals at home and abroad to say that the border region government is controlled and monopolized by the CPC … Our place has established a democratic coalition government where everyone has a position and power."

At the same time, the Border Region Government took measures to encourage people from all walks of life to express their opinions freely, striving for the full expression of the interests of the masses. In such an atmosphere, many ordinary people put aside their concerns and offered their suggestions. The Second Border Region Council alone received 399 various proposals, covering aspects such as military, politics, culture, education, health, women, and children. The government leaders listened to the opinions with an open mind and made improvements accordingly. Peasant council member Liu Defu happily said: "We farmers can criticize the government's cadres, and they can all humbly accept it. It is really an unprecedented event."

In stark contrast, Chiang Kai-shek was very sensitive to criticism from the public. According to *Huang Yanpei's Diary*, in June 1944, Chiang said at the National Consultative Council: "The surge of democratic trends from all sides is a harvest from seven or eight years of resistance against Japan. However, it is not appropriate to use this to attack the government. Apart from this point, the higher the democratic tide, the better." From this, it can be seen that although Chiang Kai-shek did not openly oppose democracy on the surface, he did not allow the public to criticize the government.

Yan'an Becomes a Beacon of Democracy

The CPC conducted large-scale general elections in the resistance base and strictly implemented the "Three-Thirds System" principle. This fully mobilized the enthusiasm of all sectors of society for participating in politics and greatly enhanced the appeal of the border region government. In retrospect, Xie Juezai summarized: "At that time, we implemented the 'Three-Thirds System' not because we had too much work to do, but to win people's hearts. This goal was achieved."

In 1941, the Second Shaanxi-Gansu-Ningxia Border Region Council was successfully convened. The sincerity shown by the CPC in implementing the "Three-Thirds System" moved many people. Xu Fanting, a patriotic general who once slit his wrists in front of Sun Yat-sen's Mausoleum in Nanjing to demonstrate his determination to resist Japan, said, "Only the CPC truly implements the Three Principles of the People." The 79-year-old non-Communist Party council member Li Dansheng also praised the CPC for its sincerity, which was "truly touching," and hoped that the CPC would "keep its promises and demonstrate its faithfulness to the world, and then the world would be theirs."

In 1944, a delegation of Chinese and foreign journalists visited Yan'an. After returning to Chongqing, Zhao Chaogou, the chief editor of the New People's Daily, wrote a book called *A Month in Yan'an*, in which he wrote: "Many people doubt the sincerity of the Communist Party in implementing the 'Three-Thirds System' and think that what they are doing is just a trick to deceive people. I am afraid that's not right. I can say that the Communist Party's implementation of the 'Three-Thirds System' is not fake because it could have monopolized power with its strength. However, quite a few non-Party members now participate in administrative work. For example, in the 'Border Region Government,' Deputy Chairman Li Dingming is a wealthy gentleman from Mizhi, Director of the Construction Department Huo Zile, Director of the Education Department Liu Shi, Deputy Director He Liancheng, and Deputy Chairman of the Council Wen Anqin are all well-known non-Party figures. This cannot but be regarded as the Communist Party's restraint on itself."

During this visit, Harrison Forman, a reporter from the United Press International, also attended a joint meeting of the Border Region Government and the Border Region Council's Standing Committee. He found that all 24 attending councilors were elected by the people, including eight Communist councilors. Li Dingming chaired the meeting, and the attending councilors included a farmer, a businessman, a landlord, a tenant farmer, an intellectual, an educator, a doctor, a military officer, a cultural worker, a shop assistant, and a Muslim. The representatives discussed issues such as the situation, afforestation plans, improving the school system, assisting military families, implementing health plans, and improving judicial litigation. Everyone spoke frankly, sincerely, equally, and freely. This made Forman extol the democratic government in the border region.

The American reporter from the *Baltimore Sun* and adviser to the KMT Central Publicity Department, Wu Dao, was initially skeptical about the CPC. However, after returning from northern Shaanxi, he wrote affirmatively: "The various institutions of the Shaanxi-Gansu-Ningxia Border Region Government are all elected by the people. The chairman and other senior officials of the Border Region Government are councilors of the border region elected by the council to hold their positions. The principle that Communist Party members only account for one-third of government personnel seems to be strictly observed."

In 1945, six representatives of the National Consultative Conference visited Yan'an. After a tour, Huang Yanpei learned, "When the Communist army arrives in an area, they must first win over the people. Their current method is to let the people stand up, gather, and freely vote for those they find satisfactory to be the local head or other public positions. The army does not intervene in local politics, allowing the local people to supervise. They believe that ordinary people can only enthusiastically contribute their efforts in this way." After Mao Zedong expounded on using democracy to break out of historical cycles, Huang Yanpei admitted inwardly: "I think this is correct. Only when the public decides on major policies can personal ambitions not arise. Only by making every local matter public to every local person can people and things be matched. Using democracy to break this cycle is likely effective."

Many foreign journalists and observers visited the resistance base during this period. In his article "Impressions of Yan'an," American *Time* magazine reporter

Theodore White wrote about the facts he saw with his own eyes: In the border regions, people have the right to vote, and the various institutions of the Shaanxi-Gansu-Ningxia Border Region Government are all elected by the people. The entire system, from elections to the border council and government, truly represents China's revolution and democracy. Here, even the least respected people in the past have the right to participate in politics. After inspecting the first People's Congress in the Jin-Cha-Ji border region, British scholar William Hinton and his wife Claire firmly believed that "the Congress fairly represents various strata of society" and is a "completely democratized representative assembly."

In addition, the democracy of Yan'an attracted many intellectuals, especially young students. These young intellectuals traveled across mountains and rivers, overcoming numerous difficulties to gather here. "Going to Yan'an" became a common choice for many passionate young people and enlightened individuals who longed for revolution. They came from all over the country and even from abroad, flooding into Yan'an like a tide, quickly forming a spectacular scene of "people's hearts from all over the world turning to Yan'an." Poet He Qifang once vividly depicted this scene in "I Sing for Yan'an": "The gates of Yan'an are open all day long, and young people from all directions come in, carrying their luggage, burning with hope, and entering this gate. They study, sing, and live tense and happy days. Then, in groups, wearing military uniforms and burning with passion, they scatter in all directions."

The reason why Yan'an became a sacred place for young intellectuals from all over the country and even from abroad is inseparable from its efforts to promote and actively practice democracy. Many people had no detailed and in-depth understanding of Yan'an before they arrived. Still, just the abstract words "freedom," "democracy," and "resistance against Japan" were enough to make their blood boil. After coming to Yan'an, they "saw real democratic politics in practice." One person who went to Yan'an at that time recalled in his later years: "In the short two months since I arrived in Yan'an, not only did I have some quite fresh perceptual understanding, but I also gained some fairly profound rational understanding. I didn't just experience the appearance of the sacred land of democracy in reality, but also from a theoretical perspective, I glimpsed the ideal realm of a democratic China."

As can be seen, during the War of Resistance, Yan'an became a beacon of democracy, attracting numerous young intellectuals, who provided strong talent and support for the continuous development of the CPC. In 1942, He Qifang wrote a poem in Yan'an.

I sing for the young men and women,
I sing of the morning,
I sing of hope,
I sing of things that belong to the future,
I sing of the growing power.

In his mind, the CPC and its representative Yan'an were these kinds of growing power.

Chapter 5

Building a Strong and Clean Party

In October 1939, Mao Zedong pointed out in the "Introducing the *Communist*" that "the united front, armed struggle and Party building are the Chinese Communist Party's three 'magic weapons.'" "The united front and armed struggle are the two basic weapons for defeating the enemy ... And the Party is the heroic warrior wielding the two weapons, the united front and the armed struggle, to storm and shatter the enemy's positions. That is how the three are related to each other. Having a correct grasp of these three questions and their interrelations is tantamount to giving correct leadership to the whole Chinese revolution." Undoubtedly, the Party's construction is dominant among these three magic weapons. Therefore, while leading the Chinese Revolution, the CPC also made unremitting efforts for this.

Solving Unprecedented Party-Building Challenges

According to Marxist theory and the Soviet Communist Party, the Proletarian Party mainly comprises the working class. However, the birth of the CPC has its own characteristics, as advanced intellectuals with Marxist thought mainly founded it. Although Marxism had begun to combine with the Chinese workers' movement during this period, this combination was not initially very close. The failure of the 1923 Beijing–Hankou Railway Strike prompted the CPC to recognize the importance of strengthening its leadership of the working class, thus further promoting the combination with the workers' movement. Since then, the May 30 Movement and the Provincial-Hong Kong Strike further demonstrated that the CPC had become the command center of the workers' movement. However, with the rapid progress of the Northern Expedition, the Party's leadership of the workers' movement somewhat lagged behind the development of the situation.

For example, in the Wuhan workers' movement, the rapid increase in union members involved industrial workers and swept thousands of laborers and handicraft workers into the revolutionary tide. Although these people had a certain revolutionary nature, most of them came from bankrupt peasants and handicraftsmen, had low cultural levels and poor ideological quality, and were influenced by guilds and trade associations for a long time, often revealing the habits of the lumpenproletariat. This brought the problem of the impure organization to the workers' movement. Liu Shaoqi, who was then leading the Wuhan workers' movement, later said, "The long-term existence of gangster organizations among workers also affected the workers' movement." At the same time, the Party's leadership was very weak, "among the 63 unions in Hankou, we only had very weak four branches." In this situation, Soviet adviser Borodin once pointed out: "In parades and demonstrations and other major events, the Communist Party has not fully demonstrated its ability to lead the mass movement."

After the failure of the Great Revolution, the CPC began to embark on the path of using rural areas to encircle the cities and seizing state power with military force. This revolutionary path was right in line with China's national conditions. Still, it also posed a huge challenge to the Party's construction: how to establish a proletarian revolutionary Party in the countryside? In October 1928, the Central Committee of CPC stated: "Now there is a widespread danger in the Party nationwide, which is the shrinking of the proletariat in the composition and leadership of the Party, and there is a serious crisis of forming a peasant Party." It should be said that this concern is not entirely superfluous. As the focus of the revolution shifted from urban to rural areas, the CPC had to seek survival and development in the vast sea of peasants. Due to their brutal exploitation and oppression, Chinese peasants had a strong revolutionary nature. Still, at the same time, they possessed the natural weaknesses of small producers, such as selfishness and disorganization. Therefore, under such historical conditions, ensuring the Party's proletarian vanguard nature and the Party's correct leadership in the Chinese revolutionary cause became an unprecedented challenge for Party-building.

For this unprecedented Party-building challenge, the Communist International and the Central Committee of CPC initially tried to find solutions regarding organizational construction, especially emphasizing family background and excluding intellectuals. At that time, the failure of the Great Revolution was completely attributed to the erroneous leadership of Chen Duxiu's "right-leaning opportunism," even believing that it was related to the Party's leading organs being "almost entirely in the hands of petty-bourgeois intellectuals." In November 1927, an expanded meeting of the Central Temporary Political Bureau pointed out that the main organizational shortcomings of the Party at present were "the Party's leading cadres are not workers, and even not poor peasants, but representatives of petty-bourgeois intellectuals." Therefore, "the most important organizational task of the CPC is to replace non-proletarian intellectual cadres with new worker-peasant cadres" and "workerize the leading cadres."

Based on this understanding, for a period after the failure of the Great Revolution, the main idea of the Central Committee of CPC in organizational construction was to make every effort to absorb industrial workers into the Party, advocating that the purity of the Party's organization should be ensured by increasing the proportion of proletarian components within the Party, ensuring the nature of the Party, and enhancing the fighting capacity of the Party. The Sixth CPC National Congress in 1928 emphasized that Party-building must focus on large cities and important industrial areas, believing that "only in these workers' centers can the proletarian foundation of the Party be established." In connection with this, the Sixth Congress also overemphasized the worker components among the delegates and members of the Central Committee. Stalin criticized at that time that the CPC was still led by a few big intellectuals like Zhang Guotao and Qu Qiubai, and more workers should be selected to work in central institutions. This view was reflected in the election of the Sixth Congress, where 21 out of the 36 elected members and alternate members of the Central Committee were of worker origin.

The biggest challenge the Party's construction faced during this period was building the Party in rural areas, and the solutions of "urban center theory" and "workerization of cadres" obviously deviated from this theme. In response to this tendency, Mao Zedong said as early as 1929: "It would be wrong to abandon the struggle in the cities, but in our opinion it would also be wrong for any of our Party members to fear the peasant strength lest it should outstrip the workers' strength and harm the revolution." However, his correct assertion did not become a consensus within the entire Party.

The thorough solution to this problem came at the Wayaobu Conference in December 1935. *The Resolution on the Current Situation and the Tasks of the Party* adopted by the conference for the first time clearly stated: "The CPC is the vanguard of the Chinese proletariat. It should absorb a large number of advanced workers and tenant farmers into the Party, creating a backbone of workers within the Party. At the same time, the CPC is also the vanguard of the entire nation. Therefore, anyone who is willing to fight for the Party's goals, regardless of their class background, can join the CPC." The implementation of this decision led to the rapid expansion of the Party's membership from over 40,000 after the failure of the fifth encirclement campaign to more than 800,000 by the end of 1940, making the CPC a truly nationwide large party.

In April 1945, Mao Zedong discussed the relationship between "background" and "joining the Party" in his oral political report at the Seventh CPC National Congress. He pointed out: "The CPC is a proletarian Party ... Of course, there are other components in the Communist Party, people from other classes, such as peasants and the petty bourgeoisie, and intellectuals from other class backgrounds. But the background is one thing. Joining the Party is another; after joining the Party, non-proletarian background becomes proletarian, and their thoughts and actions must change to those of the proletariat." This formulation further broke the constraints of the "Only Component Theory" and laid the foundation for the Party's development, growth, and successful seizure of national power.

Focusing on Building the Party from an Ideological Perspective

In theory, although the "Only Component Theory" is wrong, the Chinese Revolution has long been in an environment of rural armed struggle, and the influx of a large number of non-proletarian elements, especially peasants, has indeed brought some issues that cannot be ignored while expanding the Party's ranks. In November 1928, Mao Zedong listed many problems in the Jinggang Mountains revolutionary base in his report to the Central Government, such as localism, native and non-native issues, and speculative elements turning against the revolution. He also analyzed: "The economy of the border regions is an agricultural economy, and some places still remain in the pestle and mortar era. Social organization is generally based on family organizations with one surname as the unit. Due to living relationships, the Party's organization in the villages often consists of Party members of the same surname forming a branch, and branch meetings are almost family meetings simultaneously. Under such circumstances, constructing a 'Bolshevik Party of Struggle' is difficult." As a result, he keenly sensed: "We feel that the ideological leadership of the proletariat is very important. The parties in various counties of the border regions are almost entirely composed of peasant elements. If they are not given the ideological leadership of the proletariat, their tendency will be erroneous."

By May 1929, the Red Fourth Army led by Mao Zedong and Zhu De had 8,000 people, with 1,329 Party members. Among them, there were 311 workers, accounting for 23.4%; 626 farmers, accounting for 47.1%; 106 small businessmen, accounting for 8%; 192 students, accounting for 14.5%; and 95 others, accounting for 7%. In total, Party members from peasant and other petty-bourgeois backgrounds accounted for over 70%. Due to frequent warfare and insufficient political and ideological work, various non-proletarian ideologies and old military styles gradually spread within the Red Fourth Army, seriously hindering the implementation of the Party's line and weakening the cohesion and combat effectiveness of the army.

In light of this, Mao Zedong creatively proposed the important principle of focusing on building the Party from an ideological perspective at the Ninth Party Congress of the Red Fourth Army, also known as the Gutian Meeting, in December 1929. This is Mao Zedong's original contribution to Marxist Party-building theory. The practice has proved that this is the correct path to build a proletarian Party in line with China's national conditions, fundamentally solving the problem of building a strong proletarian Party in the long-term rural environment and the condition of Party members being mainly peasants. However, since Mao Zedong's position within the Party was not high then, this proposition was not immediately implemented throughout the Party, and the work focus of the entire Party's leading body was still on big cities.

After the nationwide War of Resistance outbreak, the Central Committee of CPC adopted the policy of expanding Party membership in large numbers to adapt to the changes in the situation and the needs of the anti-Japanese struggle, resulting in rapid growth in the number of Party members. Mao Zedong and other central leaders published a series of articles on Party-building to strengthen the political and ideological education of Party members, especially new Party members. In October

1939, Mao Zedong emphasized in "Introducing the *Communist*" that Party-building was a "great project" and proposed the task of "building up a bolshevized Chinese Communist Party, a party which is national in scale and has a broad mass character, a party which is fully consolidated ideologically, politically and organizationally."

As the main content of ideological construction, the CPC, represented mainly by Mao Zedong, gradually overcame the erroneous tendency of copying Marxism-Leninism textbooks and foreign experiences in the long and complex revolutionary struggle. After arduous exploration, they summarized an extremely rich and original revolutionary practice experience, realizing the first historical leap of the Sinicization of Marxism. This led to the formation of Mao Zedong Thought with Chinese characteristics, which was written into the Constitution of the CPC at the Seventh CPC National Congress and became the guiding ideology for the entire Party. Establishing the guiding position of Mao Zedong Thought has clarified the direction of the Party's ideological construction.

From 1942 to 1945, the Central Committee of CPC launched a vigorous Yan'an Rectification Movement throughout the Party, aiming to "learn from the past mistakes to avoid future ones, and cure the sickness to save the patient." This was done through criticism, self-criticism, and Marxist ideological education. The Yan'an Rectification Movement was a profound Marxist educational movement and a great ideological emancipation movement that broke the erroneous tendency of dogmatizing Marxism and sanctifying the resolutions of the Communist International and Soviet experiences within the Party. It was of great and far-reaching significance for all Party members, especially senior cadres, to adhere to the ideological line of starting from reality, linking theory with practice, seeking truth from facts, and adhering to the principle of Sinicization of Marxism.

After the Yan'an Rectification Movement, in April 1945, the seventh plenary session of the sixth CPC Central Committee adopted the "Resolution on Several Historical Issues," which comprehensively summarized the history since the founding of the Party, especially the period from the fourth plenary session of the sixth Central Committee to the Zunyi Conference. It pointed out the manifestations and harms of left-wing errors. It affirmed Mao Zedong's contributions to the Chinese Revolution and the significance of establishing his leadership position within the Party. Based on this, the Seventh CPC National Congress, held from April to June 1945, determined the Party's political line, stipulated Mao Zedong Thought as the guiding principle for all work, and elected the Central Committee with Mao Zedong as the leader.

After the War of Resistance and the Yan'an Rectification Movement, Mao Zedong systematically summarized the practical experience of focusing on building the Party from an ideological perspective. In 1945, he proposed at the Seventh CPC National Congress, "Therefore ideological education is the key link to be grasped in uniting the whole Party for great political struggles. Unless this is done, the Party cannot accomplish any of its political tasks." This further clarified the importance of putting ideological construction first in party building. History has proven that the CPC has put ideological construction first and established a set of effective principles, policies, and methods, ensuring that the majority of Party members join the Party not only organizationally but also ideologically and maintaining the nature of the proletarian vanguard under special historical conditions.

"Align with the Central Benchmark"

The rapid development and growth of the CPC and its successful seizure of national power can be attributed to the breakthrough of the "Only Component Theory" in organizational construction, the emphasis on building the Party ideologically, and the significant role played by institutional construction. In particular, the strict implementation of democratic centralism has institutionally ensured the correctness of the Party's political leadership and the full display of the enthusiasm and creativity of all Party members.

The CPC established democratic centralism as the Party's organizational principle and system early on. In June 1927, the Constitution of the CPC, passed by the Political Bureau of the Central Committee of CPC meeting, explicitly stated: "The guiding principle of the Party department is democratic centralism" and made many specific provisions. This was the first time the Party proposed the concept of democratic centralism and incorporated it into the Constitution of the CPC. However, the CPC was still in its infancy at that time, immature in politics, ideology, and organization. This was mainly manifested in the lack of normal democracy and centralization within the Party. The prevalence of a patriarchal system and extreme democratization resulted in painful losses to the revolutionary cause.

In response to the above tendencies, Mao Zedong systematically discussed the principles of democratic centralism in the "Resolution of the Gutian Meeting." The resolution not only clearly affirmed that democratic centralism is the organizational principle of the CPC but also comprehensively expounded its basic content, criticized various erroneous tendencies on the issue of democratic centralism, and put forward corrective measures based on the analysis of its harms and root causes.

After the Zunyi Conference in 1935, as the Party gradually consolidated and matured, the understanding of democratic centralism by the Chinese Communists represented by Mao Zedong deepened. In terms of party democracy, Mao Zedong said, "In the present great struggle, the Chinese Communist Party demands that all its leading bodies and all its members and cadres should give the fullest expression to their initiative, which alone can ensure victory." Therefore, "expanding democracy within the party should be seen as a necessary step to consolidate and develop the party, as an important weapon to make the party lively and active in the great struggle, to competently and happily grow new strength, and break through the difficult barriers of war."

At the same time, the Central Committee of CPC repeatedly emphasized political discipline and political norms, striving to maintain the authority of the central leadership. In 1938, the sixth plenary session of the sixth CPC Central Committee adopted the "Decision on the Rules and Discipline of the Central Committee's Work," the "Decision on the Rules and Discipline of the Work of Party Departments at All Levels," and the "Decision on the Provisional Organizational Structure of Party Committees at All Levels," which explored ways to strengthen the Party's political discipline and political norms. They clearly put forward the principle of "individuals obeying the organization, the minority obeying the majority, the lower levels obeying the higher levels, and the whole Party obeying the Central Committee" and pointed out: "All the Party's work is led by the Central Committee, which is the basic principle of the Party's organizational democratic centralism. Members of the Party committees at all levels must unconditionally implement this and serve as a model for all Party members and cadres."

In July 1941 and September 1942, the Political Bureau of the Central Committee of CPC adopted the "Decision on Strengthening Party Spirit" and the "Decision of the Central Committee of CPC on Unifying the Leadership of the Resistance Base and Adjusting the Relations between Various Organizations." Both decisions pointed out that, in the context of long-term decentralized and independent guerrilla warfare and a large proportion of small producers and intellectuals within the Party, there was a tendency for some Party members to violate Party spirit with "individualism," "heroism," "disorganization," "independence," and "anti-centralism." This caused great damage to the Party and the revolution. To correct these tendencies that went against the Party spirit, the Party needed to strengthen its unified leadership, enhance discipline education throughout its ranks, and strictly adhere to the basic principles of individual obedience to the organization, minority obedience to the majority, lower levels obedience to higher levels, and the entire Party's obedience to the Central Committee.

During this period, Mao Zedong repeatedly emphasized the need to abide by the Party's political discipline, saying that "the line is the 'kingly way,' discipline is the 'overbearing way,' and both are indispensable." To maintain the authority of the central leadership, he continually reiterated: "We should know that a team is often not very neat, so we often need to shout 'align,' look left, look right, look to the center; we need to align with the central benchmark." History has shown that Mao Zedong's maintenance of the central authority during the War of Resistance greatly strengthened the Party's discipline, overcame factionalism, consolidated the unity and centralization of the Party, and provided organizational and leadership guarantees for the victory of the War of Resistance.

By the time of the Seventh CPC National Congress in 1945, the Party's under-standing of democratic centralism had been further enriched and developed. In his "Report on the Revision of the Constitution of the CPC," Liu Shaoqi systematically expounded the important position of democratic centralism in the Party's organization, leadership, and state-building, clarified the scientific connotations of democratic cen-tralism, and put forward specific requirements and norms for democratic centralism. This was the first comprehensive and systematic exposition of democratic centralism in the history of the CPC, indicating that the Party's theory on democratic centralism had matured. It was under this institutional guarantee that the CPC was able to maintain the unity and normal Party life of the whole Party, fully display the initiative of all aspects, and lead the Chinese Revolution from one victory to another in the complex situation of the War of Resistance and the Liberation War with exceptionally arduous revolutionary tasks.

Strictly Punishing Corrupt Elements within the Party and Government

During the leadership of the Chinese Revolution, the CPC also emphasized the con-struction of Party integrity and a clean government, taking swift and decisive actions against various forms of corruption. Mao Zedong believed that negative phenomena and corrupt practices within the Party and government should be severely punished without mercy, and there should be no leniency. It was necessary to eliminate those who violated discipline resolutely, abused power for personal gain, and engaged in corruption from the Party and government agencies, especially those senior and meritorious members who should be treated even more seriously and punished severely to alert the entire Party. As early as the Ruijin period, he issued the "Order on Punishing Corruption and Waste," stipulating that "those who embezzle more than 500 yuan in public funds will be sentenced to death," and those who embezzle less will be sentenced according to different levels. The formulation and promulgation of these orders had a huge deterrent effect on corrupt elements and provided a reference and legal basis for the Soviet Government's anti-corruption struggle.

In 1932, the Ruijin County Soviet Government's Judicial Department received a letter from the masses accusing the Chairman of the Soviet Government in Yeping Village, Xie Busheng, of serious corruption crimes. After investigation, Xie Busheng was also found guilty of crimes such as plotting to steal someone's wife, plundering money, and secretly killing cadres. In May 1932, the Provisional Supreme Court of the Chinese Soviet Republic sentenced Xie Busheng to death. This was the first shot fired by the red regime in punishing corrupt elements, which caused a strong response in the Soviet areas and demonstrated the determination of the CPC to eradicate corruption.

From 1933 to 1934, various undertakings in the Central Soviet Area achieved considerable development, but corruption, waste, and embezzlement of public property still occurred frequently, even showing a certain expansion and spread. Given this situation, the Central Government decided to crack down and severely punish corrupt elements. In 1933, Tang Daren, the Chief of the Accounting Department of the Ruijin County Soviet, embezzled more than 2,000 yuan from 34 items, including the remaining funds from various military and political institutions, the public bonds returned by the masses, and hidden fines from landlords. Mao Zedong personally presided over the Central Government People's Committee meeting and decided to hand Tang Daren over to the court for the death penalty. In 1934, Zuo Xiangyun, Director of the General Assembly Engineering Department, was sentenced to death by the Supreme Court for embezzling 246.7 yuan in construction funds during the construction of the Central Government Hall, the Red Army Martyrs' Memorial Tower, and the Red Army Reviewing Stand. These trials upheld justice, struck down evil, and won the wholehearted support of the people in the Soviet areas.

During the Yan'an period, Mao Zedong punished corrupt and degenerate cadres like Huang Kegong and Xiao Yubi, who had made military achievements. Huang

Kegong had participated in the Jinggang Mountains struggle and the Long March and made remarkable military achievements. In October 1937, he shot and killed Liu Qian, a female student of the Shaanbei Public School, by the Yan River after a failed forced marriage attempt. After the incident, Mao Zedong personally presided over the meeting and decided to execute Huang Kegong. He also wrote a letter to Lei Jingtian, President of the High Court of the Shaan-Gan-Ning Border Region, pointing out:

"Exactly because Huang Kegong is not an ordinary person, precisely because he has been a Communist Party member for many years and has been a member of the Red Army for many years, he cannot be treated differently. ... All Communist Party members, all Red Army commanders and fighters, and all revolutionaries should take Huang Kegong as a warning from the past."

Xiao Yubi was also a hardworking and meritorious veteran of the Red Army with over 90 scars on his body. To help him recover, Mao Zedong had once specially approved a milk certificate for him. However, Xiao Yubi later became arrogant and lawless while serving as the Director of the Zhangjiapan Taxation Office in Qingjian County, Shaanxi, using his power to embezzle more than 3,000 yuan. After the case was uncovered, Mao Zedong ordered his execution without hesitation. On January 5, 1942, the *Liberation Daily* commented on the case, "There is no place for a 'Xiao Yubi'-style weed to grow on the ground of clean politics! If there is one, pull it out!" According to Lin Boqu, Chairman of the Shaan-Gan-Ning Border Region Government, the corruption rate in the border region was 5%. Xiao's execution changed the situation dramatically, and the political atmosphere in the border region noticeably improved.

In contrast, the KMT became increasingly corrupt after taking control of the national government. In 1928, a keen foreign observer, George Sokolsky, pointed out that "luxury and extravagance" had become the characteristic lifestyle of KMT officials. During the War of Resistance, American General Joseph Stilwell, who had served as Chief of Staff of the Chinese Theater of Operations, also said: "I judge the KMT and the Communist Party based on what I see. The KMT is: corruption, incompetence, chaos, economic hardship, heavy taxes, and empty words," while "the Communist Party's program is reducing taxes, rent, and interest; raising production and living standards; participating in politics; and keeping promises."

In 1944, American diplomat John S. Service in China reported to Washington: "From the top to the bottom, the government and military institutions in Chongqing are rife with unprecedented and blatant corruption and a complete breakdown of discipline." However, when he later visited Yan'an as a US military observer group member, he was surprised to find: "What I saw in Yan'an was a well-organized movement with political and economic goals, led by competent leaders who successfully carried it out. Moreover, at a time when the KMT had lost its early revolutionary spirit and was increasingly fragmented, the Communist Party, due to its continued struggle, maintained its revolutionary spirit and gradually grew stronger and more mature. People could not help but feel that this movement was powerful and successful, backed by a certain force, and established such close ties with the people that it could not be easily crushed."

After the War of Resistance victory, the KMT ransacked the people's wealth and plundered while receiving the territories. Li Zongren recalled in his memoirs that the so-called "reception" in Beijing was indeed more like "looting," as ridiculed by the newspapers at the time. The public sarcastically referred to those in charge of "receiving" as the "Five Sons of Success," meaning that they only knew how to plunder gold, houses, cars, money, and women. At the time, popular rhymes in Beijing were: "Hope for the Central Government, look forward to the Central Government, the arrival of the Central Government brings more disaster"; "Think of Chiang, hope for Chiang, when Chiang arrives, the price of rice and flour rises." Shao Yulin, an important KMT official in charge of economic reception, once told Chiang Kai-shek face-to-face: "If we continue like this, we may have recovered our territory, but we will lose the hearts of the people!" He also predicted, "A time bomb of failure has already been buried amid the sounds of victory." In response, Chiang Kai-shek said in a speech in January 1948: "Frankly speaking, no revolutionary party in the past or present, at home or abroad, has been as decadent and corrupt as we are today; nor has any party been so devoid of spirit, discipline, or moral standards. Such a party should have been eliminated and phased out long ago." In July of the same year, he said, "Our failure lies in the reception." After retreating to Taiwan, he reflected more deeply on the reasons for their failure, believing that "it was our corruption and incompetence that defeated us."

As the saying goes, "Those who win the people's hearts win the country, and those who lose the people's hearts lose the country." During the Chinese Civil War, the CPC won the hearts of most of the people because of its integrity and honesty, while the KMT lost the hearts of the people due to corruption. In 1948, the Central Research Institute of the National Government selected 81 academicians for the first session, of which nine went to Taiwan with the KMT in 1949, 12 stayed abroad, one died, and the remaining 59 chose to stay in mainland China. This shows that the support of the people is always a crucial factor in determining the fate of a political party.

— Part II —

THE SOCIALIST CONSTRUCTION PERIOD

CHAPTER 6

The Establishment of the People's Democratic Government

One of the important goals of the CPC leadership in the revolution was to enable the people to be their own masters. In 1949, the CPC won the revolution and established a people's democratic dictatorship. In accordance with China's national conditions, it implemented a system of People's Congresses that combined deliberation and execution, realizing the people as masters of their own destinies.

From Soviets to People's Congresses

Since the establishment of the CPC, it has been fighting for national independence and people's liberation and establishing a new government in which the people are their masters. Due to the establishment of the CPC being greatly influenced by Lenin and the Russian October Revolution he led, the Soviet system (which is a purely Russian term meaning "council" or "assembly") created during the revolution also had a significant impact on the CPC.

In August and September 1920, Cai Hesen, who was working and studying in France, discussed the issue of the Communist Party in detail in a letter to Mao Zedong and pointed out that the Soviets were the "political organization after the proletarian revolution" and the class struggle was about "breaking the machinery of the bourgeoisie (parliamentary government) and building the machinery of the proletariat—the Soviets."

The first Party Program adopted by the CPC in July 1921 clearly stated: "The Party recognizes the Soviet system of administration and organizes workers, peasants, and soldiers." After the split of the First KMT-CPC Cooperation in 1927, marked by Mao Zedong's leadership of the Autumn Harvest Uprising and the subsequent battles leading to the Jinggang Mountains, the Chinese Revolution embarked on a path different from the Russian Revolution, a path of encircling the cities from the countryside and seizing power through armed struggle. By June 1930, the CPC had established more than a dozen bases, covering more than 300 counties in over ten provinces, such as Jiangxi, Hunan, and Fujian, with a population of 10 million. The Soviet governments established in towns, districts, and counties in these areas were widely supported by the masses of workers and peasants. Since "Soviet" is the transliteration of Russian, the Chinese Communists at that time generally did not understand Russian and could not truly understand the meaning of "Soviet," so they used terms such as "Soviet Congress," "Soviet Workers and Peasants Republic," "Soviet People's Republic," "Sovietism," and "Sovietists" for a long time.

In November 1931, the First National Congress of the Chinese Soviets was held in Ruijin, Jiangxi. The Congress adopted the "Constitutional Outline of the Chinese Soviet Republic," which clearly stipulated: "The Chinese Soviet regime establishes a state of the democratic dictatorship of the workers and peasants. The entire Soviet power belongs to the workers, peasants, Red Army soldiers, and all laboring masses. Under the Soviet regime, all workers, peasants, Red Army soldiers, and all laboring masses have the right to elect representatives to manage state power." "The highest state power of the Chinese Soviet Republic is the Congress of Workers, Peasants, and Soldiers (Soviets)." The Congress declared the establishment of the Chinese Soviet Republic. Mao Zedong was then elected as the Chairman of the Central Executive Committee and the People's Commissar Committee. In January 1934, the Second National Congress of the Chinese Soviets was held. However, due to the failure of the fifth counter-encirclement campaign, the Central Soviet Area and other southern Soviet areas were successively lost, and the Red Army was forced to embark on the Long March.

After the Long March reached Shaanbei, the Shaan-Gan-Ning Border Region became the central area of the Chinese Soviet Republic. With the outbreak of the War of Resistance, to adapt to the new situation of the national resistance, the CPC established a new type of united front government in the resistance base—the "Three-Thirds System" government and implemented the "Three-Thirds System" of the Senate system. The Senate was an organ of public opinion, consultation, and political deliberation and the highest legislative, power, and supervision organ in the border regions, counties, and townships. Based on state-building experience during this period, the CPC proposed a preliminary concept of establishing a system of People's Congresses.

In January 1940, Mao Zedong pointed out in "On New Democracy" the so-called "political system" issue. "China may now adopt a system of people's congresses, from the NPC down to the provincial, county, district and township people's congresses, with all levels electing their respective governmental bodies." In April 1945, Mao Zedong reaffirmed in "On Coalition Government": "The organizational principle of the new-democratic state should be democratic centralism, with the people's congresses determining the major policies and electing the governments at the various levels. It is at once democratic and centralized, that is, centralized on the basis of democracy and democratic under centralized guidance. This is the only system that can give full expression to democracy with full powers vested in the people's congresses at all levels and, at the same time, guarantee centralized administration with the governments at each level exercising centralized management of all the affairs entrusted to them by the people's congresses at the corresponding level and safeguarding whatever is essential to the democratic life of the people." After discussions and deliberations, in September 1945, the Border Region Senate and the Government decided to change the Township Senate to the Township People's Congress. In April 1946, the "Constitutional Principles of the Shaan-Gan-Ning Border Region" adopted by the First Session of the Third Border Region Senate stipulated: "The Border Region, County, and Township People's Congresses (Senates) are the organs for people to manage state power"; "People universally, directly, and equally elect representatives in secret, and representatives at all levels elect government personnel"; "Governments at all levels are responsible to congresses at all levels, and representatives at all levels are responsible to their electors." This established the system of People's Congresses through legislation (constitutional principles).

As the War of Liberation progressed smoothly, in preparation for the birth of the new government in January 1948, Mao Zedong pointed out: "At this stage …

county, city, provincial or border region People's Congresses should be convened to elect governments at all levels. In the future, after the revolution is victorious nationwide, central and local governments at all levels should be elected by People's Congresses at all levels." In September 1948, Mao Zedong specifically discussed the issue of establishing the People's Congress system and criticized the past practice of copying the Soviet Union. He said, "Should we adopt the parliamentary or democratic centralism for our political system? In the past, we called it the Soviet representative system, and the Soviet was a representative conference. We called it both 'Soviet' and 'representative conference,' so 'Soviet representative conference' became 'representative conference representative conference.' This is blindly copying foreign terms. Now, we just use the term 'People's Representative Conference.' We adopt democratic centralism instead of parliamentary systems. Yuan Shikai and Cao Kun practiced the parliamentary system, which has already become disreputable. Adopting democratic centralism in China is very appropriate. We propose to convene People's Congresses, and Sun Yat-sen's Will also mentions the need to convene a national conference. The KMT recite the will daily, and they cannot oppose it. The foreign bourgeoisie could not oppose it either, as they did not oppose Chiang Kai-shek's two 'National Congresses.' … I think we can decide not to adopt the bourgeois parliamentary system and the separation of the three powers."

The core content of the People's Congress system is to convene People's Congresses to establish the Central Government, a prerequisite for state power's legitimacy. On April 30, 1948, the slogan of the Central Committee of CPC for commemorating Labor Day proposed: "All democratic parties, people's organizations, and social elites should quickly convene a Political Consultative Conference to discuss and implement the convening of the People's Congress and the establishment of a democratic coalition government."

However, under the circumstances of the civil war with the KMT, it was impossible to convene a People's Congress through comprehensive universal elections. In light of this, the Central Committee of CPC and other political parties and personages with no party affiliation unanimously thought of an alternative: a temporary Central Government could be formed directly through a Political Consultative Conference without going through the People's Congress. Therefore, on June 15, 1949, Mao Zedong officially announced at the Preparatory Meeting of the New Political Consultative Conference: "Quickly convene a new Political Consultative Conference, establish a democratic coalition government, to lead the people of the whole country, and eliminate the remaining forces of the reactionary KMT at the fastest speed and unify the whole of China." The *Common Program* confirmed this transitional arrangement, which served as a temporary constitution. The *Common Program* stipulated that the state power of the People's Republic of China belongs to the people. The highest state power organ is the National People's Congress (NPC). This established the political and legal status of the People's Congress system in China.

Representatives of the People Come from the Lathe Workshops and the Agricultural Fields

On October 1, 1949, the People's Republic of China was founded, marking a new page in Chinese history. Due to the historical environment of the nation's founding and the Central Government's formation process, the People's Republic of China did not have a state power system composed of People's Congresses at all levels at its inception. However, the *Common Program* also stipulated that before local People's Congresses convened through universal elections, local People's Representative Conferences would gradually exercise the powers of the People's Congresses, serving as local state power organs. They would elect People's Government committees (governments) and have the power to review the work reports, budgets, and final accounts of the people's governments. They could also make decisions and entrust them to the People's Government committees for implementation.

In accordance with this provision, various regions actively explored and developed the highly influential "Songjiang Experience." Songjiang County in Jiangsu Province (now Songjiang District, Shanghai) was liberated on May 13, 1949. Four months after the liberation, on September 30, 1949, Songjiang County held a conference of people's representatives from all walks of life. The conference lasted five days and was attended by 286 representatives, including workers, farmers, youth and students, educators, self-employed individuals, women, businesspeople, enlightened gentry, Party, government, and military officials. The conference's main topics were the collection of public grain, labor-capital disputes in private enterprises, and rent and interest reduction. The county mayor and county party secretary both presented reports at the conference. The conference format was simplified, and the reports were brief, with a clear purpose: to leave time for the representatives. The 286 representatives were divided into ten groups. First, they held group discussions and speeches at the plenary session. During the conference, 165 proposals were submitted by the representatives, and an additional 14 were submitted after the conference closed.

After reviewing the materials on the Songjiang Experience, Mao Zedong fully affirmed it and called for its promotion to enhance democracy and strengthen the construction of people's political power. Among some university professors with European and American study experiences, there were doubts about whether the CPC could implement democracy. Fei Xiaotong, a professor at Tsinghua University, attended the first conference of representatives from all walks of life in Beijing and later published an article in the *People's Daily*, stating that he had attended a lesson on democracy. In this "classroom," he saw participants from all aspects, including uniformed officials, workers in work clothes, women in cheongsams, democratic figures in suits, teachers in long gowns, and bosses wearing melon skin hats. These people discussed issues together and submitted more than 200 proposals.

Under the influence of the Songjiang Experience, by the end of 1952, there were more than 13 million people's representatives, with more than 80% directly or indirectly elected. People's representative conferences had exercised the powers of People's Congresses in more than two-thirds of the cities, one-third of the counties, and the vast majority of townships across all provinces and municipalities directly under the Central Government. This indicated that the People's Representative Conference had become a regular system, established from the bottom up in various regions nationwide. Based on this, the Central Committee of CPC decided in November 1952 to prepare for convening the NPC and drafting a constitution.

In December 1952, the Standing Committee of the National Committee of the CPPCC held its 43rd meeting. On behalf of the Central Committee, Zhou Enlai proposed that the National Committee of the CPPCC suggest to the Central People's Government to convene the NPC and local People's Congresses at all levels in 1953 to draft a constitution. On January 13, 1953, the Central People's Government Committee held its 20th meeting, where Mao Zedong pointed out: "In order to promote democracy, a nationwide general election, especially at the county and township levels, must be held." "The day before yesterday, I saw a speech by Eisenhower, who said that it is impossible for China to hold democratic elections. … To promote democracy, strengthen economic construction, and strengthen the struggle against imperialism, we must hold elections and establish a constitution." The meeting adopted the "Resolution on Convening the National People's Congress and Local People's Congresses at All Levels," deciding to hold general elections in 1953 and convene local People's Congresses at all levels elected by the people, followed by the NPC on this basis. The meeting also decided to establish a Constitution Drafting Committee with Mao Zedong as Chairman and an Election Law Drafting Committee with Zhou Enlai as Chairman.

In February 1953, the 22nd meeting of the Central People's Government Committee reviewed the "Election Law of the People's Republic of China for the National People's Congress and Local People's Congresses at All Levels" (Draft), with Deng Xiaoping presenting an explanatory report. The meeting finally passed the "Election Law" (Draft) and implemented it on March 1. The nationwide grassroots election work was originally scheduled to begin in May 1953, with a plan to complete it in three months. However, due to severe floods, droughts, and other factors affecting several provinces, the elections ultimately ended in June 1954.

On September 3, 1954, on the eve of the first session of the First NPC, Deng Xiaoping summarized the representative election work. He pointed out that in June and July of 1954, 150 provincial cities, 2,064 counties and autonomous counties, county-level units, and 170 districts directly under the central cities held People's Congress meetings. Some special and county-level units in minority areas where grassroots elections were temporarily not held also convened People's Representative Conferences; in these conferences, provinces, municipalities, and autonomous regions elected a total of 16,680 representatives to the People's Congresses using secret ballots. From late July to mid-August, provincial People's Congress meetings were held in each province, municipality, and the Inner Mongolia Autonomous Region, which in turn elected representatives to the NPC. Xizang and the Chamdo region elected NPC representatives through representative conferences. A total of 1,136 representatives were elected from 25 provinces, the Inner Mongolia Autonomous Region, Xizang, the Chamdo region, and 14 municipalities directly under the Central Government. The military held a military representative conference and elected 60 representatives to the NPC. The Overseas Chinese Affairs Committee elected 30 representatives to the NPC at an enlarged conference on overseas Chinese affairs with foreign overseas Chinese representatives. One thousand two hundred twenty-six representatives were elected from various regions and units to the NPC. In addition, Taiwan Province should have elected representatives to the NPC, but the quota is temporarily vacant as the province is yet to be liberated. Among the NPC representatives, there were 147 female representatives, accounting for 11.99% of the total number of representatives; minority representatives, in addition to the 150 stipulated by the election law, were also elected by various provinces and cities, totaling 27, accounting for 14.44% of the total number of representatives.

Representatives from all ethnic groups and social strata were included in the total number of representatives in proportion to their respective statuses.

During the election process of the representatives, the elected individuals felt extremely honored. Chen Shutong received a letter from Zhang Yuanji from Shanghai, saying, "It is an unparalleled honor to be elected as a representative of the NPC. I will attend the meeting in Beijing despite my illness. I will be delighted even if I die in Beijing." Zhang Yuanji was one of the most influential publishers in modern China and the only person who had met with Emperor Guangxu, Sun Yat-sen, Yuan Shikai, Chiang Kai-shek, and Mao Zedong—the "top five figures in China." At that time, he was 88 years old and bedridden due to hemiplegic paralysis. His eagerness to attend the NPC was touching.

Completing the election work for the First NPC prepared the organizational conditions for convening the Congress and the enactment and adoption of the new constitution of China.

On September 15, 1954, more than 1,200 NPC representatives gathered in Huairen Hall, Zhongnanhai, Beijing, to attend the first session of the First NPC. A report titled "Six Hundred Million People's Hearts Blossoming" in the *People's Daily* on September 16 described the scene that representatives "came from the lathe side, from the fields, from the mines, from the coast guard posts. They put down pliers, plow handles, pickaxes, pens, and compasses ... to discuss the nation's major issues with the leaders of the Party and government they love and respect." "Many of them have made outstanding contributions to the people's revolutionary cause, and many are representatives of various democratic parties and democratic strata. They express the common will of six hundred million people. Here are white-haired elders who have experienced the political turmoil of modern China, and here are advanced young people who have grown up in the new era and have just reached the voting age. They come from every province in China, from the green coast, from the grasslands of Inner Mongolia, from the Xizang Plateau above 5,000 meters, from the oasis beneath the snow peaks of the Kunlun Mountains, and from the Yunnan–Guizhou Plateau in the southwestern frontier. They are representatives of Kazakhs, Uighurs, Yi, Miao, Zhuang ... and other ethnic groups."

On September 20, 1954, the first session of the First NPC unanimously adopted the "Constitution of the People's Republic of China." The *Constitution* explicitly stipulated that the People's Republic of China is a people's democratic state led by the working class and based on the alliance of workers and farmers. All power in the People's Republic of China belongs to the people. The organs through which the people exercise state power are the NPC and the local People's Congresses at various levels. As a result, the People's Congress system was formally established as the fundamental political system of China in the form of the *Constitution*. The reason it is called the fundamental political system is explained by Dong Biwu: "Our country has many systems, such as the marriage system, tax system, judicial system, the military system, and the educational system, but these systems can only represent one aspect of our political life. Only the People's Congress or the People's Congress system can represent the whole of our political life and the source of our political power."

Establishing the Principles of People's Democracy and Socialism in the *Constitution*

The NPC is the highest state authority, with legislative and supervisory powers, and is responsible for formulating and amending the *Constitution*. Governing a country requires a fundamental law. The constitution is the fundamental law of a country, reflecting its pursuit and quality of democracy. The CPC attaches great importance to formulating and revising laws, especially the *Constitution*.

Mao Zedong personally presided over the drafting of the constitution. In November 1952, Mao Zedong convened a seminar with 18 non-party democrats to solicit opinions on the basis and role of the constitution. Most people believed that formulating the constitution would take a lot of work. Mao Zedong said that difficulties could be overcome, pointing out that during the Revolution of 1911 led by Sun Yat-sen, the *Provisional Constitution* was formulated in just a few days by 19 representatives (one from each province) after the establishment of the temporary government in Nanjing. The drafting of the *Common Program*, after discussions, actually took only about a month.

The preparatory work for drafting the *Constitution* began immediately based on Mao Zedong's opinions. Mao Zedong believed that the guiding principle for drafting the *Constitution* should be "based on facts," starting from China's actual situation at that time and referring to foreign constitutions (including socialist and capitalist ones) and past Chinese constitutions. He believed that it was absolutely necessary to refer to other countries' constitutions and China's historical constitutions when drafting the national *Constitution*. Good ideas from others, combined with China's national conditions, should be absorbed; even bad or reactionary ideas could serve as a warning. Mao Zedong read domestic and foreign constitutions and listed books for the Political

Bureau and Central Committee members in Beijing to read. This was the first time that the top leaders of the CPC systematically studied law. As China's *Constitution* belongs to the socialist type, Mao Zedong focused on studying the 1918 *Soviet Constitution*, the 1936 *Soviet Constitution*, and the constitutions of Eastern European people's democratic countries. The 1918 *Soviet Constitution* included Lenin's "Declaration of the Rights of the Exploited Working People" as the first part. Inspired by this, Mao Zedong decided to write a preamble before the general principles of the *Constitution*. The form of a "preamble" became a feature of the *Constitution of the People's Republic of China* and has been maintained until now. Mao Zedong also studied capitalist constitutions. He said, "Speaking of constitutions, the bourgeoisie was the forerunner. The bourgeoisie, whether in Britain, France or the United States, was revolutionary for a period, and it was during this period that the bourgeoisie began making constitutions. We should not write off bourgeois democracy with one stroke of the pen and deny bourgeois constitutions a place in history."

In January 1953, the Central Committee of CPC established the Drafting Committee of the Constitution of the People's Republic of China, chaired by Mao Zedong. To coordinate the discussion of the draft *Constitution*, in March 1953, the Central Committee of CPC also established the Constitution Drafting Group led by Mao Zedong, who personally participated in the work. The members included Chen Boda, Hu Qiaomu, Dong Biwu, Peng Zhen, Deng Xiaoping, Li Weihan, Zhang Jichun, and Tian Jiaying.

Based on a series of preparations, Mao Zedong led a team to draft the *Constitution* in early 1954 in Hangzhou. Mao Zedong said, "The *Constitution* is the fundamental law of a country, and everyone, from the Party Chairman and Government Chairman to ordinary people, should follow it. In the future, whoever takes my place as Party and Government Chairman must also follow it. This rule must be established." On March 23, Mao Zedong held the first meeting of the Drafting Committee of the Constitution in Beijing, deciding that the National Committee of the CPPCC, the leading organs of major administrative regions and provinces and cities, and the local organizations of various democratic parties and people's groups would all engage in extensive discussions on the draft *Constitution*. From then until June 11, over 8,000 people from the CPPCC, provincial and municipal party and government organs, military leadership organs, democratic parties, and people's groups discussed and submitted more than 5,900 amendments.

On June 11, the seventh meeting of the Drafting Committee of the Constitution was held, during which the amended draft *Constitution* was discussed and passed.

Mao Zedong said, "The drafting of the *Constitution* took almost seven months. The first draft … had seven or eight revisions. Altogether, there were probably a dozen or twenty drafts. Everyone made great efforts, and more than 8,000 people nationwide discussed and submitted more than 5,000 suggestions, adopting hundreds of them. Finally, even today, we still rely on the discussion and revision of those present. In short, we have studied it repeatedly and in detail, and after its publication, we will solicit the opinions of people across the country. The *Constitution* is drafted in such a way as to seek the opinions of the broad masses of the people. The draft *Constitution* is generally suitable for the situation of our country. After the nationwide discussion, good suggestions will be put forward, and there will be some modifications, but there will not be any major changes overall."

On June 14, the Central People's Government Committee held its 30th meeting. After enthusiastic discussions, the meeting unanimously passed the "Draft Constitution of the People's Republic of China." It announced it to the nation, calling on the masses to actively submit their opinions on amendments to the *Constitution*. Mao Zedong delivered an important speech on the "Draft Constitution of the People's Republic of China" at the meeting. He said, "A constitution is a set of general rules, it is the fundamental law. To codify the principles of people's democracy and socialism in the form of a fundamental law, in the form of the constitution, so that there will be a clear course before the people of the whole country and they will feel sure they have a clear, definite and correct path to follow—this will heighten their enthusiasm."

On June 16, the *People's Daily* published an editorial titled "Extensively Launching Discussions on the Draft Constitution of the People's Republic of China among the People Nationwide," which set off a nationwide wave of enthusiastic discussions on the draft *Constitution*. The discussion lasted nearly three months, with more than 150 million participating. The people of the whole country submitted more than 1.18 million suggestions for amendments and supplements to the draft *Constitution*, providing important evidence for the final revision before submitting it to the NPC for deliberation.

On September 9, 1954, the Central People's Government Committee held its 34th meeting. The meeting discussed and passed the "Draft Constitution of the People's Republic of China" and decided to submit it to the NPC.

On September 14, the Central People's Government Committee held a temporary meeting chaired by Mao Zedong, who also delivered a speech. He pointed out: "This is a relatively complete *Constitution*. The Central Committee of CPC first drafted it, then discussed it with more than 500 senior cadres in Beijing, followed by discussions by more than 8,000 people nationwide, and then a three-month national people's discussion. More than 1,000 NPC representatives discussed it again this time. The drafting of the *Constitution* was cautious, and every article and every character was carefully prepared, but it is not necessary to say that it is flawless and seamless. This *Constitution* is suitable for our current practical situation. It adheres to principles while maintaining flexibility."

On September 20, 1954, the First NPC held its first plenary session, which unanimously passed the *Constitution of the People's Republic of China*. One thousand one hundred ninety-seven representatives were attending the meeting, and 1,197 votes were cast, all of which were in favor. After a long struggle, the Chinese people finally had a legal document representing their interests and reflecting democratic and socialist principles. Mao Zedong pointed out: "Our draft *Constitution* combines principledness and flexibility. There are basically two principles: democratic principles and socialist principles. Our democracy is not bourgeois democracy but people's democracy, a people's democratic dictatorship led by the proletariat and based on the worker-peasant alliance. The principle of people's democracy runs through our entire *Constitution*. The other is the principle of socialism. Our country has socialism now. The *Constitution* stipulates that we must complete the socialist transformation and realize the industrialization of socialism in the country. This is principled ness." "We write what we can implement now and don't write what we can't. For example, the material guarantee of citizens' rights will be expanded when production develops, but what we write now is still 'gradually expanding.' This is also flexibility."

After promulgating the 1954 *Constitution*, it promoted the development and progress of various undertakings in China. However, due to the lack of a tradition of the rule of law and the long tradition of feudal autocracy in China, the spirit of the rule of law was not fully demonstrated for a considerable period. After the end of the "Great Cultural Revolution," the CPC learned from its painful experiences. It attached great importance to the construction of the rule of law, entering a new era of governing the country according to law.

— CHAPTER 7 —

Restoring and Developing the National Economy

The newly founded People's Republic of China faced a complex and severe international and domestic situation. How to consolidate the people's political power and quickly restore the national economy severely damaged in Old China became a major issue that the governing CPC, represented mainly by Mao Zedong, needed to solve. A series of measures were taken to consolidate the newly born democratic political power and establish a New Democratic economic system. By the end of 1952, the production of most major agricultural and industrial products had been restored to or exceeded historic highs, and the task of restoring and developing the national economy was successfully completed.

The Mess Left by the KMT

The economic development level of Old China needed to be revised. With the long-term war, the entire country's economy was on the brink of collapse when the People's Republic of China was established.

Regarding industrial production, China's pig iron output in 1949 fell to 250,000 tons, which was only 23.9% of the highest annual output in history. Steel output fell to

158,000 tons, only 17% of the highest annual output in history. The country's largest steel base, Anshan, was in ruins. Workshops were overgrown with weeds, bird nests were built on top of blast furnaces, and there were no intact workshops or working machines. Of the original 100,000 workers, only a few thousand remained. Most of the country's coal mines had also ceased production, with severely damaged equipment and flooded mine pits. In 1949, coal output was only 32 million tons, down 42.4% from the highest annual output in history. Electricity generation that year was only 4.3 billion kWh, down 28.3% from the highest annual output in history. The situation of other industrial products was: cement output was down 71.2% compared to the highest annual output in history, sulfuric acid output was down 77.4%, cotton yarn output was down 24.5%, cotton cloth output was down 32.3%, cigarette output was down 32.3%, and sugar output was down 51.9%.

Agricultural production was also severely damaged. In 1949, the number of draft animals in rural areas was 17% less than before the war, the main agricultural tools were 30% less, and the cultivated land area was reduced from 1.5 billion *mu* (one *mu* is the same as 666.67 m²) to 1.4376 billion *mu*, a decrease of about 4%. Due to the long-term disrepair of river embankments and other water conservancy facilities and war damage, the disaster situation in 1949 was dire. The affected area of farmland reached 120 million *mu*; grain output was only 113.18 million tons, down 25% from the highest annual output in history; cotton output was 444,000 tons, down 47.6% from the highest annual output in history; and oil crop output was 2.564 million tons, down 57.8% from the highest annual output in history. Flue-cured tobacco and tea output was down 76% and 81.8%, respectively, compared to the highest annual output in history. The number of pigs in that year also fell 26.5% compared to the highest number in history. People across the country faced the threat of hunger. Industrial raw materials were extremely scarce, and many factories needed help to start work.

The transportation industry was also severely damaged. A total of 20,000 kilometers of national railways (80% of the total railway length), more than 3,200 bridges (totaling 155 kilometers in length), and over 200 tunnels (totaling more than 40 kilometers in length) were severely damaged and unusable. Main lines such as Jinpu, Jinghan, Yuehan, Longhai, and Zhegan were not fully operational for over a decade. National highways were also paralyzed due to war damage. The retreating KMT mostly took away shipping and air transport vessels and aircraft to Taiwan. In contrast, those that could not be taken were either sunk or destroyed, leaving ports and airports severely damaged. Shanghai had only 145,000 tons of usable ships, accounting for 12.7% of the original tonnage.

In addition to the severe economic situation described above, at that time, the country was also facing two major challenges: soaring prices and a very difficult financial situation.

There were significant price fluctuations before and after the founding of the People's Republic of China, with four large-scale price increases occurring nationwide. The first happened in April 1949, when prices in North China rose, affecting Shandong, Northern Jiangsu, and Central China. Taking the wholesale price index of North China as an example, it was 100 in December 1948, 261 in March 1949, and it surged to 380 in May. The second wave was in July 1949. Due to the enemy's blockade of Shanghai and severe typhoon flooding, speculators shifted their focus from gold, silver, and foreign currencies to food and yarn. Shanghai experienced fluctuations for 33 days from June 27 to July 30, with the wholesale price index rising more than 1.5 times in July compared to June. The third wave was from October to November 1949. In mid-October, speculators triggered a large-scale price fluctuation, starting from Shanghai and Tianjin and spreading to Central and Northwest China, lasting for a month and a half. The focus of speculation shifted from imported goods such as hardware and chemical raw materials to yarn and food. By November 25, the wholesale price index in Shanghai had increased by 2.26 times compared to early October, while other cities saw price increases of 3 to 4 times. The fourth wave was in February 1950. On February 6 (11 days before the Spring Festival), the KMT bombed Shanghai, severely damaging the power plant and causing factories to shut down, significantly reducing yarn production. As the Spring Festival approached, speculators took advantage of the situation and hoarded goods, causing the prices of industrial products to rise. According to statistics of 25 major commodities in 15 cities, the wholesale price index was 100 in December 1949, 126.2 in January 1950, 203.3 in February, and 226.3 in March. Based on the wholesale price index of 12 major cities with December 1948 as 100, the index rose to 153 in January 1949, 1,059 in July, and 5,376 in November. Beijing's price index increased by 171% in May 1949 compared to February. In November 1949, the daily price of food, cotton yarn, hardware, and chemical products in Shanghai increased by 20%–30%. From June 1949 to February 1950, the wholesale price in Shanghai increased by about 20 times.

Before and after the founding of the People's Republic of China, the country faced great financial difficulties. A year of decisive victory in the War of Liberation and extreme financial hardship marked 1949. The reasons for this were: First, the country had not been fully liberated, and the War of Liberation was still ongoing, with military expenses accounting for about half of the fiscal revenue; Second, the Central

People's Government took over several million military and political personnel left by the KMT government, along with the Communist military and political personnel, totaling more than 9 million people, all of whom had to be supported by the state; Third, key transportation, industrial, and mining enterprises needed to be restored, and a large number of unemployed people needed relief, all of which had to be borne by the government. In 1949, the national fiscal revenue was equivalent to 30.3 billion *jin* of millet, while the fiscal expenditure reached 56.7 billion *jin*. The resulting huge fiscal deficit had to be covered by issuing more paper money. Although this approach met the needs of the War of Liberation and the restoration of production at the time, it could not prevent the price rise.

These were the material "legacies" left to the CPC by the Old China.

Win a "Huaihai Campaign" in the Economy

In the face of a difficult economic situation, some people doubted the CPC's ability to manage the economy, while others simply did not believe that the Party could manage it well. They observed, saying, "The CPC scores full marks in military affairs, eighty marks in politics, but perhaps zero in economics." However, the Central Committee of CPC faced the challenge head-on and took a series of major measures to revive the economy.

First, confiscating bureaucratic capital and establishing a state-owned economy with socialist characteristics.

The economic foundation on which the Chiang Kai-shek regime relied was the bureaucratic capital represented by the four major families of Chiang, Song, Kong, and Chen. It was estimated that after the end of the War of Resistance, the assets owned by these four families amounted to 10 to 20 billion US dollars. On the eve of the founding of New China in 1949, bureaucratic capital owned 80% of the fixed assets in the national industry, mining, and transportation sectors, monopolizing 90% of steel production, 67% of electricity, 33% of coal, 100% of non-ferrous metals and petroleum, 45% of cement, 80% of sulfuric acid, 60% of weaving machines, 38% of yarn spindles, and 90% of sugar. They also controlled the country's financial institutions, railways, highways, postal and telecommunications, aviation transportation, foreign trade, and cultural undertakings.

Confiscating bureaucratic capital and making it state-owned was one of the three major economic programs of the New Democratic Revolution. Through the confiscation of bureaucratic capital, the state-owned economy of New China had already gained a dominant position in finance and modern industry, transportation, and other fields by 1949. In the industrial sector, the output of state-owned enterprises accounted for about 50% of the total output. The state-owned economy had an absolute advantage in finance, railways, ports, aviation, and other industries. The confiscation of bureaucratic capital provided favorable conditions for establishing a state-owned economy with socialist characteristics.

Second, stabilizing the market and curbing price fluctuations.

Factors causing price fluctuations included the severe financial difficulties of the newly established country, excessive currency issuance, and speculative merchants taking advantage of the national difficulties to hoard goods, manipulate prices, and pursue exorbitant profits, exacerbating market chaos and price fluctuations. To combat speculative capital, stabilize the market, and curb price fluctuations, in July 1949, with the support of Mao Zedong, the Central Committee of CPC established the Central Finance and Economics Committee, headed by Chen Yun, which immediately engaged in the struggle on the economic front.

After the liberation of Shanghai on May 27, 1949, financial speculators triggered a surge in silver yuan prices. The black-market price of each silver yuan rose from over 600 yuan to over 1,800 yuan, driving up overall prices. As the national financial center, Shanghai greatly impacted the entire country. Stabilizing Shanghai was key to stabilizing the whole country. On June 10, with the approval of the Central Committee of CPC, the Shanghai Military Administration Committee sealed off the Securities Building, cracking down on illegal activities that disrupted the financial order and winning the "Battle of the Silver Yuan," allowing the RMB to enter the market circulation smoothly. Subsequently, the Central People's Government quickly established the absolute leadership of the People's Bank of China in the national financial industry. It stipulated that private financial institutions would be supervised and managed by the People's Bank of China.

The speculative capital in Shanghai hit during the "Battle of the Silver Yuan" was unwilling to admit defeat and soon turned to the grain, cotton yarn, and coal markets. Taking advantage of the scarcity of materials, they engaged in speculative business, triggering another nationwide wave of price increases. Some people boldly claimed: "As long as we control the 'two whites and one black' (rice, cotton yarn, and coal), we can bring Shanghai to its knees."

Under these circumstances, to defeat speculative capital, the Central Government mobilized a batch of rice, cotton, and cloth across the country, which would be directly controlled by the Central Finance and Economics Committee. They would appropriately sell these items in bulk to deal a devastating blow to the speculative capitalists. The more they sold, the cheaper the prices became, making it increasingly difficult for them to sell. Eventually, they suffered significant losses and went bankrupt, unable to make a comeback.

The struggle to combat speculative capital and curb price fluctuations achieved complete victory under the Central Committee of CPC's careful guidance and the people's support nationwide. Starting from March 1950, prices across the country gradually fell, ending the situation of soaring prices and market chaos. This struggle consolidated the newly born People's Government, enhanced the prestige of the Communist Party, and showed that the Communist Party was capable of winning the world and also skilled at governing it. Mao Zedong highly praised this struggle in the economic field, believing that its significance was no less than winning a new Huaihai Campaign.

Third, unifying national fiscal and economic policies.

The fundamental cause of price fluctuations was the large fiscal deficit of the state, and the issue of excessive currency issuance still needed to be resolved. Only by achieving a balance in national fiscal revenue and expenditure and a balance in the supply and demand of market materials could the fundamental stability of prices be ensured. Therefore, the People's Government implemented unified leadership and management of national fiscal and economic work based on the development of the situation and concentrated material resources to ensure a balance in fiscal revenue and expenditure.

In March 1950, the State Council issued the "Decision on Unifying National Fiscal and Economic Work," the main content of which was: "Unifying national fiscal revenue, concentrating the main part of national revenue in the Central Government for major national expenditures; unifying national material allocation, centralizing important materials controlled by the state from a scattered state for rational use and adjustment of surplus and shortage; unifying national cash management, requiring all military and political institutions and state-owned enterprises to deposit their cash in the national bank, except for a small amount for short-term use, for unified allocation. At the same time, the government also took measures such as tightening staffing, clearing warehouses, strengthening taxation, issuing government bonds, and saving expenditures, which all had noticeable effects."

On April 30, 1950, Mao Zedong delivered a speech at the Seventh Meeting of the Central People's Government Committee, proposing three conditions required for the fundamental improvement of the national fiscal and economic situation: "Completion of agrarian reform, proper readjustment of existing industry and commerce; and large-scale retrenchment in government expenditures." On June 6, the third plenary session of the seventh CPC Central Committee was held, with the central issue being financial and economic matters. Mao Zedong named his keynote report at the meeting (written report) "Struggling for the Fundamental Improvement of the National Fiscal and Economic Situation," setting forth the goals and tasks of the Party and the people during the period of national economic recovery. In the report, Mao Zedong clearly stated: "Three conditions are required for the fundamental turn for the better in the financial and economic situation, namely (1) completion of agrarian reform, (2) proper readjustment of existing industry and commerce, and (3) large-scale retrenchment in government expenditures. The fulfillment of these three conditions will take some time, say three years or a little longer. The whole Party and nation must strive to bring about these conditions. I believe, and so do you all, that we can surely do this in about three years. By that time, we shall be able to witness a fundamental turn for the better in the entire financial and economic situation of our country."

In his oral speech, Mao Zedong emphasized the issue of "not attacking all fronts." He said: "We must not attack all fronts. Attacking on all fronts will make the whole country tense, which is not good. We must not make too many enemies; we must make concessions to ease tensions in one aspect and concentrate our forces on attacking another aspect. We must do our work well so that workers, peasants, small artisans, and most of the national bourgeoisie and intellectuals do not oppose us. It is to eliminate the remnant KMT forces, the secret agents and the bandits, overthrow the landlord class, liberate Taiwan and Xizang and fight imperialism to the end. In order to isolate and attack our immediate enemies, we must convert those among the people who are dissatisfied with us into our supporters. Although this task is fraught with difficulties at present, we must overcome them by every possible means."

Under the influence of unified national fiscal and economic policies and measures, the prices in the country remained basically stable and slightly declined after March 1950. The increase since July was due to the outbreak of the Korean War, which caused some fluctuations in the prices of imported goods. However, the prices of people's daily necessities remained basically stable, proving that the work of unifying national fiscal and economic policies had achieved good results.

Fourth, rationally adjusting private industry and commerce.

Before and after the founding of New China, private industry and commerce played a pivotal role in the national economy. According to statistics, in 1949, the output value of the capitalist industry accounted for 63% of the country's total industrial output value. The proportion of various major industrial products was as follows: electricity 36%, coal 28%, sulfuric acid 27%, caustic soda 59%, cement 26%, machinery and machine parts 50%, cotton yarn 47%, flour 79%, cigarettes 80%, matches 81%, and paper 63%. The proportion of private commerce was even larger, with private commerce accounting for 76.1% of the total wholesale volume and 85% of the total retail volume in 1950. The role of private industry and commerce in providing products to society, promoting commodity circulation, increasing employment, and restoring and developing the national economy must be addressed.

Between March and April 1950, new economic difficulties emerged in the country, such as market depression, factory closures, and increased unemployment. The development of capitalist industry and commerce was greatly affected. The government faced a dilemma: stabilizing prices while maintaining production, appropriately slowing down tax collection and addressing the practical difficulties of private industry and commerce. In Chen Yun's words, "Now the government is carrying 'two baskets of eggs' and must not break either end."

In response to this situation, the Central Government made a timely decision to adjust industry and commerce. On April 30, Mao Zedong explicitly pointed out that the current focus of the government's financial and economic leadership was on adjusting industry and commerce. After the third plenary session of the seventh CPC Central Committee, the state's adjustment of private industry and commerce was fully launched. The guideline was: "Under build a general framework to coordinate work, gradually eliminate the blindness and anarchy in the economy, rationally adjust existing industry and commerce, effectively and properly improve the relationship between the public and private sectors, and labor and capital relations, so that various social, economic components, under the leadership of the state-owned economy of a socialist nature, can cooperate and find their proper places, promoting the recovery and development of the entire social economy."

Thanks to the correct policies and effective measures taken by the government, private industry and commerce experienced significant growth. In 1952, compared with 1949, the number of private industrial enterprises increased by 26,600, a 21.6% increase; the number of employees increased by 412,800, a 21.6% increase; and the total output value increased by 3.698 billion yuan, a 54.2% increase. Compared with 1950, the number of private commercial enterprises in 1952 increased by 280,000, a 1.9% increase; the number of employees increased by 140,000, a 2.2% increase; and the retail sales of commodities increased by 1.91 billion yuan, an 18.6% increase. The development of private capitalist industry and commerce played an important role in restoring the national economy and fundamentally improving the financial and economic situation of the country.

Fifth, launching the campaign to increase production and save resources, and the "Three-Antis" and "Five-Antis" movements.

To alleviate the severe financial and economic pressures and bear the huge military expenses brought about by the Korean War, a nationwide campaign to increase production and save resources was launched under the extensive mobilization of the Party and the government. In October 1951, an enlarged meeting of the Political Bureau of the Central Committee of CPC put forward the policy of "strengthening the army and streamlining the administration, increasing production and saving resources." On October 23, Mao Zedong pointed out in his opening speech at the Third Session of the First National People's Political Consultative Conference that resisting US aggression, aiding Korea, increasing production, and saving resources were the central tasks of the Chinese people. The campaign to increase production and save resources was then vigorously carried out nationwide, with specific measures including formulating plans for increasing production and saving resources, cleaning up assets, determining capital and production capacity, organizing production competitions, advocating rationalization proposals, and promoting advanced production experiences. The campaign achieved good economic benefits and had a positive social impact.

During the campaign to increase production and save resources, various regions exposed the "three evils" (corruption, waste, and bureaucracy) among cadres and the severe "five poisons" (bribery, tax evasion, shoddy workmanship, theft of state property, and theft of state economic intelligence) in private industry and commerce. In response to this situation, at the end of 1951, the Central Committee of CPC decided to launch the "Three-Antis" movement against corruption, waste, and bureaucracy among the staff of party and government organs, and the "Five-Antis" movement against bribery, tax evasion, shoddy workmanship, theft of state property, and theft of state economic intelligence among private industrialists and businessmen. The "Three-Antis" movement educated the majority of cadres, saved comrades who made mistakes, purified party organizations and cadre teams, resisted the erosion of decadent bourgeois ideas, and played a significant role in forming a good social atmosphere. The "Five-Antis" movement repelled the rampant attacks of unscrupulous capitalists, carried out a widespread education on law-abiding operations in private industry and commerce, and created favorable conditions for the subsequent transformation of capitalist industry and commerce.

After the outbreak of the Korean War, with the changes in the Korean War situation and domestic circumstances, the guiding principle of national financial and economic work gradually shifted from "national defense first, market stability second, and everything else third" to the policy of "fighting, stabilizing, and building simultaneously." The implementation of this policy supported and won the victory of the Korean War while maintaining the stability of domestic market prices, and in the shortest possible time, enabled the recovery and development of industrial and agricultural production, transportation, and material exchanges, thus promoting the restoration of the national economy.

The Miracle of National Economic Recovery

Under the leadership of the Party, the arduous task of restoring the national economy was successfully completed in just three years, achieving a fundamental improvement in the country's financial and economic situation.

The achievements of national economic recovery are specifically manifested in the following aspects:

First, the recovery and development of industrial and agricultural production, with the output of major products reaching or exceeding historical highs and significant improvements in technology and equipment levels.

Regarding industrial production, steel output reached 1.349 million tons in 1952, a 7.54-fold increase compared to 1949 and a 46.2% increase over the historical high. Pig iron output reached 1.929 million tons in 1952, a 6.66-fold increase compared to 1949 and a 7.1% increase over the historical high. Coal output reached 66.49 million tons in 1952, a 105% increase compared to 1949 and a 7.4% increase over the historical high. Electricity generation reached 7.26 billion kWh in 1952, a 68.1% increase compared to 1949 and a 21.9% increase over the historical high. Cotton yarn output, closely related to people's lives, reached 3.62 million pieces in 1952, a 1-fold increase compared to 1949 and a 47.8% increase over the historical high; cotton cloth output reached 3.83 billion meters in 1952, a 1.03-fold increase compared to 1949, and a 37.4% increase over the historical high.

In terms of agricultural production, the output of major products experienced significant growth, and the number of rural laborers, draft animals, agricultural tools, and cultivated land all reached or exceeded prewar levels. Grain output reached 163.92 million tons in 1952, a 36% increase compared to 1949 and a 9.3% increase over the historical high. Cotton output reached 1.304 million tons in 1952, a 1.93-fold increase compared to 1949 and a 53% increase over the historical high. Large livestock reached 76.46 million in 1952, a 27% increase compared to 1949 and a 6.9% increase over the historical high. The number of live pigs in stock reached 89,770 in 1952, a 55.2% increase compared to 1949 and a 14.3% increase over the historical high. Over the three years, the output value of rural sideline industries increased by approximately 55.1%. According to statistics, compared with 1949, the average grain yield per *mu* increased by 15%, the average cotton yield per mu increased by 41%, the average rapeseed yield per *mu* increased by 3%, and the average soybean yield per *mu* increased by 33%.

Second, the recovery and development of the transportation industry and domestic and foreign trade.

After three years of effort, China's transportation industry restored its original routes and achieved new development. In 1952, the total railway operating mileage reached 22,900 kilometers, passenger volume was 163.52 million, and freight volume was 132.17 million tons. The highway mileage reached 126,700 kilometers, passenger volume was 45.59 million, and freight volume was 131.58 million tons, with the number of heavy-duty trucks increasing from 32,000 in 1949 to 44,300 in 1952. The inland waterway mileage was 95,000 kilometers, passenger volume was 36.05 million, and freight volume was 51.41 million tons, with the cargo capacity of ships increasing from 370,000 tons in 1949 to 530,000 tons in 1952. Civil aviation routes reached 13,100 kilometers, passenger volume was 20,000, and freight volume was 2,000 tons. Except for railway passenger and freight transportation volume, which was slightly lower than the highest level before the establishment of New China, all other indicators exceeded the historical highs.

After three years of recovery, urban and rural markets across the country presented a prosperous scene of thriving buying and selling. In 1952, the total national social commodity retail sales amounted to 2.768 billion yuan, an increase of 62.3% compared to 1950. The sales of various major commodities increased in 1952 as follows, with the 1950 price index being 100: grain 271.28%, cotton yarn 171.43%, cotton cloth 245.76%, coal 141.68%, kerosene 262.67%, salt 152.89%, and cigarettes 149.41%.

Over the three years, the purchase amount of agricultural and sideline products and the supply of production materials also increased significantly. In 1952, the total purchase amount of agricultural and sideline products reached 12.97 billion yuan, an increase of 62.1% compared to 1950; the supply of agricultural production materials reached 1.41 billion yuan, an increase of 93.2% compared to 1950. The import and export trade volume in 1952 was 6.46 billion yuan, an increase of 55.5% compared to 1950.

Third, the national fiscal situation underwent a fundamental improvement.

From 1950 to 1952, the fiscal revenue and expenditure situation for the three years was as follows: In 1950, the total revenue was 6.52 billion yuan, and the total expenditure was 6.81 billion yuan, with expenditures exceeding revenue and a fiscal deficit of 290 million yuan, accounting for 4.1% of the total expenditure. In 1951, the total revenue was 13.31 billion yuan, and the total expenditure was 12.25 billion yuan, an increase of 104.9% and 79.8%, respectively, compared to 1950, with revenues exceeding expenditures, turning deficits into surpluses and a balance of 1.06 billion yuan for that year. In 1952, the total revenue was 18.37 billion yuan, and the total expenditure was 17.6 billion yuan, continuing the growth momentum, increasing by 38% and 43.7%, respectively, compared to the previous year, with revenues and expenditures offsetting each other, leaving a balance of 770 million yuan. The national finance turned from deficits to surpluses and achieved consecutive surpluses, marking a fundamental change as the country's finances had passed its most difficult period.

Fourth, the people's material and cultural living standards have significantly improved and increased.

The living standards of farmers greatly improved. According to statistics, farmers' income in 1952 increased by more than 30% compared to 1949, and the average per capita consumption level increased by about 20%. The average annual grain consumption per person was 383 *jin* (1 *jin* = 0.5 kg), edible oil 3.4 *jin*, meat 11 *jin*, and cotton cloth 13.7 *chi* (1 *chi* = ⅓ meter) increased by about 50% compared to 1949. The living conditions of urban residents also improved significantly over the three years. In 1952, compared with 1949, the total number of employees nationwide increased from 8 million to around 16 million, and the average wage of employees increased by 70%. Labor insurance systems were implemented in large enterprises, and public-funded medical systems were implemented among public education staff. In addition, the state constructed 14.62 million square meters of employee housing, improving the living conditions of employees.

Fifth, major changes occurred in the national economic structure.

As the economy recovered, profound changes occurred in the national economic structure. State-owned economy, private capitalist economy, individual economy, state capitalism, and cooperative economy all developed. Due to state support and the superiority of the socialist economy, the state-owned economy developed more rapidly. In 1949, the socialist industry accounted for 34.7% of the country's total industrial output value (excluding the handicraft industry), which increased to 56% in 1952. On the other hand, the change was that the total industrial output value (including the handicraft industry) as a proportion of the total national agricultural and industrial output value rose from 30% in 1949 to 41.5%. Among them, the output value of modern industry increased from 17% to 26.6%. In the total industrial output value, the proportion of heavy industry output value increased from 26.4% in 1949 to 35.5% in 1952. This provided an important reference for the Central Committee of CPC to decide on the transition to socialism.

In summary, the successful completion of the national economic recovery tasks from 1949 to 1952 was a strategic victory achieved by the CPC, leading the Chinese people. It is an important milestone in the history of China's socialist revolution and construction, laying the foundation for later socialist transformation and socialist industrialization construction.

CHAPTER 8

Independent and Self-Reliant Diplomatic Policy

The founding of the People's Republic of China marked a new era in Chinese diplomacy. Against the backdrop of the Cold War and in response to the hostile blockade policies adopted by Western countries against China and the doubts harbored by neighboring countries toward the new China, Chinese Communists, represented mainly by Mao Zedong, proposed a diplomatic policy of "sole alliance with the Soviet Union" and the diplomatic guidelines of "reinvent the wheel" and "cleaning up the house before inviting guests." Under these diplomatic policies and guidelines, China established a new type of equal diplomatic relations with socialist countries, nationalist countries, and capitalist countries in Northwest Europe, making a debut on the international stage and gaining a firm foothold.

"Cleaning Up the House before Inviting Guests"

On the eve of the decisive victory of the New Democratic Revolution, with the frequent reports of victories by the PLA of China on the battlefield, the KMT government quickly collapsed, and the control of the imperialist countries was also overthrown. However, they left a lot of "mud and mire" on Chinese soil that urgently needed to be cleaned up. This "mud and mire" included the treaties and agreements in the political, economic, cultural, and other fields signed between the imperialist countries and old China. The imperialist countries forced old China to cede territory and pay reparations through these treaties and agreements. It was necessary to thoroughly eliminate these "mud and mire" to avoid future problems.

To this end, Mao Zedong proposed "cleaning up the house before inviting guests." In dealing with the issue of establishing diplomatic relations with imperialist countries, especially the United States, it was preferable to wait. First, the residual forces of imperialism in China and their influence should be cleaned up, leaving no room for their activities.

From February 1 to 3, 1949, Mao Zedong talked with Stalin's representative, Mikoyan, who was sent to Xibaipo. When talking about China's foreign policy, Mao Zedong pointed out: "If we metaphorically compare our country to a family, the house is too dirty, with firewood, garbage, dust, fleas, bedbugs, lice, and so on. After liberation, we must rectify it properly. We can invite guests in when the house is clean, tidy, orderly, and well-furnished. Our real friends can enter the house early and even help us do some cleaning, but other guests must wait; we can't let them in for now."

In March, Mao Zedong further pointed out at the second plenary session of the seventh CPC Central Committee: "In each city or place where the KMT troops are wiped out and the KMT government is overthrown, imperialist political domination is overthrown with it, and so is imperialist economic and cultural domination. But the economic and cultural establishments run directly by the imperialists are still there, and so are the diplomatic personnel and the journalists recognized by the KMT. We must deal with all these properly in their order of urgency." Mao Zedong pointed out: "Refuse to recognize the legal status of any foreign diplomatic establishments and personnel of the KMT period, refuse to recognize all the treasonable treaties of the KMT period, abolish all imperialist propaganda agencies in China, take immediate control of foreign trade and reform the customs system these are the first steps we must take upon entering the big cities. When they have acted thus, the Chinese people will have stood up in the face of imperialism. As for the remaining imperialist economic and cultural establishments, they can be allowed to exist for the time being, subject to our supervision and control, to be dealt with by us after country-wide victory. As for ordinary foreign nationals, their legitimate interests will be protected and not encroached upon." Mao Zedong also pointed out: "As for the question of the recognition of our country by the imperialist countries, we should not be in a hurry to solve it now and need not be in a hurry to solve it even for a fairly long period after countrywide victory. We are willing to establish diplomatic relations with all countries on the principle of equality, but the imperialists, who have always been hostile to the Chinese people, will definitely not be in a hurry to treat us as equals. As long as the imperialist countries do not change their hostile attitude, we shall not grant them legal status in China. As for doing business with foreigners, there is no question; wherever there is business to do, we shall do it and we have already started; the businessmen of several capitalist countries are competing for such business. So far as possible, we must first of all trade with the socialist and people's democratic countries; at the same time we will also trade with capitalist countries."

After the liberation of Nanjing in April 1949, US Ambassador John Leighton Stuart did not follow the KMT to Guangzhou but tried to contact the CPC. However, one of the important preconditions for the United States to recognize the Communist government was that "the government has the ability and willingness to fulfill its international obligations." This essentially required the new regime to acknowledge the unequal treaties signed between the historical Chinese government and foreign countries and for China to continue accepting a semi-colonial international status, which the CPC could not accept.

Regarding the diplomatic guideline of "cleaning up the house before inviting guests," in April 1952, Zhou Enlai, Premier of the State Council and Foreign Minister, elaborated on it at a meeting of Chinese envoys abroad. He said: "Imperialism always wants to retain some privileges in China and wants to worm its way in. One country wants to negotiate the establishment of diplomatic relations with us. Our policy is to wait a while. First, we need to clear the residual forces of imperialism in our country. Otherwise, they will have room for activities. We must 'clean up the house' before establishing diplomatic relations and 'clean up the house before inviting guests.' However, the cleaning process should be gradual and not rushed."

Closely related to the "cleaning up the house before inviting guests" guideline is the proposal for the "starting a new stove" policy.

In January 1949, Mao Zedong proposed to review the draft instructions of the Central Committee of CPC on diplomatic issues: "We do not recognize any embassies, legations, consulates, and their affiliated diplomatic agencies and personnel of capitalist countries recognized by the KMT government before the People's Republic of China establishes diplomatic relations with these countries. We treat them only as foreign residents, but they should be effectively protected. These countries' military attachés should be treated the same way as diplomats. However, American military attachés who directly supported the KMT in the civil war should be under surveillance and not given freedom. For the embassies, legations, and their affiliated diplomatic agencies and personnel of the Soviet Union and the New Democratic countries, since their foreign policy is fundamentally different from that of capitalist countries, our attitude toward them should also be fundamentally different from that toward capitalist countries. However, since the People's Republic has not yet established diplomatic relations with them and other foreign countries, we have only informal diplomatic contacts with their diplomatic agencies in China and their affiliated military attachés."

Although Mao Zedong proposed different diplomatic policies for capitalist and socialist countries here, he emphasized that no formal diplomatic exchanges would be conducted with any country before establishing diplomatic relations with New China, showing the determination of New China to "start a new stove."

Based on this principle, in April 1949, the Central Committee of CPC sent a telegram to Deng Xiaoping, Liu Bocheng, and others who had occupied Nanjing: Regarding the embassies and legations in Nanjing, our PLA Military Administration and the municipal government should not have any formal diplomatic dealings with them, nor should they make any written or verbal acknowledgment of their ambassador or minister status. The purpose of doing so is to draw a clear line between the humiliating diplomacy pursued by successive governments of Old China as a semi-colonial state; at the same time, it also shows that newborn China will establish a new type of diplomatic relationship with all countries in the world based on mutual respect for sovereignty and equality. *The Common Program* explicitly stipulates: "The People's Republic of China must cancel all the privileges of imperialism in China." "The government of the People's Republic of China should review all treaties and agreements signed between the KMT government and foreign countries, and recognize, abolish, amend, or renegotiate them according to their content."

On October 1, 1949, Mao Zedong, on behalf of the Central People's Government of the People's Republic of China, announced to the world that it was willing to establish diplomatic relations with any foreign government that adheres to equality, mutual benefit, and mutual respect for territorial sovereignty. On the same day, Foreign Minister Zhou Enlai sent the above announcement to the governments of various countries in the form of an official letter. Zhou Enlai said in the official letter: "I believe that the People's Republic of China must establish normal diplomatic relations with all countries in the world."

New China's principled position on establishing diplomatic relations received a good response worldwide. New China's diplomacy began to take the stage of world diplomacy with a brand-new appearance.

"One-Sidedness" and the Sino-Soviet Alliance

On June 30, 1949, to celebrate the 28th anniversary of the founding of the CPC, Mao Zedong wrote an article, "On People's Democratic Dictatorship." One of the conclusions was: "The forty years' experience of Sun Yat-sen and the twenty-eight years' experience of the Communist Party have taught us to lean to one side, and we are firmly convinced that in order to win victory and consolidate it, we must lean to one side. In the light of the experiences accumulated in these forty years and these twenty-eight years, all Chinese without exception must lean either to the side of imperialism or to the side of socialism." Mao Zedong pointed out: "Unite with the Soviet Union, unite with all people's democratic countries, unite with the proletariat and the masses of other countries, and form an international united front." It is evident that China would lean toward socialism led by the Soviet Union.

On October 1, 1949, the People's Republic of China was established. On October 2, the Soviet government sent a diplomatic note, becoming the first country in the world to recognize the People's Republic of China, which was undoubtedly tremendous support for New China. In early November, Stalin invited Mao Zedong to visit the Soviet Union.

Mao Zedong's visit to the Soviet Union was well-prepared. First, he participated in the celebration of Stalin's 70th birthday and brought some "modest gifts," including vegetables and fruits: white cabbage, Laiyang pears, and onions from Jiaodong and Jinan, Shandong Province; pears and onions from Laiyang; Beijing pears; radishes from Tianjin and Shandong; Beijing red-hearted radishes, and Jiangxi kumquats. Second, he consulted directly with Stalin on major issues of common concern between the two parties and the two countries and signed relevant treaties and agreements between the two countries.

On December 6, 1949, Mao Zedong boarded a train bound for Moscow, marking his first visit abroad. A few days earlier, the Ministry of Public Security had just cracked a case involving KMT spies attempting to gather information on Mao Zedong's visit to the Soviet Union. This incident caused some concern for Mao Zedong's first foreign visit. However, Mao Zedong's character dictated that if he wanted to do something, he would definitely do it. Visiting the Soviet Union was something he had long wanted to do, and he wouldn't cancel his trip because of this small setback.

After a 10-day journey, the special train arrived in Moscow at noon on December 16. At 6:00 p.m. that evening, Stalin met with Mao Zedong at the Kremlin. This was their first meeting. The two leaders embraced warmly upon meeting. Stalin openly praised Mao Zedong, saying he looked younger and stronger than he had imagined and that he was a good son of the Chinese people who made great contributions to the Chinese revolution. After exchanging pleasantries, the two countries' leaders discussed issues of common concern.

In their first meeting, Mao Zedong explicitly expressed his hope that the Soviet Union would abolish the *1945 Sino-Soviet Treaty of Friendship and Alliance* signed with the KMT government, cancel all special interests of the Soviet Union in China, such as the Chinese Eastern Railway, Lüshun, and Dalian Port, and sign a new treaty with New China reflecting complete equality. However, Stalin pointed out that the United States and Britain had approved the signing of the 1945 treaty, and any changes to the treaty would give the two countries a pretext to attack the Soviet Union. The talks reached a deadlock. Since signing a new Sino-Soviet friendship treaty and abolishing the old one was one of the main goals of Mao Zedong's visit to the Soviet Union, he asked Stalin if it would be necessary for Zhou Enlai to come to Moscow to resolve the treaty issue. Stalin replied that the decision should be made by the Chinese themselves, and perhaps other matters might require Zhou Enlai's presence. Thus the talks came to a temporary halt.

On December 21, Mao Zedong attended the Soviet Union's celebration of Stalin's 70th birthday, receiving a high-level reception. On the 24th, Mao Zedong and Stalin held their second meeting. When Mao Zedong asked again whether Zhou Enlai should come to Moscow, Stalin said, "The chairman of the government is already here, and it might harm foreign perceptions if the prime minister comes as well." "It is still considered better for Zhou Enlai not to come to Moscow." This indicated that Stalin was still unwilling to sign a new treaty with the new China.

By the end of December, representatives from Eastern European countries returned to their countries after the celebration of Stalin's birthday, leaving only Mao Zedong behind. Stalin made daily inquiries about Mao Zedong's well-being but never discussed the signing of a treaty or met with him, much to Mao Zedong's dissatisfaction.

However, the situation suddenly changed. Internationally, countries like Burma, India, and the United Kingdom were preparing to recognize or establish diplomatic relations with the new China, and the growing number of China's "friends" prompted Stalin to seriously consider Mao Zedong's request. At the same time, British news agencies spread rumors that Stalin had put Mao Zedong under house arrest, which put the Soviet Union in a passive position. Stalin finally considered signing a new treaty with China and agreed to Zhou Enlai's visit to Moscow. It was already early January 1950. On the evening of January 2, Mao Zedong sent a telegram to the Central Committee of CPC, reporting the situation in the Soviet Union and explicitly asking Zhou Enlai to "leave Beijing on January 9 and take the train (not the plane) to Moscow."

On January 23, 1950, Zhou Enlai, who had arrived in Moscow, held talks with Mao Zedong and Stalin, marking Mao Zedong's third meeting with Stalin since arriving in Moscow. Stalin's attitude took a 180-degree turn, showing great enthusiasm for amending the treaty, which was beyond Mao Zedong's expectations. Mao Zedong reported to Liu Shaoqi in China that the work was going quite smoothly. The Chinese side proposed adding the words "mutual assistance" to the original text to differentiate the new treaty from the old one. The Soviet side accepted this proposal. Finally, the *Sino-Soviet Treaty of Friendship, Alliance, and Mutual Assistance* was concluded.

On February 14, 1950, the signing ceremony of the *Sino-Soviet Treaty of Friendship, Alliance, and Mutual Assistance* was held in the Kremlin. After the signing, following Mao Zedong's suggestion, the Chinese Embassy in the Soviet Union held a thank-you banquet. Stalin, who never attended banquets outside the Kremlin, made an exception this time out of respect for Mao Zedong and led the members of the Soviet Central Political Bureau to participate in the feast. When Stalin entered the banquet hall and embraced Mao Zedong and Zhou Enlai, the entire hall erupted with applause and cheers. This marked the People's Republic of China's entry into the socialist camp led by the Soviet Union, fulfilling Mao Zedong's diplomatic strategy of "leaning to one side."

On February 16, Stalin held a farewell banquet at the Kremlin for Mao Zedong, who was about to return to China. The next day, Mao Zedong boarded the special train to return home.

The signing of the *Sino-Soviet Treaty of Friendship, Alliance, and Mutual Assistance* was a significant accomplishment in Mao Zedong's political career. Regarding the signing, Mao Zedong said having a treaty was better than having none. Once the treaty was established, it provided a basis to rely on, allowing China to focus on other matters. With the friendship between the two countries solidified in the treaty, China could concentrate on economic development. It also had diplomatic advantages. "We are a newly established country with many difficulties, and having an ally in case of any issues can help reduce the possibility of war."

Later, as the international situation and Sino-Soviet relations evolved, and as the CPC implemented the Five Principles of Peaceful Coexistence in its dealings with other countries, the "leaning to one side" diplomatic strategy gradually became a part of history.

Taking the International Stage with a Brand-New Posture

The diplomatic history of old China is a humiliating history of "conducting diplomacy while kneeling." Zhou Enlai said, "Chinese reactionaries have always been nervous and afraid of imperialism in diplomacy. From Empress Dowager Cixi of the Qing Dynasty, Yuan Shikai of the Beiyang Government, to Chiang Kai-shek of the KMT, which one of them did not conduct diplomacy while kneeling? China's diplomatic history over the past hundred years is humiliating."

After founding the People's Republic of China, the Chinese people began to stand up and conduct diplomacy independently and autonomously. With the Soviet Union's recognition of the People's Republic of China and the establishment of equal diplomatic relations, by the end of 1949, other people's democratic countries in the socialist camp led by the Soviet Union (except the Federal People's Republic of Yugoslavia, which postponed the establishment of diplomatic relations with China due to the impact of the Cominform resolution, and the Democratic Republic of Vietnam, which established diplomatic relations with China on January 18, 1950) had established new and equal diplomatic relations with China.

According to general international practice, as long as two governments exchange recognition telegrams, it marks the beginning of diplomatic relations. However, one unique situation facing the new China was that the KMT group, supported by the United States, still occupied Taiwan and held China's seat in the United Nations. Therefore, foreign countries seeking to establish diplomatic relations with China had to follow several principles: first, to sever diplomatic ties with the KMT group in Taiwan and recognize the People's Republic of China as the sole legitimate government of China; second, to support China's restoration of its legitimate seat in the United Nations; and third, to confirm their respect for China's sovereignty through negotiations and hand over property belonging to China within their jurisdiction to the People's Republic of China. These issues did not pose problems for the countries of the socialist camp, but for other countries, they needed to be determined through negotiations. Therefore, in March 1950, when Zhou Enlai was on his way back to China from the Soviet Union and mentioned that more than ten countries had recently recognized the new China, he pointed out: "According to the provisions of the *Common Program*, diplomatic relations with the KMT must be severed first, and then we can talk about establishing diplomatic relations with us." Based on this principle, around 1950, many non-socialist countries actively sought diplomatic relations with the new China.

China and Myanmar are close neighbors, and the "Paukphaw" (brotherly) friendship between the two peoples has a long history. In December 1949, 48 organizations, including the Myanmar Chinese Chamber of Commerce, jointly issued a telegram expressing their heartfelt support for the Central People's Government, saying: "For many years, our compatriots in Myanmar have been looking forward to the birth of an independent, free, happy, and prosperous new motherland. Now, our proud days have finally arrived." Given the domestic and Myanmar situation, Tu Yuntan, the ambassador of the former KMT government to Myanmar, led all embassy staff to send a telegram to the Ministry of Foreign Affairs of the Central People's Government, expressing their disassociation from the KMT group and accepting the leadership of the Central People's Government. On December 16, 1949, Myanmar's Foreign Minister U Myint sent a telegram to Zhou Enlai, stating that the Myanmar government believed that the Chinese people supported the Central People's Government of the People's Republic of China, and Myanmar hoped to establish diplomatic relations and exchange envoys with it. At the same time, it was also expressed that the Myanmar government was willing to disarm the KMT troops who had fled to Myanmar, resolve conflicts between residents on the China-Myanmar border, and protect the rights and interests of overseas Chinese in Myanmar. On December 18 and 21, Zhou Enlai replied that after the Myanmar government severed relations with the remnants of the Chinese KMT reactionaries, they were willing to establish diplomatic relations between the two countries based on equality, mutual benefit, and mutual respect for territorial sovereignty. On the 28th, the Myanmar government announced the severance of relations with the KMT group and sent Wu Pi, the first secretary of the former embassy in Nanjing, to negotiate the establishment of diplomatic relations with China as an acting representative. On April 26, 1950, Wu Pi arrived in Beijing and immediately began negotiations with Zhang Hanfu, Deputy Foreign Minister of China. Since the Myanmar side accepted China's principles for establishing diplomatic relations, the negotiations were successfully concluded, and both sides agreed to establish diplomatic relations on June 8.

After founding the People's Republic of China, the Indian people expressed very friendly feelings toward the Chinese people. During the War of Resistance, Dr. Adel (Edward), an Indian doctor who served in the liberated areas with a medical team, congratulated Chairman Mao Zedong, saying: "Your glorious victory will not only change the face of China but also change the face of the whole world." A grand demonstration was held by the West Bengal Workers' Congress in India to celebrate the founding of the new China and demanded that the Indian National Congress government recognize the new China.

However, the Indian government hesitated. The reasons for the Indian government's hesitation were: first, they saw that the KMT group's "relocation" to Guangzhou had failed, but the contest was not over. Second, there were internal differences of opinion. At that time, the Indian Ambassador to the former KMT government, Panikkar, advised Nehru to recognize the new China early, but some people advocated postponing it. They still harbored doubts and dissatisfaction with the new China. At that time, a magazine in Shanghai criticized Nehru, saying that he "is a traitor to the national independence movement, a villain who sabotages the progress of the people's liberation movement, and a loyal servant of imperialism." However, as a politician, Nehru himself didn't think it was worth making a fuss about. He admitted that the "Chinese government is strong." He said, "Whether I like it or not, whether its structure is the same as ours or not, we will recognize it."

After much debate and with Nehru's push, the faction advocating for early recognition of the new China ultimately prevailed. On December 30, 1949, India announced severing all relations with the KMT group and recognized the new China. In March 1950, Nehru addressed this issue: "This is not a question of approval or disapproval. This is a matter of recognizing, discerning, and dealing with a major historical event."

On February 13, 1950, the representative sent by the Indian government, Y.K. Puri, arrived in Beijing. China and India began negotiations on the formal establishment of diplomatic relations and quickly agreed to establish relations on April 1. Thus, although India was the second non-socialist country to recognize the new China after Myanmar, due to the early arrival of the negotiation representative in Beijing and the smooth progress of the negotiations, India became the first non-socialist country to establish diplomatic relations with the new China.

In Europe, Nordic countries like Sweden, Denmark, Finland, and Switzerland in Central Europe belonged to the capitalist world system. Their policies were quite different from those of the United States. They advocated or leaned toward a neutral peace policy, unwilling to be involved in the disputes of major powers. They valued import and export trade with the East and believed establishing and developing relations with the new China was in their best interests. Based on this reality, Zhou Enlai pointed out that improving relations with Western countries politically meant "peace" and economically meant "trade." On this basis, relations with these countries could be established and developed on equality, mutual benefit, and mutual respect for territorial sovereignty. On January 14, 1950, Swedish Foreign Minister Östen Undén informed Zhou Enlai of Sweden's decision to recognize the new China and appointed

Ivan Kolarevic, who was stationed in Shanghai, as the temporary representative to negotiate the establishment of diplomatic relations with China.

On February 8, Li Kenong, Deputy Minister of Foreign Affairs, replied to Undén, accepting the offer. Negotiations began on March 9 and concluded on May 6, with both sides agreeing to announce the establishment of diplomatic relations on May 9. As the Swedish government quickly accepted China's principles for establishing diplomatic relations, Sweden surpassed the United Kingdom, Norway, Denmark, and Finland, which recognized China earlier, to become the first Western country to establish diplomatic relations with China. The first set of credentials presented by Geng Biao, China's first ambassador to Sweden, to the Swedish king bore the signatures of Chairman Mao Zedong and Foreign Minister Zhou Enlai, as well as the seal of the Chinese state. This was also a unique feature of the first batch of credentials from the new China. On June 12, Mao Zedong highly praised the establishment of diplomatic relations between the two countries while accepting the credentials from the first Swedish ambassador to China, Amel Stolpe, saying, "The establishment of diplomatic relations between China and Sweden will not only further consolidate the friendship already existing between the peoples of the two countries but will also contribute to lasting world peace."

At the same time as the negotiations with Sweden, China was also negotiating with Denmark. The negotiations between the two countries also began on March 9 and ended on May 8. The two countries decided to announce the establishment of diplomatic relations on May 11 and exchange envoys.

In June 1949, the United States warned the Swiss government that "it would be inappropriate to recognize a communist regime in Asia prematurely." However, in order to maintain its neutral stance and gain access to the Chinese market, the Swiss government believed that "the Communist Party's rule in China would last for a long time, so recognizing it earlier is better than recognizing it later." Based on this, Switzerland accelerated establishing diplomatic relations with China. After negotiations, the two countries simultaneously announced the establishment of diplomatic relations on September 14, 1950.

Of course, some countries established diplomatic relations with the new China without going through the negotiation process. On January 11, 1950, Prime Minister and Foreign Minister of the Republic of Indonesia, Mohammad Hatta, informed Zhou Enlai that the Republic of Indonesia had been established. On March 28, Zhou Enlai replied to Hatta, stating that the Chinese government was willing to establish normal diplomatic relations with Indonesia based on equality, mutual benefit, and mutual respect for sovereignty. On April 13, Hatta informed Zhou Enlai that the Indonesian government sincerely agreed with the Chinese government's views on establishing diplomatic relations between the two countries and welcomed the exchange of diplomatic envoys. Since Indonesia was a newly independent country with no diplomatic relations with the KMT, there was no need for a negotiation process. China established diplomatic relations with Indonesia on April 13. On January 13, 1950, Finnish Foreign Minister Carl Enckell informed Zhou Enlai that "Finland recognized the People's Republic of China today and extended its most sincere wishes for China's future." On January 16, Zhou Enlai replied, expressing his welcome and gratitude. Similarly, since Finland had no diplomatic relations with the KMT and did not participate in the United Nations, there was no issue regarding China's seat in the United Nations, so no negotiation process was required. The two sides agreed through their respective ambassadors in the Soviet Union to establish diplomatic relations on October 28, 1950.

In 1950, seven non-socialist countries, including Myanmar, India, Indonesia, Sweden, Denmark, Finland, and Switzerland, recognized the new China and established new, equal diplomatic relations with China. Thus, China ended the humiliating history of conducting diplomacy "while kneeling on the ground."

CHAPTER 9

The Great War to Resist US Aggression and Aid Korea

From October 1950 to July 1953, at the request of the Democratic People's Republic of Korea (DPRK), the People's Republic of China sent the Chinese People's Volunteer Army to Korea to participate in the war against US aggression and aid Korea. This war lasted for two years and nine months. A vigorous movement to resist US aggression and aid Korea was launched domestically to support the war effort. Both the war and the movement eventually ended in victory. The war demonstrated China's national and military prestige, thoroughly shattered the US conspiracy to expand its aggression and strangle the new China in its cradle, and greatly enhanced the international status of the new China. The new China stood tall in the East, becoming a significant political and military power that no one dared to underestimate.

Crossing the Yalu River with Pride and High Spirits

After founding the People's Republic of China, the United States continued providing military aid to Chiang Kai-shek. It supported reactionary forces in Korea and Vietnam, seeking to encircle China. Under unfavorable conditions in China's peripheral environment, an unexpected event occurred for leaders like Mao Zedong: on June 25, 1950, the Korean Civil War broke out. The South Korean army retreated under the powerful offensive of the North Korean People's Army.

After the outbreak of the Korean War, the United States intervened to maintain its leadership position and interests in Asia. On June 27, US President Harry Truman declared that the United States would send troops to Korea and ordered the US Navy's Seventh Fleet to enter the Taiwan Strait, patrolling the strait to prevent the Chinese PLA from crossing the sea to liberate Taiwan.

On July 7, the United Nations Security Council passed a US proposal without the Soviet representative, calling member states to provide necessary military assistance to South Korea. The "United Nations Forces," led by the US military, saw small contingents from fifteen other countries participating in the war. The United Kingdom, Turkey, Canada, Thailand, New Zealand, Australia, the Netherlands, France, the Philippines, Greece, Belgium, Colombia, Ethiopia, Luxembourg, South Africa, and South Korea all fell under the command of US Far East Command General Douglas MacArthur, stationed in Japan.

Faced with US interference in the Korean Peninsula and Taiwan Strait affairs, on June 28, Mao Zedong delivered a speech calling on "people all over the country and the world to unite, make full preparations, and defeat any provocation by American imperialism." On the same day, Zhou Enlai, on behalf of the Chinese government, issued a statement strongly condemning the United States' crimes of aggression in Korea, Taiwan, and interference in Asian affairs. He called on "all peace-loving, just, and freedom-loving people of the world, especially the oppressed nations and peoples of the East, to rise up and stop the new aggression of American imperialism in the East."

In response to the increasingly difficult situation in the northeastern border defense, the CPC Central Military Commission, based on Mao Zedong's proposal, held a meeting chaired by Zhou Enlai to study national defense issues. On July 13, the Central Military Commission decided to defend the northeastern border, and 255,000 troops were drawn from the 13th Army Corps and other units to form the Northeast Border Defense Army. Later, the 9th and 19th Army Corps were also mobilized as second-line forces, gathering in areas near the Tianjin-Pukou and Longhai railway lines.

To defend the country, Mao Zedong had a "bottom line" on whether or not to send troops. This "bottom line" was whether the US military would cross the 38th parallel (referred to as the "38th line"). He later said, "If the US imperialism intervenes, we won't interfere as long as they don't cross the 38th line. If they cross it, we will definitely fight back."

On September 15, the US military landed at Inchon on the southwestern coast of the Korean Peninsula and occupied Seoul on the 28th. The Korean People's Army was attacked on both sides, suffered heavy losses, and went into strategic retreat.

The situation rapidly deteriorated. On September 30, Zhou Enlai solemnly declared to the world on behalf of the Chinese government: "The Chinese people can never tolerate foreign aggression, nor can they stand idly by while imperialists wantonly invade their neighbors." On October 1, the *People's Daily* prominently published Zhou Enlai's words. However, the US government ignored the Chinese government's warning. On the morning of October 1, MacArthur issued an "ultimatum" to Kim Il-sung: surrender immediately and lay down arms. Under these severe circumstances, Kim Il-sung requested support from China. That day was the first National Day after the founding of New China. On October 3, Kim Il-sung's special envoy and DPRK Minister of Internal Affairs, Park Il Woo, brought a letter from Kim Il-sung to Mao Zedong, flying to Beijing.

From October 2 to 5, the Central Committee of CPC held consecutive meetings of the Secretariat and expanded meetings of the Political Bureau to discuss the Korean War situation.

While the Central Committee was discussing whether to send troops to Korea, diplomatic efforts were also being made. Since China and the United States had not yet established diplomatic relations, on October 3, Zhou Enlai urgently met with the Indian Ambassador to China, K. M. Panikkar, and warned the United States through him, saying: "The US military is attempting to cross the '38th line' and expand the war. If the US military does so, we cannot stand idly by; we will interfere." To emphasize the word "interfere," Zhou Enlai instructed the translator in advance: "This word should carry considerable weight when translated into English. Think it through carefully and make sure it is accurate in translation." That same day, Truman learned of Zhou Enlai's conversation. He believed that "Zhou Enlai's statement was nothing more than intimidation against the United Nations"; Panikkar was a Communist sympathizer, "at best a mouthpiece for the Communist Party's Publicity."

On the afternoon of October 4, the Central Political Bureau continued to hold an expanded meeting, with most people still having various concerns about sending troops. The reasons were that China had just ended the war, and the economy was very difficult; the PLA's weapons and equipment were far behind those of the US military, with no air or sea control; some cadres and soldiers harbored peace-seeking and war-weary thoughts; the long-term burden of the war would be unbearable, and so on. After listening, Mao Zedong said: "What you have said has its reasons, but when others are in a state of national crisis, we cannot just stand by and watch. No matter what we say, we would feel uneasy in our hearts." That day, Peng Dehuai, the Commander of the Northwest Military Region and Deputy Commander of the PLA, who had just arrived in Beijing from Xi'an, was late to the meeting due to a flight delay and did not speak after entering the conference room. After the meeting, Peng Dehuai thought a lot, and he believed: "The American 'tiger' wants to eat people. When it eats depends on its appetite!"

On the morning of October 5, Mao Zedong asked Deng Xiaoping to bring Peng Dehuai to Zhongnanhai for a private conversation. Mao asked Peng for his opinion, and Peng replied that he supported sending troops to aid Korea. Mao then asked who should lead the forces, and Peng mentioned that the Central Committee had already decided on Lin Biao. Mao stated that Lin Biao could not go and that the Central Committee hoped Peng would take responsibility. Peng expressed his obedience to the Central Committee's decision, and Mao felt relieved, asking Peng to present his views at the Political Bureau meeting that afternoon.

In the afternoon of October 5, the Expanded Political Bureau Meeting continued with differing opinions. Peng Dehuai argued that sending troops to aid Korea was necessary and that, at most, it would only delay the victory of the liberation war by a few years. If the US military was positioned on the banks of the Yalu River and in Taiwan, it could launch an invasion at any time, always finding an excuse. He believed that if the US occupied the Korean Peninsula, future problems would be more complicated, so it was better to fight sooner rather than later. In response to concerns about the highly modernized US military and its possession of atomic bombs, Mao Zedong said, "They have their atomic bombs, I have my hand grenades, and I believe my hand grenades will defeat their atomic bombs." After discussions, the Central Committee finally reached a consensus and made a strategic decision to "resist America, aid Korea, and defend the homeland," appointing Peng Dehuai to lead the Volunteer Army into battle in Korea. At the same time, Zhou Enlai was sent to meet with Stalin to seek Soviet military support.

On October 7, the US forces crossed the 38th parallel and advanced northward, reaching the China-North Korea border. On October 8, Mao Zedong issued the order to form the Chinese People's Volunteer Army and enter the war in Korea.

When Kim Il-sung learned that China had decided to send troops, he excitedly opened a bottle of wine and asked to toast with the Chinese ambassador to North Korea, Ni Zhiliang.

On the same day that Mao Zedong issued the order on October 8, Peng Dehuai flew to Shenyang to prepare the Volunteer Army for entering Korea. However, just a few days into the preparations, there was a change in the Central Committee's plans. On October 12, Mao Zedong sent a telegram to Peng Dehuai: (1) The 13th Army Corps should continue training in place and not advance. (2) Gao Gang and Dehuai should come to Beijing tomorrow or the day after for a discussion.

The assembly call had been sounded on October 8, so why was there a halt now? It turned out that Zhou Enlai's talks with Stalin in Moscow were not going smoothly. Zhou Enlai asked for Soviet air force support to cover the Volunteer Army and for assistance with supplying aircraft, artillery, tanks, and other weapons to China. Stalin agreed to provide weapons but said the Soviet air force was not yet ready and could only assist in two and a half months.

Stalin's reluctance to deploy air force support for the Volunteer Army surprised Mao Zedong and Zhou Enlai. Later, Zhou Enlai discussed this situation, saying: "When the US military approached the Yalu River, we were determined to discuss it with Stalin. There were two opinions: either send troops or not send troops; these were Stalin's words. We asked: Can you help with the Air Force? He wavered, saying that China was in difficulty and could choose not to send troops. He said that even if North Korea were lost, we would still be socialist, and China would still exist. We talked for a day, and we had to make a decision in the evening, so we immediately sent a telegram to Chairman Mao." On October 13, Mao Zedong replied that the Political Bureau unanimously believed it was advantageous for the Chinese army to deploy to Korea, stating, "We believe that we should join the war and must join the war. The benefits of joining and the losses of not joining are enormous."

On October 15, Pyongyang was in imminent danger. Just as the Chinese army was about to set out, Stalin retreated again, instructing Molotov to inform Zhou Enlai that the Soviet Union had decided to only send air forces to the north bank of the Yalu River within Chinese territory. They did not plan to enter North Korea to cover the Volunteer Army's operations even after two or two and a half months. Zhou Enlai was very unhappy. On October 16, he left Moscow with regret toward the Soviet Union and returned to China.

On the 18th, Mao Zedong chaired a Political Bureau meeting to study further the issue of sending troops. Mao said the enemy was now besieging Pyongyang, and they would reach the Yalu River in a few days. Regardless of the enormous difficulties, the deployment of the Volunteer Army across the Yalu River to aid Korea could not be changed, and the timing could not be postponed. The meeting decided that the Chinese People's Volunteer Army would enter Korea for combat as planned on October 19.

On October 19, Pyongyang fell. On the night of October 19, 260,000 personnel from four armies, three artillery divisions, and one anti-aircraft artillery brigade of the Chinese People's Volunteer Army secretly crossed the Yalu River under darkness and entered North Korea. This marked the beginning of the great war to resist America and aid Korea.

Drive the Aggressors Back South of the 38th Parallel

After the Chinese People's Volunteer Army entered Korea, from October 25, 1950, to June 10, 1951, the Volunteer Army and the Korean People's Army carried out five consecutive strategic campaigns, pushing the American aggressors back south of the 38th parallel and stabilizing the situation in Korea.

The first campaign started on October 25, 1950, and ended on November 5, 1950.

On the eve of the Volunteer Army's departure, the enemy had occupied Pyongyang, Wonsan, and other places and had concentrated four armies with 130,000 troops from Wonsan and Pyongyang in two separate eastern and western fronts (with the main force on the western front), advancing toward the Sino-Korean border. Their goal was to reach the Sino-Korean border by November 23, annihilate the Korean People's Army in one fell swoop, and achieve the occupation of the entire Korean peninsula. In response to this situation, Mao Zedong and Peng Dehuai decided that the main strategy for the Volunteer Army's first phase would be mobile warfare, combined with some positional warfare and guerrilla warfare behind enemy lines. On October 21, Mao Zedong emphasized in a telegram to Peng Dehuai: "Now is the time to seize the opportunity, not to deploy defenses first and then talk about attacking."

The Volunteer Army decided to strike a heavy blow to the enemy before the "United Nations Forces" discovered their entry into the Korean War. On October 25, the Volunteer Army launched the first campaign of the Korean War, with the main force of one army cooperating with the Korean People's Army on the eastern front to carry out a blockade while concentrating five armies and one division on the western front to deliver a surprise blow to the "United Nations Forces," driving them from the Yalu River to the south of the Chongchon River. This thwarted the "United Nations Forces" plan to occupy the whole of Korea by Thanksgiving (November 23) and initially stabilized the situation in Korea. The Volunteer Army annihilated more than 15,000 enemy troops in the first campaign.

The second campaign started on November 25, 1950, and ended on December 24, 1950, lasting one month.

The sudden appearance of the Chinese People's Volunteer Army on the Korean battlefield shocked the United States. However, they believed that the Volunteer Army's involvement was merely to defend the border. From November 6 onwards, the enemy on the western front began probing attacks to ascertain the strength and intentions of the Volunteer Army. Peng Dehuai ordered his troops to retreat from the Chongchon River, deliberately showing weakness to the enemy. General MacArthur believed the Volunteer Army was "poorly equipped and cowardly in battle" and ordered his troops to advance northward. With the cooperation of the Korean People's Army, the Volunteer Army lured the "United Nations Forces" led by the United States and their South Korean counterparts to the predetermined battlefield. They then launched a surprise counterattack under the full moon on the night of November 25. After a series of fierce battles, the "United Nations Forces" were defeated on the western front along the banks of the Chongchon River and on the eastern front at the Chosin Reservoir. They were forced to abandon Pyongyang and Wonsan, retreating south of the 38th parallel via land and sea routes.

In this campaign, the Volunteer Army fought tenaciously. When one observes the overall situation on the battlefield, it becomes evident that the enemy was caught in a pincer movement by the Volunteer Army from the north and south. However, in the local battlefields of Sariwon and Ryongyonri on the western front, the Volunteer Army was also caught in the enemy's pincer movement from the south and north. If these two places were lost, the enemies west and north of the Chongchon River would all flee southward, and the goal of annihilating the enemy in the second campaign would be missed. The 38th Army of the Volunteer Army withstood the coordinated attacks of various enemy forces, preventing the enemy from fleeing south and reinforcing the north, with a distance of less than one kilometer between them. This significantly boosted the morale of the Volunteer Army and deeply moved Commander Peng Dehuai, who exclaimed, "Long live the 38th Army" in his congratulatory telegram. In the second campaign, the Volunteer Army annihilated more than 36,000 enemy troops, and the Volunteer Army and the People's Army gained the initiative to switch from defense to offense. Unfortunately, on November 25, the day the second campaign was launched, Mao Zedong's eldest son, Mao Anying, lost his young life due to enemy bombing. After a difficult decision, this news was not relayed to Mao Zedong until after New Year's Day 1951 by Zhou Enlai, Peng Dehuai, and the confidential secretary Ye Zilong. Suppressing his grief, Mao Zedong said, "Alas! War always has casualties." With Mao Zedong's approval, Mao Anying and millions of Volunteer Army martyrs rest in peace on the soil of Korea, symbolizing the friendship between the Chinese and Korean peoples.

The third campaign began on December 31, 1950, and ended on January 8, 1951.

After the second campaign, the Volunteer Army, with one week of preparation, concentrated six armies on December 31, 1950, and, with the cooperation of three army corps of the People's Army, launched a full-scale attack on the "United Nations Forces" defending the established positions along the 38th parallel. On January 4, they occupied Seoul. On January 5, they crossed the Han River, and on January 8, they recaptured Incheon, pushing the enemy back from the 38th parallel to the area near the 37th parallel north. The third campaign annihilated more than 19,000 enemy troops. In this campaign, the Volunteer Army occupied Seoul, dealt a new blow to the enemy, deepened their internal contradictions and feelings of failure, and boosted the Korean people's movement to resist America and aid Korea in defending their homeland. It was a great victory in both military and political terms.

The fourth campaign began on January 25, 1951, and ended on April 21, 1951, lasting nearly three months.

After three consecutive campaign victories, the main force of the Chinese and Korean armies shifted to rest and reorganization. The "United Nations Forces" discovered that the Volunteer Army had difficulties with supplies and insufficient frontline troops, so they quickly replenished personnel and materials, adjusted deployment, and resumed the offensive on January 25, 1951. The Chinese People's Volunteer Army and the Korean People's Army switched to defensive operations, resisting the enemy along the Han River by relying on field fortifications. With a portion of the troops stubbornly fighting on the western front, six armies concentrated on the eastern front in the Hwachon area to launch a counterattack. Still, they failed to break the "United Nations Forces" offensive in the main direction. In this situation, to trade space for time and cover the arrival of subsequent military units, the Chinese and North Korean forces shifted to a mobile defense along the entire front, resisting and wearing down the "United Nations Forces."

On March 7, the "United Nations Forces" concentrated more than 200,000 troops and launched a full-scale attack on the positions of the Chinese and Korean armies with the support of hundreds of aircraft. On March 13, the Chinese and Korean troops voluntarily withdrew from Seoul. By the end of March, the front line gradually moved north of the 38th parallel, but due to the stubborn resistance of the Chinese and Korean armies, the enemy found it difficult to advance even half a step. By the end of the campaign on April 21, a total of more than 78,000 enemy troops were killed, wounded, or captured (including more than 53,000 by the Volunteer Army), causing the "United Nations Forces" to pay a price of nearly 1,000 casualties per day to advance 1.3 kilometers. The Volunteer Army also suffered more than 42,000 casualties. In this campaign, the Chinese and Korean armies completed their defensive tasks, won time, covered the assembly of the subsequent Volunteer Army Corps, and created favorable conditions for the launch of the fifth campaign.

At this time, there were serious disagreements between MacArthur and the Truman administration on invading Korea. MacArthur prioritized military victories, and Truman did not approve of many of his actions on the Korean Peninsula, with some even going against Washington's decisions. On April 11, Truman decided to relieve MacArthur of his position as Supreme Commander, with Ridgway taking over.

The fifth campaign began on April 22, 1951, and ended on June 10, 1951.

During the fourth campaign, the United States attempted to land on the flanks and rear of the Chinese and Korean armies, launch a pincer attack from the north and south, and regain the initiative on the battlefield. The Chinese and Korean armies launched the fifth campaign to thwart this plan. They first concentrated 11 Volunteer Army divisions and one People's Army Corps on the western front to launch a major assault, crossing the 38th parallel again and pushing toward Seoul. Then, the Volunteer Army shifted its forces to the eastern front. Finally, the Chinese and Korean armies voluntarily moved northward. By June 10, the front line stabilized north and south of the 38th parallel, forming a seesaw situation. The Volunteer Army and the People's Army annihilated more than 82,000 "United Nations Forces" troops, with their combat losses exceeding 85,000, surpassing the "United Nations Forces" for the first time. In this campaign, the 180th Division of the Volunteer Army suffered severe losses due to untimely withdrawal and indecisive handling.

The Days When a Few Cannons Could Dominate a Country's History Are Gone Forever

While the Chinese People's Volunteer Army was defending their homeland and fighting in Korea, a massive nationwide movement of resisting the United States and aiding Korea was launched in China.

On July 10, 1950, the Chinese People's Movement Committee against the US Invasion of Taiwan and Korea was established in Beijing. On July 14, it issued a notice on "Movement Week against the US Invasion of Taiwan and Korea," the movement of resisting the United States and aiding Korea began to spread nationwide.

After the Volunteer Army went to Korea, on October 26, 1950, the Central Committee of CPC issued a *Directive on Current Affairs Publicity*, reviewed and revised by Mao Zedong. It immediately launched a nationwide publicity campaign to resist the United States and aid Korea. On the same day, the Chinese People's Committee for the Defense of World Peace and Opposition to US Aggression (hereinafter referred to as the "Committee for Resisting the United States and Aiding Korea") was established. Administrative districts and provinces successively established branches or merged existing Committees for the Defense of World Peace and Committees against US Aggression into branches for Resisting the United States and Aiding Korea.

On November 4, the CPC and various democratic parties jointly issued a declaration "Vowing to fully support the just demands of the people of the whole country and support the people's sacred mission of resisting the United States and aiding Korea voluntarily for the defense of our homeland." From November 4 to 11, the National Association of Natural Sciences, the National Association of Popular Science, the Social Science Research Association, the All-China Women's Federation, the All-China Youth Federation, and other people's organizations issued declarations in support of the joint declaration of the CPC and various democratic parties, calling on the masses to actively participate in the movement of resisting the United States and aiding Korea to defend their homeland. On November 27, the CPPCC held a joint meeting with various democratic parties. It issued a notice on the "Agreement on the Movement to Console the Chinese People's Volunteer Army and the Korean People's Army by Various Democratic Parties and People's Organizations" on December 1.

On January 14, 1951, the Committee for Resisting the United States and Aiding Korea issued a notice on "Consoling the Chinese People's Volunteer Army and the Korean People's Army and Aiding Korean Refugees." On January 15, the *People's Daily* published an editorial entitled "Collecting Consolation Goods and Relief

Goods is an Important Political Task," calling on the people of the whole country to actively participate in the patriotic donation campaign. By May 30, people across the country had donated over 118.6 billion yuan, more than 770,000 consolation bags, and over 1.26 million consolation items. From early April to mid-May, delegations of representatives from various democratic parties, people's organizations, and people from all walks of life visited multiple parts of Korea to console the Chinese People's Volunteer Army, the Korean People's Army, and the people.

On February 16, the CPPCC issued a telegram calling for the movement to resist the United States and aid Korea to be "further popularized and deepened in every rural area, every organ, every school, every factory, every shop, every street, and every region inhabited by various nationalities." On March 14, the Committee for Resisting the United States and Aiding Korea issued a notice, urging "efforts to popularize and deepen the practical work and publicity and education work of resisting the United States and aiding Korea, so that every place and every person throughout the country receives this patriotic education and actively participates in this patriotic action." Subsequently, the movement of Resisting the United States and Aiding Korea entered a stage of even broader popularization and deeper development.

On June 1, 1951, the Committee for Resisting the United States and Aiding Korea issued a notice, calling on people from all walks of life across the country to donate aircraft and artillery. Subsequently, the All-China Federation of Trade Unions, the All-China Women's Federation, the Central Committee of the Communist Youth League, the All-China Youth Federation, and the Chinese Red Cross, among other people's organizations, issued declarations and notices, urging people from all walks of life to donate actively. By September 25, 2,481 aircraft were presented, and the donated funds reached 997 billion yuan.

The domestic movement to resist the United States and aid Korea was a strong backing for the victorious battles of the Chinese People's Volunteer Army in Korea.

After more than seven months of military confrontation, the US government realized that if its main forces were bogged down in the Korean battlefield for a long time, it would be highly unfavorable for its Europe-focused global strategy. Coupled with the rising anti-war sentiment at home and abroad, the US shifted to a defensive stance and prepared for negotiations with China and North Korea based on strength, seeking a ceasefire.

After five battles, China and North Korea deeply felt that their forces were still at a disadvantage regarding technical equipment, and it would be difficult to annihilate the enemy's heavy troops in a short time. Given that the US had expressed its willingness to negotiate, the two sides began Korean ceasefire negotiations on July 10, 1951, after multiple channels of communication. From then on, the war entered a situation of fighting and negotiating simultaneously for more than two years.

On July 27, the ceasefire negotiations reached a stalemate over the issue of the military demarcation line. China and North Korea proposed the 38th parallel as the military demarcation line. Still, the other side rejected the proposal, seeking to gain more land under the pretext of "compensation" for their naval and air superiority. After their demands were denied, the US openly threatened with force, saying, "Let the bombs, cannons, and machine guns debate."

From August 18 to October 22, the "United Nations Forces" adopted a step-by-step offensive, gradually advancing tactics, launching successive local offensives in summer and autumn. Starting in August, they implemented a 10-month air blockade of transportation lines, aiming to cut off the supply of food and ammunition to the front lines of the Chinese and Korean People's Army and force China and North Korea to accept their negotiation terms. After the battles between the Chinese and Korean armies, the enemy's offensive was crushed by late October. The "United Nations Forces" suffered more than 150,000 casualties, forcing them to return to the negotiating table.

In early 1952, the US military blatantly violated international conventions by spreading a large number of animals and insects carrying plague, cholera, typhoid, and other infectious diseases in Northern Korea and Northeastern China, attempting to fundamentally weaken the combat effectiveness of the Chinese and Korean military and civilians through biological warfare. On March 8, Zhou Enlai issued a statement protesting the use of biological weapons by the US government and its violation of Chinese airspace. The US bacteriological warfare provoked great indignation among people worldwide. On April 28, Ridgway was replaced by US General Clark as the "UN Forces Commander." Meanwhile, the "United Nations Forces" proposed the so-called voluntary repatriation principle for detaining Chinese and Korean prisoners of war, opposing the full repatriation proposed by China and North Korea, causing the ceasefire negotiations to reach another deadlock.

To support the negotiations and constantly inflict damage on the enemy, forcing them to concede eventually, the Chinese People's Volunteer Army launched a full-scale tactical counterattack on September 18, 1952. The battle lasted 44 days until October 31, annihilating more than 25,000 enemy troops and causing over 10,000 casualties among the Volunteer Army.

To reverse the situation and force China and North Korea to accept US nego-tiation terms, General Clark commanded the Battle of Triangle Hill on October 14, 1952. In the 43 days of fierce fighting, the US military fired 1.9 million shells and 5,000 bombs at Triangle Hill, which covered an area of less than 3.7 square kilometers and launched more than 900 assaults. Triangle Hill was bombarded to a depth of one to two meters, turning it into scorched earth. However, the Volunteer Army soldiers defended their positions tenaciously, and many war heroes emerged. On October 19, Huang Jiguang sacrificed his young life by blocking an enemy bunker's gun hole with his chest, opening the way for the Volunteer Army to capture the central peak during his mission to blow up the bunker. In this battle, the Volunteer Army suffered more than 11,000 casualties. Still, it annihilated over 25,000 enemy troops, once again demon-strating the formidable offensive and defensive capabilities of the Chinese People's Volunteer Army, and the US military never relaunched any significant offensives.

From December 1952 to April 1953, the US-led "United Nations Forces" and South Korean troops under their command attempted amphibious landings on Korea's east and west coasts. In response, the Chinese People's Volunteer Army and the Korean People's Army prepared actively for battle, forcing the "United Nations Forces" to abandon their plans for military adventure and resume ceasefire negotiations with China and North Korea on April 26, 1953, after a six-month hiatus.

During the continued negotiations, South Korea strongly opposed the talks, claiming they would advance north alone. From mid-May to mid-June 1953, the Chinese People's Volunteer Army launched two offensive operations supporting the ceasefire negotiations, mainly targeting the South Korean army and annihilating more than 40,000 enemy troops. On July 13, the Chinese and Korean People's Armies launched the Battle of Kumsong, annihilating nearly 80,000 South Korean troops and recovering 167 square kilometers of land. Under these circumstances, on July 19, the US issued a statement guaranteeing the implementation of the ceasefire and putting pressure on South Korea. Subsequently, the South Korean government issued a statement accepting the ceasefire agreement.

On July 27, 1953, representatives from both sides of the war signed the "Agreement on Military Ceasefire in Korea" at Panmunjom, marking the end of the more than three-year-long Korean War and the victorious conclusion of the great war to Resist US Aggression and Aid Korea.

Regarding this war, "United Nations Forces" commander General Clark later wrote in his memoirs: "In carrying out my government's orders, I gained an unenviable distinction: I became the first US Army commander in history to sign a ceasefire agreement without victory. I felt a disappointment and pain, and I think my predecessors, Generals MacArthur and Ridgway, must have shared the same sentiment." In September 1953, Peng Dehuai, Commander of the Chinese People's Volunteer Army, pointed out in a report on the work of resisting US aggression and aiding Korea that the victory in the war "eloquently proves that the era when Western aggressors could dominate a country by setting up a few cannons on the coast of the East is gone forever." He also stated that the victory "eloquently proves that an awakened nation, daring to fight for the glory, independence, and security of its motherland, is invincible."

CHAPTER 10

Transition from New Democracy to Socialism

The goal of achieving socialism in China has been a struggle determined by the CPC since its founding. From 1953 onwards, under the guidance of the general line for the transition period, China began the socialist transformation of agriculture, handicrafts, and capitalist industry and commerce. By 1956, the transformation tasks were completed, and the basic socialist system was established.

Concepts and Changes in the Transition to Socialism

From the early 1940s, when Mao Zedong published "On New Democracy," to 1949, the consensus within the Party was that after the revolution's victory, a new democratic transitional stage would be necessary before entering socialism. Based on this judgment, the resolution of the second plenary session of the seventh CPC Central Committee in March 1949 proposed, "After the victory of the revolution, quickly restore and develop production to deal with foreign imperialism and steadily transform China from an agricultural country to an industrial country and from a new democratic country to a socialist country." This view was reflected in the *Common Program*. The first article of the *Common Program* stipulates that "The People's Republic of China is a new democratic or people's democratic country," without mentioning the socialist future.

After the founding of the People's Republic of China in June 1950, Mao Zedong concluded the Second Session of the First National People's Political Consultative Conference, saying, "Our country is advancing steadily, through war and new democratic reforms, and when various conditions are met, and the whole nation has matured and agreed, we can calmly and properly enter the new era of socialism."

However, by 1952, Mao Zedong's judgment had changed. At the September 24, 1952, meeting of the Central Committee of CPC Secretariat, Mao Zedong initially proposed the guiding ideology and general conception of "how China will gradually transition to socialism from now on." This was a significant change in strategic deployment, and the discussion was no longer about when to take socialist steps but about how many years it would take to complete the transition to socialism from now on.

Why did Mao Zedong change his original conception and propose the transition to socialism just three years after the founding of New China?

This was not a whim of Mao Zedong. At this time, the ratio of state-owned and private industrial production value had fundamentally changed. In 1949, the state-owned and private ratios of China's total industrial output value were 43.8% and 56.2%, respectively. By September 1952, the state-owned ratio had risen to 67.3%, and private had dropped to 32.7%, with the state-owned economy surpassing the private economy, providing China with the main material basis for gradually transitioning to socialism. In addition, after land reform, the cooperative movement in rural areas developed widely. These practices show that in some areas, the initial work of socialist transformation had already begun.

Another crucial point was that the main contradiction in Chinese society began to change. In June 1952, as the "Three-Antis" and "Five-Antis" campaigns were about to end, and the nationwide land reform was basically completed, Mao Zedong pointed out: "With the overthrow of the landlord class and the bureaucrat capitalist class, the contradiction between the working class and the national bourgeoisie has become the principal contradiction in China; therefore the national bourgeoisie should no longer be defined as an intermediate class." Treating the bourgeoisie as the target of revolution signified the imminent start of the socialist revolution and put socialist transformation on the Party's agenda.

In summary, the proposal of the general line for the transition period has a reasonable historical basis, and it also conforms to the psychological needs of the majority of people at that time and the needs of the international communist movement. Establishing a socialist society has been the ideal proclaimed by the CPC since its founding. Since the transition to a socialist society is inevitable sooner or later, and the conditions are now in place, why not make the transition quickly? Why not take a step directly into a socialist society?

After a considerable period of brewing, on June 15, 1953, Mao Zedong put forward the Party's general line and overall task for the transition period at a meeting of the Central Political Bureau, stating: "The general line or the general task of the Party for the transition period is basically to accomplish the industrialization of the country and the socialist transformation of agriculture, handicrafts and capitalist industry and commerce in ten to fifteen years, or a little longer." The Political Bureau accepted this formulation.

Subsequently, the National Committee of the Political Consultative Conference officially announced the general line for the transition period in the slogan celebrating the 4th anniversary of the founding of the People's Republic of China. From Mao Zedong's first proposal in September 1952 to the official announcement, the entire process took a full year, showing the cautious attitude and prudent steps the Central Committee of CPC took in formulating and announcing the general line.

A nationwide publicity campaign was launched after announcing the general line for the transition period. To adapt to the needs of learning and publicity, in December 1953, Mao Zedong asked the Central Publicity Department to draft a learning and publicity outline, which gave a complete statement of the general line: "The general line or the general task of the Party for the transition period is basically to accomplish the industrialization of the country and the socialist transformation of agriculture, handicrafts and capitalist industry and commerce in ten to fifteen years, or a little longer. This general line is a beacon illuminating our work in all fields. Do not depart from this general line, otherwise 'Left' or 'Right' mistakes will occur."

In February 1954, the fourth plenary session of the seventh CPC Central Committee passed a resolution, officially approving the Party's general line for the transition period. In September of the same year, the *Constitution of the People's Republic of China* adopted by the first plenary session of the first NPC incorporated the general line for the transition period into its general principles.

Mutual Aid Groups, Primary Cooperatives, and Advanced Cooperatives

The proposal of the Party's general line for the transition period is directly related to the changes in rural China at that time. This change is manifested in the widespread development of mutual aid and cooperation in rural areas.

Old China was a backward agricultural country dominated by small-scale peasant individual economies with a shallow level of productivity. To resist natural disasters, develop production, and solve the difficulties of insufficient labor, draught animals, and incomplete agricultural tools, farmers had a spontaneous tradition of mutual aid in agricultural production. The *Common Program* stipulates: "In all areas where land reform has been thoroughly implemented, the people's government should organize farmers and all labor forces that can engage in agriculture to take the development of agricultural production and its sideline industries as the central task, and should guide farmers to gradually organize various forms of labor mutual aid and production cooperation on the principles of voluntariness and mutual benefit."

In accordance with this spirit, by 1950, there were 2.724 million mutual aid groups in agriculture nationwide, with 11.313 million households joining, accounting for 10.7% of the total number of households nationwide. However, the Party had different understandings of how to treat farmers' enthusiasm to develop individual economies and mutual aid cooperation.

To strengthen the leadership of rural work, in November 1952, the Central Committee of CPC decided to establish the Rural Work Department and appointed Deng Zihui as the Minister. In February 1953, the Central Rural Work Department was established to guide the development of agricultural mutual aid and cooperation movement.

In the spring and summer of 1953, with the launch of large-scale planned economic construction, Mao Zedong advocated strengthening the transformation of the small-scale peasant economy and accelerating the pace of agricultural mutual aid and cooperation. For this reason, the Third National Agricultural Mutual Aid and Cooperation Conference held from October to November 1953 clearly stated the path of transformation of individual agriculture, namely, guiding individual farmers through mutual aid groups with socialist sprouts to semi-socialist primary cooperatives and then to fully socialist advanced cooperatives. In the process of socialist transformation in agriculture, the principle of "active leadership and steady progress" should be implemented, opposing laissez-faire and any forced orders and deprivation of farmers' rights.

Since then, rural mutual aid and cooperation development has entered the stage of widespread development of primary cooperatives and pilot projects for advanced cooperatives from the stage of widespread expansion of mutual aid groups and pilot projects for primary cooperatives.

In response to the new situation, in April 1954, the Central Rural Work Department held the Second National Rural Work Conference. The conference determined that by 1955, the number of agricultural production cooperatives would develop to 300,000 or 350,000, and by 1957, it would develop to 1.3 million or 1.5 million, with participating households accounting for about 35% of the total households nationwide. During the Second Five-Year Plan, around 1960, the goal was to achieve cooperativization in the basic regions of the country. By the autumn of 1954, 114,000 agricultural production cooperatives participated in the autumn harvest distribution, and more than 115,000 cooperatives were established in various places before the autumn harvest, reaching a total of over 229,000 agricultural production cooperatives in early October.

In mid-to-late October 1954, the Central Rural Work Department held the Fourth National Mutual Aid and Cooperation Conference. The conference raised the goal of developing 300,000 or 350,000 cooperatives by 1955, as proposed at the Second National Rural Work Conference, to 600,000 cooperatives before the 1955 spring plowing.

However, some regions tended to rush and take risks during cooperatives' rapid development. This caused psychological panic among farmers, who feared their means of production would be nationalized. They began slaughtering pigs, cattle, and sheep and selling livestock; meanwhile, there were serious incidents of farmers cutting down trees and destroying agricultural tools.

In early March 1955, Mao Zedong met with Deng Zihui and others to address this situation. He pointed out, "The relations of production must adapt to the requirements of the development of the productive forces; otherwise, the productive forces will revolt. The current killing of pigs and cattle by farmers is an example of the productive forces revolting." He affirmed the measures taken by the Rural Work Department in rural work and summarized them as "the three-word guideline: stop, shrink, and expand."

However, between April and May 1955, Mao Zedong's inspection tour and the situations he observed led to a change in his understanding of the development of agricultural cooperatives. He believed that the claims of farmers' production being passive only applied to a small portion of them. "I saw wheat growing half a person deep along the way. Is that passive production?" The Central Rural Work Department's reports on the difficulties faced by some cooperatives were considered "rumor-mongering."

On May 17, the Central Committee of CPC held a meeting of 15 provincial and municipal committee secretaries in Hangzhou. Although Mao Zedong reiterated the "stop, shrink, expand" three-word guideline in his speech, he emphasized "expanding." This significant change in his views on agricultural cooperatives became known as the "May Change."

In late June 1955, Mao Zedong met with Deng Zihui and proposed that the number of agricultural production cooperatives should double from the existing 650,000 to around 1.3 million by the following year. Deng Zihui insisted it would be better to stick to the original plan of 1 million cooperatives. The two argued for several hours without resolution and parted on bad terms. On July 11, Mao Zedong met with Deng Zihui again, reaffirming his opinions and proposals, but Deng Zihui still held his ground. Furious, Mao Zedong told Deng Zihui, "Your thoughts need to be bombarded by artillery."

On July 31, 1955, the Central Committee of CPC held a meeting of provinces, municipalities, and autonomous regions secretaries. Mao Zedong delivered a report on "Issues Concerning Agricultural Cooperativization" and indirectly criticized Deng Zihui and others for being "conservative" and "right-leaning." He exaggerated the debate within the Party over the pace of agricultural cooperativization into a divergence of two lines. In October, the Expanded sixth plenary session of the seventh CPC Central Committee adopted the "Resolution on Agricultural Cooperativization," which officially characterized Deng Zihui's and the Central Rural Work Department's so-called "mistakes" as "rightist opportunism." After the sixth plenary session, a nationwide upsurge of agricultural cooperativization occurred.

From September to December 1955, Mao Zedong presided over the compilation of *The Socialist Upsurge in China's Countryside*, continuing to criticize the so-called "rightist opportunism sharply." Amidst the "anti-rightist" campaign, the development of agricultural cooperatives accelerated rapidly.

By the end of 1955, the number of households joining primary agricultural production cooperatives had surged from over 16 million in the spring to 75.45 million. Provinces and cities such as Hebei, Shanxi, Liaoning, Heilongjiang, Jilin, Anhui, Henan, Hunan, Hubei, Qinghai, Gansu, Beijing, Shanghai, and Tianjin had basically achieved semi-socialist primary cooperativization. By early 1956, the number of households joining primary agricultural production cooperatives nationwide had reached 106.67 million, accounting for 90% of the total households. This essentially achieved semi-socialist primary cooperativization across the country.

Following this, starting in January 1956, a new upsurge focused on developing advanced cooperatives swept across rural China, with primary cooperatives transforming into advanced cooperatives. By June 1956, Beijing, Tianjin, Shanghai, Hebei, Shanxi, Liaoning, Jilin, Heilongjiang, Henan, Guangxi, and Qinghai had achieved full socialist advanced cooperativization, with 90% to 95% of the households in these provinces joining advanced cooperatives. In the autumn, Hunan, Jiangxi, Anhui, Jiangsu, Zhejiang, and Hubei followed suit, with over 80% of the households in each province joining advanced agricultural production cooperatives.

By the end of 1956, except for some remote mountain households and hunters and some ethnic minority areas, cooperativization had been almost universally achieved. The number of households joining cooperatives reached 117.82 million, accounting for 96.3% of the total households in the country, of which 107.42 million households joined advanced cooperatives, accounting for 87.8% of the total households. About 10.4 million households joined primary cooperatives, accounting for 8.5% of the total households, and approximately 4 million households still needed to join agricultural production cooperatives, accounting for 3.7% of the total households.

Peaceful Redemption of National Industries and Commerce

During the formation of the overall transitional period strategy, to summarize the experiences of the state's utilization and restriction policies on capitalist industries and commerce since the founding of the new China, Li Weihan, the Minister of the United Front Work Department of the Central Committee of CPC, led an investigation team to Wuhan, Nanjing, Shanghai, and other places in March and April 1953. Subsequently, they submitted an investigation report to the Central Government. The report pointed out that state capitalism is the main form of transforming the capitalist industry to gradually transition to socialism and the main link in transforming the bourgeois elements.

Mao Zedong endorsed Li Weihan's report. In September 1953, Mao Zedong invited representatives from some democratic parties and the industrial and commercial sectors for a discussion. He stated, "With more than three years of experience behind us, we can say with certainty that accomplishing the socialist transformation of private industry and commerce by means of state capitalism is a relatively sound policy and method." He proposed a series of policies for the transformation of capitalist industries and commerce: in terms of form, adopting joint public-private ventures, processing and order, and procurement; in terms of profit distribution, implementing the "Four Horses Share the Spoils" policy, with income tax accounting for 34.5%, welfare funds 15%, public reserve funds 30%, and capital dividends 20.5%.

In January 1954, the Central Finance and Economics Committee held an expanded meeting on the industrial plan for joint public-private ventures, which clarified the working guidelines for expanding public-private joint ventures in the industry: "consolidate the position, focus on expansion, set examples, and strengthen preparations." From 1954, the expansion of public-private joint ventures was carried out with focus and planning.

The development of joint public-private enterprises began with the merger of large enterprises, referred to as "eating apples," which meant merging one by one; then "eating grapes," gradually expanding to small and medium-sized enterprises. At the same time, it expanded from major industries to general industries and from large cities to small and medium-sized cities. After the merger of large enterprises, the state could not disperse more funds and materials to numerous small and medium-sized enterprises due to the need to ensure key construction projects. As a result, small and medium-sized enterprises struggled and actively sought joint public-private ownership. From December 1954 to January 1955, the State Council held the Second National Conference on Expanding Joint Public-Private Industrial Planning. The conference finally decided to adopt the "big leading small, advanced leading backward" method in joint public-private ownership in various industries, first restructuring and merging small and medium-sized enterprises according to different conditions and then implementing joint public-private ownership.

The socialist transformation of private commerce also gradually became clear. In July 1954, the Central Committee of CPC issued the "Instructions on Strengthening Market Management and Transforming Private Commerce," stipulating the method of "moving forward and making arrangements step by step," gradually transforming existing private wholesalers and retailers into various forms of state capitalist commerce. After that, the transformation of private commerce and industry was carried out in parallel.

Following the nationwide sensation of the agricultural cooperativization upsurge in the summer of 1955, the upsurge of handicraft cooperativization soon followed. National capitalists were concerned about this situation. If they actively embraced the coming transformation upsurge, they feared losing their existing economic interests and social status; if they were not proactive, they feared being criticized and facing more significant impacts.

In response to this situation, on October 27 and 29, 1955, Mao Zedong twice invited representatives of the industrial and commercial sectors to attend the First Executive Committee Meeting of the All-China Federation of Industry and Commerce to hold discussions. Mao Zedong likened the attitude of the industrial and commercial sectors toward changing private ownership to "fifteen buckets drawing water, seven up and eight down." He asked capitalists to reduce their "bucket drawing," stabilize their emotions, understand the development trend of society, stand on the side of socialism, and take control of their own destiny. In the discussion on October 29, Mao Zedong elaborated on the policy of continuing peaceful transformation and gradual redemption for capitalist industries and commerce.

> The socialist transformation of capitalist industries and commerce we are implementing now is actually the redemption policy put forward by Marx, Engels, and Lenin in the past. It is not the state purchasing the private property of capitalists (not consumer goods, but means of production, such as machinery and factory buildings) with a lump sum of money or issuing government bonds, nor is it carried out suddenly but gradually, extending the transformation period, say, 15 years. Workers will produce part of the profits for industrial and commercial workers during this period. This part of the profit is a portion of the workers' made profit allocated to private individuals. There is such an account for the national capitalists' fixed asset valuation: 2.5 billion yuan in industry and 0.8 billion yuan in commerce, totaling 3.3 billion yuan. I think that if we add the three-year recovery period to the fifteen years, making a total of eighteen years, the profits produced by the working class for the middle class will exceed this figure ... There are mainly two arrangements for capitalists: one is the job position, and the other is the political status, which should be comprehensively arranged ... Do you think you have a chance to become part of the working class? There definitely is hope, and I can write you a check for that. This is a bright political status and a bright future. Once individual private ownership and capitalist private ownership are abolished, only the working class, the peasantry, and the intellectuals will remain in society. Only then will the entire nation have a brighter future and more excellent development prospects.

Mao Zedong's speech greatly alleviated the concerns and doubts of representatives from the industrial and commercial sectors about their future and destiny, and many people expressed their support on the spot.

In early November 1955, the First Executive Committee of the All-China Federation of Industry and Commerce held a meeting to convey Mao Zedong's speech. Many industrialists and businessmen spoke out, criticizing their own history of exploitation and realizing that only by being determined to take the socialist path could they control their own destiny and achieve a bright future. From November 16 to 24, the Political Bureau of the Central Committee of CPC convened a meeting on the transformation of capitalist industry and commerce, with representatives from the provincial, municipal, and autonomous region party committees attending. The meeting passed the "Resolution on the Issue of the Transformation of Capitalist Industry and Commerce" (Draft), pointing out that the transformation of industry and commerce should be advanced to a new stage, the stage of implementing public-private partnerships in whole or in large part.

Driven and influenced by the aforementioned meeting, the climax of public-private partnerships across industries was unstoppable. On November 23, 1955, the retail stores of the cotton and department store industries in Nanjing implemented public-private partnerships across the entire industry; on November 24, 160 of the 165 factories in the cotton spinning, wool spinning, hemp spinning, papermaking, cigarette, flour, and rice milling industries in Shanghai completed economic restructuring and implemented public-private partnerships for 100 factories across the industry. On November 26, public-private partnerships were realized in five industries in Beijing, including flour, pharmaceuticals, electrical machinery, papermaking, and machine dyeing.

After New Year's Day in 1956, Beijing was the first to see a wave of public-private partnerships across industries. From January 8 to 10, Beijing approved the public-private partnership applications of all capitalist industrial and commercial households in three days, with 3,990 industrial households and 13,973 commercial households realizing public-private partnerships simultaneously. On January 15, more than 200,000 people from all walks of life in Beijing held a celebration of the successful transformation at Tiananmen Square. Mao Zedong, Liu Shaoqi, Zhou Enlai, and others attended the meeting and received enthusiastic reports from various industries. On January 21, a celebration of the success of socialist transformation was held in Shanghai. Subsequently, major cities nationwide followed suit, with a constant stream of parades of capitalists and private enterprise employees applying for partnerships and celebratory meetings announcing the implementation of public-private partnerships across industries.

By the end of 1956, 99% of the national private industrial households (more than 88,000 households) and 82.2% of the private commercial households (more than 2.4 million households) were incorporated into public-private partnerships or cooperatives.

After the implementation of public-private partnerships across industries, capitalists were no longer the owners of their original enterprises but were accepted as employees of the enterprises according to their abilities. The state paid the fixed interest they received at a fixed rate according to the private share assets determined at the time of the partnership, regardless of the enterprise's profit or loss, and had no connection with the original enterprise's profits. By the end of 1956, after public-private partnership enterprises' clearing and asset verification, the private share capital was determined to be 2.41864 billion yuan. Starting from January 1, 1956, the state issued fixed interest to 1.14 million private shareholders at a fixed annual interest rate of 5% (slightly higher than the bank interest rate at that time), with an annual fixed interest amount of over 0.12 billion yuan. The original fixed interest was set to remain unchanged for seven years, but in 1962, it was decided to extend it to ten years. In September 1966, the fixed interest was canceled. This marked the peaceful redemption of the national industrial and commercial sectors. During this process, the state successively paid more than 3 billion yuan to private industrial and commercial entrepreneurs as the price of peaceful redemption through the "Four Horses Share the Spoils" and fixed interest, which exceeded their original total asset value.

The Institutional Basis for China's Development and Progress

While carrying out reforms in agriculture, industry, and commerce, the transformation of handicraft industries was also carried out in parallel and successfully completed.

By 1956, the socialist transformation was essentially completed, bringing about profound changes in the ownership of the means of production in China. The small private ownership of peasants and handicraftsmen had largely been transformed into collective ownership by the working masses. The capitalist private ownership had essentially been transformed into state ownership or ownership by the whole people. Comparing 1956 with 1952, the share of the state-owned economy in the national income increased from 19.1% to 32.2%. The share of the cooperative economy rose from 1.5% to 53.4%, and the share of the joint public-private economy rose from 0.7% to 7.3%.

In contrast, the share of the individual economy decreased from 71.8% to 7.1%, and the share of the private capitalist economy decreased from 6.9% to nearly zero. The share of the socialist public ownership economy reached a total of 92.9%. In the total industrial output value, comparing 1956 with 1952, the share of socialist state-owned industry increased from 56% to 67.5%, national capitalist industry from 26.9% to 32.5%, and capitalist industry decreased from 17.1% to nearly zero. In the total retail sales of social commodities, the share of state-owned commerce and supply and marketing cooperative commerce increased from 42.6% to 68.3%, national capitalist commerce and cooperative commerce formed by former small private merchants increased from 0.2% to 27.5%, and private commerce decreased from 57.2% to 4.2%. That is to say, in the entire national economy, the two forms of socialist public ownership, ownership by the whole people and collective ownership by the working masses, have occupied a dominant position. The fundamental change in the ownership structure indicates that the economic foundation of socialism has been initially established in China.

The historical contribution of the socialist transformation of agriculture, handicrafts, and capitalist industry and commerce must be fully affirmed.

First, it basically eliminated the exploitative system of private ownership of the means of production and established a socialist economic system with public ownership of the means of production and distribution according to contribution as its main form and characteristic. Together with the socialist political system of the people's democratic dictatorship led by the working class established at the beginning of the founding of the People's Republic of China, it ensured the establishment of the socialist system in China, thus realizing the greatest and most profound social transformation in thousands of years and creating and laying the institutional foundation for China's progress and development. Second, as a major transformation of social systems involving hundreds of millions of people, it avoided the usually inevitable large-scale social unrest and damage to the productive forces. It promoted the unity of the people of all ethnic groups and the development of social productive forces. As the *Resolution on Several Historical Issues of the Party since the Founding of the People's Republic of China*, passed by the sixth plenary session of the 11th CPC Central

Committee, stated, during this period, "economic development was relatively fast, economic effects were relatively good, and the proportions among major economic sectors were relatively coordinated. Markets were prosperous, and prices were stable. People's lives improved significantly." Finally, it created a series of transformation forms from low to high levels and embarked on a path of socialist transformation with Chinese characteristics, enriching and developing Marxist theory on socialist transformation. In particular, the socialist transformation of capitalist industry and commerce, using various forms of state capitalism and combining the transformation of enterprises with the transformation of people, successfully realized the peaceful buyout policy of the bourgeoisie envisioned by Marx and Lenin. The transformation of capitalists into self-reliant workers was a great victory.

At the same time, it should be recognized that there were shortcomings and deviations in the socialist transformation of agriculture, handicrafts, and capitalist industry and commerce. The *Resolution on Several Historical Issues of the Party since the Founding of the People's Republic of China* pointed out: "After the summer of 1955, the requirements for agricultural cooperation and the transformation of handicrafts and individual commerce were too urgent, the work was rough, the changes were too rapid, and the forms were too simplistic and uniform, leaving some problems for a long time."

Chapter 11

Exploring China's Own Path to Construction

After the socialist transformation was basically completed in 1956, the task of large-scale socialist construction was placed before the Chinese Communists. How to build socialism in China, a poor, backward, populous, and highly distinctive oriental country, is a very difficult and complex issue. The CPC started exploring the construction path well but later made some mistakes and took some detours.

From Learning from the Soviet Union to Drawing Lessons from the Soviet Experience

After founding the People's Republic of China, learning from the Soviet Union's construction experience was a realistic choice under the "leaning to one side" diplomatic policy as China's revolution was about to succeed.

On June 30, 1949, in the article "On the People's Democratic Dictatorship," Mao Zedong openly announced the "leaning to one side" policy and expressed his willingness to learn from the Soviet Union. Shortly after the founding of the New China,

Liu Shaoqi pointed out at the founding conference of the Sino-Soviet Friendship Association on October 5: "The Chinese people's revolution in the past was learning from the Soviet Union, 'taking Russia as a teacher,' and thus achieving today's victory. In the future, we must also 'take Russia as a teacher' and learn from the Soviet people's experience in nation-building." As a result, "learning from the advanced experience of the Soviet Union" and "the Soviet Union's today is our tomorrow" became the slogans and goals for various sectors of Chinese society.

After Lenin's death, under Stalin's leadership, the Soviet Union underwent 20 years of development and gradually formed a highly centralized socialist model, mainly managed through administrative means, known as the "Soviet model" or "Stalin model." When learning from the Soviet Union's construction experience in the early days of the founding of New China, China was also influenced by this model.

Mao Zedong believed that a dialectical and analytical attitude should be adopted toward "learning from the Soviet Union" and copying the Soviet model. First, "copying" was necessary since there were no other alternatives, and it indeed played a positive role in the rapid recovery of the national economy. Second, Mao was not satisfied with completely "copying" the Soviet model. He later said, "After the liberation, we were ignorant of construction during the three-year recovery period. Then, during the First Five-Year Plan, we were still ignorant of construction and could only copy the Soviet approach. But we always felt dissatisfied and uneasy." To change this situation, at the end of 1955, Mao Zedong explicitly raised the issue of "drawing lessons from the Soviet Union" and hoped to explore a new path of socialist construction that suited China's characteristics outside the Soviet model.

While the CPC was exploring China's own path of socialist construction, in February 1956, the 20th Congress of the Communist Party of the Soviet Union (CPSU) was held. On the eve of the closing of the congress, Nikita Khrushchev, the General Secretary of the CPSU, convened a secret meeting that had not been previously arranged and delivered a secret report, "On the Cult of Personality and Its Consequences," revealing the serious consequences of Stalin's creation of a cult of personality. Once disclosed, the report's content immediately caused huge political shockwaves in the international community, especially within the socialist camp. The exposure of the Stalin issue made people see that the Soviet socialist model, which had long been worshipped, had serious drawbacks. Blindly imitating the Soviet method could not replace self-exploration, which greatly promoted the reflection on the Soviet model by Communist parties in various countries, including the CPC, and serious consideration of their own construction path.

After the 20th Congress of the CPSU, Mao Zedong's idea of "drawing lessons from the Soviet Union" became clearer.

From February to April 1956, to discuss various problems in socialist construction and summarize experiences, Mao Zedong personally listened to the work reports of 34 departments in central industry, agriculture, transportation, and commerce. He listened to reports as soon as he got up and went to bed after listening to them. Only mealtime was considered leisure time. He called this a "bed-up, bed-down" life. He worked intensely like this for more than two months.

Based on the opinions of everyone, on April 25, Mao Zedong delivered a report on "On the Ten Major Relationships" at an enlarged meeting of the Political Bureau of the Central Committee. The basic principle determined in the report was to mobilize all positive factors at home and abroad to serve the socialist cause. The ten issues discussed in the report were raised based on summarizing China's economic construction experience and taking the Soviet Union's experience as a warning. Given the lessons from the Soviet Union's neglect of agriculture and light industry and the one-sided emphasis on heavy industry, causing imbalanced development of agriculture, light, and heavy industries, the report proposed that China's economic plan should be adjusted appropriately in the future, with more emphasis on developing agriculture, light industry, and coastal industries, reducing the proportion of military and political expenses as much as possible, and focusing more on economic construction. These ideas actually involved the issue of China's path to industrialization. The report also discussed the relationship between the state, production units, and individual producers, the relationship between the central and local governments, and began to involve economic system reform; it also expounded on the relationships between the Han and minority nationalities, the party and non-party members, revolution and counterrevolution, right and wrong, and China and foreign countries in the political life.

Mao Zedong pointed out, "Particularly worthy of attention is the fact that in the Soviet Union certain defects and errors that occurred in the course of their building socialism have lately come to light. Do you want to follow the detours they have made? It was by drawing lessons from their experience that we were able to avoid certain detours in the past, and there is all the more reason for us to do so now." He said, "Our guideline is to learn from the strengths of all nations and countries, and everything that is truly good in politics, economy, science, technology, literature, and art," including "learning from the advanced science and technology of capitalist countries and the scientific aspects of enterprise management methods."

The speech "On the Ten Major Relationships" took the lessons of the Soviet Union as a warning and put forward the historical task of exploring a socialist construction path suitable for China's national conditions. In March 1958, Mao Zedong pointed out at the Chengdu Conference: "In April 1956 I put forward the 'Ten Major Relationships' which made a start in proposing our own line for construction. This was similar to that of the Soviet Union in principle but had our own content." In June 1960, he wrote in "A Summary of Ten Years": "For the first eight years, we copied foreign experiences. But since 1956, when the Ten Major Relationships were proposed, we began to find a path suitable for China."

Preliminary Achievements of Exploration

From the first half of 1956 to the summer of 1957, before the anti-rightist struggle was severely expanded, the first generation of the central leadership of the CPC, with Mao Zedong as its core, carried out a relatively comprehensive examination of many major theoretical and practical issues in China's socialist construction and achieved a series of valuable intellectual achievements.

First, the guiding ideology and basic principles for exploration were proposed. Mao Zedong emphasized the guiding ideology in "On the Ten Major Relationships": "Our theory combines the universal truth of Marxism-Leninism with the concrete practice of the Chinese revolution." On the basic principles, Mao Zedong pointed out in "On the Ten Major Relationships": "We should mobilize all forces, whether direct or indirect, and strive to make China a powerful socialist country."

Second, correct analysis and judgment were made on the main social contradictions, and a strategic decision was made to shift the focus of work. This is the most important theoretical contribution of the 8th CPC National Congress. The resolution on the political report made by Liu Shaoqi, which the 8th National Congress passed, pointed out that after the socialist system was basically established, the main contradiction within the country was no longer between the proletariat and the bourgeoisie. "The main contradiction within the country has become the contradiction between the people's demand for building an advanced industrial country and the reality of a backward agricultural country; it has become the contradiction between the people's need for rapid economic and cultural development and the current economic and cultural situation that cannot satisfy the people's needs." Therefore, the focus of the Party's work is to lead the people in socialist economic construction, vigorously develop productive forces, realize national industrialization, and gradually meet the people's growing material and cultural needs.

Third, new ideas for economic construction and economic system reform were proposed. First, a principle of economic construction was formulated that is both anti-conservative and anti-adventurous, which is to move forward steadily in a comprehensive balance. Second, the idea of reforming the overly centralized and unified planned economic system was put forward. In "On the Ten Major Relationships," Mao Zedong proposed the idea of expanding local power and increasing the "independence" of factories and enterprises. Chen Yun put forward the idea of "three main bodies, three supplements" (planned production as the main body of industrial and agricultural production, supplemented by free production within the scope permitted by the state plan according to market changes; the state market as the main body, supplemented by a certain range of free markets under state leadership; state-owned and collective economies as the main body of industrial and commercial production and operation, supplemented by a certain number of individual economies).

Fourth, the basic contradictions of socialist society and the theory of two types of contradictions were creatively expounded. In February 1957, in his speech "On the Correct Handling of Contradictions among the People," Mao Zedong pointed out that the basic contradiction in socialist society was still the contradiction between the productive forces and the relations of production and between the economic base and the superstructure. There are still two types of contradictions in socialist society: the contradiction between the enemy and ourselves and the contradiction among the people. These two types of contradictions have different natures and need to be correctly distinguished and dealt with. Coercive and dictatorial methods must resolve the contradiction between the enemy and ourselves. In contrast, the contradiction among the people can only be resolved through democratic, persuasive, and educational methods and the approach of "unity-criticism-unity." He clearly pointed out that the correct handling of contradictions among the people is the theme of the country's political life, and "our policy is to take everything into consideration and make appropriate arrangements."

Fifth, several important ideas were put forward to strengthen socialist democratic politics and the construction of the legal system. With the completion of the socialist transformation and the elimination of the bourgeoisie, the issue of whether the various democratic parties should continue to exist under the new historical conditions of socialism was raised. Mao Zedong clearly pointed out in "On the Ten Major Relationships." China does not follow the Soviet-style one-party system or the Western two-party system but adheres to the multi-party cooperation system led by the Communist Party, implementing the policy of "long-term coexistence and mutual supervision." Regarding the construction of the legal system, Dong Biwu put forward the ideas of "having laws to follow" and "abiding by the law." In addition, Zhou Enlai proposed the idea of "continuing dictatorship and expanding democracy"; Liu Shaoqi discussed how to prevent state leaders from becoming a special class.

Sixth, the correct policy was put forward for ideological and cultural construction. In January 1956, Zhou Enlai, on behalf of the Central Committee of CPC, announced at the conference on the intellectual issue: "The vast majority of them have become state workers, serving socialism, and are already part of the working class." Socialist construction "must rely on the close cooperation of physical and mental labor and the alliance of workers, peasants, and intellectuals." In March, the Central Government approved the establishment of the National Science Commission, responsible for formulating the 1956–1967 long-term plan for science and technology. On April 28, at an expanded meeting of the Central Political Bureau, Mao Zedong proposed the policy of "letting a hundred flowers bloom and a hundred schools of thought contend" in scientific and cultural work.

In addition, the eighth CPC National Congress also put forward important guidelines for strengthening the construction of the Party under the national governance, requiring more emphasis on promoting the Party's fine tradition of the mass line, being vigilant against the governing Party's detachment from the masses and reality; promoting democracy within the Party and opposing personality cult.

In general, the exploration of the road to socialist construction that began in 1956 had a good start, was in the right direction, and many valuable experiences and brilliant ideas laid a certain foundation for the comprehensive and highly effective exploration carried out by the CPC after the third plenary session of the eleventh Central Committee.

"Great Leap Forward" and the "Great Cultural Revolution"

Regrettably, the correct ideas and decisions put forward in the exploration of 1956 were mostly unable to be well adhered to in practice. As Deng Xiaoping said, 20 years of "leftism" occurred. "After 1957, 'leftist' thinking began to rise and gradually gained the upper hand. In 1958, the 'Great Leap Forward' and the rapid development of people's communes took place, with a one-sided emphasis on 'one big, two publics' and eating from the same big pot, which brought about a great disaster. The 'Great Cultural Revolution' is even more needless to mention. ... It is basically due to the persistence of 'leftist' mistakes, which continued until 1978." Deng Xiaoping pointed out: "For a full twenty years, the income of farmers and workers increased very little, the living standards were very low, and there was not much development of productivity."

Why was this so? As mentioned earlier, starting in 1956, Mao Zedong wanted to break free from the constraints of the Soviet model and find a fast and good path for socialist construction. From the founding of New China to the basic completion of socialist transformation, a series of victories in just a few years made people believe that the goal of China's socialist construction might be achieved relatively quickly. As Mao Zedong pointed out: "In the past seven or eight years, we have seen hope for our nation," "that is, we hope our country will become a big and strong country." "I think our nation is now like breaking the atomic nucleus and releasing heat energy."

Under such circumstances, due to the lack of experience in socialist construction, insufficient understanding of the laws of economic development and the basic situation of the Chinese economy, and, more importantly, because Mao Zedong, the Central Government, and many local leaders grew complacent in the face of victory, and as a result exaggerated the role of personal subjective will, the "Great Leap Forward" campaign was rashly launched in 1958 without serious investigation, research, and pilot projects.

During the "Great Leap Forward," there was a prevalence of high targets, blind command, false reporting, exaggeration, and the "communist wind." In agriculture, the slogan "the bolder the people, the greater the production" was promoted, and grain yields per acre were raised layer by layer, reaching 800 billion *jin* (actually only 400 billion *jin*) in 1958. In industry, there was a one-sided pursuit of high steel production targets; the slogan "surpassing the UK and catching up with the US" was put forward, and a nationwide "mass steelmaking" campaign was launched, with tens of millions of people participating; steel was regarded as the key, driving the "Great Leap Forward" in other industries. The "Great Leap Forward" disrupted the order of the national economy and wasted a large amount of human and material resources.

Beginning in October 1958, Mao Zedong became aware of and began to correct the problems that had emerged in the "Great Leap Forward." To this end, the Central

Committee of CPC successively convened meetings to adjust economic targets, achieving some results. The Lushan Conference in 1959 was originally intended to correct leftist errors, but it eventually turned from correcting leftism to attacking rightism, branding Peng Dehuai and others who criticized the "Great Leap Forward" as an "Anti-Party Clique" and then launched a new "Great Leap Forward" campaign.

In the continuation of the "Great Leap Forward," due to the more serious mistakes of high targets and "communist wind" in the second half of 1959, especially in 1960, compared to the errors of 1958, the scope of the impact was even wider. In addition, some regions experienced natural disasters, and the Soviet government treacherously tore up aid contracts (prompting China to smelt "defiant steel," exacerbating the mistake of "taking steel as the key"). The national economy faced serious difficulties, and the number of abnormal deaths in rural areas increased in many provinces. According to official statistics, the total population in 1960 was 10 million less than the previous year. Moreover, the "Great Leap Forward" caused huge economic losses, lost valuable development opportunities, and widened the gap between China and other countries. It is estimated that the direct economic loss caused by the "Great Leap Forward" reached 120 billion yuan.

In January 1961, the Central Committee of CPC convened the ninth plenary session of the eighth Central Committee, officially approving the implementation of adjustments to the national economy, following the guideline of "adjustment, consolidation, enrichment, and improvement." The "Great Leap Forward" campaign came to an end.

After several years of effort, just as the task of adjusting the national economy was basically completed, the "Great Cultural Revolution" broke out in 1966 and lasted for ten years.

Regarding the historical period from the "Great Leap Forward" to the "Great Cultural Revolution," Deng Xiaoping pointed out that the political "leftism" led to the economic "Great Leap Forward" in 1958, which caused great damage to production and made people's lives very difficult. 1959, 1960, and 1961 were very difficult; people could not even get enough to eat, let alone anything else. In 1962, things began to improve and gradually returned to the previous level. However, the ideological issues were not resolved, and as a result, the "Great Cultural Revolution" began in 1966, which lasted for ten years and was a great disaster.

The mistakes of the "Great Leap Forward" and the comprehensive, long-term left-leaning errors of the "Great Cultural Revolution" caused huge losses to the Party, the country, and the nation, and the lessons learned are extremely profound. From the Party's perspective exploring its own path of socialist construction, the two have commonalities, which reflect the serious deviation between subjective understanding and objective reality and between motivation and effect.

Mao Zedong launched the "Great Leap Forward" to quickly change the backward appearance of the country, enable China to become a powerful and developed country as soon as possible, and catch up with developed countries. This motivation and purpose are beyond reproach. Huang Kecheng, who was labeled as a member of the "Anti-Party Group" for agreeing with Peng Dehuai's views at the Lushan Conference and was wronged for twenty years, pointed out after his return: "Chairman Mao's ambition in his later years was still very great, and he wanted to accomplish things that would take hundreds of years to achieve within a few years or decades. As a result, some chaos emerged. Although this chaos brought misfortune and trauma to our Party and people, from his original intention, he still wanted to do the people's affairs well and push the revolutionary cause forward. He worked hard for this ideal for a lifetime."

Similarly, Mao Zedong's subjective desire to launch the "Great Cultural Revolution" was to build an ideal socialist new society and prevent the restoration of capitalism. As pointed out in *The Cambridge History of the People's Republic of China*:

Mao tirelessly pursued the purity of the revolution after its victory, which was his motivation for launching the "Great Cultural Revolution"; Mao's pursuit of revolutionary purity led him to exaggerate and wrongly estimate the problems China faced in the 1960s. In Mao Zedong's view, the greatest threat to the success of the socialist revolution was not an external attack but the restoration of capitalism within the country. Mao believed that the experience of the Soviet Union after Stalin's death proved that if revisionist elements gained power within the governing Communist Party, capitalism would be restored. It was necessary to constantly struggle against the "Party members in power" who might take the capitalist road to avoid this situation. In fact, after the nationalization of industry and the collectivization of agriculture, this would be the main form of class struggle in a socialist society. This method of conducting class struggle would "boldly arouse the masses at the grassroots level" in a cultural revolution, not only criticizing the revisionist elements in power within the Party but also criticizing the selfish and liberal tendencies in their own thoughts. Since the root of revisionism lies in human selfishness, a cultural revolution lasting for decades is necessary to preserve the purity of a socialist society.

Maintaining the purity of the revolution and building an ideal socialism are impeccable motivations. The problem lies in the fact that the goals needed to be more detached from reality, and the methods and means to achieve these goals needed to be revised. In 1967, when Mao Zedong talked about why he launched the "Great Cultural Revolution," he emphasized that it was because the past struggles in the countryside, factories, the cultural field, and the socialist education movement "could not solve the problem." Therefore, the "Great Cultural Revolution" had to be implemented, focusing on "class struggle" and achieving "great order under great chaos." History has proven that this can only cause serious chaos, destruction, and regression.

Significant Achievements and Their Impact

Despite the mistakes of the "Great Leap Forward" and the "Great Cultural Revolution" while exploring the socialist construction path, a specific and objective analysis of this period should acknowledge that China's various undertakings in socialist construction have achieved significant achievements recognized worldwide.

The "Great Leap Forward" caused tremendous destruction and waste in industrial and agricultural production and construction. However, many tasks in industrial construction, scientific research, and the development of cutting-edge defense technology, as well as farmland water conservancy construction and the development of agricultural mechanization and modernization, were initiated during those years. Among them, the development of the oil industry and the research and development of cutting-edge defense science and technology are particularly prominent. China used to be considered an oil-deficient country, with fuel imported from foreign countries as "foreign oil." In 1959, technicians discovered industrial oil flow in Daqing, northeastern China. In 1960, during the most challenging time in the national economy, the Central Committee of CPC decided to draw workers, cadres, and technicians from various aspects to concentrate on exploration and development in the vast grasslands. In just one year, the oilfield area was explored and tested, and within three years, China's largest oil base was built, producing two-thirds of the country's total oil output. By

1965, China's demand for oil was entirely self-sufficient, and the era of relying on "foreign oil" was over for the Chinese people.

Work in cutting-edge defense science and technology also began in 1958. In 1961, the Central Committee of CPC made a significant decision to accelerate the development of defense research and industry centered on developing "two bombs" (atomic bomb and missile). On October 16, 1964, China successfully detonated its first atomic bomb; in October 1966, the combined test of the atomic bomb and missile succeeded; on June 17, 1967, the first hydrogen bomb airburst test succeeded; on April 24, 1970, the first artificial satellite ("Dongfanghong-1") was successfully launched. In October 1988, Deng Xiaoping pointed out: "If China had not developed atomic bombs and hydrogen bombs since the 1960s and launched satellites, China could not be called a major country with significant influence, nor have its current international status. These things reflect the capabilities of a nation and are also a symbol of the prosperity and development of a nation and a country."

Therefore, the *Resolution on Several Historical Issues of the Party since the Founding of the People's Republic of China* adopted by the sixth plenary session of the 11th CPC Central Committee in June 1981 pointed out the achievements of the ten-year construction (1956–1966) including the "Great Leap Forward": "The material and technical foundation that we now rely on for modernization was built largely during this period; the backbone forces and their working experience in various fields of national economic and cultural construction were also cultivated and accumulated during this period. This is the leading aspect of the Party's work during this period."

The *Resolution on Several Historical Issues of the Party since the Founding of the People's Republic of China* discusses the ten years of the "Great Cultural Revolution," in addition to the "Great Cultural Revolution" movement and Mao Zedong's later mistakes, it also states: "Although our national economy has suffered huge losses, progress has still been made" and through "implementing correct foreign policies," our "foreign work has also opened up a new situation." This judgment is also in line with reality.

During the "Great Cultural Revolution," China's national economy suffered huge losses, but significant progress was still made with the joint efforts of the majority of cadres and the masses. Grain production maintained relatively stable growth, reaching 572.6 billion *jin* in 1976, an increase of 183.5 billion *jin* from 1965. Important achievements were made in industrial transportation, infrastructure, and science and technology. Crude oil production in 1976 was 6.7 times that of 1965. Some new railways with challenging engineering tasks and the Nanjing Yangtze River Bridge were completed and opened to traffic. Some technologically advanced large-scale enterprises were put into operation. Rich achievements were made in cutting-edge scientific and technological research, such as nuclear technology, artificial satellites, and carrier rockets. In 1972 and 1973, the production of the vast majority of industrial products increased, and investment in infrastructure remained higher than the average level from 1966 to 1969. Even in 1972, when a severe drought caused a reduction in grain production, agricultural harvests increased slightly. In 1974 and 1976, some important industrial products declined, but the production of energy and various other products continued to grow even during the politically turbulent years. Therefore, even in a year of chaos like 1976—when both Zhou Enlai and Mao Zedong passed away, and the Tangshan Earthquake occurred—the economic work was not subject to lasting impact, the extent of its influence was comparable to that of 1967–1968 and even lower than the impact of the "Great Leap Forward."

More notably, during the "Great Cultural Revolution," Mao Zedong and Zhou Enlai made a timely assessment of the situation, adapted to the changing circumstances, and transformed China's diplomatic work. On October 25, 1971, the 26th United Nations General Assembly passed a resolution to restore the People's Republic of China's lawful seat in the United Nations. In February 1972, US President Nixon visited China, and the "Sino-US Joint Communiqué" signed in Shanghai on February 28 after talks between the two sides marked the beginning of the normalization of relations between the two countries. The easing of Sino-US relations directly promoted the improvement of Sino-Japanese relations, and China also saw a climax in establishing diplomatic relations with many Western European countries. Exchanges with the outside world gradually increased, creating external conditions for the reform that began in China in the late 1970s.

Looking back on the 20 years of tortuous development history, renowned theorist Hu Sheng pointed out: "If we say that there is nothing to be gained from the past 35 years and that it is all an accumulation of mistakes, then we cannot correctly interpret the history of those 35 years. Of course, the third plenary session of the 11th Central Committee is a major turning point, but the foundation of past production development also contributes to the formation of this turning point. Therefore, the history since the country's founding is not an accumulation of mistakes." Hu Qiaomu, who served as Mao Zedong's secretary for a long time, also pointed out: "During the 20 years of left-leaning mistakes, the country's economy has generally developed. We fundamentally reject the 'Great Cultural Revolution,' but there were also achievements during that decade that did not belong to the 'Great Cultural Revolution,' in science and technology, and diplomacy."

History cannot be severed. In January 2013, General Secretary Xi Jinping pointed out: "Our Party has led the people in socialist construction in two historical periods, before and after reform and opening-up. These are two interconnected periods with significant differences, but they are essentially both practices and explorations of socialist construction led by our Party. Socialism with Chinese characteristics was initiated in the historic new era of reform and opening-up, but it was also initiated based on establishing the socialist basic system in New China and more than 20 years of construction." "Without the establishment of New China in 1949 and the carrying out of socialist revolution and construction, important ideological, material, and institutional conditions would not have been accumulated, and it would be difficult for the reform and opening-up to proceed smoothly." "We cannot deny the historical period before the reform and opening-up with the historical period after the reform and opening-up, nor can we deny the historical period after the reform and opening-up with the historical period before the reform and opening-up. The socialist practice exploration before the reform and opening-up has accumulated conditions for the socialist practice exploration after the reform and opening-up, and the socialist practice exploration after the reform and opening-up is a continuation, reform, and development of the previous period. In the exploration of socialist practice before the reform and opening-up, we must adhere to the ideological line of seeking truth from facts, distinguish between the mainstream and tributaries, adhere to the truth, correct mistakes, carry forward experience, and learn lessons, and continue to push forward the cause of the Party and the people on this basis." At the same time, when it comes to the evaluation of Mao Zedong, it should also be analyzed in the context of the era and social historical conditions in which he lived. In December 2013, General Secretary Xi Jinping pointed out in his speech at the symposium commemorating the 120th anniversary of Comrade Mao Zedong's birth: "We cannot simply attribute the success in favorable historical circumstances to individuals, nor can we simply blame the setbacks in adverse historical circumstances on individuals. We cannot measure and demand our predecessors with today's conditions, development level, and understanding level, nor can we demand that they achieve what only later generations can achieve."

PART III

REFORM AND OPENING-UP AND SOCIALIST MODERNIZATION

Chapter 12

Taking Reform as the Driving Force for Development

Based on a profound understanding of the fate of the Party and the country, a profound summary of the experience of socialist revolution and construction, a deep insight into the trend of the times, and a deep understanding of the expectations and needs of the people, the third plenary session of the 11th CPC Central Committee held at the end of 1978 made a decisive decision to implement reform and opening-up and shift the focus of the Party's work from class struggle to socialist modernization. This marked a significant turning point in the history of the Party since the founding of the People's Republic of China and ushered in a new era of reform, opening-up, and socialist modernization. Since then, reform has become a powerful driving force for China to forge ahead through the waves, profoundly changing China and the entire world.

Household Contract Responsibility System and Expansion of Enterprise Autonomy

After the curtain of reform was lifted, rural reform made a breakthrough first. In the winter of 1978, some farmers in Anhui Province secretly experimented with contracting land to households to overcome drought and fill their stomachs. Among them, 18 households in Xiaogang Village, Liyuan Commune, Fengyang County, pressed red fingerprints and promised to keep it a secret. At the same time, the Sichuan Provincial Party Committee was supporting farmers in contracting production to groups and allowing and encouraging members to engage in legitimate sideline businesses. Similar practices were adopted in other provinces in China. These bold attempts marked the beginning of rural reform.

The remarkable achievements of rural reform gained high recognition from the people and prompted the Central Committee of CPC to deepen the reform efforts further. For example, in 1979, Sichuan Province produced 64 billion *jin* of grain, 4 billion *jin* more than the historical highest year of 1978. Xiaogang Village in Fengyang County, Anhui Province, was once a well-known "beggar village" and "bachelor village" that had not handed in public grain for more than 20 years and relied on grain reselling. After contracting production to households in 1978, they reaped a bumper harvest in 1979, began to hand in public grain in 1980, and witnessed pleasing changes such as building new houses and marrying brides in 1981. However, some people worried that this would deviate from socialism. Some discussions appeared in society, making some farmers uneasy about contracting production to households, and some places took back the land. On May 31, 1980, Deng Xiaoping pointed out, "After the rural policy was relaxed, some areas suitable for contracting production to households did so, and the results were good, and the changes were rapid. In Feixi County, Anhui Province, most production teams contracted production to households, and the increase in production was significant. In Fengyang County, sung in 'Fengyang Flower Drum,' most production teams carried out the big contracting, and it was a turnaround in one year, changing the face. Some comrades are worried that this will affect the collective economy. I think this worry is unnecessary."

In this context, at the First Secretary Symposium of the Provinces, Municipalities, and Autonomous Regions held by the Central Committee of CPC in September 1980, it was decided to allow remote mountainous areas and poverty-stricken areas to implement contracting production to households, a big step forward from the previous regulation of "no contracting production to households, no separate land cultivation." In December 1981, the National Rural Work Conference was held to discuss some new issues raised by the vast majority of farmers in practice since the third plenary session of the 11th CPC Central Committee and to propose solutions and form conference summaries. On New Year's Day in 1982, the No. 1 Document of the Central Committee of CPC approved the "Summary of the National Rural

Work Conference." Clearly, it stated that contracting production to households and contracting to households were the production responsibility systems of the socialist collective economy. This new regulation reassured farmers and promoted the widespread implementation of the household contract responsibility system across the country. Subsequently, the Central Committee of CPC issued four consecutive No. 1 documents to deepen rural reform continuously. Before the reform, farmers worked without enthusiasm and wasted time; after the reform, farmers understood their responsibilities, and their enthusiasm for farming was greatly stimulated. Coupled with factors such as improved crop varieties, the use of chemical fertilizers, and hybrid technology, grain production increased steadily. In 1984, the national grain output reached 814.6 billion *jin*, with a per capita output of 781 *jin*, effectively solving the long-standing problem of food and clothing for Chinese farmers.

At this time, the people's commune system implemented in rural areas could no longer adapt to reality after the transformation of the rural economic system. In 1983, the Central Committee of CPC and the State Council abolished the people's commune system and established township governments based on pilot projects. In just over half a year, more than 92,000 townships were established. In the early 1980s, the song "On the Field of Hope" was sung across the country, expressing the joy and happiness of farmers after the loosening of restrictions and reflecting the tremendous changes taking place in rural areas at that time.

The development of any country can be challenging, and China is no exception. China's rural development also encountered some difficulties. In the mid-to-late 1990s, grain prices fell relatively, making it difficult for farmers to increase their income and dampening their enthusiasm for planting. The Party Central Committee emphasized solving "issues relating to agriculture, rural areas, and farmers" and held meetings to study and solve them. Entering the 21st century, the Central Government issued more than ten consecutive "No. 1 Documents" to deploy rural work continuously. At the same time, it changed its working approach, establishing the scientific development concept of cities supporting rural areas, and promoted the resolution of "issues relating to agriculture, rural areas, and farmers" through the construction of a socialist new countryside, large-scale promotion of new rural cooperative medical care, reduction and exemption of agricultural taxes, and other measures.

Under the influence of rural reform, urban reform also continued to advance. Unlike the spontaneity of rural reform, urban reform was initially deployed by the Central Government, with the primary goal of expanding enterprise autonomy to stimulate the enthusiasm of enterprises and employees. At the end of 1978, the third plenary session of the 11th CPC Central Committee proposed to start the reform of the planned economic system. The Central Working Conference in April 1979 further proposed to expand the autonomy of enterprises, link the success of enterprise operations to the material interests of employees, and appropriately divide the management authority between the central and local governments to mobilize the enthusiasm of local management under the unified leadership of the Central Government. In accordance with the spirit of this conference, pilot projects for urban economic system reform began, gradually expanding enterprise autonomy.

The pilot project to expand enterprise autonomy began in Sichuan Province. In October 1978, the Sichuan Provincial Committee and the Provincial Government decided to select six representative enterprises from different industries, including Ningjiang Machine Tool Factory and Chongqing Iron and Steel Company, for the pilot project. These enterprises were granted profit targets on a case-by-case basis, with specified annual production and income targets, allowing them to retain a small portion of profits as enterprise funds after completing the plan and distributing a small portion of funds to employees. On June 25, 1979, Ningjiang Machine Tool Factory published an advertisement in the *People's Daily*, announcing, "We have machine tools for sale here" to the whole country, quickly turning their backlog into best-selling products. The advertisement also stated they could accept direct orders from domestic and foreign customers. Products were not purchased and stored by the materials department, nor did they occupy state funds, but they were directly ordered by users, which significantly impacted the exploration of new forms of production and sales integration.

Based on the initial experience of the reform, in May 1979, six departments, including the State Economic Commission, decided to carry out pilot projects to expand the autonomy of eight enterprises, such as the Capital Steel Company, Tianjin Bicycle Factory, and Shanghai Diesel Engine Factory in Beijing, Tianjin, Shanghai, and other places. This decision had the effect of mobilizing the enthusiasm of enterprises for production and increasing output and income. In July, the State Council issued five documents, including "Several Provisions on Expanding the Operation and Management Autonomy of State-owned Industrial Enterprises," to guide the pilot projects to expand enterprise autonomy. After the reform achieved good results, enterprise reform gradually expanded from developing autonomy to implementing the economic responsibility system. Subsequent state-owned enterprise reforms went through stages such as contracting and shareholding, and in December 1986, the trial of the bankruptcy law allowed state-owned enterprises to go bankrupt.

Since the 1990s, state-owned enterprises have gradually established a modern enterprise system and withstood the severe test of more than 30 million laid-off workers due to reform. In the 21st century, enterprise reform continues, with measures such as optimizing the allocation of state-owned assets and diversifying the forms of public ownership emerging. As reforms continue to be explored, China's large state-owned enterprises are becoming increasingly competitive globally. They occupy an increasingly prominent position among the world's top 500 enterprises. Of course, urban reform involves enterprise expansion or restructuring and includes social security, housing, financial management, tax, and financial systems. The city-county management system also evolved gradually.

The rapid development of the private economy is unexpected good news brought about by economic reform. In terms of both employment and tax contributions, the achievements of the private economy are surprising and exciting. In order to support and protect the development of the private economy, the national constitution has been explicitly stipulated to guide, supervise, and manage private enterprises, thereby legally protecting the legitimate rights and interests of these enterprises. The Central Committee of CPC and the State Council have repeatedly expressed their unwavering support for developing the non-public economy, proposing the policy of "two unwavering" support. Since the 1980s, many private enterprises have grown rapidly, like bamboo shoots after a spring rain. Huawei, Sany Heavy Industry, DJI, Tencent, Alibaba, and Xiaomi have become famous Chinese and world-renowned enterprises. The rise of these enterprises has excited China and surprised the world.

Socialism Can Also Practice a Market Economy

The most outstanding achievement of China's economic reform is to break through the opposition between the planned economy and the market economy, combine the socialist system with the market economy, implement the socialist market economy, and give full play to the role of the "invisible hand." This is the greatest theoretical and practical innovation of China's economic reform, reflecting the courage and boldness of the Chinese Communists. The practice has shown that implementing the socialist market economy in China is successful.

The establishment of the socialist market economy system has been a long-term effort. Deng Xiaoping proposed reforming the planned management system at the Central Working Conference held from November to December 1978. In March

1979, after long-term contemplation, Chen Yun wrote an outline on the relationship between planning and the market, pointing out that the common problem in the socialist construction of the Soviet Union and China was the presence of only "planned proportions" without market regulation. In the future, we must adhere to a planned economy as the main focus but also have market regulation; the former is primary and secondary, but it is necessary. His idea was supported by Li Xiannian, another member of the Political Bureau Standing Committee of the Central Committee of CPC and Vice Premier of the State Council, who had long been involved in economic management. In November 1979, Deng Xiaoping told an American guest during a meeting that "China can also practice market economy."

Under the impetus of reform, opening-up practice, and the economic theory community, the Party Central Committee continued promoting economic system reform. In the second half of 1984, a breakthrough was made in economic system reform. On October 20 of that year, the third plenary session of the twelfth CPC Central Committee was held in Beijing, and the meeting passed the "Decision of the Central Committee of CPC on Economic System Reform." The "Decision" clearly pointed out that the main drawbacks of the traditional planned economic system are the confusion of government and enterprise responsibilities, fragmentation, excessive and rigid control of enterprises by the state, neglecting the role of commodity production, value law, and the market, and serious egalitarianism in distribution. This has caused the initially vibrant socialist economy to lose its vitality to a large extent. Reforming the economic system means reforming a series of interconnected links and aspects in the relations of production and the superstructure that are not conducive to developing productive forces under the premise of adhering to the socialist system. This kind of reform is the self-improvement and development of the socialist system. "To reform the planning system, we must first break through the traditional concept of opposing planned economy and commodity economy and recognize that the socialist planned economy must consciously follow and apply the law of value, which is a planned commodity economy based on public ownership. The full development of the commodity economy is an insurmountable stage of social and economic development and a necessary condition for realizing China's economic modernization." This breaks the concept of opposing planned economy and commodity economy and confirms that the nature of China's economy is a "planned commodity economy based on public ownership," thus pointing out the direction for economic system reform. Deng Xiaoping highly praised this "Decision": "My impression is that it is a draft of political economy, which is a political economy that combines the basic principles of Marxism with China's socialist practice."

In February 1987, Deng Xiaoping pointed out that we used to learn from the Soviet Union and engage in a planned economy. Later, we proposed that the planned economy should be the main focus, and we should refrain from talking about this anymore. Following Deng Xiaoping's opinion, the 13th CPC National Congress did not stick to the question of who the main and auxiliary focus was. Instead, it proposed the reform idea of "the state guiding the market, the market guiding enterprises," breaking through the debate on whether the plan or the market is the main focus.

In the late 1980s and early 1990s, many events occurred. Internationally, the disintegration of the Soviet Union and the dramatic changes in Eastern Europe led to the loss of governing positions by the Communist Party in these countries, and the international communist movement fell into a trough. China also experienced political turmoil. At a pivotal historical moment, the 88-year-old Deng Xiaoping, undeterred by age or fatigue, embarked on a significant inspection tour in early 1992. He visited places like Shenzhen, Zhuhai, and Shanghai, during which he delivered his influential "Southern Tour Talk." He mentioned that a planned economy does not equal socialism, and capitalism also has plans; a market economy does not equal capitalism, socialism can also engage in the market, and both the market and planning are means that can be used by socialism and capitalism. This groundbreaking assertion summarizes Deng Xiaoping's decades of governance wisdom, reflecting a politician's profound vision and global perspective. Under the enormous influence of the Southern Tour Talk, in 1992, the 14th CPC National Congress not only made a strategic decision to seize the opportunity to accelerate development but also clearly stated that China's economic system reform aimed to establish a socialist market economic system. With Deng Xiaoping's Southern Tour Talk and the 14th CPC National Congress as a milestone, China's reform and opening-up entered a new stage.

After more than ten years of practical exploration and theoretical innovation, the CPC continuously liberated its thinking, broke away from historical inertia, dared to break old frameworks, and put forward the new idea of a socialist market economy with extraordinary courage. In 1993, the third plenary session of the fourteenth CPC Central Committee adopted the "Decision of the Central Committee of CPC on Several Issues Concerning the Establishment of a Socialist Market Economic System," which began the construction of the framework for the socialist market economy. After following this blueprint for ten years, in 2003, the third plenary session of the 16th CPC Central Committee adopted the "Decision of the Central Committee of CPC on Several Issues Concerning the Improvement of the Socialist Market Economic System," which provided a roadmap for the further improvement of the socialist market economic system. In November 2012, the 18th CPC National Congress proposed the major issue of properly handling the relationship between the government and the market. It emphasized accelerating the transformation of government functions.

Although China has experienced a long period of exploration in the combination of socialism and market economy, the establishment of a socialist market economic system has indeed brought huge dividends. After 1992, China's economic development entered the fast lane, with the economy growing at double-digit rates, and by 2010, its economic aggregate surpassed Japan to become the world's second-largest economy. The practice has fully shown that establishing a socialist market economic system is one of the greatest decisions in the history of the CPC.

Actively and Prudently Promoting Political System Reform

With the unfolding of economic system reform, political system reform was also put on the agenda. In August 1980, Deng Xiaoping explicitly proposed promoting the Party and state leadership system reform. In June 1986, he said, "Political restructuring should be included in the reform-indeed, it should be regarded as the hallmark of progress in the reform as a whole." On June 28, he said at the Standing Committee of the Central Political Bureau, "If we only carry out economic system reform and do not carry out political system reform, the economic system reform will not work because the first obstacle encountered is human." "Whether all our reforms can ultimately succeed still depends on the reform of the political system."

From September to November 1986, Deng Xiaoping repeatedly emphasized the issue of political system reform in several talks. He pointed out, "Now, with every step forward in economic system reform, we deeply feel the necessity of political system reform. Without reforming the political system, we cannot guarantee the results of economic system reform, nor can we continue to advance economic system reform, which will hinder the development of productive forces and the realization of the four modernizations." Deng Xiaoping also emphasized that political system reform involves a wide range of people and issues, is profound, and will encounter many obstacles requiring caution. He clearly pointed out that China's political system reform should be aimed at three goals: "The first goal is always to maintain the vitality of the Party and the state"; "The second goal is to overcome bureaucracy and improve work efficiency"; "The third goal is to mobilize the enthusiasm of grassroots, workers, peasants, and intellectuals." These ideas have pointed the way for political system reform.

According to Deng Xiaoping's opinions and suggestions, in September 1986, the Central Committee of CPC established the Central Political System Reform Research Group. After conducting special research, the group eventually formed the "Overall Plan for Political System Reform" (Draft). The seventh plenary session of the 12th CPC Central Committee, held on October 20 of the same year, fully discussed and agreed in principle to the "Overall Plan for Political System Reform" and decided to incorporate the main content of the document into the report of the 13th CPC National Congress. The 13th CPC National Congress, held in October 1987, devoted a special section to the issue of political system reform. The report clearly stated that political system reform aims to promote the development of a socialist democratic political system with Chinese characteristics. The long-term goal of the reform is to build a highly democratic, legally sound, efficient, and vibrant socialist political system. The short-term goal of political system reform is to establish a leadership system conducive to improving efficiency, enhancing vitality, and mobilizing the enthusiasm of all parties. The political system reform has been gradually carried out since then, and the construction of democratic politics has made continuous progress.

Since the 1990s, especially after entering the 21st century, the CPC has actively and prudently promoted political system reform. People's democratic rights have been fully guaranteed. In 2004, the constitution included "the state respects and protects human rights"; in March 2010, the *Election Law* was amended, clearly stipulating that the election of deputies to the National People's Congress should be conducted according to the same population ratio in urban and rural areas. By the end of 2010, our socialist system of laws with Chinese characteristics had been formed, reflecting the full protection of people's democratic rights. Judicial system reform has also made progress. In December 2008, the Central Committee of CPC forwarded the "Opinions of the Central Political and Legal Affairs Commission on Several Issues Concerning Deepening Judicial System and Working Mechanism Reform." People's enthusiasm for orderly political participation has surged, and China has made great efforts to build a "transparent government." The implementation of the Government Information Disclosure Regulations in 2008, the open legislation of the National People's Congress at all levels, the holding of public hearings by government departments, the gradual disclosure of "three public expenses," and the booming development of "online inquiries" have all ensured people's right to know, participate, express, and supervise, and have enabled the people to exercise extensive decision-making power.

The government's operation has rapidly moved toward legalization and standardization. After entering the 21st century, China implemented two concentrated administrative management system reforms in 2003 and 2008. The State Council has undergone five clean-ups, canceling and adjusting 2,183 administrative approval items. The construction of the administrative reconsideration and administrative litigation system has made it possible for citizens to sue officials; the implementation of the Government Information Disclosure Regulations has gradually accustomed the government to working under the supervision of the people; and the accountability of leading cadres and administrative law enforcement errors has put a "tight hoop" on power. Some social organizations have also begun to participate in social management, and state power has partially shifted to specific social organizations. During this stage, the National Anti-Corruption Bureau was established, a punishment and prevention system focusing on prevention was formulated, and some places tried the "separation of powers of supervision, decision-making, and execution," etc., which are all useful attempts in terms of power restraint and supervision.

Balancing Reform, Development, and Stability

Compared with the shock therapy adopted during the Soviet Union's reform, China's reform has more distinct gradualist features and is often called incremental reform. The basic characteristics of this reform model are to start with easier tasks before moving on to more difficult ones, proceed step by step, improve the system, and transition through pilot projects and fine-tuning. Its advantage is that it is relatively easy to control the pace of reform, combining top-down strategic deployment with grassroots bottom-up creativity and enthusiasm, summarizing experiences and lessons through trial and error, and adjusting the steps of reform to ensure social stability while deepening reform.

From the endless vitality of the rural household contract responsibility system, the sudden emergence of township and village enterprises, and the vigorous development of small towns to the gradual unfolding of state-owned enterprise reform, many grassroots reform experiences have been condensed. Another feature of China's incremental reform is its expansion and advancement from economic to political, social, and cultural fields. Reforms in the employment system, social security system, income distribution system, household registration system, danwei system, legislative system, grassroots democracy construction, intra-party democracy construction, cultural industry development, etc., are all continuously underway.

China's reform has gone from a dual-track price system and dual-track investment system to a gradual transition to a floating exchange rate system. Incrementalism remains an important feature of China's reform to this day. Over time, people have realized that incremental reform should be an effective way for a large country to avoid reform risks under the constraint of "stability first." The experience of China's incremental reform shows that the relationship between reform, development, and stability must be properly handled to succeed in reform.

China is a developing, generally poor country with a population of over a billion. Any small issue multiplied by a population of more than a billion becomes a huge issue. Therefore, China must maintain both economic and social development and basic social stability. Development is the key, as without development, basic needs cannot be met, and people cannot achieve a well-off life. Without a stable situation, nothing can be accomplished, and development will encounter difficulties. For development to occur, reforms must be carried out, which may break various vested interests and easily breed instability. Therefore, how to properly handle the pace of reform and the people's ability to bear it while maintaining social stability is a concern for every leader. The correct handling of the relationship between reform, development, and stability is a test of the wisdom and ability of those in power. Many years of reform practice have shown that the CPC has withstood this test.

Reform is a new great revolution, and its impact is bound to be extensive and far-reaching. However, it is also essential to recognize that reform is not smooth sailing and comes with a cost. For example, some original state-owned departments, such as tobacco, alcohol, sugar, tea companies, and state-owned cotton mills, gradually lost their advantageous positions in the reform, and the interests of workers in these departments were damaged to varying degrees. In the reform of state-owned enterprises in the 1990s, tens of millions of workers were laid off, many of whom experienced the pain of reform. However, it is precisely through reform that China has overcome the shortages of the planned economy era and promoted the historic leap of the Chinese people from mere subsistence to moderate prosperity and from standing up to becoming wealthy.

CHAPTER 13

Growing Stronger through Opening-Up

Adhering to opening-up to the outside world is a distinct feature of China's development and progress under the leadership of the CPC. In contemporary China, even in a small rural supermarket, one can feel the atmosphere of openness, as many foreign company names can be seen on the shelves of daily necessities. The distribution of brands for household appliances and mobile terminals in ordinary people's homes also has a robust global flavor. Over the past few decades, China has continuously developed and grown stronger through opening-up.

China's Development Cannot Be Separated from the World

More than a hundred years ago, Marx and Engels said that large-scale industry "has for the first time created world history by making the satisfaction of the needs of each civilized country and each person in these countries dependent on the whole world, and by abolishing the naturally formed closed and self-sufficient state of each country." Indeed, with the development of social productivity, the Earth where humans live have become increasingly "small" and "flat." The whole world is becoming increasingly interconnected and interdependent, making the development of each country increasingly intertwined and inseparable.

With the advent of the third wave of the technological revolution and the rapid development of information technology, the world's connections have become even closer, and no country can stand outside the "world." Deng Xiaoping keenly grasped this objective historical development process, pointing out that "the world is now an open world." China's modernization construction should be examined in the context of the international environment and the general trend of human development. Deng Xiaoping first proposed opening-up in October 1978. During a meeting with a delegation of German journalists, he pointed out that China had contributed to the world in history but had long stagnated and developed slowly. It was time for China to learn from advanced countries in the world. In answering questions from guests, the 74-year-old Deng Xiaoping used the term "opening-up" for the first time and emphasized that good traditions must be preserved, but new policies should be determined according to new situations. We introduce advanced technology to develop productivity and improve people's living standards, which benefits our socialist country and system.

The Chinese leadership reached a consensus on opening-up, related to the many senior officials who went abroad for study tours and visits after the end of the "Great Cultural Revolution." Among the many study groups, the delegation headed by Gu Mu, Deputy Prime Minister of the State Council, which visited France, Denmark, Switzerland, Belgium, and West Germany from May 2 to June 6, 1978, was the most eye-catching. After founding the People's Republic of China, this was the first delegation to visit the five Western European countries for economic inspection. The delegation experienced firsthand the advanced management experience of Western developed countries, such as that France's Charles de Gaulle Airport could complete aircraft takeoff and landing in just one minute. At the same time, Beijing Capital Airport took half an hour. Gu Mu's delegation saw the huge gap between China and the West and the willingness of Western developed countries with surplus capital to cooperate with China, which has a vast market. Before the visit, Deng Xiaoping specifically encouraged Gu Mu to observe and learn more. On June 30, 1978, Gu Mu reported his observations and thoughts on the visit to the Party Central Committee. The report lasted from 3:00 to 11:00 p.m., nearly eight hours. The leaders expressed that they should not wait any longer and start working first. From July to September 1978, the State Council held a meeting on speeding up development and opening-up, which was discussed enthusiastically. In his closing speech, Vice Premier Li

Xiannian proposed boldly reforming all aspects of the superstructure that do not adapt to the economic foundation and all production relations that do not adapt to the productive forces and actively introducing advanced foreign technology. This laid some foundation for deciding to open up. The third plenary session of the 11th CPC Central Committee held in the same year made a major decision on reform and opening-up. When attending the APEC meeting held in Beijing in 2014, former Australian Prime Minister Bob Hawke said that implementing the reform and opening-up policy was a major move that changed China and influenced the world.

The key step in opening-up was the establishment of four special economic zones, including Shenzhen and Xiamen. At the Central Work Conference held in April 1979, Xi Zhongxun, the head of the Guangdong Provincial Committee, suggested to the Central Government to give Guangdong some special preferential policies, allowing Guangdong to take advantage of its geographical proximity to Hong Kong and Macau and set up some export processing zones to develop rapidly. The head of the Fujian Provincial Committee made a similar suggestion. After careful consideration, the Central Government sent Gu Mu to investigate Guangdong and Fujian provinces. Based on the investigation report, the Central Government gave particular preferential policies to Guangdong and Fujian. On August 26, 1980, the 15th meeting of the Standing Committee of the National People's Congress deliberated and passed the Guangdong Special Economic Zone Regulations, deciding to establish Shenzhen, Zhuhai, and Shantou as special economic zones. In October of the same year, Xiamen in Fujian was also approved as a special economic zone. As the windows of China's opening-up, these four zones have been committed to innovation and bold reform and played a pioneering role in opening-up. Shenzhen's slogan, "time is money, efficiency is life," shocked people's hearts, and the "Shenzhen speed" of building one floor every three days became famous nationwide. In the context of overcoming difficulties and achieving remarkable results in developing special economic zones, in May 1984, the Central Committee of CPC and the State Council decided to open up 14 coastal port cities, such as Dalian, Tianjin, Qingdao, and Shanghai. The opening-up expanded significantly from points to lines. In 1985, the Liaodong Peninsula and the Jiaodong Peninsula were opened, and the Yangtze River Delta, Pearl River Delta, and Xiamen-Zhangzhou-Quanzhou Triangle were designated open zones. By then, 150 million people along the southeast coast were involved in the opening-up, and China initially formed a multi-level, wide-ranging, and all-round opening-up pattern.

Deng Xiaoping made it clear that self-seclusion would not work. During the "Great Cultural Revolution," there was an incident with the "Fengqing Ship," where he quarreled with the "Gang of Four." It was just a 10,000-ton ship, what's the big deal! In 1920, when he went to study in France, he took a 50,000-ton foreign mail ship. If not for the opening-up, our car production would still be like the past, hammering and beating with hammers. Now, it's completely different, which is a qualitative change.

In April 1990, the development and opening-up of Pudong, Shanghai, directly drove the economic development of the Yangtze River Basin, China's golden waterway. At the 15th CPC National Congress in 1997, Jiang Zemin pointed out: "We must strive to improve the level of opening-up to the outside world. Opening-up is a long-term basic national policy. Facing the trend of economic and technological globalization, we must adopt a more proactive attitude toward the world, improve the all-round, multi-level, and wide-ranging pattern of opening-up, develop an open economy, enhance international competitiveness, and promote the optimization of the economic structure and the improvement of the quality of the national economy." In 2000, Jiang Zemin also proposed the opening-up strategy of "bringing in" and "going out" at the same time. At the end of 2001, after 15 years of arduous negotiations, China finally joined the World Trade Organization (WTO), integrating deeply into the tide of globalization. In a speech in 2002, Jiang Zemin further pointed out: "We must adapt to the new situation of economic globalization and China's accession to the WTO, participate in international economic and technological cooperation and competition at a larger scale, a wider range, and a higher level, expand the space for economic development, and comprehensively improve the level of opening-up to the outside world."

In October 2007, at the seventh plenary session of the 16th CPC Central Committee, Hu Jintao explicitly proposed that opening-up to the outside world is China's basic national policy. Under the increasingly close connection between domestic and international markets, China must have a broad global perspective, strive to improve the level of openness, accelerate the transformation of foreign trade growth mode, actively and effectively utilize foreign investment, and implement a win-win opening-up strategy. At the 17th CPC National Congress, Hu Jintao proposed new requirements for "expanding the breadth and depth of opening-up and improving the level of an open economy." He also stated that China should adhere to the basic national policy of opening-up, better combine "bringing in" and "going out," expand the scope of opening-up, optimize the structure of opening-up, improve the quality of opening-up, and perfect a safe, efficient, mutually beneficial, and win-win open economic system. He also emphasized the need to "pay attention to preventing international economic risks." During this period, the opening-up strategy based on mutual benefit and win-win was proposed, and the utilization of foreign investment increased, further deepening the opening-up process.

Absorbing the Achievements of Human Civilization

In June 1988, Deng Xiaoping pointed out: "China must open up to seek development, get rid of poverty and backwardness. Opening-up is not only about developing international exchanges but also about absorbing international experience." In his 1992 Southern Tour Talk, he strongly called for "socialism to win the advantage in comparison with capitalism, we must boldly absorb and learn from all the achievements of human civilization created by society, and absorb and learn from all the advanced management methods and methods reflecting the laws of modern socialized production in the world today, including those in capitalist developed countries."

Since the beginning of opening-up to the outside world, China has been paying attention to learning from and drawing on foreign management experience and introducing advanced foreign technologies. A typical example of absorbing human civilization achievements in opening-up is in the economic field, such as issuing stocks, reforming enterprises through shareholding, and implementing modern enterprise systems. On November 26, 1990, with the authorization of the State Council and the approval of the People's Bank of China, the Shanghai Stock Exchange was officially established. This was the first stock exchange to open in mainland China since the People's Republic of China was founded. Subsequently, on July 3, 1991, the Shenzhen Stock Exchange also officially opened. The operation of the two exchanges centralized stock trading and formed a national security trading market, effectively promoting the development of the shareholding system. To the outside world, this was a leap in China's implementation of its open-door policy. In the exquisite and splendid window display of the New York Stock Exchange, various symbolic items record the development process of capital markets worldwide. Among them is a beautifully made Chinese stock, the first stock issued since the founding of the People's Republic of China—Feile Audio stock. In November 1986, Deng Xiaoping presented this stock to John Phelan, then President of the New York Stock Exchange, to demonstrate China's great determination to reform and opening-up to the world.

The shareholding system, once suspected of taking the capitalist road, encountered a bottleneck in the mid-1980s. Influenced by rural reforms, Chinese enterprises turned to the contracting system. However, as an institutional arrangement, the contracting system has inherent defects. After transferring part of the residual control rights and residual claim rights to the contractors, the definition of enterprise property rights becomes unclear and even more ambiguous. Conflicts of interest between the issuer and the contractor intensify, and both parties' infringement actions become more likely. The contracting system cannot and will not grant enterprises full autonomy or achieve the separation of government and enterprises and equal competition among enterprises. Instead, it solidifies the existing system to some extent and increases the difficulty of reform. In early 1992, Deng Xiaoping addressed the debate on the shareholding system in his Southern Tour Talk, saying, "Allow observation, but be determined to try." After Deng Xiaoping's southern tour, Jiang Zemin specifically discussed the shareholding system with Li Yining of Peking University, Wang Jiafu of the Chinese Academy of Social Sciences, and Lu Baifu, deputy director of the Development Research Center of the State Council. Wang Jiafu talked from a legal perspective, Li Yining from an economic perspective, and Lu Baifu from a policy research perspective. They all believed that the shareholding system was necessary and feasible. Jiang Zemin said he supported the shareholding system and that only small enterprises were practicing it; large enterprises should also implement it. In October 1992, the 14th CPC National Congress report officially established the reform goal of building a socialist market economic system. Deng Xiaoping's Southern Tour Talk and the report of the 14th National Congress greatly advanced the transformation of China's shareholding system. In 1992, nearly 400 pilot shareholding enterprises were approved and established in cities nationwide, with more than 3,700 shareholding enterprises nationwide. At the same time, the State Council also approved nine state-owned enterprises to reorganize into shareholding companies and list them in Hong Kong and abroad.

To continue promoting state-owned enterprise reform, the 15th CPC National Congress in 1997 explicitly stated that establishing a modern enterprise system was the direction of state-owned enterprise reform. It also clarified that "a shareholding system is a form of capital organization for modern enterprises, conducive to the separation of ownership and management rights, and conducive to improving the operation efficiency of enterprises and capital. Both capitalism and socialism can use it. It cannot be broadly stated whether the shareholding system is public or private; the key is who holds the controlling rights." This groundbreaking theory was the first major revision of the traditional ownership theory in an official document of the Central Committee of CPC. By liberating the thinking on the forms of public ownership and expanding the scope of public ownership, including the shareholding system, there is no need to debate whether it is "socialist" or "capitalist."

Of course, learning from the achievements of capitalist civilization is not only about economic management methods and experiences but also includes the introduction of advanced technologies. Since the reform and opening-up, China has introduced a large number of advanced technologies from the West in areas such as high-speed railways, electronic information, and metal smelting, which has greatly helped accelerate national economic development and improve technological innovation capabilities.

Develop and Open Up the Pudong Area

In the 1990s, China decided to develop and open up the Pudong area in Shanghai. This significant decision changed Shanghai and had far-reaching effects on China. The practice has proven that this major decision not only promoted the development of Shanghai but also directly impacted the development of the Yangtze River Delta and even the entire Yangtze River basin, influencing and driving the overall Chinese economy.

The development and opening-up of Pudong in Shanghai underwent a brewing process. The 1980s were a time of great strides and significant achievements in China's reform and opening-up. Shanghai, which had become the central city of the Far East as early as the 1930s, found itself in an extremely awkward position in the 1980s. It not only widened the gap with the East Asian "Four Little Dragons" but also had many shortcomings compared to surrounding provinces and cities. What made Shanghai even more uneasy was that economic development encountered constraints of urban transformation and limited development space. In the decades since the founding of New China, the urban area expanded only slightly. At the same time, the population nearly doubled, industrial output increased more than tenfold, and the city faced traffic congestion, crowded housing, and environmental pollution.

To solve these problems, Shanghai began exploring new paths. During Wang Daohan's tenure as mayor of Shanghai, he actively explored and submitted a report outline on Shanghai's economic development strategy to the State Council in 1984, proposing to plan for the development strategy of the new era and create conditions for the development of Pudong. In February 1985, the State Council approved the report outline. After identifying the development of Pudong as a strategic direction, Shanghai carried out extensive preparatory work. On June 1, 1987, Jiang Zemin, then Secretary of the Shanghai Municipal Party Committee, presided over the 19th Executive Meeting of the Shanghai Municipal Government to discuss the development of Pudong. He emphasized that, based on scientific research and analysis and in line with the principle of being active and cautious, the development plan should be submitted to the Central Government as soon as possible after considering political, economic, and technical factors. In April 1988, when Zhu Rongji was nominated as mayor of Shanghai, he pointed out at the Fourth Meeting of the first plenary session of the ninth Shanghai People's Congress that Pudong was the future hope of Shanghai and a "new Shanghai" should be built there to alleviate the pressure on the "old Shanghai." "This construction is a magnificent plan, which cannot be achieved in a short period, but we must work hard, and we will enjoy the fruits of our labor later." This revealed the predicament faced by Shanghai and pointed out the direction for Shanghai's development.

To gain the Central Government's support, Zhu Rongji took the opportunity of Deng Xiaoping's visit to Shanghai during the Spring Festival in 1990 to make a special report to him. Deng Xiaoping said, "I have always advocated being bolder. Over the past ten years, I have advocated opening-up and being bolder. There is nothing to be afraid of, and nothing is extraordinary. Therefore, I support your development of Pudong." Deng Xiaoping said, "You are late," but immediately added, "It's also fast now. The people of Shanghai are smart." This was a great encouragement to Shanghai.

On the morning of February 17, 1990, when discussing the development of Pudong, Deng Xiaoping said to Li Peng, "You are the Premier; you should be in charge of the development of Pudong." That afternoon, Li Peng instructed He Chunlin, Deputy Secretary-General of the State Council responsible for special zone work, to call Shanghai and talk about some issues to be aware of during reform, opening-up, and expressing some opinions. At the same time, he asked Zhu Rongji, "Do you have something?" Zhu Rongji replied, "We have been discussing the report for two or three months but are unsatisfied. If you want to urge us, I will work overtime tonight and send it to you." The report was revised that night and sent the next day.

On February 26, Zhu Rongji also reported to Qiao Shi, who was inspecting Shanghai, "We now hope to strengthen the Central Government's determination to approve this report. We guarantee that we will do our best and die without regret, contributing to the overall situation and allowing Shanghai to make its due contribution to the national chess game. We have this determination."

On February 26, 1990, the Shanghai Municipal Party Committee and Municipal Government submitted the "Report on the Development of Pudong" to the Central Government, which received attention from the Central Committee of CPC and the State Council. In early March, Deng Xiaoping mentioned during a conversation with Jiang Zemin and other central leaders, "Shanghai is our trump card, and developing Shanghai is a shortcut." Subsequently, Li Peng instructed Vice Premier Zou Jiahua to convene relevant State Council departments to study Pudong's development.

From March 28 to April 8, entrusted by the Central Committee of CPC and the State Council, Yao Yilin, then a member of the Political Bureau Standing Committee and Vice Premier of the State Council, led a delegation of responsible comrades from the State Council's Special Zone Office, the National Planning Commission, the Ministry of Finance, the Ministry of Commerce, the People's Bank of China, the Ministry of Foreign Economic Relations and Trade, and the Bank of China to Shanghai to conduct a special investigation and research on the development of Pudong. Zhu Rongji reported the relevant situation three times. In his report on March 29, Zhu Rongji said, "Comrade Wang Daohan is the most active in raising the issue of Pudong development, much more active than I am. When Comrade Xiaoping and Comrade Shangkun came to Shanghai, we reported twice, and it was Comrade Guodong who first raised the issue." "Comrade Yilin, you have come to Shanghai once in two years. I hope you can thoroughly solve the problem this time and not come again in two years. You don't need to come if there are still problems by then. That will be an inspection, just to take a look." In the report on April 2, Zhu Rongji said, "The comrades from the Central Committee have been very thoughtful and steady in helping Shanghai and have given us great support. This truly reflects the care of the Party Central Committee and the State Council for Shanghai and the understanding and support of Comrade Yilin and other comrades for Shanghai. I want to say this from the bottom of my heart." In his report, Zhu Rongji mentioned that the development of Pudong requires the construction of some infrastructure and funding, and he hoped that the Central Government would provide support. After a detailed investigation, the inspection team submitted the "Report Outline on Several Issues Concerning the Development of Pudong in Shanghai" to the Central Government, which elaborated on the adoption of economic development zones and the implementation of certain special economic zone policies for the development of Pudong, as well as a series of supporting measures. This quickly received the Central Government's approval and consent.

On April 18, 1990, Premier Li Peng announced Pudong's development and opening-up. A little over a month later, *People's Daily* reported this groundbreaking event, which shook both Shanghai and the world, with the headline "The Dawn of the Western Pacific." On June 2, the Central Committee of CPC and the State Council agreed to the Shanghai Municipal Party Committee and Municipal Government's request on the issue of developing and opening-up Shanghai's Pudong, pointing out that it was a major initiative in deepening reform and further implementing the opening-up policy, which would have a significant impact on the political stability and economic development of both Shanghai and the entire nation. At that time, the international community doubted whether China would continue to adhere to its reform and opening-up policy. The development of Pudong demonstrated China's unwavering commitment to opening-up.

In early 1991, Deng Xiaoping inspected Shanghai and remarked, "We say Shanghai's development has been late; we must work hard at it!" He also stated, "Shanghai people are smart and of good quality. If an economic special zone had been established in Shanghai at the time, things would be different now. Shanghai was just one of the fourteen coastal port cities, nothing special. If Pudong had been developed a few years earlier, like the Shenzhen Special Economic Zone, it would have been better. Developing Pudong has great significance, and it's not just about Pudong itself but concerns Shanghai's development and the utilization of Shanghai as a base to develop the Yangtze River Delta and the Yangtze River basin. Hasten the development of Pudong, without wavering, until it's completed." Subsequently, Pudong underwent earth-shattering changes, and a modern new city emerged, achieving one "first in China" after another.

On June 21, 2005, the State Council approved Pudong for a comprehensive supporting reform pilot. Reforms in pricing, state-owned enterprises, and finance were all part of specific reforms. Comprehensive supporting reforms were necessary to make the market economic system more perfect, and this reform mission was assigned to Pudong. In May 2009, the State Council approved incorporating the former Nanhui District into Pudong, marking a new stage of Pudong's second venture. The global financial crisis unfolded then, and the Central Government issued a document on building Shanghai's "two centers." Pudong's mission was to coordinate the "three ports, three zones" strategic resources, accelerate the construction of the "two centers," and promote the development of the southern region. In September 2013, the Shanghai Free Trade Zone was established. In December 2014, the Shanghai Free Trade Zone was expanded, ushering Pudong into the era of the Free Trade Zone making new contributions to building a new open economic system for the country.

Shanghai adheres to the policy of "Developing Pudong, Revitalizing Shanghai, Serving the Nation, and Facing the World." After 30 years of hard work and struggle, Pudong has become the "symbol of China's reform and opening-up" and the "epitome of Shanghai's modernization." On November 12, 2020, General Secretary Xi Jinping pointed out in his speech at the 30th-anniversary celebration of Pudong's development and opening-up that Pudong's economy has achieved leapfrog development. The GDP jumped from 6 billion yuan in 1990 to 1.27 trillion yuan in 2019, and total fiscal revenue has increased from 1.1 billion yuan at the beginning of development and opening-up to over 400 billion yuan in 2019. With only one eight-thousandth of the nation's land area, Pudong created one-eightieth of the national GDP and one-fifteenth of the total value of goods imports and exports.

As a pioneer in China's reform and opening-up, Pudong has given birth to the first financial trade zone, the first bonded zone, the first free trade experimental zone and Lingang New Area, and the first wholly foreign-owned trading company, among other "national firsts." Its core competitiveness has been significantly enhanced, forming a modern industrial system mainly based on modern services, led by strategic emerging industries and supported by advanced manufacturing, bearing essential functions for constructing Shanghai's international economic, financial, trade, shipping, and technological innovation centers. The overall standard of living for the people has soared. In 2019, urban and rural residents per capita disposable income reached 71,647 yuan, the average life expectancy increased from 76.10 years in 1993 to 84.46 years, and the per capita urban housing construction area increased from 15 square meters in 1993 to 42 square meters.

The achievements of 30 years cannot be fully reflected by numbers alone. For example, in terms of image, Pudong has built an outward-oriented, multi-functional, and modern new urban area based on farmland, constructed a group of hub-type, networked infrastructure, and established central business districts such as Lujiazui. In terms of function, Pudong has broken through a series of key core technologies based on agriculture and simple processing industries, developed a competitive new industrial system, possessed the function of allocating resources such as capital, currency, labor, and bulk commodities, and built a relatively complete social undertakings and public service system. In terms of environment, Pudong has not only built a first-class development hardware environment but also initially formed a development software environment aligned with international practices. According to a survey, the success rate of foreign investment entering China since the reform and opening-up is about one-third, while Pudong is two-thirds, twice the national average. It can be said that the most important achievement of Pudong's development and opening-up over the past 30 years is not numbers, not images, but the environment, which is Pudong's core competitiveness and what makes people most proud.

Joining the World Trade Organization

The World Trade Organization (WTO) is one of today's most important international economic organizations. Its predecessor was the General Agreement on Tariffs and Trade (GATT), established in 1948. China is one of the founding members of GATT, but due to various reasons, it did not restore its GATT contracting party status for a period of time after the founding of the People's Republic of China. To adapt to the needs of reform and opening-up, in July 1986, the Chinese government decided to apply for the restoration of China's GATT contracting party status and established a specialized agency to organize external negotiations. During the negotiations, GATT was replaced by the WTO in 1995, and the accession negotiations were subsequently referred to as negotiations for joining the WTO.

During the negotiation process, many representatives believed that China, as a large country with rapid development, should not be considered a developing country. Based on this, Jiang Zemin proposed three principles that must be adhered to in the negotiations: joining the WTO is necessary for China's economic development and reform and opening-up, and the WTO also needs China; as an international organization, the WTO is incomplete without the participation of a large developing country like China, which is also not conducive to the development of the world economy; China is a developing country with underdeveloped social productivity, so it can only join the WTO under the conditions of a developing country; when China joins the WTO, rights and obligations must be balanced. The Chinese representatives insisted on these three principles throughout the negotiations. China sent four successive heads of delegations to participate in bilateral and multilateral negotiations. After continuous efforts and difficult negotiations, and overcoming various obstacles, China finally reached an agreement with the relevant parties. On November 10, 2001, the Fourth WTO Ministerial Conference held in Doha, Qatar, unanimously adopted the decision on China's accession to the WTO. China signed the *Protocol of Accession to the WTO*, and on December 11 of the same year, China officially joined the WTO as its 143rd member. This day marked 15 years since China's formal application to restore its GATT contracting party status in July 1986. As then-Premier Zhu Rongji said, the negotiators' hair turned from black to white during the negotiations, which shows the hardship of the negotiation process.

For China, joining the WTO is beneficial for expanding its opening to the outside world, winning a better international environment, promoting economic system reform and strategic adjustment of the economic structure, enhancing national economic development vitality and international competitiveness, and is in line with the country's fundamental and long-term interests. At the same time, joining the WTO is also a major test for China. The competition in the international market will be more deeply integrated with the domestic market competition, and China's economic risks will significantly increase. In this regard, Jiang Zemin pointed out: "Continuing to promote reform, opening-up, and modernization construction under the new situation of joining the WTO is a new learning process and a new test for our entire Party. What is being tested? It is our Party's learning, coping, competitiveness, decision-making, and innovation ability. In short, this will be a very practical and specific test of the wisdom and strength of all Party comrades. This is a difficult hurdle for all Party comrades, but we must overcome it, and we can only succeed, not fail."

The year 2011 marked the 10th anniversary of China's accession to the WTO. Hu Jintao gave a speech at the High-level Forum on China's WTO Accession 10th Anniversary, summarizing China's achievements. He said that in the ten years since joining the WTO, China has fully implemented its commitments, significantly enhancing the level of trade and investment liberalization and facilitation. China has expanded market access for agriculture, manufacturing, and the clothing industry, reduced import tariffs on products, abolished all import quotas, licenses, and other non-tariff measures that do not comply with WTO rules, fully liberalized foreign trade rights, and significantly lowered the threshold for foreign investment. China's overall tariff level has decreased from 15.3% to 9.8%, meeting and exceeding the WTO's requirements for developing countries. China's service trade opening has reached 100 sectors, approaching the level of developed countries. China has carried out large-scale reviews and revisions of laws and regulations, with the Central Government reviewing over 2,300 laws, regulations, and departmental rules and local governments reviewing more than 190,000 local policies and regulations. China's opening-up policy's stability, transparency, and predictability have continuously improved.

Over the past decade, China has adhered to a policy of opening-up based on equality, mutual benefit, and win-win cooperation, providing a strong impetus for global economic development. China has fully enjoyed the rights of WTO members, and its economic development has gained favorable external conditions. The breadth and depth of exchanges and cooperation with countries worldwide in economy, trade, technology, and culture have continuously expanded. China's global ranking in goods trade has risen from sixth to second, with export volume ranking first and accumulated import volume reaching 7.5 trillion US dollars; accumulated foreign direct investment reached 759.5 billion US dollars, ranking first among developing countries; annual growth of outbound direct investment exceeded 40%, reaching 68.8 billion US dollars in 2010 and ranking fifth globally. China imports an average of 750 billion US dollars of goods each year, creating a large number of jobs and investment opportunities for trading partners. Foreign-invested enterprises in China have remitted 261.7 billion US dollars in profits, with an annual growth rate of 30%.

In the past decade, China has actively assumed its international responsibilities and striven to promote the common development of all countries. We have actively adopted a series of major policy measures, worked with the international community to respond to the global financial crisis, and vigorously promoted strong, sustainable, and balanced growth of the world economy. We firmly support the WTO Doha Round negotiations, participate in international macroeconomic policy coordination, participate in the construction of global economic governance mechanisms such as the G20, and are committed to the reform and improvement of the international monetary system, international trading system, and the price formation mechanism of commodities, as well as promoting economic globalization and regional economic integration. We uphold the banner of free trade, oppose all forms of protectionism, and promote establishing a fair, reasonable, and non-discriminatory international trading system. We actively promote the establishment of a more equal and balanced new global development partnership, strengthen North-South dialogue and South-South cooperation, increase foreign aid efforts, and have provided more than 170 billion yuan in various forms of aid over the past decade, canceled nearly 30 billion yuan in due debts of 50 heavily indebted poor countries and least developed countries, pledged to grant zero-tariff treatment to 97% of the tariff lines of products from the least developed countries that have diplomatic relations with China, and trained more than 60,000 personnel from 173 developing countries and 13 regional international organizations, enhancing the self-development capabilities of aid recipient countries. These achievements demonstrate the great success of China's accession to the WTO and its full integration into globalization. It can be said that accession to the WTO has changed China and influenced the world.

In addition, China's opening-up has experienced a remarkable transformation from primarily "bringing in" to both "bringing in" and "going out." In the early stages of reform and opening-up, China was technologically backward and lacked capital. Most coastal areas opened up by introducing capital and technology, mainly through "three import, and one compensate," which refers to "processing with supplied materials, processing with supplied samples, assembly with supplied parts, and compensation trade." This strategy indeed brought capital to China and provided significant support for improving China's technological capabilities.

As the 1990s began, China's development accelerated in various aspects, with its technological innovation and business operation capabilities gradually increasing. Based on an in-depth analysis of the international and domestic political and economic situation, the Central Committee of the CPC made the significant decision to implement the "going out" strategy. On December 24, 1997, Jiang Zemin first proposed "going out" as an important strategy when meeting with National Foreign Investment Conference representatives. He said that "bringing in" and "going out" are two closely linked and mutually promoting aspects of our basic policy of opening-up to the outside world, and neither can be neglected. "This is a major strategy, both an important strategy for opening-up to the outside world and for economic development."

In December 2011, Hu Jintao pointed out that "bringing in" and "going out" are essential aspects of China's opening-up and effective means for deepening foreign economic and trade cooperation and promoting joint development with countries worldwide. China will continue to expand the openness of various fields, strengthen the coordination of industrial policies and foreign investment policies, continue to welcome investors from all countries to invest and start businesses in China, encourage foreign businesses to establish research and development centers in China, and use global technological and intellectual resources to promote domestic technological innovation. China will accelerate the implementation of the "going out" strategy, guide enterprises to carry out overseas investment and cooperation in an orderly manner following the principles of market orientation and corporate autonomy, attach importance to cooperation that benefits the livelihood of underdeveloped countries, and enhances their self-development capabilities, assume social responsibilities, and benefit local people. This demonstrates the Central Government's insistence on emphasizing "going out" and "bringing in."

Under the guidance of this idea, while achieving significant results in foreign trade and utilizing foreign investment, Chinese enterprises have taken firm steps in "going out." More and more Chinese companies are expanding through various means, such as cross-border mergers and acquisitions and overseas listings, continuously broadening their investment fields and enhancing their cooperation levels. China's foreign investment now covers more than 170 countries and regions. From 2001 to 2010, China's outward direct investment (non-financial direct investment flow) maintained a growth trend for nine consecutive years, with an average annual growth rate of about 50%, increasing from less than 1 billion to 59 billion US dollars and the accumulated outward direct investment stock exceeded 300 billion US dollars over ten years. According to the United Nations Conference on Trade and Development's "2011 World Investment Report," in 2010, China's outward direct investment accounted for 5.2% of the global annual flow, ranking fifth globally, surpassing traditional foreign investment powers such as Japan and the UK for the first time. China's foreign investment has played a promotional role in many countries' economic recovery and development.

To improve the level of opening-up and achieve the sustainable and healthy development of China's economy, the Central Committee of CPC has also proposed and implemented a mutually beneficial and win-win opening-up strategy. The purpose is to create a favorable international environment, achieve a win-win situation, promote common development, and make full use of both domestic and foreign resources and markets to promote the sound and rapid development of China's economy.

CHAPTER 14

The World-Shaking Chinese Miracle

Since the reform and opening-up, China's economy and society have developed rapidly under the strong leadership of the CPC. In 2010, China's economy surpassed Japan's to become the world's second-largest economy. Since then, it has remained the second largest in the world. The fact that a poor and backward country with a population of more than one billion has achieved such tremendous accomplishments is truly a Chinese miracle. The miracle is closely related to China's unwavering taking economic development as the central task, formulating development strategies in line with national conditions, and emphasizing balanced and sustainable economic and social development.

Focusing on Economic Development

Faced with the sluggish national economic development after the end of the "Great Cultural Revolution" and the unresolved subsistence problem for over 200 million farmers, Deng Xiaoping first proposed in September 1978 during his inspection tour of the three northeastern provinces to stop the "Gang of Four" campaign and shift the focus to socialist modernization as soon as possible. During the inspection, he "lit fires everywhere," repeatedly emphasizing that the key issues were seeking truth from facts, combining theory with practice, and proceeding from reality. He strongly encouraged local officials in the northeast to free their minds and focus on production. His far-sighted and popular proposal was approved by other Political Bureau Standing Committee members, creating favorable conditions and laying a solid foundation for the subsequent Central Working Conference and the historic decision of the third plenary session of the 11th CPC Central Committee to shift the focus of the Party and state work to economic construction and implement reform and opening-up.

In December 1978, the third plenary session of the 11th CPC Central Committee re-established Marxism's ideological, political, and organizational lines, achieving a strategic shift in the focus of Party and state work and resolving the issue of shifting priorities that had not been properly addressed since 1957. During the meeting, some delegates pointed out that even if a war occurred, the central task of economic construction must be upheld after the war. After the meeting, Deng Xiaoping repeatedly emphasized the importance of concentrating on economic construction, reform, and opening-up. In early 1980, Deng Xiaoping emphasized in his speech at a cadre meeting convened by the Central Committee of CPC: "The task of modernization construction is multifaceted, and all aspects need to be balanced comprehensively. We cannot just focus on one aspect. However, in the end, we still have to take economic construction as the center. Without focusing on economic construction, losing the material foundation is dangerous. All other tasks must be subordinate to this center. We must not interfere with or impact it around this center."

Achieving modernization is China's most significant political goal. In 1982, the 12th CPC National Congress clearly proposed that "the overall task of the CPC in the new historical period is to unite the people of all ethnic groups across the country, rely on our own efforts, work hard, and gradually achieve modernization of industry, agriculture, national defense, and science and technology, and build our country into a highly civilized and highly democratic socialist country." In 1986, the sixth plenary session of the twelfth CPC Central Committee further proposed that the overall layout of China's socialist construction is to focus on economic construction, unswervingly carry out economic system reform, unswervingly carry out political system reform, and unswervingly strengthen the construction of spiritual civilization, and coordinate and promote these aspects mutually. This again emphasizes the importance of economic construction.

Based on summarizing the ten-year experience of reform and opening-up, the 13th CPC National Congress, held in 1987, clearly outlined and comprehensively expounded the Party's basic line in the primary stage of socialism in accordance with the theory of the primary stage of socialism. The basic line, briefly referred to as "one center, two basic points," emphasizes economic construction as the center and vigorously develops social productivity. Even in the face of complex domestic and international situations in the late 1980s and early 1990s, Deng Xiaoping particularly emphasized "to adhere to the line, principles, and policies since the third plenary session of the 11th Central Committee, and the key is to adhere to the 'one center, two basic points.' Without adhering to socialism, reform and opening-up, economic development, and improving people's livelihood, there is only a dead end. The basic line must be maintained for a hundred years and not shaken. Only by adhering to this line will the people believe in and support you."

Since the 1990s, whether facing major floods, serious financial crises, major epidemic disasters, or significant natural disasters such as earthquakes, or proposing the "Three Represents" important thought or implementing the Scientific Outlook on Development, the Party Central Committee has always emphasized focusing on economic construction and stressed that development is the top priority for governing and rejuvenating the country. For example, the report of the 18th CPC National Congress points out that the entire Party must more consciously regard promoting economic and social development as the primary task of implementing the Scientific Outlook on Development, firmly grasp the center of economic construction, concentrate on construction and development, strive to grasp the laws of development, innovate development concepts, and solve development problems. We must deepen the implementation of the strategies for invigorating the country through science and education, making the country strong through talent and sustainable development, accelerate the formation of development methods and institutional mechanisms in line with the requirements of scientific development, continuously liberate and develop productive forces, and continuously achieve scientific, harmonious, and peaceful development, laying a solid foundation for adhering to and developing socialism with Chinese characteristics.

The Three-Step Strategic Plan

Formulating practical and feasible development strategies is a valuable experience for the CPC in governing the country. In the 1950s, China proposed the construction of a socialist power and later put forward the "Four Modernizations" goals, which are the manifestations of the CPC's emphasis on strategic planning in governance. Deng Xiaoping is known as the chief architect of China's reform and opening-up, mainly because he proposed and implemented many major strategies and designs that are crucial to China's fate.

On December 6, 1979, when meeting with Japanese Prime Minister Masayoshi Ohira, Deng Xiaoping first proposed the Chinese-style modernization concept of "*xiaokang*" (moderately prosperous). He said: "By the end of this century, even if China's four modernizations have achieved some goals, our per capita GDP will still be very low. To reach the level of a slightly wealthier country in the Third World, such as a per capita GDP of 1,000 US dollars, we still have to make great efforts. Even if we reach that level, we will still be backward compared to the West." This is a pragmatic performance and a result of summarizing China's development experience and lessons. In January 1980, Deng Xiaoping further proposed a strategic plan for achieving Chinese-style modernization in the next 20 years, divided into two decades, in his speech at the Central Committee of CPC. In April 1981, when meeting with a visiting delegation from the Japan-China Friendship Parliamentarian Association, Deng Xiaoping again introduced his economic strategic vision to the guests: "Through our efforts, we expect to double in ten years and quadruple in two decades, that is, to achieve a per capita GDP of 1,000 US dollars."

In September 1982, the 12th CPC National Congress formally established the strategic goal of quadrupling by the end of the 20th century and achieving a moderately prosperous society. The 12th National Congress report pointed out that from 1981 to the end of this century, the overall goal of China's economic construction was to strive to double the total industrial and agricultural output value on the premise of continuously improving economic efficiency, increasing it from 710 billion yuan in 1980 to about 2.8 trillion yuan by 2000. Upon achieving this goal, the income of urban and rural people will grow multiple times, and people's material and cultural life will reach a moderately prosperous level. The report also pointed out that in order to achieve the 20-year goal, the strategic deployment should be divided into two steps: laying a solid foundation, accumulating strength, and creating conditions in the first ten years; entering a new period of economic revitalization in the second ten years. Since then, "quadrupling and striving for a moderately prosperous society" has become a hot topic of concern and discussion among the whole Party and the people nationwide.

Whether the moderately prosperous strategy can be achieved on schedule depends on local development. From February 6 to 9, 1983, Deng Xiaoping came to Suzhou for an on-the-spot investigation of constructing a moderately prosperous society.

Deng Xiaoping was very concerned about whether Jiangsu could quadruple by 2000. Comrades from Jiangsu told him that places like Suzhou were preparing to achieve the goals set by the Central Committee five years ahead of schedule. After returning to Beijing, he said, "I went from Jiangsu to Zhejiang and then from Zhejiang to Shanghai. Along the way, I saw a good situation. People were beaming with happiness, many new houses were built, the market was rich in materials, and the cadres were full of confidence. It seems that there is great hope for the Four Modernizations."

Based on research and investigation, Deng Xiaoping gradually clarified China's economic development strategy of "approaching the level of developed countries by the middle of the 21st century." In his speech during a meeting with Chinese and foreign representatives attending the discussion on Sino-foreign economic cooperation in October 1984, he pointed out that achieving a moderately prosperous society was only a phased grand goal for China. On this basis, China would strive to gradually approach the level of developed countries in two steps. "The first step is to double the size of the economy, which will take 20 years. Then there's the second step, which will take 30 to 50 years, probably 50 years, to approach the level of developed countries. The two steps together add up to 50 to 70 years." This prepared the groundwork for the later complete "Three-Step" development strategy proposal.

According to Deng Xiaoping's strategic conception and China's national conditions, the 13th CPC National Congress officially established the "Three-Step" economic development strategy: "Since the third plenary session of the 11th CPC Central Committee, China's economic construction has been generally divided into three steps. The first step was to double the gross national product compared to 1980 and solve the problem of people's food and clothing, which has been basically achieved. The second step is to double the gross national product again, with per capita living standards reaching a moderately prosperous level. The third step is to reach the level of moderately developed countries in terms of per capita gross national product by the middle of the next century, with people enjoying relatively affluent lives and achieving basic modernization. Then continue to advance on this basis." The formation and determination of this economic development strategy planned the grand blueprint for China's socialist modernization construction, answered major issues related to the overall goal and steps of China's modernization construction, and pointed out the direction for China's economic development.

After arduous efforts, from 1987 to 1997, through ten years of struggle, the gross national product achieved a "doubling" on the basis of the 1980s. By 2000, the per capita gross national product exceeded 800 US dollars, achieving the second step of the "Three-Step" economic development strategy. The 15th CPC National Congress made new arrangements for the third step of the "Three-Step" economic development strategy, proposing: "As we look forward to the next century, our goal is to double the gross national product compared to 2000 in the first decade, make people's moderately prosperous life more comfortable, and form a perfect socialist market economic system; after another ten years of effort, by the 100th anniversary of the founding of the Party, the national economy will be more developed and various systems will be perfect; by the 100th anniversary of the founding of the People's Republic of China in the middle of the century, we will basically achieve modernization and build a prosperous, strong, democratic, culturally advanced and harmonious modern socialist country."

"Two Major Situations" and the Strategy of Rejuvenating the Country through Science and Education

The Central Committee of CPC adopted Deng Xiaoping's idea of allowing some people and some regions to get rich through hard work to stimulate and drive the development of other regions, ultimately achieving common prosperity. This approach has achieved significant results in practice.

Initially, the Central Government adopted the strategy of prioritizing the development of the eastern region. The Yangtze River Delta and Pearl River Delta in the southern part of mainland China, taking advantage of their geographical location and central policy support, along with their diligence and hard work, developed rapidly. Within a short span of ten years, cities and factories sprang up in these areas, and the eastern region took the lead in entering the fast track of development. In response to the widening gap between the economic and social development of the central and western regions and the eastern regions, Deng Xiaoping put forward the idea of "two major situations" in the late 1980s: "Coastal areas should speed up opening-up to the outside world, so that the vast region with a population of 200 million can develop faster and, in turn, drive the better development of inland areas. This is a matter of great importance, and the inland areas should consider this. Conversely, when development reaches a certain stage, coastal areas must devote more effort to help inland development, which is also a major situation. At that time, coastal areas should also comply with this situation." Based on Deng Xiaoping's ideas, the Central Government formulated the policy of "encouraging early prosperity, promoting later prosperity, joint development between the east and west, and achieving common prosperity" and "adapting measures to local conditions, reasonable division of labor, each showing its strengths, complementary advantages, and joint development." Deng Xiaoping repeatedly emphasized that the socialist path means gradually achieving common prosperity. After a certain level of prosperity is achieved in some areas, the focus should be on accelerating the development of less-developed regions.

To promote the rapid development of the western region, on March 3, 1999, Jiang Zemin formally proposed the strategic concept of "Great Western Development" in his speech at the Party member leaders' meetings of the Second Session of the Ninth National People's Congress and the Second Session of the Ninth CPPCC. In October 2000, the fifth plenary session of the 15th CPC Central Committee established the implementation of the Great Western Development Strategy (developing west China, revitalizing old industrial bases in the northeast and other parts of the country, and spurring the rise of the central region) and the promotion of regional coordinated development as a strategic task, emphasizing that "implementing the Great Western Development strategy and accelerating the development of the central and western regions are crucial measures for achieving the third step of the strategic goal, as they relate to economic development, national unity, social stability, regional coordinated development, and the ultimate realization of common prosperity." In March 2001, the Fourth Session of the Ninth National People's Congress approved the "Outline of the Tenth Five-Year Plan for National Economic and Social Development of the People's Republic of China," which again made specific arrangements for implementing the Great Western Development Strategy.

The western region refers to 12 provinces, autonomous regions, and municipalities, including Shaanxi, Gansu, Ningxia, Qinghai, Xinjiang, Sichuan, Chongqing, Yunnan, Guizhou, Xizang, Guangxi, and Inner Mongolia. The Xiangxi Tujia and Miao Autonomous Prefecture in Hunan Province, Enshi Tujia and Miao Autonomous Prefecture in Hubei Province, and Yanbian Korean Autonomous Prefecture in Jilin Province also enjoy relevant western development policies. The implementation of the Great Western Development strategy aims to rely on major transportation arteries such as the Eurasian Land Bridge, the Yangtze River waterway, and the southwest sea channels, leverage the role of central cities, connect points with lines, and bring areas together, gradually forming characteristic economic belts in China's western region that span administrative regions, such as the Xilonghai-Lanzhou-Xinjiang Line, the upper reaches of the Yangtze River, Nanning-Guiyang, Chengdu-Kunming, and other areas, driving the development of other regions and advancing the Great Western Development step by step and with focus.

On the morning of July 8, 2010, at a press conference held by the State Council Information Office, Du Ying, Deputy Director of the National Development and Reform Commission, introduced the implementation of the Great Western Development, the main tasks, policy measures, and other aspects of deepening the Great Western Development strategy. He pointed out that over the past ten years, under the correct leadership of the Central Committee of CPC and the State Council, various regions and departments, especially the vast number of cadres and masses in the western region, have made remarkable achievements in the Great Western Development through pioneering innovation, hard work, and solid work. First, the economic strength has been significantly improved. From 2000 to 2009, the GDP of the western region increased from 1.6655 trillion yuan to 6.6868 trillion yuan, with an average annual growth rate of 11.9%. Local fiscal revenue increased from 112.7 billion yuan to 605.5 billion yuan, with an average annual growth rate of 19.4%. The total fixed asset investment of the whole society increased from 611.1 billion yuan to 4.97 trillion yuan, with an average annual growth rate of 24.8%. The total retail sales of consumer goods increased from 599.7 billion yuan to 2.3039 trillion yuan, with an average annual growth rate of 15.4%. The total import and export trade increased from 17.2 billion US dollars to 91.5 billion US dollars, with an average annual growth rate of 20.9%. Second, breakthrough progress has been made in infrastructure construction. By the end of 2009, a total of 120 key projects had been started, with a total investment scale of 2.2 trillion yuan. An additional 972,000 kilometers of new highway mileage was opened to traffic, including 16,000 kilometers of new expressways. The "Five Vertical and Seven Horizontal" national trunk line sections in the western region, totaling 16,000 kilometers, were completed, with a total highway mileage of 1.5045 million kilometers. The accessibility rate of highways in towns (townships) and administrative villages reached 99.06% and 88.54%, respectively.

An additional 11,000 kilometers of railway operating mileage was added, bringing the total railway operating mileage to 32,800 kilometers. Forty-eight main and branch line airports were renovated or expanded, and 23 new airports were built, bringing the total number of civil transport airports to 81, accounting for 48.8% of the total number of airports in the country. A series of large-scale water conservancy projects were completed and put into operation, solving the drinking water difficulties and safety issues for 94.37 million rural residents. An additional 18,630 kilometers of oil and gas pipelines were added. The total installed power generation capacity reached

266.07 million kilowatts, and power infrastructure construction in areas without electricity continued to progress steadily. An additional 230,000 kilometers of long-distance optical cable lines and 4.98 million kilometers of long-distance optical cable cores were added.

Third, the overall trend of ecological environment deterioration has been preliminarily curbed. Successive major ecological projects such as turning farmland into forests, turning farmland into grasslands, and natural forest protection have been implemented, with significant local ecological improvements. Currently, the forest area in the western region is 116.81 million hectares, with a forest coverage rate of 17.1%, an increase of 6.7 percentage points compared to 1999; the forest stock volume has reached 8.27 billion cubic meters, an increase of nearly 1.3 billion cubic meters. The project of returning farmland to forests has become the largest, most extensive, and most effective major ecological project in the history of New China, with a total of 15.793 million hectares of forests created in the western region, accounting for 34% of the total afforestation area during the same period nationwide. The project of returning grazing land to grasslands has cumulatively arranged for the construction of 45.07 million hectares of grassland fences in the western region and has supported the improvement and reseeding of 8.133 million hectares of severely degraded grasslands, with an average increase of 14 percentage points in vegetation coverage and an average increase of 68% in grass yield. The Natural Forest Resources Protection Project has effectively protected 63.8 million hectares of natural forest resources in the western region, accounting for 32.6% of the total national forest area, and commercial logging of natural forests has been completely halted in the 13 provinces (regions and cities) along the upper reaches of the Yangtze and Yellow rivers. Projects such as the Beijing-Tianjin sandstorm source control, the fourth phase of the "Three-North" shelterbelt system construction, the Qinghai Sanjiangyuan region, the Gannan Yellow River important water source replenishment area, comprehensive treatment of karst rocky desertification, and the management of the Tarim River, Heihe River, and Shiyang River basins are progressing steadily. Water pollution prevention and control have been actively promoted, and the deterioration trend of water quality in key river basins has been controlled. Chemical oxygen demand and sulfur dioxide emissions have been significantly reduced.

Fourth, the construction of people's livelihood projects has been strengthened. The "two basics" (basic education and basic medical care) battle plan was completed as scheduled, with 397 counties passing the "two basics" inspection and the "two basics" population coverage rate reaching 99.5%. A total of more than 6 million illiterate people were eliminated, and 48.8 million students enjoyed the "two exemptions and one subsidy" policy. The number of ordinary colleges and universities increased from 251 in 1999 to 542 in 2008, with the number of students enrolled increasing more than four times. The total number of beds in health institutions reached 1.081 million, with 16,440 township health centers and nearly 180,000 village health clinics built. The participation rate in the new rural cooperative medical system was 91.5%. A number of key national laboratories and other scientific and technological infrastructure-sharing platforms were built. An additional 179 museums, 151 cultural centers, and 1,421 comprehensive cultural stations were established. The comprehensive radio coverage rate reached 96%, and the television coverage rate reached 97%. The number of insured urban workers under basic medical insurance reached 36.89 million, and the number of insured urban residents under basic medical insurance reached 24.4 million. The Central Government invested in constructing more than 1.72 million low-rent housing units, covering more than 82.86 million square meters.

Fifth, the construction of new rural areas has made solid progress. By 2009, more than 4.2 million hectares of low- and medium-yield fields had been transformed, the effective irrigation area in the western region increased by a net of 5.07 million hectares, and the water-saving irrigation area increased by 3.9 million hectares. Nearly 6 million household biogas units and 2,988 livestock breeding areas and joint biogas units were newly built. Nearly 40,000 village-level organization activity venues were built, and more than 98% of administrative villages had telephone access. In 2009, the per capita net income of rural residents in the western region reached 3,817 yuan. The total rural poor population was reduced by 33.593 million, accounting for 57.6% of the total poverty reduction in China during the same period.

Sixth, the reform and opening-up continue to deepen. The pace of reform, reorganization, and transformation of state-owned enterprises has accelerated, and individual, private, and small and medium-sized enterprises have played an important role in invigorating the urban and rural economy, expanding social employment, and optimizing the economic structure. Comprehensive supporting reform pilot areas for urban and rural coordination have been established in Chongqing and Chengdu, and the reform of coordinating scientific and technological resources in Xi'an has been actively promoted. Rural comprehensive reform has steadily advanced, collective forest rights system reform has been actively promoted, and the grassland household contract responsibility system has been fully implemented. International regional cooperation, such as the China-ASEAN Free Trade Area and the Shanghai Cooperation Organization, has been further promoted, the Greater Mekong Subregion economic cooperation and Central Asia regional economic cooperation have steadily developed, and a new pattern of all-round foreign development has initially formed. By the end of 2009, about 200,000 enterprises from the eastern regions had invested and started businesses in the western regions, with a total investment of nearly 3 trillion yuan; 15 eastern provinces (cities), planned municipalities, and special administrative region cities established poverty alleviation cooperation relationships with 11 western provinces (regions, cities); 20 provinces (cities) supported the reconstruction after the Wenchuan earthquake, with a contribution of 67.37 billion yuan to the reconstruction projects. The Western China International Fair, Western China Expo, China-ASEAN Expo, etc., have become important platforms for East-West interactive cooperation and attracting foreign investment. In addition, characteristic and advantageous industries have shown good development momentum, key regions have accelerated development, and talent development has been further promoted. Entering the 21st century, we have successively implemented strategies such as revitalizing old industrial bases in the northeast and other parts of the country and the rise of the central region, promoting China's regional development to become coordinated gradually.

Science and technology are the primary productive forces, and education cultivates talents for development. Hence, with an eye on enduring, robust, and sustainable progress, the nation has meticulously crafted and executed a strategy centered on invigorating the country through advancements in science, education, and the cultivation of exceptional talent. On May 6, 1995, the Central Committee of CPC and the State Council made the "Decision on Accelerating Scientific and Technological Progress" to explicitly propose the strategy of rejuvenating the country through science and education. The "Decision" points out: "Rejuvenating the country through science and education means fully implementing the idea that science and technology are the primary productive forces, adhering to education as the foundation, placing science and technology and education in important positions in economic and social development, enhancing the country's scientific and technological strength and the ability to transform scientific and technological achievements into real productive forces, improving the scientific and technological literacy of the entire nation, shifting economic construction to relying on scientific and technological progress and improving the quality of the workforce, and accelerating the realization of national prosperity and strength." On May 26 to 30 of the same year, the Central Committee of CPC and the State Council held the National Science and Technology Conference in Beijing. The conference required party committees and governments at all levels to earnestly implement the decisions of the Central Committee and the State

Council, combine the realities of various regions and departments, regard promoting scientific and technological progress as a major task, put it on the important agenda, and formulate feasible measures.

The fifth plenary session of the 14th CPC Central Committee held in 1995 included the implementation of the strategy of invigorating the country through science and education as one of the important guidelines for accelerating the construction of socialist modernization in China in the next fifteen years and into the 21st century, in its proposal on the "Ninth Five-Year Plan" for national economic and social development and the 2010 long-term goals. In September 1997, the 15th CPC National Congress reaffirmed the importance and urgency of implementing the strategy of invigorating the country through science and education. It emphasized the need to put education and science and technology in a strategic position for priority development and regarded the development of education and science as the foundation of cultural construction. In March 1998, at the press conference for Chinese and foreign journalists at the First Session of the Ninth National People's Congress, Premier Zhu Rongji solemnly declared: "Invigorating the country through science and education is the biggest task of this government." After the meeting, the National Science and Technology Education Leadership Group was established, with Zhu Rongji personally serving as the group leader.

Since 1997, ten major tasks have been carried out to promote the central link, and significant progress has been made in some key issues. The central link is always focused on promoting the integration of science, education, economic development, and social progress and persistently implementing the strategy of invigorating the country through science and education. To fully implement the strategy, the state has placed education in a strategic position for priority development. Great efforts have been made in implementing nine-year compulsory education, basically achieving compulsory education. Free lunch programs have been implemented in difficult areas. In terms of university education, expansion of enrollment, university mergers, and higher education enrollment rates have significantly increased. In order to establish high-level universities, the state has implemented the "211 Project" and the "985 Project." In order to address the difficulties and costs of attending school, the state has taken many measures. In terms of strengthening school safety, related systems are also being established. The "National Medium and Long-Term Education Reform and Development Plan (2010–2020)" was adopted, outlining the guiding principles for education development in the next ten years. The state has made great efforts to improve college entrance examination policies, and the construction of kindergartens has been continuously strengthened.

In terms of science and technology, after 1992, the science and technology system underwent reform pilot projects focusing on structural adjustment, talent diversion, and mechanism transformation under the principle of "stabilizing one end and opening-up a wide range." After the National Science and Technology Conference held by the Central Committee in 1995, the reform of the science and technology system entered a new stage in which structural adjustment and mechanism transformation promoted each other. In the promotion of more than ten years of reform, China's scientific and technological work has initially formed a strategic pattern of focusing on the main battlefield of economic construction, developing high-tech industries and strengthening basic research; a series of major scientific and technological actions have been implemented, such as key basic research planning, science and technology tackling plans, the 863 Program, the Torch Program, the Spark Program, the Prairie Fire Program, the National Engineering Research Center Construction Plan, and the National Key Industrial Experimental Plan. Key equipment updates for some national key laboratories have been carried out, and the construction of major national scientific projects has been organized and implemented. The role of scientific and technological progress in economic and social development has been increasingly strengthened.

As we stepped into the 21st century, the Central Government emphasized the pivotal role of innovation, championing the mission of transforming China into a hub of ingenuity. The nation adopted a strategy prioritizing talent, recognizing human capital as its foremost resource and leveraging talent acquisition programs at various levels to propel national advancement. Recent milestones, from breakthroughs in manned space missions and deep-sea explorations to the rapid expansion of high-speed rail and the enhanced safety of nuclear power plants, underscore China's ascent to new zeniths in scientific and technological prowess.

Building a Harmonious Socialist Society

Focusing on social construction is a reflection of the continuous expansion of the layout of socialist construction driven by the practice of reform and opening-up. In the last two decades of the 20th century, the CPC, in the process of leading the construction of socialist modernization, experienced a transformation in the layout of socialist construction from focusing on both material and spiritual civilization to building political, economic, and cultural systems. In the 1980s, Deng Xiaoping proposed that we should grasp both material and spiritual civilization with one hand, "both hands must be firm." The sixth plenary session of the 12th CPC Central Committee adopted the resolution on strengthening the construction of socialist spiritual civilization and made detailed arrangements for the construction of spiritual civilization. The nation carried out the "Five Talks, Four Beauties, Three Loves" and the Learning from Lei Feng campaign to advance the construction of spiritual civilization. Many heroic and exemplary figures, such as Zhang Haidi, emerged during this period. The "Strike Hard" campaign was also launched to crack down on criminal offenses, significantly improving the social atmosphere. After Deng Xiaoping's Southern Tour Talk in 1992 and the 14th CPC National Congress, the state gradually established and improved the socialist market economic system and strengthened the construction of the social security system. The 15th CPC National Congress in 1997 explicitly proposed the basic program for the primary stage of socialism and made specific arrangements to construct socialism with Chinese characteristics in politics, economy, and culture.

As the 21st century began, social construction gradually became an integral part of the overall layout of socialism with Chinese characteristics. When the 16th CPC National Congress deployed the comprehensive construction of a moderately prosperous society in 2002, it clearly put forward the goal of "a more harmonious society," which was the first time in the reports of the Party Congress. The fourth plenary session of the 16th CPC Central Committee held in 2004 further proposed the task of building a harmonious socialist society, emphasizing that forming a society in which all people do their best and live in harmony is the inevitable requirement for consolidating the Party's governing foundation and realizing the historical mission of the Party's rule. It is necessary to adapt to the profound changes in our country's society, place a harmonious society in an important position, and clarify the main content of building a harmonious socialist society. In February 2005, the Central Committee of CPC held a special seminar on improving the ability of provincial and ministerial-level leading cadres to build a harmonious socialist society. Hu Jintao pointed out in his speech that with the continuous development of China's economy and society, the overall layout of socialism with Chinese characteristics has become more clearly a Four-Sphere Integrated Plan development of socialist economic, political, cultural, and social construction. Building a harmonious socialist society is a major task put forward by our Party from the overall perspective of building a well-off society in an all-round way and creating a new situation in the cause of socialism with Chinese characteristics. It meets the objective requirements of our country's reform and development entering a critical period and reflects the fundamental interests and common aspirations of the broad masses of the people. The meeting proposed that the harmonious socialist society we want to build should be a society of democracy and the rule of law, fairness and justice, honesty and love, full of vitality, stability, and order, and harmony between man and nature. The sixth plenary session of the 16th CPC Central Committee held in 2006 specifically studied and deployed the construction of a harmonious socialist society. The meeting not only proposed the construction goals and main tasks for 2020 but also considered social harmony as the essential attribute of socialism with Chinese characteristics and an important guarantee for national prosperity, national rejuvenation, and people's happiness. This marks the enrichment and expansion of the overall layout of socialism with Chinese characteristics from a three-in-one combination of politics, economy, and culture to a four-in-one combination of politics, economy, culture, and society. The 17th CPC National Congress, held in 2007, emphasized accelerating the promotion of social construction focused on improving people's livelihood, striving to ensure that all people have access to education, work, medical care, old-age care, and housing, and promoting the construction of a harmonious society.

Entering the 21st century, social construction focusing on improving people's livelihood has gradually strengthened. In terms of the five-year plan, the "Eleventh Five-Year Plan" (2005–2010) has never before placed such a high emphasis on people's livelihood issues: among the twenty-two indicators, eight involve public services and people's lives, with two of them included in the plan as binding indicators for the first time. By the end of 2010, all eight livelihood indicators were achieved—urban and rural residents' incomes increased significantly, free nine-year compulsory education was fully implemented, the number of people covered by urban basic pension insurance and the coverage rate of the new rural cooperative medical system met the targets ahead of schedule, and 55 million new urban jobs were created nationwide. At the end of the "Eleventh Five-Year Plan," the per capita income of urban and rural residents in China reached 19,109 yuan and 5,919 *yuan*, respectively. Even during the most severe impact of the international financial crisis from 2007 to 2009, the annual growth rate of urban and rural residents' income was higher than the 5% plan target.

The public's praise is better than gold and silver trophies. As the measures to benefit the people were implemented, the CPC gained even more support from the people. For example, in 2006, the Central Committee of CPC abolished the agricultural tax that had lasted for more than 2,600 years, reducing the burden on farmers. In gratitude to the CPC's commitment to the people, Wang Sanni, a farmer in Lingshou County, Hebei Province, spent 80,000 yuan to cast a bronze tripod named "Farewell to the Land Tax Ding." In 2011, the self-written and self-directed lantern play "Ten Thanks to the Communist Party" by the farmers of Tianjia Gully, Longfeng Village, Xinglong Town, Meitan County, Zunyi City, Guizhou Province, not only became popular in the villages of Guizhou but also entered the CCTV Spring Festival Gala. The short "Ten Thanks to the Communist Party" reflected the popularity of the Party's economic and social development policies and the construction of a socialist harmonious society in line with public opinion.

During this period, cultural undertakings and industries developed rapidly, presenting a gratifying trend of prosperity in cultural construction. Through implementing a series of major environmental protection projects, the structure of ecological civilization also made significant progress, and the socialist modernization construction showed an all-round development trend.

Chapter 15

Promoting the Construction of Democracy and Rule of Law

Since the reform and opening-up, the CPC has summarized the positive and negative experiences in the development of socialist democratic politics and clearly put forward that without democracy, there would be no socialism and no socialist modernization. The essence and core of socialist democratic politics is that the people are the masters of the country. It is also proposed to adhere to the unity of the Party's leadership, the rule of law, and the People's being the masters of the country, making significant progress in developing socialist democratic politics.

The Restoration and Development of the People's Congress System

The People's Congress system is the fundamental political system of contemporary China. During the "Great Cultural Revolution," the People's Congress could not function normally, and the timing of its meetings was uncertain. In February and March 1978, the First Session of the Fifth National People's Congress was held, adopting the *Constitution of the People's Republic of China*, electing Ye Jianying as the Chairman of the Standing Committee of the National People's Congress, reappointing Hua Guofeng as the Premier of the State Council, and appointing Deng Xiaoping, Li Xiannian, and 13 others as Vice Premiers. The convening of this Congress indicated that the work of the NPC had basically returned to normal, but there were some issues with the *Constitution* adopted at this meeting, mainly due to the strong color of class struggle. According to the suggestion of the Central Committee of CPC, on July 1, 1979, the Second Session of the Fifth National People's Congress adopted the "Resolution on Amending Certain Provisions of the Constitution of the People's Republic of China" and the *Organization Law of Local People's Congresses and Local People's Governments at All Levels*, explicitly stipulating that the Standing Committees of People's Congresses at the county level and above should be established, changing the previous situation where there were no permanent institutions of the People's Congress at the county level, marking a significant development of the People's Congress system.

The National People's Congress is China's highest legislative body, bearing the major task of legislation. Based on summarizing historical experience, Deng Xiaoping believed that laws were reliable and proposed the guiding principle for the construction of the socialist legal system, namely, laws must be available, laws must be followed, law enforcement must be strict, and lawbreakers must be prosecuted. To achieve the availability of laws, strengthening legislation is necessary. The first major action to strengthen legislation was amending the *Constitution*. At the enlarged meeting of the Political Bureau of the Central Committee of CPC held in August 1980, Deng Xiaoping announced that the Central Committee would propose to amend the *Constitution* at the Third Session of the Fifth National People's Congress. In September 1980, the Third Session of the Fifth National People's Congress accepted the suggestion of the Central Committee of CPC and decided to establish a Constitution Amendment Committee. The Constitution Amendment Committee was headed by Ye Jianying, with Song Qingling and Peng Zhen as deputy directors. Peng Zhen was specifically responsible for amending the *Constitution*. Based on the suggestions of the Central Committee of CPC, the guiding ideology for amending the *Constitution* was determined as the Four Basic Principles, and the focus was to shift the focus of the country's work to socialist modernization and economic construction. All work should revolve around this focus and serve this focus. At the same time, full attention should be paid to the construction of socialist spiritual civilization and the development of socialist democracy. Specific principles included taking the 1954 *Constitution* as the basis; incorporating the Four Basic Principles into the *Constitution*; placing citizens' rights and obligations before state institutions; not implementing a bicameral system, establishing the position of the President of the country; setting up the Central Military Commission; abolishing the lifelong tenure system for leadership positions; retaining the Supreme People's Procuratorate; establishing administrative supervision organs; adhering to the system of regional ethnic autonomy; and providing a constitutional basis for the "One Country, Two Systems" principle, etc. During the drafting process of this *Constitution*, the Constitution Amendment Committee held five meetings, three of which involved detailed discussions and amendments on each chapter, section, and article. The Central Political Bureau and the Secretariat held eight special meetings for discussion, and a four-month nationwide discussion was held before submitting it to the Fifth Session of the Fifth National People's Congress.

On December 4, 1982, the Fifth Session of the Fifth National People's Congress adopted the new *Constitution*, the famous 1982 *Constitution*. The 1982 *Constitution* legally confirmed the achievements of the Chinese people of all ethnic groups, defined the fundamental system and tasks of the state, and became the general charter for managing state affairs. The implementation of the 1982 *Constitution* has a milestone significance, marking the entry of socialist democracy and socialist legal system construction into a new stage and serving as the highest legal basis for establishing and improving the People's Congress system in the new era.

Since 1978, the People's Congress system has been fully restored and continuously reformed, with new developments and improvements in many aspects. For example, the powers of the Standing Committee of the National People's Congress have been expanded; the organizational structure and working system of the National People's Congress and its Standing Committee have been improved; the Standing Committees of the People's Congresses at the county level and above have been established; it has been stipulated that provincial-level People's Congresses and their Standing Committees have the power to enact local regulations; it has been stipulated that the People's Congresses of larger cities and their Standing Committees can enact local regulations (which need to be implemented after approval by the Standing Committees of the provincial People's Congresses). The election system has been improved, among other things. In 2012, for the first time, the 18th CPC National Congress put forward that the People's Congress system is an institutional guarantee of socialism with Chinese characteristics, clarifying the status and role of the People's Congress system in socialism with Chinese characteristics.

"Those who know the house leaks are under the eaves; those who know the political losses are in the grassroots." When determining whether a political system is democratic or superior, the key is to see whether the will of the vast majority of the people is fully reflected, whether the right of the vast majority of people to be the masters of the country is fully realized and whether the legitimate rights and interests of the vast majority of the people are fully protected. In decades of practice, the People's Congress system has ensured the people's right to be the masters of the country, mobilized all the people to devote themselves to socialist construction as the masters of the country, ensured the coordinated and efficient operation of state organs, maintained national unity and ethnic solidarity, and brought together the strength of all the people to the greatest extent, under the leadership of the CPC, moving toward the national development goals with unity and efficiency. Facts have proved that this fundamental political system is reliable for realizing, safeguarding, and developing the fundamental interests of the vast majority of the people and for our country to withstand various risks and challenges and overcome various difficulties.

The Multi-Party Cooperation and Political Consultation System under the Leadership of the CPC

The multi-party cooperation and political consultation system in China is led by the CPC, which is different from the two-party or multi-party competition system in Western countries and the one-party system practiced in some countries. It is a new party system suitable for China's national conditions. The basic characteristics of this party system are "the CPC leads, multi-parties cooperate; the CPC governs, and multi-parties participate in politics."

In 1982, the 12th CPC National Congress expanded the eight-character policy of "long-term coexistence and mutual supervision" between the CPC and democratic parties, which was established in the 1950s, into the 16-character policy of "long-term coexistence, mutual supervision, sharing weal and woe, and working together closely" as the basic policy for multi-party cooperation in the new era and the basic principle for handling relations between the CPC and democratic parties. This 16-character policy later became the policy of the CPPCC.

In December 1989, the Central Committee of CPC issued the "Opinions of the Central Committee of CPC on Adhering to and Improving the Multi-Party Cooperation and Political Consultative System Led by the CPC," further clarifying that the multi-party cooperation and political consultation system led by the CPC is a basic political system in China, clarifying the status of democratic parties as participating parties in the state power of China, and proposing various institutional measures for the democratic parties to participate in politics and supervision.

Cheng Siwei, former Chairman of the Central Committee of the China Democratic National Construction Association, once used a special analogy to explain the relationship between the CPC and the democratic parties. He said: "Some friends from overseas asked me, since you are an independent party, why do you accept the leadership of the CPC? I explained to them that the Western party system is like 'playing rugby,' where one must overpower the other. Our party system is like 'singing a chorus.' The cooperation between the democratic parties and the CPC is for a common goal and to maintain social harmony. There must be a conductor to sing a chorus; historically and in reality, this conductor can only be the CPC. For a chorus to be sung, there must be a main melody, and this main melody is building socialism with Chinese characteristics."

In 1992, the 14th CPC National Congress made improving the multi-party cooperation and political consultation system led by the CPC one of the main contents of building socialism with Chinese characteristics and political system reform. In 1993, the constitutional amendment adopted by the First Session of the Eighth National People's Congress included "the multi-party cooperation and political consultation system led by the CPC will exist and develop for a long time" in the *Constitution*. In 2006 and 2007, the Central Committee of CPC successively issued two documents on the construction of the multi-party cooperation and political consultation system, namely the "Opinions of the Central Committee of CPC on Further Strengthening the Construction of the Multi-Party Cooperation and Political Consultative System Led by the CPC" and the "Opinions of the Central Committee of CPC on Strengthening the Work of the CPPCC." These two documents are the programmatic documents for the United Front work in the new era. These two documents emphasize the importance of democratic parties participating in politics, fulfilling their functions, and providing institutional guarantees. In July 2006, the Central Committee of CPC issued the "Opinions of the Central Committee of CPC on Consolidating and Expanding the United Front in the New Century and New Stage." In 2012, the Central Committee of CPC issued the "Opinions of the Central Committee of CPC on Strengthening the Construction of Non-CPC Representatives' Team under New Circumstances." This series of guiding documents marks the in-depth development of the regularization and proceduralization of China's multi-party cooperation and political consultation system.

The increasingly advancing process of democratization in China has led to the continuous development and growth of Chinese democratic parties and the CPPCC organizations. At the beginning of the founding of the People's Republic of China, there were a total of 11,000 members of various democratic parties, which increased to over 100,000 in 1956. By the time their activities were fully resumed in 1978, there were about 65,000 members. As of 2007, the total number of members of various democratic parties reached over 707,000, with 3,160 local CPPCC organizations at all levels and 615,000 CPPCC members at all levels.

After more than half a century of development, the functions of the CPPCC have become increasingly clear, and its operating mechanism has become increasingly mature, making it the main channel and form of consultative democracy in China. The main functions of the CPPCC are political consultation, democratic supervision, and participation in political decision-making. In March 1993, Li Ruihuan, then-Chairman of the CPPCC National Committee, pointed out in his speech at the closing session of the First Session of the Eighth CPPCC National Committee: "The democratic consultation method practiced by the CPPCC helps to fully absorb the opinions of various democratic parties, allowing both the leadership role of the CPC and the participation of democratic parties to be brought into play; it helps to broaden the channels for the public to express their opinions, respecting both the common wishes of the majority and the reasonable demands of the minority; it helps to promote democracy under the premise of unity and stability and consolidate and develop a stable political situation in the process of promoting democracy. This democratic consultation method is a great creation in China's democratic political construction and a major feature and advantage of China's socialist democratic system."

Political consultation with democratic parties on major decisions, important documents, and major personnel arrangements has become a political convention in China. According to statistics, from 1990 to the end of 2006, more than 230 consultation meetings, symposiums, and information briefing sessions were held by the Central Committee of CPC, the State Council, and relevant departments entrusted with the task, of which the General Secretary of the Central Committee of CPC chaired 74. In addition, central committees of various democratic parties and non-party representatives submitted more than 200 major written opinions and suggestions to the Central Committee of CPC, covering a wide range of areas such as economy, politics, society, education, science and technology, culture, health, national defense, diplomacy, Hong Kong, Macao, Taiwan, and overseas Chinese affairs.

After examining the actual operation of the CPPCC, Anders Powell, a professor of media studies at Stockholm University in Sweden, sincerely said: "Practice has proved that the National People's Congress and the CPPCC system are suitable for China's national conditions and conducive to China's development." Zhou Tienong, the then-Chairman of the Central Committee of the Revolutionary Committee of the Chinese KMT, who has served as Vice-Chairman of the 9th and 10th CPPCC National Committee and Vice-Chairman of the Standing Committee of the 11th National People's Congress, criticized the "vase theory" of democratic parties with his "personal experience." "There is always this argument that Chinese participating parties are just vases, merely decorations." "But for those of us who are truly working within the participating parties, our personal experience is completely different. When we see the strong support from the Central Government for the issues we want to solve, we feel that the 'multi-party cooperation' system has indeed played a significant role in China!"

The Establishment of Community-Level Self-Governance

The vigorous rural reforms during the early stages of reform and opening-up quickly impacted the highly integrated system of the people's communes, which combined the functions of government agencies, economic organizations, and grassroots society. In a short time, a power vacuum emerged in the countryside, and rural public affairs such as social security, social welfare, and land management were left unattended—the vast rural areas called for a new governance model.

Hezhai, a small village located at the junction of Yishan (now Yizhou District), Liujiang, and Xincheng counties in Guangxi, experienced chaos characterized by "six more, one less" after the abolition of the people's commune: more gambling and disturbances, more cattle and horse thefts, more random logging, more obscene songs, more unrestrained cattle and horses, more feudal superstitions, and fewer people in charge. The villagers were very dissatisfied with the chaotic security situation. Under the leadership of the village party organization, at the end of 1980, 85 farmers in Hezhai Village spontaneously organized elections for village officials and established the first villagers' committee in China. Based on the actual situation in the village, the Hezhai Village Villagers' Committee formulated village rules and regulations, set up management regulations, and democratically managed public affairs within the village in accordance with the law, pioneering grassroots democratic political construction in New China. "The village rules and regulations are good; there is no gambling or theft in the village. Public affairs are managed, and disputes have become fewer. We work on the four modernizations during the day and sleep peacefully at night." This self-composed folk song sung by the villagers is a spontaneous praise for village self-governance. The Central Government and the Ministry of Civil Affairs fully affirmed the self-governance initiative of Hezhai Village. It was subsequently promoted as an autonomous organization for grassroots rural masses. The 1982 *Constitution* explicitly stipulated the status and role of urban residents' committees and rural villagers' committees as grassroots mass self-governing organizations. By the end of 1982, similar organizations to villagers' committees had emerged in many regions nationwide.

In November 1987, the 23rd meeting of the Sixth National People's Congress Standing Committee adopted the *Organic Law of the Villagers' Committees of the People's Republic of China (Trial)* to standardize further and promote the development of villagers' committees. The law was implemented nationwide on June 1, 1987. A large number of farmers actively participated in the democratic election and construction of village committees according to the law. In 1991, Ping'an Village, Shuanghe Township, Lishu County, Jilin Province, adopted an open selection process to elect the village committee director. First, all eligible villagers participated in a secret ballot to nominate preliminary candidates. Then, the official candidates were determined by another secret ballot of all villagers. Finally, the formal election was held. The leaders selected through such a multi-stage process were like "finding a needle in a haystack," hence the term "open selection." No organization or individual was allowed to interfere in the entire election process. This was a great creation by the farmers. By 1992, grassroots democratic elections had been implemented in rural areas nationwide. In 1998, the *Villagers' Committee Organization Law* was revised and implemented, providing a legal basis for the standardization and institutionalization of village committee elections and grassroots democracy. Subsequently, all 31 provinces, autonomous regions, and municipalities directly under the Central Government completed three rounds of village committee elections. Seventeen provinces piloted or implemented the "open selection" method on a larger scale, where the villagers chose candidates by direct voting and decision-making.

As the 21st century began, rural areas creatively introduced new election methods, such as the two-vote and double recommendation systems, making further progress in grassroots democracy. The 16th CPC National Congress report pointed out, "Expanding grassroots democracy is the fundamental work of developing socialist democracy." The 17th CPC National Congress, for the first time, incorporated the grassroots mass self-government system into the basic category of the socialist democratic political system with Chinese characteristics, clearly stating, "The people exercise their democratic rights directly according to the law, manage grassroots public affairs and public welfare undertakings, implement self-management, self-service, self-education, and self-supervision, and exercise democratic supervision over officials. This is the most effective and widespread approach for the people to be masters of their own affairs and must be prioritized as a fundamental project for the development of socialist democratic politics."

Affected by the rural governance reforms, urban self-government has also gradually become institutionalized. In September 1986, after the promulgation and implementation of the "Regulations on the Workers' Representative Conference of State-Owned Industrial Enterprises" by the Central Committee of CPC and the State Council, workers began to participate in enterprise management through workers' representative conferences on an institutionalized basis. In accordance with the relevant provisions of the 1982 *Constitution*, by the end of 1986, more than 80,000 residents' committees had been established nationwide. After direct elections emerged in rural areas, scattered cases of direct elections of community residents' committees appeared in some large and medium-sized cities in the late 20th century. In 1998, the second and sixth residents' committees of Ruichang Road Street in Sifang District, Qingdao, initiated the direct election of urban community committees. In 2000, the Ministry of Civil Affairs began to promote community construction nationwide. It advocated the principles of expanding democracy and residents' self-government, requiring urban communities to implement democratic elections, democratic decision-making, democratic management, and democratic supervision, and gradually achieve community residents' self-management, self-education, self-service, and self-supervision. From 2002 onwards, community direct elections gradually became widespread. To further promote the development of urban grassroots democracy, starting in 2006, the Ministry of Civil Affairs encouraged the election behavior of community residents' committees, including adopting various forms such as public speeches, meetings, wall newspapers, and broadcasts, and standardized specific procedures such as open voting and on-the-spot announcement of election results. In 2008, more than 70% of Shenzhen's community residents' committees began direct elections.

The 17th CPC National Congress report regarded the "grassroots mass self-government system" as an important part of the development path of socialist politics with Chinese characteristics, and the grassroots democratic self-government system has become increasingly perfected. In 2010, the *Organic Law of Villagers' Committees* was amended, establishing the village affairs supervision committee system, putting democratic elections, democratic decision-making, democratic management, and democratic supervision into practice. In fact, the prototype of the villagers' supervision committee system was born on June 18, 2004, in Houchen Village, Wuyi County, Jinhua City, Zhejiang Province. In June 2005, Xi Jinping, then Secretary of the Zhejiang Provincial Party Committee, visited Houchen Village to investigate and study the village affairs supervision committee system, affirming their practices and requiring promotion.

Admittedly, there are various problems in the grassroots democracy system, but grassroots democracy has taken solid steps, and the democratic consciousness of the grassroots masses has been cultivated and trained. With the increasing improvement of the urban and rural grassroots self-governance system, China has established a grassroots democratic self-governance system consisting mainly of rural villagers' committees, urban residents' committees, and workers' representative assemblies in enterprises and institutions. Hundreds of millions are managing their affairs according to the law and actively participating in democratic practice activities.

Implementation of the Basic Strategy of Governing the Country according to Law

Following the requirements for strengthening democracy and the rule of law proposed by the third plenary session of the eleventh CPC Central Committee, the Party and the state have taken a series of important measures since 1979. In February 1979, the Sixth Session of the Standing Committee of the Fifth National People's Congress (NPC) decided to establish the Legal Affairs Committee of the NPC Standing Committee. In June of the same year, the Second Session of the Fifth NPC discussed and passed seven important laws. In August 1980, the NPC Standing Committee initiated a great project of democracy and the rule of law construction, the revision of the *Constitution*. In November 1982, the Constitutional Amendment Committee held two plenary meetings and unanimously agreed to submit the "Draft Amendment to the Constitution of the People's Republic of China" and the report on the draft amendment to the Fifth Session of the Fifth NPC for deliberation. The 1982 *Constitution*, which is the current *Constitution*, has played a significant role in governing the country and ensuring its stability.

To adapt to the new situation and new requirements of the rapid development of reform and opening-up and socialist modernization, legislative work and legal popularization work have been significantly strengthened. In November 1985, the

Central Committee of CPC and the State Council issued a notice on the "Five-Year Plan for Basic Legal Popularization among All Citizens" proposed by the Central Publicity Department and the Ministry of Justice. Subsequently, the Sixth NPC Standing Committee adopted the "Resolution on Basic Legal Popularization among Citizens" and decided to carry out legal education nationwide in 1986. The judicial departments carried out legal popularization activities in various forms, including producing TV dramas and films and inviting experts to give lectures on the rule of law. A lecture on the rule of law was held in Zhongnanhai to promote the popularization of law. On the morning of July 3, 1986, the first legal lecture for central leaders was held at Huairen Hall in Zhongnanhai. Central leaders listened to Sun Guohua, then associate professor of Renmin University of China, on "Several Points of Understanding on the Nature and Function of Law." Starting this year, carrying out legal education in the form of a "Five-Year Plan" has become an important part of China's rule of law construction.

Since the fourth plenary session of the thirteenth CPC Central Committee, the Central Committee of CPC has attached great importance to the construction of the rule of law and accelerated the process of governing the country according to law and building a socialist country under the rule of law. On September 26, 1989, Jiang Zemin pointed out, "We must never substitute the Party for the government, nor should we substitute the Party for the law." "We must follow the principle of the rule of law." In his Fourteenth CPC National Congress report, Jiang Zemin stated that strengthening legislative work was an "urgent requirement for establishing a socialist market economic system." While legislative work was constantly being strengthened, from December 1994 to July 2001, the Central Committee of CPC held 12 legal lectures, demonstrating the central committee's emphasis on the construction of the rule of law. Among them, the lecture on "The Theory and Practice of Governing the Country according to Law and Building a Socialist Country under the Rule of Law" held on February 8, 1996, was proposed by Jiang Zemin. In his concluding speech at the lecture, he pointed out that implementing and adhering to the rule of law was significant for promoting sustained, rapid, and healthy economic development, comprehensive social progress, and ensuring national long-term stability. In March 1996, the Fourth Session of the Eighth National People's Congress included "governing the country according to law" as the goal and direction of China's political system reform in the "Outline of the Ninth Five-Year Plan for National Economic and Social Development and the 2010 Long-term Objectives" approved by the conference.

The Fifteenth CPC National Congress held in 1997 established governing the country according to law as a national strategy. The report of the Fifteenth Congress pointed out: "Governing the country according to law, building a socialist country under the rule of law. Governing the country according to law means that the broad masses of the people, under the leadership of the Party, manage state affairs, economic and cultural undertakings, and social affairs in accordance with the *Constitution* and laws and ensure that all aspects of national work are carried out according to law, gradually realizing the institutionalization and legalization of socialist democracy, making such systems and laws unchanged due to changes in leadership and changes in leaders' opinions and focus. Governing the country according to law is the basic strategy of the Party leading the people in governing the country." In March 1999, the Second Session of the Ninth NPC passed the constitutional amendment, which added the content of "governing the country according to law and building a socialist country under the rule of law" and established it in the form of the basic strategy of the state. After the Fifteenth CPC National Congress, the construction of the rule of law in China was further strengthened. By 2001, in addition to the *Constitution*, the NPC and its Standing Committee had enacted 284 laws, 117 decisions on legal issues, and two explanations, totaling 403; the State Council had issued or approved the issuance of 913 administrative regulations by departments. These laws and regulations further improved the basic legal content in criminal, civil, and state institutions.

In 2007, the Seventeenth CPC National Congress proposed to adhere to the path of political development of socialism with Chinese characteristics, adhere to the organic unity of the Party's leadership, the people being the masters of the country, and governing the country according to law, further pointing out the direction for the construction of the rule of law. The legislative work in this stage has achieved remarkable results. By the end of 2010, in addition to the *Constitution* and its four amendments, China had enacted 236 currently valid laws, 690 administrative regulations, and more than 8,600 local regulations. The legal departments covering all aspects of social relations have been completed, the basic and major laws in each legal department have been enacted, the corresponding administrative regulations and local regulations are relatively complete, and the overall internal legal system has achieved scientific and harmonious unity. A socialist legal system with Chinese characteristics, based on China's national conditions and realities, adapting to the needs of reform and opening-up and socialist modernization, reflecting the will of the Party and the people, with the *Constitution* as the commander, the *Constitution*-related laws, civil and commercial laws, and other legal departments' laws as the mainstay, and composed of legal norms at various levels, such as laws, administrative regulations, and local regulations, has been formed, enabling all aspects of national construction to have laws to follow.

Chapter 16

National Unity, Diplomacy, and National Defense

S ince the reform and opening-up, under the strong leadership of the CPC, the great cause of national unity has taken important steps, with Hong Kong and Macau returning to the motherland's embrace and the cross-strait relations progressing amid waves. China has always adhered to the path of peaceful development, showing the world the image of a major power pursuing peaceful development, persisted in the path of building a powerful military, and made significant achievements in national defense and military construction.

The Proposal and Practice of the "One Country, Two Systems" Principle

National unity is the common aspiration of all Chinese people. Since the emergence of the Taiwan issue in 1949, the CPC has always regarded resolving the Taiwan issue and completing the great cause of national unity as its sacred duty, making unremitting efforts for a long time. In the 1950s and 1960s, China experienced a process of moving from the military liberation of Taiwan to the peaceful liberation of Taiwan, which eventually formed the proposal for the peaceful resolution of the Taiwan issue summarized by Mao Zedong and Zhou Enlai, known as the "One Guideline, Four Points."* After the reform and opening-up, the CPC continued to dedicate itself to the cause of national unity. In light of the changing domestic and international situation and considering the fundamental interests of the Chinese nation and the overall strategy of national development, Deng Xiaoping creatively put forward the great concept of "One Country, Two Systems," making a historic contribution to the establishment of the principle of "peaceful unification and One Country, Two Systems." The "One Country, Two Systems" concept was first successfully practiced in the cases of Hong Kong and Macau. Influenced by this, cross-strait relations also developed relatively quickly.

January 1, 1979, was an extraordinary day, as described by Deng Xiaoping. He said, "It is extraordinary because it has three distinct features compared to previous New Year's Days: first, the focus of our national work has shifted to the construction of the four modernizations; second, Sino-US relations have been normalized; and third, the great cause of reunifying Taiwan with the motherland and completing national unity has been put on a specific agenda." On this day, the Standing Committee of the National People's Congress issued the "Message to Taiwan Compatriots," stating that the reunification of China was the aspiration of the people and the trend of the times, and solemnly declared the major policy of peaceful reunification of the motherland. At the same time, the Ministry of National Defense announced the cessation of the decades-long bombardment of Jinmen, and the mainland continuously sent out peaceful signals. On the eve of National Day in 1981, Ye Jianying, Chairman of the Standing Committee of the National People's Congress, elaborated on the nine principles of the Chinese government regarding Taiwan's return to the motherland and the achievement of peaceful unification in a speech to Xinhua News Agency reporters. On January 11, 1982, Deng Xiaoping commented on Ye Jianying's nine principles, stating that this was essentially "One Country, Two Systems," under the premise of national unity, the country's main body implementing the socialist system,

---

* The "One Guideline" refers to "as long as Taiwan returns to the motherland, all other issues will be properly handled with full respect for the President's and Brother's opinions." The "Four Points" include "After Taiwan's return to the motherland, except that foreign affairs must be unified with the central government, all military and political powers and personnel arrangements will be fully handled by the President and Brother; all military, political, and construction expenses, if insufficient, will be allocated by the central government; social reforms in Taiwan can proceed slowly, and must wait for conditions to mature, and then be carried out in consultation with and respect for the opinions of the President and Brother; both sides mutually agree not to send people to undermine the unity of the other party."

See Jin Chongjin, *The Biography of Mao Zedong (1949–1976)*, vol. 1 (Beijing: Central Literature Publishing House, 2003), 881.

and Taiwan implementing the capitalist system. The widely significant and important summary of "One Country, Two Systems" was thus formed. The principle of "One Country, Two Systems" and the peaceful reunification of the motherland was officially proposed and passed in the "Government Work Report" of the Second Session of the Sixth National People's Congress on May 15, 1984. "One Country, Two Systems" became a basic national policy with legal effect. The mainland opened the door to cross-strait exchanges with Taiwan compatriots. In November 1987, under strong public demand, the Taiwan authorities allowed Taiwan residents to visit the mainland for family reunions. The 38-year-long separation across the strait was finally broken. Since then, "family reunion" and "root-seeking" have become the most popular terms between the two sides for many years. Millions of people traveling between the two sides of the Taiwan Strait for family reunions and tourism have built numerous air bridges to maintain the stability of cross-strait relations.

"One Country, Two Systems" was first applied to solve the Hong Kong and Macau issues. After arduous negotiations, China and the United Kingdom, China and Portugal agreed on the return of Hong Kong and Macau. On June 30, 1997, China and the UK held a handover ceremony for Hong Kong's sovereignty at midnight. On July 1, the Hong Kong Special Administrative Region of the People's Republic of China was officially established. This dazzling pearl of the Orient finally returned to the motherland's embrace, marking the end of a century of humiliation for the Chinese nation. At midnight of December 19, 1999, China and Portugal held a handover ceremony for Macau's sovereignty. On December 20, the Macau Special Administrative Region of the People's Republic of China was officially established, taking another important step forward in the great cause of national unity. The smooth return of Hong Kong and Macau is a milestone event in the process of the great cause of national unity.

The Central Committee of CPC has always considered the development of Hong Kong and Macau within the nation's overall development, providing policy support and favoritism to Hong Kong and Macau. In March 2006, the Tenth National People's Congress approved the "Outline of the Eleventh Five-Year Plan for National Economic and Social Development," which explicitly incorporated Hong Kong and Macau into the overall national planning, fully demonstrating the Central Committee's concern and support for the Hong Kong and Macau Special Administrative Regions and reflecting their important positions in the national development strategy. In October 2010, the Central Committee specifically planned for the development of Hong Kong and Macau in its "Twelfth Five-Year Plan" proposal, the most important of which was supporting Hong Kong in consolidating and enhancing its status as an international financial, trade, and shipping center, strengthening its industrial innovation capabilities, and promoting coordinated economic and social development. It also supported Macau in building a world tourism and leisure center and promoting moderately diversified economic development.

Since the return of Hong Kong and Macau, China has adhered to the principles of "One Country, Two Systems," supporting Hong Kong and Macau in integrating their own development into the overall development of the country and a high degree of autonomy. Although some issues remain to be addressed, Hong Kong and Macau have maintained a stable development trend overall.

With the resolution of the Hong Kong and Macau issues, to promote the development of cross-strait relations, the mainland's authorized civilian organization, the Association for Relations Across the Taiwan Straits (ARATS), was established in Beijing on December 16, 1991, with Wang Daohan as its president, and actively carried out its work. In November 1992, ARATS and the Straits Exchange Foundation of Taiwan held talks and political dialogue on common issues such as dispute resolution and crime prevention across the strait, reaching a consensus that both sides recognized the "One China Principle" but expressed it differently, which was called the "1992 Consensus." On August 31, 1993, the Taiwan Affairs Office of the State Council and the Press Office jointly issued the white paper *The Taiwan Issue and China's Reunification*, which systematically expounded on the major policies of the CPC and the Central Government on the peaceful reunification of the two sides of the strait.

In January 1995, Jiang Zemin delivered a speech titled "Continue to Strive for the Completion of the Great Cause of Peaceful Reunification of the Motherland," putting forward eight proposals to advance the process of peaceful reunification. On March 4, 2005, during a joint discussion with members of the Democratic League, Taiwan League, and Taiwan Federation, Hu Jintao put forward four points on developing cross-strait relations under the new situation. These proposals significantly impacted both sides of the strait and the international community. To curb and combat the "Taiwan independence" forces' attempt to split the country, promote the peaceful reunification of the motherland, and maintain peace and stability in the Taiwan Strait region, on March 14, 2005, the Third Session of the Tenth National People's Congress deliberated and passed the *Anti-Secession Law*, declaring the strong will of the Chinese people to uphold national unity and territorial integrity for the first time in the form of national legislation. The Central Government has also taken practical actions to encourage Taiwan businesses to invest and set up factories on the mainland, promoting economic and cultural exchanges between the two sides of the strait and between political parties. The Chairmen of the KMT of China, Lian Zhan, the People First Party of Taiwan, Song Chuyu, and the New Party of Taiwan, Yu Muming, visited the mainland in succession, highlighting the shared roots and origin across the strait and strengthening the consciousness of One China.

During the process of cross-strait exchanges, economic and trade interactions have been the most eye-catching. In April 2006, the cross-strait economic and trade forum was held in Beijing, and the mainland announced 15 policy measures to promote cross-strait exchanges and cooperation and benefit the Taiwan people. On October 17 of the same year, the cross-strait agricultural cooperation forum was held in Boao, Hainan, and the mainland introduced 20 policy measures to expand and deepen cross-strait agricultural cooperation. From 2007 onward, the forum has been named the "Cross-Strait Economic, Trade and Cultural Forum" by both the CPC and the KMT. More than ten forum sessions have been held so far, promoting economic, trade, and cultural exchanges between the two sides of the strait. Mutual assistance reflects the affection between the people on both sides of the strait. When Taiwan's fruit sales were sluggish, the mainland actively extended a helping hand to help them solve practical problems. When the devastating earthquake struck Wenchuan, Sichuan, in 2008, the Taiwan rescue team did not take the Spring Festival charter flight detouring through Hong Kong but directly flew to Chengdu Shuangliu Airport, joining the earthquake relief efforts at the first moment, reflecting the blood ties and shared destiny between the people on both sides of the strait.

On December 31, 2008, at a symposium commemorating the 30th anniversary of the "Message to Taiwan Compatriots," Hu Jintao comprehensively and systematically expounded on the ideas of peaceful development of cross-strait relations and put forward six opinions on promoting the peaceful development of cross-strait relations in the new century and at the new stage, namely: adhering to one China and enhancing political mutual trust; promoting economic cooperation for common development; carrying forward Chinese culture and strengthening spiritual ties; enhancing personnel exchanges and expanding exchanges among all sectors; safeguarding national sovereignty and negotiating foreign affairs; ending the hostile state and reaching a peace agreement. These six opinions fully demonstrated the sincerity of peacefully resolving the Taiwan issue and caused a significant response across the strait.

The Cross-Strait Economic Cooperation Framework Agreement was signed on June 29, 2010, to promote cross-strait economic exchanges further. This was a milestone in the normalization and institutionalization of cross-strait economic relations, marking a new historical starting point for cross-strait economic relations.

Stick to the Path of Peaceful Development

Since the reform and opening-up, the rapidly developing China has become a focus of continuous attention worldwide. When China's development faced difficulties, some people claimed that China was about to collapse, putting forward the so-called "China Collapse Theory." When China overcame obstacles and achieved development, some people said that China posed a threat, concocting the so-called "China Threat Theory." In the face of great international attention, the CPC has always upheld the banner of peaceful cooperation and development, adhered to the fine tradition of peaceful development, repeatedly expressed its determination to follow the path of peaceful development, and elevated the path of peaceful development to the level of national strategy.

In the 1980s, Deng Xiaoping emphasized, "To achieve the Four Modernizations, carry out reform and opening-up, we need a stable and united political situation domestically and a peaceful environment internationally. We put forward our foreign policy based on this situation: opposing hegemonism, safeguarding world peace, promoting international cooperation and common prosperity." Under Deng Xiaoping's leadership, China insisted on independence and autonomy, adhered to principles in international affairs, and kept its promises. As a permanent member of the UN Security Council, China played an important role in promoting the resolution of major regional conflicts such as the Iran-Iraq War, the Cambodian issue, and the Six-Party Talks on North Korea's nuclear issue. China has participated in major international organizations such as the World Bank and the International Monetary Fund (IMF), positively impacting the environment, food, crime prevention, drug control, and refugees. In international human rights, China advocates dialogue, opposes confrontation, and forcefully counters the erroneous views put forward by Western countries.

Pursue an independent and peaceful foreign policy. In May 1984, Deng Xiaoping summarized China's foreign policy as an independent foreign policy, pointing out that "China's foreign policy is independent," and it is "truly non-aligned," specifically manifested as "four nos and one comprehensive": non-alignment, non-isolation, non-confrontation, not targeting any third country, and comprehensively engaging in diplomatic activities. The core is non-alignment. Later, Deng Xiaoping repeatedly said that China should not be afraid of anyone but should not offend anyone. Friends should be made, priorities should be clear, and China should focus on its affairs. Establishing diplomatic relations between China and the United States in the late 1970s and improving Sino-Soviet relations in the 1980s are examples of China's independent foreign policy. For instance, from May 15 to 18, 1989, Mikhail Gorbachev, the top leader of the Soviet Union, visited China. Deng Xiaoping carefully considered and decided on the theme of the meeting: "Ending the past and opening up the future." Through this high-level meeting, China and the Soviet Union, two major neighboring countries, finally ended their abnormal state for decades.

In the 1990s, the disappearance of the Soviet Union led to the formation of a new international pattern featuring "one superpower (referring to the United States) and several strong powers (referring to China, Russia, the European Union, Japan, etc.)." Against the backdrop of great turbulence in the international situation, China still adhered to peaceful development, with its independent diplomacy becoming more flexible and pragmatic. During this stage, Sino-US relations experienced ups and downs, including the "Yinhe Incident," the Taiwan Strait Crisis, and the US Bombing of the Chinese Embassy in Yugoslavia. During this period, China actively developed international relations. The Shanghai Cooperation Organization, formed with Russia and Central Asian countries, was a political and security alliance against terrorism, religious extremism, and separatism.

The China-ASEAN Free Trade Area, built with Southeast Asian countries, was an economic and tariff alliance. At the same time, China was strengthening traditional and non-traditional security cooperation with Southeast Asian countries, and so on. Whether it is conducive to China's national interests, international peace, and world development has become the only criterion for China's independent diplomacy today. In dealing with relations with small and medium-sized countries and developing countries, China is now pursuing a win-win policy based on the development of the international situation and its existing national strength. China adheres to its national interests while properly taking care of and assisting developing countries. It does not act arrogantly but assumes certain responsibilities for the stability of the East Asian political and economic situation. China's performance during the Southeast Asian financial crisis, its efforts to actively integrate regional economies, and its signing of the "Declaration on the Conduct of Parties" with relevant countries in the South China Sea fully demonstrate China's understanding and attitude toward regional responsibilities. In short, with Jiang Zemin as the main representative, the Chinese

Communists creatively inherited and developed Deng Xiaoping's diplomatic thought, pushing China's diplomacy forward and achieving new successes. In constructing the framework of major power relations, China promoted the establishment of a new type of cooperative relationship with major powers oriented toward the 21st century. In actively developing good-neighborly friendships, China achieved full diplomatic relations with Asian countries and created a favorable peripheral environment. In strengthening solidarity and cooperation with developing countries, China widely participated in international affairs, safeguarded world peace, and promoted common development.

In the 21st century, China continues to adhere to peaceful development. The 16th CPC National Congress pointed out that peace and development are the "common aspirations" of the people of all countries, and China should work together with the people of all countries to "jointly maintain" and "jointly promote" the cause of peace and development. China should "jointly consult" with other countries on world affairs, safeguard the "common interests" of all mankind, and achieve the "common prosperity" of all countries. In response to some erroneous international arguments that suppress or flatter China, such as the "China Threat Theory" and the "China Responsibility Theory," China put forward new ideas for promoting the construction of a harmonious world and continued to follow the path of peaceful development unswervingly. The 17th CPC National Congress in 2007 reaffirmed that no matter how the international situation changes, the Chinese government and people will always uphold the banner of peace, development, and cooperation, pursue an independent and peaceful foreign policy, safeguard national sovereignty, security, and development interests, adhere to the diplomatic policy of maintaining world peace and promoting common development, and emphasized that "China will always follow the path of peaceful development," and "this is a strategic choice made by the Chinese government and people based on the trend of the times and their fundamental interests."

Actions speak louder than words. The Beijing Summit of the Forum on China-Africa Cooperation is a typical manifestation of China's practice of the concept of peaceful development. On November 4, 2006, representatives from 48 African countries gathered in the Great Hall of the People, including 35 heads of state, six heads of government, one vice president, six high-level representatives, and the chairperson of the African Union Commission. South African President Mbeki lamented that some African leaders had not attended African Union summits for years, but this time, they came to Beijing, making it even more well-attended than African Union meetings themselves. The summit was significant for consolidating and developing friendly relations between China and African countries and demonstrating China's peaceful development concept to the world. On December 26, 2008, in accordance with relevant resolutions of the United Nations Security Council and with the approval of the State Council and the Central Military Commission, the Chinese Navy sent its first fleet from the Hainan Sanya Military Port to the Gulf of Aden and Somalia for escort missions. This was the first time since the founding of New China that the Chinese military had organized naval forces to go overseas to fulfill international humanitarian obligations, attracting great attention at home and abroad and showcasing China's responsible great power image in maintaining peace. On May 13, 2012, the leaders of China, South Korea, and Japan announced in Beijing that the three countries agreed to launch negotiations on a China-Japan-Korea Free Trade Area within the year. This meant that after a decade of efforts, the three East Asian countries, with a combined economy accounting for one-fifth of the global total, officially embarked on the process of building a free trade area. These major initiatives are important measures taken by China to adhere to its peaceful development diplomatic policy and promote the construction of a harmonious world.

Modernization of National Defense and the Armed Forces

Building an iron Great Wall and a strong, modernized national defense force has been an important national defense and military construction goal since the reform and opening-up. In January 1979, the Central Military Commission held a symposium, during which Defense Minister Marshal Xu Xiangqian pointed out that shifting the focus to the Four Modernizations for the military meant modernizing national defense. After 1985, the Central Military Commission of the CPC studied and adjusted some specific contents of the "active defense" military strategic guideline, adding more era-specific contents, such as strengthening containment of war, maintaining peace, and dealing with small-scale local wars and emergencies. In December 1988, the expanded meeting of the Central Military Commission re-established the "active defense" military strategic guideline in its entirety.

The restoration of the military rank system and the implementation of the civilian cadre system in the military were carried out in the 1980s. In July 1988, the Third Session of the Seventh Standing Committee of the National People's Congress passed the "Regulations on Military Ranks of the People's Liberation Army of China," restoring the military rank system and deciding that all officers and soldiers would wear new military rank insignia starting from October 1, 1988. In April 1988, the Central Military Commission officially issued the "Interim Regulations of the People's Liberation Army of China for Civilian Cadres." By August 30 of that year, the work of converting the first batch of active-duty military officers to civilian cadres in the PLA was successfully completed, with a total of more than 100,000 people being transferred to civilian cadres. The implementation of this system was beneficial to the stability of the professional and technical cadre team within the army. Under the guidance of the idea of advancing toward a professional military, the PLA also underwent a series of significant adjustments and reforms in its organizational structure.

In the face of the dramatic changes in the international situation in the 1990s, the rapid development of the new global military revolution, and the trend of widening gaps in military development at home and abroad, China has established its military strategic guidelines for the new era. After Jiang Zemin became Chairman of the Central Military Commission, he put forward the overall requirements for the construction of the armed forces in the new era in December 1990, namely that the entire army must be politically qualified, militarily proficient, have excellent style, strict discipline, and strong support. In January 1993, the expanded meeting of the Central Military Commission made a major adjustment in military strategy, shifting the focus of military struggle preparation from dealing with local wars under general conditions to winning local wars under modern, especially high-tech conditions. This new-era military strategic guideline provided a scientific basis for national defense and military construction and pointed out the direction for development. The Central Committee of CPC also solemnly presented the two historical issues of winning and not degenerating to the whole army based on the new historical conditions. At the beginning of the 21st century, the Central Military Commission, based on the scientific judgment that high-tech warfare is essentially information warfare, enriched the connotation of the new-era military strategic guidelines and adjusted the focus of military struggle preparation to winning local wars under informed conditions.

To implement the new-era military strategic guidelines, in 1997, the Central Military Commission put forward the strategic concept of "three steps" for the cross-century development of national defense and military modernization: the first step is to strive to achieve the various requirements put forward by the new-era military strategic guidelines from now until 2010 and lay a solid foundation for national defense and military modernization over a decade. The second step is to accelerate the pace of military quality construction in the second decade of the 21st century, along with the growth of the country's economic strength and the corresponding increase in military spending, appropriately increase the development of high-tech weapons and equipment, improve the weapons and equipment system, comprehensively improve the quality of troops, further optimize the system and establishment, and achieve greater development of national defense and military modernization. The third step is to achieve national defense and military modernization by the middle of the 21st century after another thirty years of effort. Subsequently, the Central Committee of CPC further clarified that the basic benchmark for achieving national defense and military modernization is informatization. In April 1998, the Central Military Commission formulated the reform plan for the military system and establishment during the "Ninth Five-Year Plan" period. In that year, at the suggestion of Jiang Zemin, the Chairman of the Central Military Commission, the General Equipment Department was officially established, realizing the centralized and unified leadership of military weapons and equipment construction. During this period, the ideological and political construction of the military was strengthened, the commercial activities of various military branches and armed police forces were halted, the strategy of building a strong army through science and technology was proposed, the "two fundamental changes" were implemented,** and the conscription system, non-commissioned officer system, military housing system, military insurance system, and others were reformed, presenting a new outlook for national defense and military construction.

Since the 16th CPC National Congress, the Central Committee of CPC has accurately grasped the new requirements for national defense and military construction in the new century and the new stage, scientifically expounded on the historical mission of our army in the new century and the new stage, and clearly put forward the important guiding principle of using the scientific development concept to strengthen national defense and military construction, providing fundamental guidance for promoting the scientific development of national defense and military construction from a higher starting point. In September 2004, the fourth plenary session of the 16th CPC Central Committee agreed to Jiang Zemin's request to resign as Chairman of the CPC Central Military Commission and decided that Hu Jintao would be the Chairman of the CPC Central Military Commission. In October 2006, Hu Jintao put forward the requirement of "building a revolutionary army that follows the Party's command, serves the people, and is brave and good at fighting." In October 2007, the

---

** In terms of military combat readiness, there has been a shift from preparing for localized warfare under general conditions to preparing to win localized warfare under modern technological conditions, especially high-tech conditions. In terms of military construction, there has been a transformation from a quantity and scale model to a quality and efficiency model, and from labor-intensive to technology-intensive.

17th CPC National Congress pointed out that we must stand at the height of the overall situation of national security and development strategy, coordinate economic construction and national defense construction, and realize the unity of a wealthy country and a strong army in the process of building a well-off society in an all-round way. During this stage, the Central Committee of CPC persisted in building a strong military through science and technology, vigorously implemented the talent strategy project, promoted military training under informed conditions, and established and improved the weapon and equipment research and production system and the joint logistics support system of the military, continuously improving the scientific level of military construction.

The number of soldiers is not the key, but their quality and effectiveness are crucial. Entering the new period of reform and opening-up, the Central Military Commission made three major force reductions based on the judgments of the international situation, the central task of the Party, and the actual situation of our army. The first one was in 1985, personally decided by Deng Xiaoping. The expanded meeting of the Central Military Commission held that year made a major decision to reduce the military personnel by one million after discussion. Deng Xiaoping pointed out, "Reducing the number of the Chinese PLA by one million is a manifestation of the strength and confidence of the CPC, the Chinese government, and the Chinese people." By early 1987, the task of reducing the army by one million was successfully completed. Through this streamlining and restructuring, not only was the total size of the military effectively compressed, reducing the total number of troops from 4.236 million to 3.235 million, but the proportion of military establishment was also adjusted and optimized. The second time was in 1997 when Jiang Zemin announced at the 15th CPC National Congress that based on reducing the army by one million in the 1980s, another 500,000 personnel would be cut within the next three years. The third time was in 2003, when the Central Committee of CPC and the Central Military Commission decided to reduce the number of military personnel by 200,000 before 2005, keeping the army's total scale at 2.3 million. The three major force reductions kept pace with the global military revolution and laid a solid foundation for embarking on the path of building a highly skilled and efficient military with Chinese characteristics.

Since the reform and opening-up, the PLA has carried out military exchanges with many countries' armies worldwide and actively participated in major domestic events, playing an important role in peacetime. In the new century and the new stage, the army actively participated in combating the SARS epidemic and disaster relief efforts, such as the Wenchuan and Yushu earthquakes. For example, after the massive

Wenchuan earthquake in 2008, the army rushed to the disaster area in no time, effectively playing the role of a pioneering pathfinder, and gained valuable time for rescuing disaster victims and fighting against the earthquake. Especially on May 14, 2008, at 11:47 a.m., seven of the 15 paratroopers took the lead in fearlessly jumping from a height of 4,999 meters above the earthquake-stricken area. At that time, dozens of hours had passed since the Wenchuan earthquake occurred. The area beneath their feet, one of the hardest-hit areas in Sichuan, Mao County, had lost communication and was cut off from the outside world, becoming an isolated island. But this was a "suicidal" parachute jump, unprecedented in the history of world military aviation, as it was carried out from about 5,000 meters under "three nos" conditions—no meteorological data, no ground markers, and no command guidance. Half an hour later, the disaster situation of the epicenter's isolated island was reported for the first time. The soldiers risked their lives to maintain the peaceful situation in China. During this stage, the PLA successfully completed the military parade celebrating the 60th anniversary of the founding of the People's Republic of China and major tasks such as security support for the Beijing Olympics and Shanghai World Expo. The PLA's execution of various tasks, large-scale deployment, and frequent troop dispatches was rare since the reform and opening-up, embodying the saying "train troops for a thousand days, use troops for a moment." The PLA also actively participated in and supported local economic construction, such as participating in the development of the western region, the construction of a new socialist countryside, key local infrastructure projects, and ecological and environmental construction. These "most lovable people" have won the praise of the general public with their practical actions and truly deserve to be regarded as a civilized and mighty force.

CHAPTER 17

The New Great Project of Party Building

The key to handling China's affairs lies in the Party. The CPC faces constant changes in the world, national, Party, and people's sentiments, as well as numerous challenges from within and outside the Party. The CPC must continuously adjust itself and strengthen its self-construction. The practice of reform and opening-up and the construction of socialist modernization in the new era shows that the CPC has withstood complex and severe tests through strict governance and self-discipline.

Governing the Country Must Start with Governing the Party

As the leadership core of China's socialist undertakings, the quality of the CPC's self-construction is closely related to China's future and destiny. The CPC has been able to stand tall through hardships and become stronger through trials because it has always insisted on governing the Party strictly, focusing on strengthening its self-construction and ensuring its own integrity.

In the early stage of reform and opening-up, the CPC Central Commission for Discipline Inspection took the lead in formulating the "Several Guidelines on Party's

Internal Political Life," which explicitly emphasized the maintenance of the Party's centralization and unity, strict adherence to Party discipline, and played a positive role in maintaining a serious political life within the Party. In response to issues such as special treatment for cadres being discussed by the masses, the Central Committee of CPC formulated the "Several Regulations on the Living Allowances of Senior Cadres" to rectify the Party's style and improve people's customs, using regulations to standardize the living allowances of senior cadres. The 12th CPC National Congress in 1982 first proposed the overall goal and requirements of Party building in the new era: to build the Party into a strong core leading the cause of socialist modernization, thus pointing out the direction for the Party building in the new era.

With the progress of reform and opening-up, some corrupt elements emerged, damaging the Party's internal atmosphere and social customs. Deng Xiaoping resolutely advocated severe punishment for these corrupt elements. To strengthen the Party's construction and improve the Party's leadership, the Central Committee of CPC decided to carry out party rectification in 1983, focusing on a comprehensive rectification of the Party's style and organization. The report of the 13th CPC National Congress in 1987 pointed out that "strengthen Party's discipline, besides expelling a few corrupt elements from the Party, it is also necessary to focus on educating the vast majority of Party members and improve their quality." During the rectification period, the CPC made a firm decision to crack down on "official profiteering," and some high-ranking children who violated national laws were severely dealt with, causing a huge impact on society. The political turmoil in 1989 exposed weak links in the Party's construction. On June 16 of that year, Deng Xiaoping told the central leaders: "The comrades of the Standing Committee must focus on Party building. It's time to strengthen the Party, and it can no longer be delayed."

After Jiang Zemin was elected as the Central Committee General Secretary, he kept Deng Xiaoping's political instructions in mind and paid close attention to the Party's construction. On August 28, 1989, the Political Bureau of the Central Committee of CPC passed the "Notice of the Central Committee of CPC on Strengthening Party Building," further deploying Party-building efforts. In the late 1980s and early 1990s, as many long-governing political parties in the world, especially communist party organizations, successively fell from power, the dissolution of the CPSU drew the attention and reflection of the CPC. The CPSU seized power with 200,000 members and perished with nearly 20 million members, which taught a painful lesson. We must not take the detours others have taken. In early 1992, during the Southern Tour Talk,

Deng Xiaoping warned the whole Party that "if there is a problem in China, it will still come from within the Communist Party."

In order to properly manage and govern the Party, the Central Committee of CPC carried forward the fine traditions formed during Mao Zedong's era and put forward the idea of a new great project of Party building. In 1994, the fourth plenary session of the 14th Central Committee of the CPC adopted the "Decision on Several Major Issues Concerning Strengthening Party Building," which, for the first time in the new era of reform and opening-up, put forward the goals and tasks of building a new great project of the Party. That is, to build our Party into a Marxist Party armed with the theory of socialism with Chinese characteristics, wholeheartedly serving the people, being completely consolidated in ideology, politics, and organization, capable of withstanding all kinds of risks, and always standing at the forefront of the times. In 1997, the 15th CPC National Congress reiterated: "To build the Party into a Marxist Party armed with Deng Xiaoping Theory, wholeheartedly serving the people, being completely consolidated in ideology, politics, and organization, capable of withstanding all kinds of risks, always standing at the forefront of the times, and leading the people of the whole country in building socialism with Chinese characteristics." In 2002, the 16th CPC National Congress emphasized that in a large developing multi-ethnic country like ours, in order to unite the will and strength of all the people, comprehensively build a well-off society, accelerate the promotion of socialist modernization, we must unswervingly strengthen and improve the Party's leadership, and comprehensively promote the new great project of Party building.

To advance the new great project of Party building, the Central Committee of CPC has adopted a series of measures, such as the "Opinions on Strengthening Party Conduct and Building a Clean Government" and the "Notice on Urgently Training and Selecting Outstanding Young Cadres," which clarify the ideas and requirements for Party building under the new situation. From 1994 to 2000, 365,000 underperforming village Party branches were rectified nationwide. On October 10, 1996, the fourth plenary session of the 14th Central Committee of the CPC made a decision to conduct centralized Party spirit and Party conduct education focusing on "learning, politics, and integrity" among county-level and above leading cadres, referred to as the "Three Stresses" education. The 15th CPC National Congress reaffirmed this in 1997. On November 21, 1998, the Central Committee of CPC issued the "Opinions on Thoroughly Carrying Out Party Spirit and Party Conduct Education Focusing on 'Learning, Politics, and Integrity' among Party and Government Leading Groups and Leading Cadres at the County Level and Above," requiring the promotion of the "Three Stresses" education to encourage county-level and above Party and government leading groups and cadres to study Deng Xiaoping Theory and the spirit of the 15th CPC National Congress in-depth and improve their work style. From the end of November 1998 to the end of 2000, the two-year "Three Stresses" education campaign progressed smoothly with remarkable results. Through the "Three Stresses" education, the majority of cadres received a profound Marxist education, underwent strict party life training, and their awareness of implementing the Party's guidelines and the principles of democratic centralism was enhanced. In September 2001, the fifth plenary session of the 16th CPC Central Committee also deliberated and adopted the decision on strengthening and improving the Party's work style, which is another major measure taken by the Central Committee of CPC to strengthen the Party's work style construction and promote the great project construction.

Since the 16th CPC National Congress, the Central Committee of CPC, with Comrade Hu Jintao as General Secretary, has put forward and implemented major strategic thoughts such as the Scientific Outlook on Development, taken the Party's governing capacity and advanced nature construction as the main line, and continuously advanced the Party's ideological construction, organizational construction, work style construction, system construction, and anti-corruption and clean governance construction with the spirit of reform and innovation, creating a new situation for the new great project of Party building.

Strictly Governing the Party

Strictly governing the Party is a fine tradition of the CPC. Strictly governing the Party requires Party organizations at all levels to strictly demand, educate, and supervise Party members and cadres and resolutely overcome the negative and corrupt phenomena within the Party. Mao Zedong and Deng Xiaoping repeatedly emphasized that the Party must be governed strictly. Under market economy conditions, the Central Committee of CPC pays more attention to strictly governing the Party.

In October 1992, the 14th CPC National Congress report pointed out: "In the new historical period, the environment and tasks facing the Party have changed greatly, and the ideological, political, organizational, and style construction of the Party faces many new situations and new problems. We must combine the reality of the Party, follow the Party's guidelines, adhere to the Party's self-governance and strictly govern the Party, strengthen and improve Party building, and strive to improve the Party's governance and leadership levels so that our long-tested Marxist Party can better play a leading role in the great cause of building socialism with Chinese characteristics." In a speech at the graduation ceremony of the provincial and ministerial classes of the Party School of the Central Committee of CPC on May 31, 2002, Jiang Zemin further emphasized the purpose and significance of adhering to strict Party governance, requiring adherence to the principles of the Party's self-governance and strict Party governance, further addressing the two major historical issues of improving the Party's leadership level and governance level, and enhancing the ability to resist corruption, prevent degeneration, and resist risks, while always maintaining close ties between the Party and the masses.

Entering the 21st century, the CPC continues to adhere to Party self-governance and strict Party governance principles. In 2004, the fourth plenary session of the 16th CPC Central Committee emphasized that Party self-governance and strict Party governance must be followed. In 2009, the fourth plenary session of the 17th CPC Central Committee passed the "Decision of the Central Committee of CPC on Several Major Issues Concerning Strengthening and Improving Party Building under the New Situation," which pointed out in summarizing the basic experience of Party building during the 60 years of the Party's governance: To govern the country, the Party must first govern itself and must be strict in doing so. Implement the Party-building work responsibility system, adhere to strict demands, strict education, strict management, strict supervision, carry out criticism and self-criticism, sound Party conduct, and clean government of affecting the people's hearts and the Party's life and death, persevere in the fight against corruption, resolutely correct the unhealthy tendencies that harm the interests of the masses, constantly address the problems within the Party, and always maintain the Party's advanced nature and purity. In his 2011 "July 1" speech, Hu Jintao pointed out that under the new situation where the world, the nation, and the Party have undergone profound changes, the Party's construction faces many unprecedented new situations, new problems, and new challenges. The tests of governance, reform and opening-up, market economy, and external environment not only exist for a long time but are also complex and severe. The dangers of spiritual slack, insufficient ability, detachment from the masses, and negative corruption are more sharply placed before the entire Party. The task of implementing Party self-governance and strict Party governance is more arduous and urgent than at any time in the past.

On May 14, 2012, the National Bureau for Corruption Prevention's website posted information stating that from 1982 to 2011, over the course of thirty years, more than 420,000 Party and government officials were disciplined for violating Party and political rules; among them, 465 were provincial and ministerial-level officials. Over 90 provincial and ministerial-level officials were held legally responsible for corruption. This fully demonstrates the CPC's fulfillment of the political commitment to "govern the Party with strict discipline."

Governing Capacity Building and Advancement Construction

If a person lacks the ability, they will be eliminated in fierce competition. Similarly, the people in social development will eliminate a Party without ability. As a governing Party, it is essential to constantly strengthen and improve itself and continuously enhance its leadership level and governance capabilities. The CPC adheres to the main line of governance capacity building and pioneering nature of the CPC. It has taken several measures to strengthen and improve its construction.

In November 2002, the 16th CPC National Congress proposed "strengthening the Party's governance capacity building." In September 2004, the fourth plenary session of the 16th CPC Central Committee proposed that the Party's governance capacity refers to the ability of the Party to propose and apply correct theories, lines, principles, policies, and strategies, lead the formulation and implementation of the constitution and laws, adopt scientific leadership systems and methods, mobilize and organize the people to manage national and social affairs, economy and culture according to law, effectively govern the Party, the country, and the army, and build a modern socialist country.

In order to strengthen the Party's governance capacity, improving the ability to make scientific judgments on the situation, the ability to control the market economy, the ability to cope with complex situations, the ability to govern according to law, and the ability to grasp the overall situation is necessary. The Central Committee of CPC focuses on improving the ability to resist corruption, prevent degeneration, and resist risks. It strengthens the Party's ideological, organizational, and institutional construction, reforms and improves the Party's leadership methods and governance methods, leadership system, and working system, and continuously improves the Party's leadership and governance levels.

While strengthening the Party's governance capacity building, the Central Committee of CPC regards strengthening the pioneering nature of the CPC as the focus of comprehensively promoting Party building. Since January 2005, a nationwide education campaign to maintain the advanced nature of Communist Party members, with the main content being the practice of the "Three Represents" important thought, has been launched for a year and a half. In the advanced education campaign, the whole Party has conducted in-depth research on the laws of the pioneering nature of the CPC and enriched the theory of the pioneering nature of the CPC. On January 14, 2005, the Central Committee of CPC held a special report meeting on maintaining the advanced nature of Communist Party members in the new period. Hu Jintao first clearly proposed the Party's pioneering nature in his speech. He pointed out that a pioneering nature is the essential attribute of a Marxist Party and the source of life and strength for a Marxist Party. On June 30, 2006, in his speech at the celebration of the 85th anniversary of the founding of the CPC and the summary of the education campaign to maintain the advanced nature of Communist Party members, Hu Jintao profoundly expounded the theory of the Party's pioneering nature construction. He pointed out that the CPC, as a Marxist Party, has an unparalleled pioneering nature in essence compared to non-Marxist Parties. This pioneering nature is mainly manifested in adhering to the guidance of Marxist scientific theories, adhering to the realization of socialism and communism in line with the laws of human social development as a firm belief and lofty ideal, adhering to the essential requirements of serving the public good and exercising power in the interests of people, adhering to the democratic centralism as the fundamental organizational system and leadership system, and adhering to the broad masses of the people as the fundamental source of strength.

He emphasized that history and reality have shown that a Party's past pioneering nature does not necessarily mean it is currently advanced, and current pioneering nature does not guarantee eternal pioneering nature. It is not easy for a Marxist Party to achieve a pioneering nature, and it is even more difficult to maintain and develop a pioneering nature in complex domestic and international environments and under long-term governance. We must regard strengthening the Party's pioneering nature construction as a major strategic task, making it more prominent and urgent for the whole Party.

To consolidate the achievements of the advanced education campaign and further implement the scientific development concept, the 17th CPC National Congress clearly proposed a campaign to deepen the study and practice of the scientific development concept throughout the Party. The study and practice campaign officially started in September 2008 and was carried out in three batches from top to bottom. By the end of February 2010, more than 3.7 million Party organizations and over

75 million Party members participated. Through the joint efforts of the whole Party, the study and practice campaign basically achieved the goals of improving ideological understanding, solving outstanding problems, innovating institutional mechanisms, promoting scientific development, and strengthening grassroots organizations, with notable results. According to the deployment of the 17th CPC National Congress, the "Creating Excellence" campaign was launched in April 2010 and continued until the 18th National Congress in 2012. The main forms of the campaign were to create advanced grassroots party organizations and strive to be outstanding Communist Party members, with a number of positive achievements.

Complementary to maintaining the Party's pioneering nature and improving the Party's governance capacity building is strengthening the Party's work style and clean government construction. Entering the new century stage, the Central Committee of CPC has attached great importance to anti-corruption system construction and innovation, focusing on preventing and solving corruption problems from the source. In October 2003, the third plenary session of the 16th CPC Central Committee proposed establishing and improving a punishment and prevention system for combating and preventing corruption that emphasizes education, institutions, and supervision and is compatible with the socialist market economy system. In September 2004, the fourth plenary session of the 16th CPC Central Committee put forward the principle of "combining treatment of symptoms and root causes, comprehensive governance, and equal emphasis on punishment and prevention, with a focus on prevention" for Party style and clean government construction and anti-corruption struggle under the new situation. In January 2005, the Central Committee of CPC issued the "Outline for the Implementation of Establishing and Improving the Punishment and Prevention System for Combating and Preventing Corruption," clarifying the guiding ideology, main objectives, and working principles for establishing the punishment and prevention system for combating and preventing corruption. In October 2007, the 17th CPC National Congress clearly put forward the concept of anti-corruption and clean government construction and made it one of the important contents of Party building. In June 2008, the Central Committee of CPC issued the "2008–2012 Work Plan for Establishing and Improving the Punishment and Prevention System for Combating and Preventing Corruption" to promote the construction of a punishment and prevention system for combating and preventing corruption.

Strengthening the Party's work style and clean government construction, together with maintaining the advanced education campaign for Communist Party members and improving the Party's governance capacity building, has mutually promoted the enhancement of the CPC's ability to resist corruption and degeneration and withstand risks under the conditions of developing a socialist market economy. This has comprehensively promoted the great new project of Party building.

Improving the Scientific Level of Party Building

Science is about being in accordance with laws. Scientific Party building means that the Party's construction must follow these laws. The first mention of the scientific Party building was at the fourth plenary session of the 17th CPC Central Committee held in September 2009.

The plenary session put forward six main tasks to strengthen and improve Party building and enhance the scientific level of Party building. First, to build a Marxist learning-oriented Party, improve the ideological and political level of the entire Party, and focus on the urgent strategic task of building a Marxist learning-oriented Party according to the requirements of being armed with scientific theory, having a global perspective, being good at grasping laws, and being rich in innovative spirit; second, to adhere to and improve democratic centralism and actively develop intra-party democracy; third, to deepen the reform of the cadre and personnel system and build a high-quality cadre team that is good at promoting scientific development and social harmony; fourth, to strengthen the grassroots and lay a solid foundation for the Party's governance; fifth, to promote the Party's fine work style and maintain the close ties between the Party and the masses; sixth, to accelerate the construction of the punishment and prevention system for combating and preventing corruption and carry out the anti-corruption struggle in depth.

To improve the scientific level of Party building, the Central Committee of CPC has made great efforts to promote the construction of learning-oriented Party organizations. The Central Committee issued the "Opinions on Promoting the Construction of Learning-Oriented Party Organizations," established a working coordination group for the construction of learning-oriented Party organizations led by the Publicity Department, and set up offices of the working coordination group for the construction of learning-oriented Party organizations at the central and provincial, regional, and municipal levels to strengthen guidance, coordination, and service for the construction of learning-oriented Party organizations. The Theoretical Bureau of the Publicity Department and the Cadre Education Bureau of the Organization Department have recommended six batches of more than 30 books, guiding Party members and cadres to read more books, love reading, and read good books. A reading craze has been instituted among most Party members and cadres.

In July 2011, in his speech at the celebration of the 90th anniversary of the founding of the CPC, Hu Jintao further elaborated on the requirements for improving the scientific level of Party building under new historical conditions. He pointed out that to improve the scientific level of Party building under new historical conditions, we must adhere to the emancipation of the mind, seeking truth from facts, and keeping pace with the times, vigorously promote the Sinicization, modernization, and popularization of Marxism, and improve the ideological and political level of the entire Party; we must adhere to the principles of "drawing talent from all sources and appointing people on their merits," adhere to the standard of selecting and appointing people with both moral integrity and professional competence, and give priority to moral integrity, and bring outstanding talents from all aspects into the Party and the country's cause; we must adhere to the people-centered and people-serving concept, firmly establish the Marxist mass viewpoint, consciously implement the Party's mass line, and always maintain the close ties between the Party and the masses; we must adhere to the principle of treating both the symptoms and root causes, comprehensive management, equal emphasis on punishment and prevention, and focus on prevention, and carry out the construction of Party style and clean government and the anti-corruption struggle in depth, and always maintain the pioneering nature and purity of the Marxist political Party; we must adhere to managing power, affairs, and people with institutions, improve democratic centralism, and continuously promote the institutionalization, standardization, and proceduralization of Party building.

In short, the CPC, in leading the reform and opening-up and the construction of socialist modernization, has always focused on upholding the Party's leadership, attaching great importance to Party building, clarifying the main line of Party construction, and forming a layout of Party construction that includes ideological construction, organizational construction, style construction, system construction, and anti-corruption and integrity-building. The emphasis on leading by example and gentle persuasion in ideological construction and style construction has increased, the scientific level of organizational construction and system construction has noticeably improved, and anti-corruption and integrity-building have paid more attention to institutionalized and systematic construction. The ability to govern and manage the Party has noticeably strengthened, and the Party's mass base and governing foundation have become more stable, thus ensuring that the reform, opening-up, and socialist modernization progress in the right direction.

Part IV

NEW ERA OF SOCIALISM WITH CHINESE CHARACTERISTICS

CHAPTER 18

Realizing the Chinese Dream of the Great Rejuvenation of the Chinese Nation

A s the governing Party of the world's second-largest economy, the largest developing country, and a rapidly rising socialist power, the CPC has attracted much attention, especially in the conferences where the top leaders are elected. On November 15, 2012, the first plenary session of the 18th CPC Central Committee was held, electing a new Political Bureau Standing Committee and Xi Jinping as the General Secretary of the Central Committee of CPC. Xi Jinping had already been working in China's core decision-making circle for five years as a member of the 17th CPC Political Bureau Standing Committee, but his first appearance as China's top leader left people wondering what he would say to China and the world and what his policy strategies would be.

The Aspiration of the People to Live a Better Life Must Always Be the Focus of Our Efforts

At 11:56 a.m. on November 15, 2012, the 18th CPC Political Bureau Standing Committee members met with Chinese and foreign journalists who had been waiting for some time. Xi Jinping, General Secretary of the Central Committee of CPC, first expressed his heartfelt thanks to the journalists on behalf of the 18th National Congress Secretariat, saying, "Sorry to keep you waiting." He then introduced his six colleagues from the Political Bureau Standing Committee. He expressed his gratitude on behalf of the new central leadership for the trust placed in them by the entire Party, pledging to do their utmost to be trustworthy and fulfill their mission. Xi Jinping then delivered a brief but important speech, conveying a wealth of information.

Xi Jinping pointed out, "The trust of our comrades in the Party and the expectations of people of all ethnic groups in the country are both a tremendous inspiration for us to do our work well and a great responsibility on our shoulders." Regarding responsibility toward the people, Xi Jinping clearly stated, "The aspiration of the people to live a better life must always be the focus of our efforts." He also said, "Our people are great. In the long course of history, the Chinese have relied on their hard work, courage, and wisdom to create a harmonious and beautiful home for the nation and nurture a long-lasting and ever-renewing outstanding culture. Our people love life and look forward to better education, more stable jobs, more satisfactory income, more reliable social security, higher-level medical and health services, more comfortable living conditions, and a more beautiful environment. They hope that their children will grow up better, work better, and live better." These ten "betters" accurately summarize the new CPC Central Committee's understanding of the people's aspirations for a better life.

All the world's splendor comes from enduring hardship; every happiness in human life is created through hard work. To realize people's aspirations for a better life, it requires the CPC to unite and lead the entire Party and people of all ethnic groups in the country, continue to liberate their minds, adhere to reform and opening-up, constantly liberate and develop the productive forces of society, strive to solve the difficulties in the production and living conditions of the masses, and unswervingly pursue the path of common prosperity. Xi Jinping stated: "Responsibility is heavier than Mount Tai, and the task is long and arduous. We must always be in sync with the people, share their joys and sorrows, and struggle together with them, working diligently and tirelessly to provide a satisfactory answer to history and the people."

General Secretary Xi Jinping once said in an interview with a Russian television station, "The CPC insists on governing for the people, and the people's aspirations for a better life are our goals. My governing philosophy can be summarized as serving the people and assuming the responsibilities I should bear." It is this profound and sincere commitment to the people that the Central Committee of CPC, with Comrade Xi Jinping at its core, has always placed the people at the highest position in their hearts, adhered to the people-centered development concept, strived to provide a satisfactory education for the people, focused on employment as the foundation of people's livelihood, and improved social security as the basis. The people's living standards have significantly improved, and their sense of happiness, gain, and security have been noticeably enhanced.

The Greatest Dream of the Chinese People since Modern Times

On November 29, 2012, at the National Museum of China on the east side of Tiananmen Square in Beijing, Xi Jinping, General Secretary of the Central Committee of CPC and Chairman of the Central Military Commission, along with Political Bureau Standing Committee members Li Keqiang, Zhang Dejiang, Yu Zhengsheng, Liu Yunshan, Wang Qishan, and Zhang Gaoli, visited the exhibition *Road to Rejuvenation*. The exhibition reviews the various explorations for national rejuvenation since the Opium War in 1840, when China fell into the abyss of a semi-colonial and semi-feudal society, especially the glorious course of the CPC leading people of all ethnic groups in the country to fight for national independence, people's liberation, national prosperity, and people's happiness, fully demonstrates how history and the people chose Marxism, the CPC, the socialist road, and reform and opening-up, and why it is necessary to always uphold the great banner of socialism with Chinese characteristics unswervingly.

During the visit, General Secretary Xi Jinping delivered a speech, explicitly proposing to realize the Chinese dream of the great rejuvenation of the Chinese nation. He said, "Now, everyone is discussing the Chinese Dream. In my opinion, achieving the rejuvenation of the Chinese nation has been the greatest dream of the Chinese people since the advent of modern times. This dream embodies the long-cherished hope of several generations of the Chinese people, gives expression to the overall interests of the Chinese nation and the Chinese people, and represents the shared aspiration of all the sons and daughters of the Chinese nation." He also said, "Our struggles in the over 170 years since the Opium War have created bright prospect for achieving the rejuvenation of the Chinese nation. We are now closer to this goal, and we are more confident and capable of achieving it than at any other time in history." This is the goal of struggle proposed by the new central leadership, marking the collective pursuit and work direction of the CPC for the next period.

What does the Chinese Dream mean? Whose dream is it? How can it be achieved? In March 2013, at the First Session of the 12th National People's Congress,

Xi Jinping, newly elected President of the People's Republic of China, responded. He said that realizing a moderately prosperous society in all respects, a prosperous, strong, democratic, culturally advanced, and harmonious socialist modern country, and realizing the Chinese Dream of the great rejuvenation of the Chinese nation is to achieve national prosperity, national rejuvenation, and people's happiness. He also said, "The Chinese Dream is ultimately the dream of the people and must rely on the people to realize it, and it must continuously benefit the people." This points out the connotation of the Chinese Dream from the three dimensions of the country, the nation, and the people and highlights the essential feature of the Chinese Dream is the people's dream.

To realize the Chinese Dream, we must follow the Chinese path, promote the Chinese spirit, and unite Chinese strength. Among them, the Chinese path is the path of socialism with Chinese characteristics. This path has not come easily. It has emerged from more than forty years of great practice of reform and opening-up, more than seventy years of continuous exploration since the founding of the People's Republic of China, a profound summary of the development process of the Chinese nation since modern times for more than 180 years, and the inheritance of the Chinese nation's five-thousand-year-old splendid civilization. It has deep historical roots and a broad practical basis. The Chinese nation is a nation with extraordinary creativity. We have created the great Chinese civilization and can continue to explore and follow the development path suitable for China's national conditions. People of all ethnic groups across the country must strengthen their confidence in the theory, path, and system of socialism with Chinese characteristics and resolutely advance along the correct Chinese path with courage.

The Chinese spirit is the national spirit with patriotism at its core and the spirit of the times with reform and innovation at its core. This spirit unites the people and pools their strength. Patriotism has always been the spiritual force that unites the Chinese nation, and reform and innovation have always spurred us to advance with the times in reform and opening-up. People of all ethnic groups across the country must carry forward the great national spirit and the spirit of the times, continuously strengthen the spiritual ties of unity and self-improvement, and always stride toward the future with vigor and vitality.

The Chinese strength is the strength of unity among all ethnic groups in China. The Chinese Dream is the dream of the nation, as well as the dream of every Chinese person. As long as we unite closely and work together for a common dream, the power to realize the dream will be unparalleled, and each of us will have a vast space to strive for our own dreams. The Chinese people living in our great motherland and great era share the opportunity to shine in life, the opportunity to realize dreams, and the opportunity to grow and progress with the motherland and the times. With dreams, opportunities, and struggles, everything beautiful can be created. People of all ethnic groups across the country must remember their mission, think and work together, and gather the invincible, immense power of 1.3 billion people with their wisdom and strength.

Realizing the Chinese Dream will be challenging and cannot be achieved by simply beating gongs and drums. In the face of major changes unseen in a century, realizing the Chinese Dream requires great struggles, great projects, and the advancement of great causes. As General Secretary Xi Jinping pointed out, "In the great practice of socialism with Chinese characteristics in the new era, with the strong leadership of the Party and the tenacious struggle, we should inspire all the Chinese people to keep moving forward, consolidating the mighty force of working together to build the Chinese Dream!"

"Five-Sphere Integrated Plan" and "Four Comprehensives"

Entering a new era and facing new situations, how does the CPC plan and promote the advancement of its cause? Under the Central Committee of CPC's leadership with Comrade Xi Jinping's core, the CPC has formed and coordinated the overall layout of the "Five-Sphere Integrated Plan," promoting economic, political, cultural, social, and ecological civilization construction. It has also formed and coordinated the strategic layout of the "Four Comprehensives": comprehensively building a modern socialist country (before the fifth plenary session of 19th CPC Central Committee in 2020, the expression was "comprehensively building a moderately prosperous society"), deepening reform, governing the country according to law, and strictly governing the Party. The "Five-Sphere Integrated Plan" overall layout and the "Four Comprehensives" strategic layout mutually promote and coordinate, establishing the strategic planning and deployment for adhering to and developing socialism with Chinese characteristics in the new era.

The "Five-Sphere Integrated Plan" overall layout is an important achievement of the CPC in deepening its understanding and practice of the laws of socialist construction. Since the reform and opening-up, with the development of the economy and society, the layout has evolved from the "two civilizations" of material and spiritual civilization in the 1980s to the "three in one" of economic, political, and cultural construction in the 1990s, to the "four in one" of economic, political, cultural, and social construction in the early 21st century, and finally to the "Five-Sphere Integrated Plan" of economic, political, cultural, social, and ecological civilization construction proposed at the 18th CPC National Congress. This reflects the gradual deepening of the CPC's understanding of the laws of socialist construction. The "Five-Sphere Integrated Plan" aspects are interconnected, mutually promoting, and indivisible, together forming the overall picture of socialism with Chinese characteristics. In accordance with the overall goals of the "Five-Sphere Integrated Plan" layout, it is necessary to adhere to the central role of economic construction, promote the coordination of all aspects of economic, political, cultural, social, and ecological civilization construction, and promote the adaptation of the relations of production to the productive forces and the superstructure to the economic base, to achieve comprehensive development and progress in socialism with Chinese characteristics.

After the 18th CPC National Congress, the Central Committee of CPC, with Comrade Xi Jinping at its core, increasingly clarified the major ideas and new features of governing the country. In August 2014, General Secretary Xi Jinping expounded on the relationship between comprehensively promoting the rule of law, building a moderately prosperous society, and deepening reform, requiring a good grasp of the logical connection of these "three comprehensives." In December, during an inspection and research trip in Jiangsu, General Secretary Xi Jinping added "strict governance of the Party" to the "three comprehensives." He called for the coordinated promotion of comprehensively building a moderately prosperous society, deepening reform, promoting the rule of law, and governing the Party strictly, aiming to elevate reform and opening-up and socialist modernization to a new level.

This was the first time the "Four Comprehensives" were proposed. On February 2, 2015, at the opening ceremony of the seminar for provincial and ministerial-level leading cadres held at the Party School of the Central Committee of CPC, General Secretary Xi Jinping explicitly stated: "Since the 18th CPC National Congress, the Central Committee of CPC, starting from the overall situation of upholding and developing socialism with Chinese characteristics, has proposed and formed the strategic layout of comprehensively building a moderately prosperous society, comprehensively deepening reforms, comprehensively governing the nation according to law, and comprehensively strictly governing the Party." This was the first time the "Four Comprehensives" strategic layout was put forward.

The "Four Comprehensives" strategic layout has strategic goals and measures. Each "comprehensive" has a close internal logic with one another, representing an orderly unfolding of an overall strategic deployment and the strategic choice of the CPC to promote reform and opening-up, socialist modernization, and adherence to and development of socialism with Chinese characteristics in the new era. The third, fourth, fifth, and sixth plenary sessions of the 18th CPC Central Committee have successively conducted thematic studies on comprehensively deepening reform, comprehensively governing the country according to law, comprehensively building a moderately prosperous society, and comprehensively governing the Party strictly, completing the top-level design of the "Four Comprehensives" strategic layout. The CPC has made arduous efforts to coordinate and promote the "Four Comprehensives" strategic layout according to the aforementioned "blueprint."

General Secretary Xi Jinping attaches great importance to reform. His first research trip outside Beijing was to Guangdong, where he climbed Lotus Mountain in Shenzhen to present flowers to the bronze statue of Deng Xiaoping. He said that the reason for choosing Guangdong, which took the lead in reform and opening-up, was to pledge that the reform would continue and the opening-up would not come to a standstill. Under the leadership of General Secretary Xi Jinping, the CPC launched the most extensive and comprehensive deepening of reforms in decades. To carry out this highly challenging reform, the Central Committee of CPC established the Central Leading Group for Comprehensively Deepening Reform (renamed the Central Commission for Comprehensively Deepening Reform in March 2018), led by Xi Jinping himself, to coordinate and promote the comprehensive deepening of reforms. As of December 2020, 40 meetings of the Central Leading Group for Comprehensively Deepening Reform and 17 meetings of the Central Commission for Comprehensively Deepening Reform were held, reviewing and approving 599 important reform documents and introducing 2,485 reform plans in various aspects.

Over the years, the Central Committee of CPC has steadfastly promoted reforms, resolutely eliminating various institutional and mechanism drawbacks, consolidating the foundation, and building the framework while emphasizing comprehensive promotion and accumulating momentum. Reforms have been fully implemented, with breakthroughs in multiple points and deepened progress, and the systematic, holistic, and synergistic aspects of reform have been continuously strengthened. The goals and tasks set by the third plenary session of the 18th CPC Central Committee have been comprehensively advanced, the basic institutional framework in various fields has been established, and historical changes, systemic reshaping, and holistic construction have been achieved in many fields. This lays a solid foundation for the formation of a complete, scientifically standardized, and effective institutional system and makes the institutions in various fields more mature and better established, achieving historic great achievements in comprehensively deepening reform. In the future, we must strengthen our confidence in reform, gather the strength of reform, make persistent efforts, forge ahead, and promote greater breakthroughs and achievements in reform.

Faced with new requirements in the new era, the Central Committee of CPC adheres to the overall working principle of pursuing progress while maintaining stability, coordinates the promotion of the "Five-Sphere Integrated Plan" overall layout, coordinates the promotion of the "Four Comprehensives" strategic layout, grasps strategic priorities, and achieves key breakthroughs. In order to better implement the "Five-Sphere Integrated Plan" overall layout and the "Four Comprehensives" strategic layout, the Central Committee of CPC has implemented a series of major strategies, including the innovation-driven development strategy, regional coordinated development strategy, and sustainable development strategy, to present a new outlook for reform, opening-up, and socialist modernization.

Guided by Xi Jinping Thought on Socialism with Chinese Characteristics for a New Era

Based on the new historical position, the Central Committee of CPC, with Comrade Xi Jinping at the core, adheres to the principles of liberating thought, seeking truth from facts, keeping pace with the times, and being pragmatic and realistic. Upholding dialectical materialism and historical materialism, the Party closely integrates new era conditions and practical requirements, deepening its understanding of the laws of governance for the CPC, the construction of socialism, and the development of human society with a new perspective. Through arduous theoretical exploration, the Party has achieved major theoretical innovations and established Xi Jinping Thought on Socialism with Chinese Characteristics for a New Era. This thought was established as the Party's guiding ideology at the 19th CPC National Congress and was incorporated into the Constitution of the CPC. In March 2018, it was written into the *Constitution*, thus becoming the guiding ideology for the whole Party and the entire nation.

The content of Xi Jinping Thought on Socialism with Chinese Characteristics for a New Era is rich, systematically answering the major questions of what kind of socialism with Chinese characteristics to adhere to and develop in the new era and how to adhere to and develop it, from the integration of theory and practice. It covers the overall goals, tasks, layout, strategic layout, development direction, development methods, development momentum, strategic steps, external conditions, and political guarantees of adhering to and developing socialism with Chinese characteristics in the new era. It also provides new theoretical summaries and strategic guidance for various aspects such as economy, politics, the rule of law, science and technology, culture, education, people's livelihood, nationality, religion, society, ecological civilization, national security, national defense, and military, "One Country, Two Systems" and the reunification of the motherland, united front, diplomacy, and Party building based on new practices.

The core content of Xi Jinping Thought on Socialism with Chinese Characteristics for a New Era consists of "Eight Clarifications" and "Fourteen Persistences." The "Eight Clarifications" are: first, to adhere to and develop socialism with Chinese characteristics, with the overall task of achieving socialist modernization and the great rejuvenation of the Chinese nation, and to build a prosperous, strong, democratic, civilized, harmonious, and beautiful socialist modernized powerful country in two stages on the basis of comprehensively building a moderately prosperous society; second, to clarify that the main contradiction in our society in the new era is the contradiction between the people's ever-growing needs for a better life and unbalanced and insufficient development, and we must adhere to the people-centered development philosophy and continuously promote the all-round development of people and the common prosperity of all; third, to clarify that the overall layout of the cause of socialism with Chinese characteristics is "Five-Sphere Integrated Plan" and the strategic layout is "Four Comprehensives," emphasizing firm confidence in our path, theory, system, and culture; fourth, to clarify that the overall goal of comprehensively deepening reform is to improve and develop the socialist system with Chinese characteristics and promote the modernization of the national governance system and capacity; fifth, to clarify that the overall goal of comprehensively promoting the rule of law is to build a socialist legal system with Chinese characteristics and build a socialist country under the rule of law; sixth, to clarify that the goal of strengthening the army in the new era is to build a people's army that listens to the Party's command, can win battles, and has an excellent style, and to build the people's army into a world-class army; seventh, to clarify that China's diplomacy with its characteristics as a major country should promote the construction of a new type of international relations and the building of a community with a shared future for mankind; eighth, to clarify that the most distinctive characteristic of socialism with Chinese characteristics is the leadership of the CPC, and the greatest advantage of the socialist system with Chinese characteristics is the leadership of the CPC. The Party is the highest political leading force. It puts forward the overall requirements for Party building in the new era and emphasizes the important position of political construction in Party building.

The "Fourteen Persistences" are: to persist in the Party's leadership over all work, to persist in putting people at the center, to persist in comprehensively deepening reform, to persist in the new development concepts, to persist in the people being masters of the country, to persist in comprehensively promoting the rule of law, to persist in the socialist core value system, to persist in ensuring and improving people's livelihood in the course of development, to persist in the harmonious coexistence of people and nature, to persist in the overall national security concept, to persist in the Party's absolute leadership over the people's army, to persist in "One Country, Two Systems" and the promotion of the reunification of the motherland, to persist in promoting the construction of a community with a shared future for mankind, and to persist in comprehensively and strictly governing the Party.

The "Eight Clarifications" and "Fourteen Persistences" are organically integrated and unified, embodying the valuable experience of the CPC in adhering to and developing socialism with Chinese characteristics, reflecting the deepening, expansion, and sublimation of the understanding of the laws of socialism with Chinese characteristics by the Central Committee of CPC with Comrade Xi Jinping at its core, and embodying the distinct features of the integration of theory and practice and the unity of epistemology and methodology, with many original contributions. This thought is the golden key to solving the main contradictions in Chinese society in the new era and a powerful ideological weapon for guiding the Chinese nation in realizing the Chinese Dream.

Xi Jinping Thought on Socialism with Chinese Characteristics for a New Era is an inheritance and development of Marxism-Leninism, Mao Zedong Thought, Deng Xiaoping Theory, the important thoughts of "Three Represents," and the Scientific Outlook on Development. It is the latest achievement of the Sinicization of Marxism, a crystallization of the practical experience and collective wisdom of the Party and the people, an important part of the theoretical system of socialism with Chinese characteristics, contemporary Chinese Marxism, and 21st-century Marxism. It is the action guide for the whole Party and the people of the entire country to strive for the great rejuvenation of the Chinese nation and must be adhered to and developed over the long term.

The international community has paid close attention to China's theoretical innovation and the 19th CPC National Congress. Monica Valente, executive secretary of the São Paulo Forum, believes that "Xi Jinping Thought on Socialism with Chinese Characteristics for a New Era takes into account economic growth, social justice, and environmental protection and has strong reference value for the Latin American region." The Russian *Nezavisimaya Gazeta* also pointed out in its commentary on the 19th CPC National Congress that "the Chinese experience is worth learning from for those countries that wish to accelerate their development and maintain their independence."

CHAPTER 19

Building a Modernized Economic System

Since the outbreak of the international financial crisis in 2008, the global economic situation has not emerged from the downturn. In the context of economic globalization, China, as a major world trading nation, could hardly remain unscathed. Faced with a pessimistic international and domestic economic situation, the Central Committee of CPC calmly made a significant judgment that economic development has entered a new normal, insisted on guiding development with new concepts, vigorously promoted supply-side structural reform, actively built a new development pattern, established a modernized economic system, promoted high-quality development and achieved steady progress. When China announced its 2020 report card, it sparked a global debate. On January 21, 2021, Russia's TASS published an article titled "China's GDP Growth in 2020 Exceeds Expectations." *The Wall Street Journal* and *The New York Times* in the United States both wrote that, in 2020, the global economy was hit by the COVID-19 pandemic, and China's economy achieved a perfect "V-shaped recovery," allowing China's national rejuvenation ambitions to continue to move forward. Japanese economic experts say that China's GDP breaking the 100 trillion yuan mark is of epoch-making significance.

Grasping the Big Logic of Economic Development in the New Normal

After the 18th CPC National Congress, in the face of the complex situation of the overlapping "three periods" of growth rate shift, structural adjustment pain, and digestion of previous stimulus policies, the Central Committee of CPC made a comprehensive analysis of the world economic long cycle and China's developmental stage characteristics and their interaction, making a major strategic judgment that China's economic development has entered a "new normal."

In December 2014, General Secretary Xi Jinping pointed out: "Entering the new normal manifests the inevitable periodic nature of China's economic development. Understanding the new normal, adapting ourselves to the new normal, and guiding the new normal are major tasks in the present and future stages of our economic development." The new normal of China's economy has several distinct features: First, economic development has shifted from high-speed growth to medium-high-speed growth; Second, the economic structure is continuously optimized and upgraded, with the tertiary industry and consumer demand gradually becoming the main body, urban-rural regional gaps gradually narrowing, residents' income ratio rising, and development achievements benefiting a broader population; Third, it has shifted from factor-driven and investment-driven to innovation-driven.

There are still some discussions in society about the decline in economic growth. However, just like a person, from the age of 10 to 18, one grows rapidly in height, and after the age of 18, the speed of growth slows down. Economic development is the same. As a major economy, China can only sometimes advance at high speed. Low-end industries need to be concentrated and digested, while medium- and high-end industries need to accelerate development. The days of making money by producing anything and selling any amount are gone forever. It should also be noted that China's labor advantage, low-cost resources, and factor input-driven force have significantly weakened, and the export situation is also changing. Both domestic and foreign situations show that high-speed growth is challenging, and economic growth needs to be driven by innovation and consumer demand.

At the same time, it is also necessary to see that under the new normal of economic development, although China's economy is facing considerable downward pressure, the fundamentals of long-term economic improvement have not changed, the basic characteristics of good economic resilience, sufficient potential, and ample room for maneuver have not changed, and the good foundation and conditions for sustained economic growth, the advancing trend of economic structural adjustment and optimization have not changed. It can be said that the shift in gear and speed reduction do not lose momentum. To adapt to the new normal, it is necessary to promote economic system reform resolutely and change development ideas.

On July 1, 2016, General Secretary Xi Jinping pointed out: "We must adhere to the central focus on economic construction, adhere to the guidance of the new development concept in leading the new normal of economic development, accelerate the transformation of economic development mode, adjust the economic development structure, improve the quality and efficiency of development, vigorously promote supply-side structural reform, promote the economy to develop more efficiently, with higher quality, more equitably, and more sustainably, and accelerate the formation of mechanisms and environments that advocate innovation, emphasize coordination, promote green development, cultivate openness, and advance sharing, and continuously strengthen our country's economic strength and comprehensive national power." This accurate judgment and clear directive on the state of economic development have pointed the way for reforms in the economic field.

Promoting Supply-Side Structural Reform

Promoting supply-side structural reform is a major innovation in adapting to, grasping, and leading the new normal of economic development. It is the proactive direction and main line of China's economic work in the process of promoting economic system reform and is also an inevitable requirement for China's economy to achieve high-quality development.

The third plenary session of the 18th CPC Central Committee, held in November 2013, pointed out that economic system reform is the focus of comprehensively deepening reform. The core issue is properly handling the relationship between the government and the market, allowing the market to play a decisive role in resource allocation and better play the role of the government. This is the first time the Central Committee of CPC explicitly proposed allowing the market to play a decisive role in resource allocation. Making this significant judgment is conducive to establishing a correct concept of the relationship between the government and the market in the entire Party and society, conducive to transforming the mode of economic development, transforming government functions, and curbing negative corruption phenomena. Developing a socialist market economy requires both the effective functioning of the market and the active role of the government, but the functions of market forces and government roles are different. To better play the role of the government is to emphasize scientific macro-control and effective government governance; it is to emphasize that the government's responsibilities and roles are mainly to maintain macroeconomic stability, strengthen and optimize public services, ensure fair competition, strengthen market supervision, maintain market order, promote sustainable development, and promote common prosperity, and to remedy market failures. This accurate positioning of the government and the market is an inevitable requirement for economic reform and a reform goal.

A breakthrough in deepening economic system reform is to actively promote supply-side structural reform. Since 2010, China's economic growth rate has fluctuated downward for several years, and the economic operation has shown different situations and characteristics from the past. The imbalance and disharmony between supply and demand have become increasingly prominent, with the adaptation of the supply side to changes in the demand side lagging behind. This requires accelerating supply-side structural reform while moderately expanding total demand. Supply-side structural reform aims to promote structural adjustment through reform, reduce inefficient and low-end supply, expand effective and medium-to-high-end supply, enhance the adaptability and flexibility of the supply structure to the demand structure, and improve total factor productivity. This requires all regions and departments to adapt to the new normal of economic development, implement the overall ideas of stable macro policies, accurate industrial policies, flexible micro policies, practical reform policies, and bottom-line social policies, focusing on the five major tasks of cutting capacity, destocking, deleveraging, reducing costs, and strengthening weaknesses, and implementing them firmly, boldly, and accurately.

The steel industry is a key industry for capacity reduction. To implement the spirit of the Central Committee of CPC, in February 2016, the State Council issued the "Opinions on Resolving Excess Capacity in the Steel Industry and Achieving Relief Development," which clearly proposed that from 2016, crude steel production capacity would be reduced by 100 million to 150 million tons in five years. At the end of 2016, China Baowu Steel Group was established, insisting on supply-side structural reform as the main line, vigorously reducing excess capacity by more than 10 million tons, resolutely shutting down loss-making production lines, and withdrawing inefficient capacity. In the first half of 2017 alone, the company doubled its total profits.

To promote supply-side structural reform and achieve sustained economic development, the Central Committee of CPC has intensified efforts to deepen the reform of state-owned enterprises. On October 24, 2014, the Central State-owned Enterprise Reform Leading Group was established, marking a new stage in SOE reform. On August 24, 2015, the "Guiding Opinions on Deepening the Reform of State-owned Enterprises of the Central Committee of CPC and the State Council" were promulgated and implemented, clearly pointing out that the guiding ideology of the reform is to "deeply study and implement the spirit of General Secretary Xi Jinping's series of important speeches, adhere to and improve the basic economic system, adhere to the direction of socialist market economy reform, adapt to the new situation of marketization, modernization, and internationalization, take the liberation and development of social productivity as the standard, focus on improving the efficiency of state-owned capital and enhancing the vitality of state-owned enterprises, improve the modern enterprise system with clear property rights, clear rights and responsibilities, separation of government and enterprises, and scientific management, improve the state-owned asset supervision system, prevent the loss of state-owned assets, comprehensively promote the rule of law in enterprises, strengthen and improve the Party's leadership over state-owned enterprises, make state-owned enterprises stronger, better and larger, continuously enhance the vitality, control, influence, and risk resistance of the state-owned economy, actively adapt to and lead the new normal of economic development, and make positive contributions to promoting the sustained and healthy development of the economy and society and realizing the great rejuvenation of the Chinese nation and the Chinese Dream." The document detailed the deployment of key issues in SOE reform, such as properly handling the relationship between government and enterprises, reasonably arranging compensation systems, and managing state-owned capital. This is China's new top-level design for promoting state-owned enterprise reform, drawing up a blueprint, timetable, and roadmap for state-owned enterprise reform.

On July 4, 2016, a symposium on the reform of state-owned enterprises was held in Beijing. General Secretary Xi Jinping made an important directive, emphasizing that state-owned enterprises are an important force for strengthening the comprehensive national power and safeguarding the common interests of the people. They must be unswervingly developed to be stronger, better, and larger, continuously enhancing their vitality, influence, and ability to resist risks and realizing the preservation and appreciation of state-owned assets. We must unswervingly deepen the reform of state-owned enterprises, focus on innovating systems and mechanisms, accelerate the establishment of modern enterprise systems, and bring into play the enthusiasm, initiative, and creativity of all types of talents in state-owned enterprises, stimulating the vitality of all factors. We must follow the requirements of the new development concept of innovation, coordination, green, openness, and sharing, promote structural adjustment, innovation, and development, and optimize the layout so that state-owned enterprises can play a leading role in supply-side structural reform. We must strengthen supervision and resolutely prevent the loss of state-owned assets. We must adhere to the Party's self-governance and strict governance, strengthen and improve the Party's leadership over state-owned enterprises, and fully play the political core role of Party organizations. This important directive further points out the direction for the reform of state-owned enterprises. In October 2016, a national conference on Party building in state-owned enterprises was held in Beijing, deploying efforts to strengthen and improve the Party's leadership over state-owned enterprises, strengthen and improve Party building in state-owned enterprises, and make state-owned enterprises the most reliable support force for the Party and the country. This provides organizational guarantees for maintaining the correct direction of enterprise reform.

While promoting reforms in the economic field, the Central Committee of CPC attaches great importance to the "issues relating to agriculture, rural areas, and farmers" and urbanization issues. General Secretary Xi Jinping pointed out that for China to be strong, agriculture must be strong; for China to be beautiful, rural areas must be beautiful; for China to be rich, farmers must be rich. In recent years, the Central Committee has issued an Agricultural No. 1 Document every year. (The theme of the 2013 No. 1 Document is "accelerating the development of modern agriculture and further enhancing rural development vitality"; the theme of the 2014 No. 1 Document is "comprehensively deepening rural reform and speeding up agricultural modernization"; the theme of the 2015 No. 1 Document is "increasing reform and innovation efforts and speeding up agricultural modernization construction"; the theme of the 2016 No. 1 Document is "implementing new development concepts and speeding up agricultural modernization to achieve the goal of building a moderately prosperous society in all respects"; the theme of the 2017 No. 1 Document is "deepening the supply-side structural reform of agriculture and accelerating the cultivation of new driving forces for agricultural and rural development"; the theme of the 2018 No. 1 Document is "implementing the rural revitalization strategy"; the theme of the 2019 No. 1 Document is "adhering to the priority development of agriculture and rural areas and doing a good job in the 'issues relating to agriculture, rural areas, and farmers'; the theme of the 2020 No. 1 Document is "focusing on key tasks in the 'issues relating to agriculture, rural areas, and farmers' and ensuring the realization of a moderately prosperous society on schedule"; the theme of the 2021 No. 1 Document is "comprehensively promoting rural revitalization and accelerating agricultural and rural modernization.") These important documents have been implemented precisely, targeting the problems in rural areas and agriculture, promoting significant and noticeable progress in "agriculture, rural areas, and farmers" work. The Central Committee of CPC has also focused on promoting people-centered new urbanization construction, gaining valuable experience, and providing a good foundation for the further implementation of economic reform.

After the 18th CPC National Congress, from the central to local governments, supply-side structural reform has been taken as the main theme, continuously pushing the reform deeper, focusing on resolving the structural contradictions and problems in economic operation, promoting the macroeconomic operation to always stay within a reasonable range, and also promoting the steady improvement of the quality and efficiency of economic development.

Unswervingly Implement the New Development Concept

On the basis of the basic completion of the "Twelfth Five-Year Plan," in October 2015, the fifth plenary session of the 18th CPC Central Committee deliberated and adopted the "Proposal of the Central Committee of CPC on Formulating the Thirteenth Five-Year Plan for National Economic and Social Development." According to this proposal, the State Council formulated the "Outline of the Thirteenth Five-Year Plan for National Economic and Social Development (Draft)." In March 2016, the Fourth Session of the Twelfth National People's Congress approved this planning outline.

The "Outline" clarifies the main line of development for the next five years: to implement the new development concept and adapt to and grasp the new normal of economic development, it is necessary to moderately expand the total demand while focusing on promoting supply-side structural reform, making the supply capacity meet the growing, upgrading, and individualized material, cultural, and ecological environment needs of the vast majority of people. It is necessary to use reform methods to promote structural adjustment, increase market-oriented reform efforts in key areas and critical links, improve a fair competition and survival-of-the-fittest market environment and mechanism, optimize resource allocation, promote industrial structure upgrading, expand effective and high-end supply, enhance the adaptability and flexibility of supply structure, and improve total factor productivity. It is necessary to aim at improving the quality and efficiency of the supply system, implement the policy pillars of stable macro policies, accurate industrial policies, flexible micro policies, practical reform policies, and bottom-line social policies, reduce overcapacity, destock, deleverage, lower costs, and fill shortcomings, accelerate the cultivation of new development momentum, transform and upgrade traditional comparative advantages, consolidate the foundation of the real economy, and promote the overall improvement of the level of social productivity. At the same time, the "Outline" emphasizes that to achieve the development goals of the "Thirteenth Five-Year Plan" period, overcome development difficulties, and foster development advantages, it is necessary to firmly establish and effectively implement the development concept of innovation, coordination, green, openness, and sharing. This is a profound transformation related to China's overall development.

The 19th CPC National Congress made adherence to the new development concept a basic strategy for adhering to and developing socialism with Chinese characteristics in the new era. It expanded the connotation of development in an all-around way with new era characteristics and elevated the thoughts and theories on development to a new height. Innovation is the primary driving force for development, coordination is the inherent requirement for sustainable and healthy development, green is the necessary condition for sustainable development, openness is the essential path for national prosperity and development, and sharing is the essential requirement of socialism with Chinese characteristics. The new development concept of innovation, coordination, green, openness, and sharing is a systematic theoretical system with inherent connections. It answers a series of theoretical and practical questions about the purpose, driving force, methods, and paths of development, clarifies major issues such as political stance, value orientation, development model, and development path, and is a concentrated reflection of China's development ideas, directions, and focal points for the "Thirteenth Five-Year Plan" and even longer periods. It is the main content of Xi Jinping's Economic Thought on Socialism with Chinese Characteristics in the New Era, deepens and expands the Party's understanding of the laws of economic development under socialism with Chinese characteristics, enriches and develops the political economy of socialism with Chinese characteristics, and must run through all aspects and links of economic and social development.

On January 11, 2021, General Secretary Xi Jinping further pointed out at the opening ceremony of a special seminar on studying and implementing the spirit of the fifth plenary session of the 19th CPC Central Committee for provincial and ministerial-level leading cadres held at the Party School of the Central Committee of CPC that "the whole Party must comprehensively, accurately, and completely implement the new development concept." We should grasp the new development concept from the fundamental purpose, problem orientation, and awareness of potential risks. Since the 18th CPC National Congress, various regions have actively implemented the new development concept, China's economic strength has reached a new level, and its economic growth rate ranks among the forefront of major economies in the world, becoming the main driving force and stabilizer for world economic growth. There has been a major change in the economic structure, the promotion of supply-side structural reform, and the achievement of the supply-demand balance. The reform of the economic system continues to advance, making the economy more dynamic and resilient.

Accelerate the Construction of a New Development Pattern

The CPC has implemented a series of major strategies to promote economic development in line with the new development concept, such as the Beijing-Tianjin-Hebei Coordinated Development Strategy, the Yangtze River Economic Belt, and the Construction of the Guangdong-Hong Kong-Macao Greater Bay Area, among others. Another significant move is the establishment of the Xiong'an New Area. On February 23, 2017, General Secretary Xi Jinping traveled more than 100 kilometers from Zhongnanhai in Beijing to this magical land on the North China Plain. "The construction of Xiong'an New Area is a historical project," General Secretary Xi Jinping clearly positioned it. With thousands of tower cranes and over a hundred thousand builders, Xiong'an New Area has become the world's largest construction site, growing every day. Today, the city of the future, carrying the millennial plan and national events, presents a vigorous construction scene.

That year, the highly-anticipated 19th CPC National Congress was held. What new development ideas does the Central Committee of CPC have in store for everyone? General Secretary Xi Jinping clearly proposed new ideas for promoting high-quality economic development by building a modern economic system at the Party Congress. The 19th CPC National Congress report pointed out that China's economy has shifted from a stage of rapid growth to one of high-quality development and is in a critical period of changing development methods, optimizing economic structure, and transforming growth drivers. Building a modern economic system is an urgent requirement and strategic goal for China's development. We must adhere to quality first and efficiency first, take supply-side structural reform as the main line, promote the transformation of economic development quality, efficiency, and driving force, improve total factor productivity, focus on accelerating the construction of an industrial system with coordinated development of the real economy, technological innovation, modern finance, and human resources, and focus on building an economic system with effective market mechanisms, dynamic micro-entities, and measured macro-regulation, continuously enhancing China's economic innovation and competitiveness.

To promote the construction of a modern economic system and high-quality economic development, the Central Committee of CPC vigorously promoted supply-side structural reforms, accelerated the construction of an innovative country, implemented the rural revitalization strategy, implemented regional coordinated development strategies, accelerated the improvement of the socialist market economy system, and promoted the formation of a new pattern of comprehensive opening-up, achieving remarkable achievements in China's economic construction.

General Secretary Xi Jinping inspected Zhejiang from March 29 to April 1, 2020, to coordinate epidemic prevention, control, and economic and social development. During the inspection, he found that due to the outbreak of COVID-19, the supply chain had been broken, and the world economic situation was different from the past, as the conditions for large inflows and outflows had changed. In April, General Secretary Xi Jinping proposed the idea of constructing a new development pattern. The Standing Committee of the Political Bureau of the Central Committee held on May 14 proposed "to give full play to China's super-large-scale market advantage and domestic demand potential and build a new development pattern of domestic and international dual circulation that promotes each other." On May 23, General Secretary Xi Jinping pointed out when visiting economic committee members attending the CPPCC meeting: "In order to cultivate new strengths for China's participation in international cooperation and competition, we need to ensure smooth production, distribution, circulation, and consumption, and gradually form a double development dynamic with the domestic economy as the mainstay and the domestic economy and international engagement providing mutual reinforcement." The new development pattern was emphasized at the entrepreneurs' symposium held on July 21, and the Political Bureau meeting held on July 30. The "Fourteenth Five-Year Plan" proposal presented at the fifth plenary session of the 19th CPC Central Committee also set forth the establishment of a new development pattern as a major strategic task. This strategic arrangement and preemptive move are aimed at seizing the initiative in future development. It requires accurate understanding and active advancement from a comprehensive perspective.

The key to building a new development pattern lies in the unobstructed circulation of the economy. Therefore, it is necessary to deepen the main line of supply-side structural reform, continue to complete the important tasks of "three reductions, one reduction, and one supplement," comprehensively optimize and upgrade the industrial structure, enhance innovation capability, competitiveness, and comprehensive strength, strengthen the resilience of the supply system, form a more efficient and higher-quality input-output relationship, and achieve a dynamic balance of the economy at a high level. The most essential feature of the new development pattern is to achieve a high level of self-reliance and self-strengthening. More emphasis must be placed on independent innovation, comprehensively strengthening the deployment of technological innovation, gathering advantageous resources, vigorously and orderly promoting the "listing and leading" system and mechanism for innovation breakthroughs, and strengthening the connection between the innovation chain and the industrial chain. It is necessary to establish an effective system for expanding domestic demand, releasing the potential of domestic demand, accelerating the cultivation of a complete domestic demand system, strengthening demand-side management, expanding household consumption, improving consumption levels, and making the construction of a super-large domestic market a sustainable historical process.

The CPC's proposal on the new development pattern has attracted widespread international attention. According to *Xinhua News Agency*, Jim O'Neill, Chairman of the Royal Institute of International Affairs in the UK, said that China's in-depth exploration of the potential of its 1.4 billion population market would not only provide the impetus for its own economic recovery but also make an important contribution to the global economic recovery. Gu Qingyang, a scholar at the National University of Singapore, said that domestic and international circulation are mutually coordinated and promote each other. The stability of China's domestic circulation system is conducive to the stability of global economic circulation. Participating in international circulation helps Chinese enterprises carry out global layouts and provides external momentum for domestic economic circulation, creating more opportunities.

Because the CPC can always grasp the subtleties and creatively propose solutions to economic problems, China achieved positive growth in the extremely unusual year of 2020, being the only major economy in the world to achieve positive growth. In 2020, China's GDP exceeded 100 trillion yuan, and China's per capita GDP exceeded 10,000 US dollars, firmly ranking as the world's second-largest economy. The gap between the total economic volume of China and the world's largest economy, the

United States, is narrowing, and the confidence of the Chinese people is even more sufficient.

Looking around the world, in the context of the global economic downturn and the global challenges of COVID-19 pandemic control, China must rely on its own reality, unblock domestic circulation, and strive to develop an invincible and indestructible body in order to stand firm amid the changing international landscape and always maintain a vibrant survival and development. In practice, it is necessary to guard against cognitive misunderstandings, accelerate the construction of a new development pattern, and enhance one's own survival, competitiveness, development, and sustainability in various foreseeable and unforeseeable storms and waves, ensuring that the revitalization process of the Chinese nation is not interrupted.

— CHAPTER 20 —

Developing Socialist Democratic Politics

The CPC has always pursued democracy and promoted its development. When an American journalist visited Yan'an in the 1930s, he was impressed by the democratic style of the CPC. Attilio Massimo Iannucci, a former Italian ambassador to China, said, "China's democratic political framework has been initially established, and the Chinese government has put forward the task of gradually improving social democracy. Grassroots democracy has also been developed." Entering a new era, China regards people's democracy as the lifeblood of socialism, not only expanding people's democracy but also striving to build a socialist consultative democracy, promoting the extensive and multi-level institutionalization of consultative democracy. At the same time, significant progress has been made in comprehensively governing the country according to law, modernizing the national governance system and governance capabilities, and China's democratic political construction has achieved historical achievements.

Continuously Expanding the People's Democracy

Since the 18th CPC National Congress, the Central Committee, with Comrade Xi Jinping at its core, has focused on enhancing the Party's ability and determination to guide, plan, set policies, and promote reform. In national political life, the Party takes a leading position, strengthens the centralized and unified leadership of the Party, supports the National People's Congress, the government, the CPPCC, and the supervisory, court, and procuratorial organs to perform their functions according to law and regulations, carry out work, and play a role, focusing on unifying the two aspects. The Party's leadership and governance styles are improved to ensure the effective governance of the country by the Party leading the people. The People's Congress system is constantly improved to keep pace with the times and strengthen the system to guarantee that the people are masters of the country. The People's Congress system is a fundamental political system arrangement that organically unifies the Party's leadership, the people being masters of the country and governing the country according to law, and must be adhered to and continuously improved for a long time; the people being masters of the country is the essence and core of socialist democratic politics.

The people being masters of the country is solidly implemented. General Secretary Xi Jinping pointed out: "Ensuring and supporting the people being masters of the country is not just a slogan or an empty talk; it must be implemented in the political and social life of the country." In 2013, for the first time in sixty years, urban and rural areas elected deputies to the National People's Congress according to the same population ratio. In the 12th National People's Congress, the proportion of Party and government leaders decreased by 6.93% compared with the previous one; the proportion of grassroots workers and farmer representatives increased by 5.18%, and more representatives came from the grassroots frontline. On September 5, 2014, at the celebration of the 60th anniversary of the founding of the National People's Congress, General Secretary Xi Jinping pointed out: "The People's Congress system is an important part of the socialist system with Chinese characteristics and the fundamental political system supporting China's national governance system and governance capabilities. Under the new situation, we must unswervingly adhere to the People's Congress system and keep pace with the times to improve the People's Congress system."

The power of the National People's Congress has been significantly strengthened. In 2014 and 2018, the Standing Committee of the National People's Congress amended the *Budget Law* to strengthen the responsibilities of the National People's Congress in budget review and supervision. In April 2015, the Standing Committee of the National People's Congress issued "Several Opinions on Improving and Perfecting the Work of Special Inquiries," and every year, special inquiries were conducted on several major issues, with leaders of the State Council reporting to the Standing Committee of the National People's Congress, answering inquiries, and listening to opinions. To enhance the authority of the National People's Congress, China strictly enforces election discipline and seriously investigates and deals with cases such as the Hengyang election sabotage case in Hunan, the vote-buying and bribery case in Nanchong, Sichuan, and the vote-buying and bribery case in Liaoning, ensuring that the 2016 nationwide county and township-level National People's Congress representatives' renewal work maintains a clean and upright atmosphere. In 2017, the General Office of the Central Committee issued the "Implementation Opinions on Improving the System of Major Decisions Discussed and Decided by the National People's Congress and Reporting Major Decisions to the National People's Congress at the Same Level before They Are Issued by Governments at All Levels," taking an important step in the institutional construction of the people being masters of the country.

The exercise of state power by the people through the National People's Congress is supported and guaranteed. The leading role of the National People's Congress and its Standing Committee in legislative work is further played, the organization system and work system of the National People's Congress are improved, the exercise of legislative power, supervisory power, decision-making power, and appointment and removal power by the National People's Congress according to law is supported and guaranteed, and the role of the National People's Congress representatives is better played. At all levels, the National People's Congress and its Standing Committee have become representative organs that maintain close ties with the masses and assume all responsibilities conferred by the *Constitution* and laws.

In June 2020, Shen Jilan, who was re-elected as a representative of the 13th National People's Congress, passed away. As a grassroots female representative, she not only witnessed the development of Chinese people's democracy but also embodied the people's representatives' elegance, being a legendary Chinese woman. This ordinary farmer from the Taihang Mountain Village met Mao Zedong several times, visited Zhou Enlai's home, took photos with Deng Xiaoping, and was called "rare as phoenix feathers and unicorn horns" by Jiang Zemin. She was awarded the "National Model Worker" title three times. She was the only representative from the

First to the Thirteenth National People's Congress, known as the "living fossil of the People's Congress system." Despite her numerous honors, Shen Jilan always followed the "six nos" agreement: not changing her household registration, not being assigned a rank, not receiving a salary, not asking for housing, not adjusting work relations, and not being separated from labor. Whether as the Director of the Shanxi Women's Federation or as the Deputy Director of the Changzhi Municipal People's Congress Standing Committee, she always considered herself an ordinary farmer, never forgetting the people and labor, always fighting on the road to leading villagers out of poverty and striving for a moderately prosperous society, leading everyone to develop mushroom greenhouses, cultivate new industries, introduce Zhangze photovoltaic power generation, and develop green ecological tourism. In 2019, after participating in the National Day series of events in Beijing and returning to Xigou, she got busy again. She told the comrades in Xigou Village: "We must insist on scientific and green development, insist on high-quality development. No pretty words, just one word, 'do'!" She also said, "As an old Party member and representative, we have only one goal: to work with the masses and realize the people's dreams."

Adhere to and improve the system of regional ethnic autonomy, achieving "two combinations."

In December 2014, General Secretary Xi Jinping emphasized at the Central Ethnic Work Conference that we should adhere to and improve the system of regional ethnic autonomy by combining unity with autonomy and combining ethnic factors with regional factors. After the meeting, the Central Committee of CPC and the State Council issued the "Opinions on Strengthening and Improving Ethnic Work under New Circumstances," putting forward 25 opinions in six aspects: unswervingly following the correct path of solving ethnic problems with Chinese characteristics, promoting economic and social development in ethnic areas focusing on improving people's livelihood, promoting exchanges and integration among all ethnic groups, building a common spiritual home for all ethnic groups, improving the ability to manage ethnic affairs according to law, and strengthening the Party's leadership in ethnic work, pointing out the direction for ethnic work in the new era.

Adhere to and improve the grassroots mass self-government system and comprehensively strengthen grassroots democracy construction. Since the 18th CPC National Congress, the Party has strengthened its leadership in grassroots democracy construction; promoted the legalization of grassroots democracy, guaranteeing people's direct exercise of democratic rights according to law; innovated the forms of grassroots democracy realization; expanded channels for grassroots consultative democracy; and continuously improved grassroots democratic management mechanisms. Ninety-eight percent of villages in the country have formulated village rules and agreements or village self-government regulations, and urban communities have generally implemented residents' agreements or self-government regulations; significant progress has been made in constructing grassroots democratic systems. In 2017, the Fifth Session of the 12th National People's Congress reviewed and adopted the *General Provisions of the Civil Law of the People's Republic of China*, clarifying that village committees and resident committees have the special legal person qualifications of grassroots mass self-governing organizations and can engage in civil activities necessary for performing their functions.

Properly handling the relationship between consistency and diversity and doing a good job in the united front work under the new situation; fully strengthening the CPC's leadership in the United Front work is an important feature of the United Front work in the new era. In May 2015, the Central United Front Work Conference was held, and the Central Committee of CPC issued the "Regulations on the United Front Work of the Communist Party of China (Trial)." In July, the Political Bureau of the Central Committee of CPC decided to establish the Central United Front Work Leading Group. Since then, united front work leading groups led by the main person in charge of the Party committees have been established at all levels from the central to local levels to ensure the stable, orderly, and efficient operation of united front work, forming a united front pattern of concentrating and optimizing resources, with party committees, governments, people's organizations, and social organizations jointly promoting united front work. During this stage, new paths have been explored to broaden democratic supervision and increase supervision in implementing major reform measures and important policies. General Secretary Xi Jinping personally entrusted eight democratic parties to connect with eight provinces and regions in the central and western regions with large populations and high poverty incidence for special supervision of the poverty alleviation implementation. In September 2019, General Secretary Xi Jinping emphasized at the Central CPPCC Work Conference that in developing socialist consultative democracy, we should make good use of the advantages of democratic centralism, carry forward the fine tradition of "unity-criticism-unity," promote the full expression and in-depth exchange of different ideological viewpoints, respect each other and consult equally without imposing, follow rules and orderly consultation without speaking their own minds, be understanding and inclusive, sincerely consult without being radical or paranoid, and create a good atmosphere for consultation that is both free-spoken and rational, legal and compliant.

Create a new situation in the Party's mass organization work. In January 2015, the Central Committee of CPC issued the "Opinions on Strengthening and Improving the Party's Mass Organization Work." The "Opinions" profoundly expounded the importance and urgency of strengthening and improving the Party's mass organization work under the new situation, scientifically summarized the path of socialist mass organization development with Chinese characteristics, and put forward clear requirements and a series of policy measures for strengthening and improving the Party's political leadership, ideological leadership, and organizational leadership over mass organizations, giving play to the role of mass organizations and promoting the reform and innovation of mass organizations. It is a programmatic document for guiding and promoting the continuous development of the Party's mass organization work. In July, the Central Party's Mass Organization Work Conference was held. General Secretary Xi Jinping delivered an important speech, emphasizing the need to effectively maintain and enhance the political, advanced, and mass nature of the Party's mass organization work and create a new situation for the Party's mass organization work under the new situation. After the meeting, the General Office of the Central Committee of CPC successively issued the "National Federation of Trade Unions Reform Pilot Program," "Communist Youth League Reform Program," "National Women's Federation Reform Program," and others, comprehensively deploying and carrying out mass organization reforms, presenting a new atmosphere for mass organization work.

Promote the Extensive and Multi-level Institutional Development of Consultative Democracy

Strengthening the construction of consultative democracy is a major feature of socialist democratic political construction in the new era. Consultative democracy is an important way to realize the Party's leadership, a unique form and distinctive advantage of Chinese socialist democratic politics. The CPPCC is an institutional arrangement with Chinese characteristics and an important channel and specialized institution for socialist consultative democracy.

Since the 18th CPC National Congress, the CPPCC has focused on the central tasks of the Party and the country, revolving around the themes of unity and democracy, with consultative democracy running through political consultation, democratic supervision, and participation in political affairs. The content and form of consultative democracy have been continuously improved. Starting from October 2013, the 12th National Committee of the CPPCC began to hold bi-weekly consultative seminars, innovating the form of political consultation. In January 2015, the Central Committee of CPC issued the "Opinions on Strengthening the Construction of Socialist Consultative Democracy," making comprehensive arrangements for carrying out consultative democracy under the new situation and promoting the extensive, multi-level, and institutionalized development of socialist consultative democracy.

Expanding the pattern of political consultation and strengthening party consultation. Specifically, party consultation refers to the important democratic form of the CPC directly conducting political consultations with democratic parties based on common political goals, major policies, and important matters of the Party and the country before decision-making and during decision-making implementation. Strengthening party consultation is conducive to expanding the orderly political participation of democratic parties and non-party members, facilitating the expression of opinions, enhancing political consensus, gathering people's hearts and strength, promoting scientific and democratic decision-making, and advancing the modernization of the national governance system and governance capacity. In December 2015, the General Office of the Central Committee of CPC issued the "Implementation Opinions on Strengthening Party Consultation." This is the first time in the history of the CPC that specific implementation opinions on party consultation have been put forward, and it is a programmatic document for the CPC to strengthen cooperation with democratic parties in the new era. The opinion stipulates the main contents of the party consultation between the Central Committee of CPC and the central committees of democratic parties, including important documents of the CPC National Congress and the Central Committee of CPC; suggestions for amendments to the *Constitution*, and suggestions for the formulation and amendment of important laws; proposed candidates for state leaders; medium and long-term plans for national economic and social development, and annual economic and social development situations; important issues related to reform, development, and stability; major issues in the united front and multi-party cooperation; and other important issues that need to be consulted. The method of consultation is also stipulated. All these are conducive to the smooth development of party consultation.

Play the role of CPPCC think tank and actively offer suggestions and advice. The CPPCC includes more than 30 sectors, bringing together elites from all walks of life across the country, making it a highland of wisdom and the most intelligent think tank. The Central Committee of CPC has long recognized this role of the CPPCC.

Since the release of opinions on strengthening the construction of think tanks in 2015, the CPPCC's think tank construction has been fruitful. Through solid research and active discussions, many good suggestions have been made to the Central Committee of CPC. General Secretary Xi Jinping has also held several symposiums with non-party members to solicit opinions from the central committees of various democratic parties and non-party representatives.

For example, on December 8, 2020, the Central Committee of CPC held a symposium with non-party members at Zhongnanhai to listen to the opinions and suggestions of the central committees of various democratic parties, leaders of the All-China Federation of Industry and Commerce, and non-party representatives on the 2020 economic situation and economic work in 2021. Xi Jinping, General Secretary of the Central Committee of CPC, chaired the symposium, and Li Keqiang, Wang Yang, Wang Huning, and Han Zheng, members of the Political Bureau Standing Committee of the Central Committee of CPC, attended the symposium. Li Keqiang reported on the relevant situation of economic work on behalf of the Central Committee of CPC and introduced the relevant considerations for the economic work in 2021. At the symposium, speeches were successively delivered by Wan Exiang, Chairman of the Central Committee of the Revolutionary Committee of the Chinese KMT; Ding Zhongli, Chairman of the Central Committee of the China Democratic League; Hao Mingjin, Chairman of the Central Committee of the China National Democratic Construction Association; Cai Dafeng, Chairman of the Central Committee of the China Association for Promoting Democracy; Chen Zhu, Chairman of the Central Committee of the Chinese Peasants and Workers Democratic Party; Wan Gang, Chairman of the Central Committee of the Jiusan Society; Wu Weihua, Chairman of the Central Committee of the Taiwan Democratic Self-Government League; Su Hui, Chairman of the Central Committee of the Zhi Gong Party; Gao Yunlong, Chairman of the All-China Federation of Industry and Commerce; and Ouyang Changqiong, representative of non-party individuals. They agreed with the Central Committee of CPC's analysis of the current economic situation and considerations for next year's economic work. They made suggestions on promoting the construction of new smart cities, improving the top-level design of the national scientific and technological innovation system, promoting the implementation of carbon-neutral goals, promoting the equalization of public cultural services, cultivating and expanding new growth points for domestic demand, promoting the construction of community health institutions, improving grassland productivity to ensure grassland ecological restoration, guiding private enterprises to participate in rural revitalization and promoting common prosperity, and promoting the rapid development of the digital economy. After carefully listening to everyone's speeches, General Secretary Xi Jinping delivered an important speech. He said: "Everyone fully affirmed the achievements of this year's economic work in their speeches and put forward many constructive opinions and suggestions on studying and implementing the spirit of the fifth plenary session of the 19th CPC Central Committee, correctly understanding the current economic situation, and doing well in next year's economic work. We will seriously study and actively absorb them." He also emphasized that 2020 was an extraordinary year in the history of New China. Faced with a complex international situation, arduous and heavy domestic reform, development, and stability tasks, especially the severe impact of the COVID-19 pandemic, we maintained strategic focus, accurately judged the situation, carefully planned and deployed, decisively took action, made arduous efforts, and delivered a satisfactory and eye-catching answer sheet to the people and the world. During this period, the central committees of all democratic parties, the All-China Federation of Industry and Commerce, and non-party members consciously focused their work on the decision-making and deployment of the Central Committee of CPC. They closely followed the central work of the Party and the state, researching and investigating major issues such as promoting reform and innovation, enhancing governance capabilities, stimulating new momentum for economic development, and safeguarding and improving people's livelihood. Through flexible research methods such as organizational linkage and information technology, they gathered firsthand information, listened to frontline voices, and made efforts to understand the situation, identify problems, and propose practical countermeasures. They submitted various research reports, opinions, and suggestions to the Central Committee of CPC and the State Council, providing important references for scientific decision-making and effective policy implementation of the Central Committee of CPC. General Secretary Xi Jinping expressed his heartfelt thanks to everyone on behalf of the Central Committee of CPC. Similar symposiums are held every year and even multiple times a year. Through such channels, the CPC and other democratic parties maintain regular contact, which is beneficial for scientific and democratic decision-making.

Comprehensively Advancing the Rule of Law in China

Since the 18th CPC National Congress, the Central Committee of CPC, with Comrade Xi Jinping as its core, has placed greater emphasis on the rule of law and has clearly put forward the strategic task of comprehensively promoting the rule of law and accelerating the construction of a socialist country under the rule of law. The progress in scientific legislation, strict law enforcement, judicial justice, and the rule of law for all has been deepened, and the construction of a country, government, and society under the rule of law has been mutually promoted. The socialist legal system with Chinese characteristics has been increasingly improved, and the legal awareness of the whole society has been significantly enhanced.

Adhere to the path of the socialist rule of law with Chinese characteristics. In February 2013, General Secretary Xi Jinping pointed out in his speech at the Fourth Collective Study Session of the 18th CPC Central Committee Political Bureau that the comprehensive building of a moderately prosperous society puts forward higher requirements for the rule of law. We should fully implement the spirit of the 18th CPC National Congress, comprehensively promote scientific legislation, strict law enforcement, judicial justice, and the rule of law for all, and "persist in the rule of law, law-based governance, and law-based administration, promote the construction of a country, government, and society under the rule of law, and continuously create a new situation for the rule of law." In October of the same year, the third plenary session of the 18th CPC Central Committee put forward the goal of "promoting the construction of a law-based China." In October 2014, the fourth plenary session of the 18th CPC Central Committee, themed on comprehensively promoting the rule of law, put forward the guiding ideology, overall objectives, and basic principles for comprehensively promoting the rule of law and answered a series of major theoretical and practical issues related to the relationship between the Party's leadership and the rule of law, especially the significant assertion that we should adhere to the path of socialist rule of law with Chinese characteristics and build a socialist legal system, which has vigorously promoted the construction of a socialist country under the rule of law.

The essence of the path of the socialist rule of law with Chinese characteristics mainly includes three aspects: upholding the leadership of the CPC, adhering to the socialist system with Chinese characteristics, and implementing the socialist legal theory with Chinese characteristics. The socialist legal theory with Chinese characteristics is broad and profound, with rich connotations, and it profoundly answers the questions of what the socialist rule of law is and how to build it. The socialist legal theory with Chinese characteristics provides scientific theoretical guidance and solid academic support for comprehensively promoting the rule of law and building a law-based China.

There are countless roads to take, but the most effective one comes first. Throughout history, both in China and abroad, there is no universally applicable path to the rule of law in the world. There is no optimal model or standard version on the issue of the rule of law, only the choice that suits oneself. The path of the socialist rule of law with Chinese characteristics is the only correct path for China's rule of law, and we must resolutely follow it.

Clarifying the overall goal of comprehensively advancing the rule of law. In October 2014, the fourth plenary session of the 18th CPC Central Committee adopted the "Decision of the Central Committee of CPC on Several Major Issues Concerning Comprehensively Advancing the Rule of Law," which clearly put forward the overall goal of comprehensively advancing the rule of law as building a socialist legal system with Chinese characteristics and a socialist country under the rule of law. The Decision elaborates on the overall goal of comprehensively advancing the rule of law: under the leadership of the CPC, adhering to the socialist system with Chinese characteristics, implementing socialist legal theory with Chinese characteristics, forming a completely legal and regulatory system, an efficient rule of law implementation system, a strict rule of law supervision system, a strong rule of law guarantee system, a sound Party-internal regulatory system, persisting in the rule of law, law-based governance, and law-based administration, promoting the integrated construction of a country, government, and society under the rule of law, realizing scientific legislation, strict law enforcement, judicial justice, and the rule of law for all, and promoting the modernization of the national governance system and governance capacity. The proposal of the overall goal of comprehensively advancing the rule of law not only clarifies the nature and direction of comprehensively advancing the rule of law but also highlights the focus and main thrust of comprehensively advancing the rule of law, which has a guiding significance for comprehensively advancing the rule of law.

First, accelerate the improvement of the socialist legal system with Chinese characteristics. Law is an essential tool for governing the country, and good laws are the prerequisite for good governance. Since the 18th CPC National Congress, the Central Committee of CPC has prioritized legislation, deepening scientific, democratic, and lawful legislation and continuously improving the socialist legal system with Chinese characteristics, with the *Constitution* as its core. Improve the implementation and supervision system of the *Constitution*. For example, establishing the National Constitution Day and the Constitution Oath system. In November 2014, the 11th Meeting of the 12th National People's Congress Standing Committee adopted the

"Decision on the Establishment of the National Constitution Day," setting December 4 as National Constitution Day. In July 2015, the 15th Meeting of the 12th National People's Congress Standing Committee adopted the "Decision of the Standing Committee of the National People's Congress on Implementing the Constitution Oath System," requiring state functionaries elected or appointed by the People's Congresses at all levels and their standing committees at or above the county level to take a public oath to the *Constitution* when taking office. In addition, to ensure the strict implementation of laws, the Standing Committee of the National People's Congress has continuously strengthened and improved law enforcement inspection work.

Second, improve the legislative system. First, strengthen the leadership of the CPC in the legislative work. Continuously improve the system of reporting legislative work to the Central Committee of CPC, and major issues in drafting and amending important laws and other significant matters in legislative work shall be promptly reported to the Central Committee by the Party Group of the National People's Congress Standing Committee. Second, give full play to the leading role of the National People's Congress and its Standing Committee in legislative work. The revision of the *Legislation Law* in 2015 standardized the authority of departmental regulations and local government regulations, granted local legislative power to all cities with districts and clearly stated that cities with districts can formulate local regulations on urban and rural construction and management, environmental protection, historical and cultural protection, and other matters, making significant adjustments to the local legislative system. As of October 2017, among the 240 cities, 30 autonomous prefectures and four prefecture-level cities without districts newly endowed with local legislative power, 456 local regulations and 193 local government rules had been formulated.

Third, strengthen legislation in key areas. Since the 18th CPC National Congress, the National People's Congress and the State Council have insisted on legislation as a priority, actively playing a leading and promoting role in legislation and successively introducing a series of laws and regulations. *The General Provisions of Civil Law*, passed by the Fifth Session of the 12th National People's Congress in March 2017, marked the solid first step in compiling China's Civil Code. In May 2020, the Third Session of the 13th National People's Congress deliberated and passed the *Civil Code*, marking a new stage in the construction of China's rule of law. The *Civil Code* is an "encyclopedia of social life," the basic market economy law, a declaration of civil rights protection, and a culmination of civil legislation in New China. Its promulgation has a milestone significance in the history of China's rule of law construction. It will bring more positive, comprehensive, and standardized impacts on constructing a country, government, and society under the rule of law. It will also provide sufficient legal protection for upholding and improving the socialist system with Chinese characteristics, promoting the modernization of the national governance system and governance capacity, and safeguarding the well-being and happiness of the people. As General Secretary Xi Jinping said, "The *Civil Code* has an important position in the legal system of socialism with Chinese characteristics and is a fundamental law that solidifies the foundation, stabilizes expectations, and benefits the long term."

In addition, the level of scientific legislation, democratic legislation, and lawful legislation has been further improved. For example, in December 2013, the Standing Committee of the National People's Congress passed a decision to repeal legal provisions on re-education through labor, which legally abolished the re-education through the labor system that had been in place for more than 50 years. The Legislative Affairs Commission of the Standing Committee of the National People's Congress actively researched proactive and passive reviews. From 2013 to 2016, 42 administrative regulations and 98 judicial interpretations that were newly promulgated were reviewed and studied, and those found to be in violation of the *Constitution* and laws were revoked and corrected according to law and regulations.

Comprehensively promote the construction of the rule of law. Accelerate the construction of a government under the rule of law. In October 2014, the fourth plenary session of the 18th CPC Central Committee put forward the overall goal of building a government under the rule of law, namely, a government with scientific functions, legally defined powers and responsibilities, strict law enforcement, openness and fairness, integrity and efficiency, and law-abiding integrity. In December 2015, the Central Committee of CPC and the State Council issued the "Outline for the Implementation of the Construction of a Government under the Rule of Law (2015–2020)," further clarifying the timetable and roadmap for the construction of a government under the rule of law and promoting the steady progress of the construction of a government under the rule of law. In February 2016, the General Office of the Central Committee of CPC and the General Office of the State Council issued the "Opinions on Comprehensively Promoting Government Affairs Openness" and implementation details, requiring adherence to the principle of openness as the norm and non-disclosure as the exception, and promoting the openness of administrative decision-making, execution, management, service, and results. Relying on the Internet government information data service platform and convenient service platform, various regions and departments have promoted the standardization and normalization of government affairs openness, improving the effectiveness and convenience of government affairs openness. Governments at all levels have actively improved the government spokesperson system and the information release system for emergencies, timely responding to public concerns.

Comprehensively deepen judicial reform and build a high-quality team for the rule of law. Judicial fairness plays an important leading role in social justice, while judicial injustice has a fatal destructive effect on social justice. General Secretary Xi Jinping has called for enhancing the credibility of the judiciary. Since the 18th CPC National Congress, legal and political institutions at all levels have deeply promoted judicial system reform under the strong leadership of the Central Committee of CPC, continuously improving the judiciary's credibility. This includes comprehensively implementing the reform of the judicial accountability system, implementing a classified management system for judicial personnel, and dividing the staff of courts and procuratorates into judges and prosecutors, judicial assistants, and judicial administrative personnel according to the characteristics and requirements of their profession, realizing proper roles and responsibilities for each. On February 27, 2019, the Supreme People's Court released the white paper "Judicial Reform of Chinese Courts (2013–2018)" in Beijing, disclosing that since the 18th CPC National Congress, the People's Courts have corrected 34 major criminal wrongful cases, such as the cases of Nie Shubin, Hugejiletu, and Zhang's uncle and nephew, through the trial supervision process, boosting society's confidence in judicial fairness.

Protect the litigation rights and interests of the people. Actively and comprehensively implement the case filing registration system, improve the people's assessor and people's supervisor system, and improve the state compensation and judicial aid system. Vigorously promote judicial openness. The people's courts have built four major platforms: open trial process, open court activities, open judicial documents, and open enforcement information; the procuratorial organs have built a case information public system, operating four major platforms for case procedural information inquiry, legal document publication, important case information release, and defense and agency appointment applications. An open, dynamic, transparent, and convenient sunshine judicial mechanism is gradually taking shape.

Build a high-quality team for the rule of law. In accordance with the requirements of strong political, professional, responsible, disciplined, and style performance, build a politically and legally dedicated, people-oriented, daring to take responsibility, and clean and honest team. Improve the national unified legal professional qualification system and support the leadership of the CPC and the socialist rule of law as the basic requirements for lawyers to practice. Establish an open selection system for legislative workers, judges, and prosecutors and a hierarchical selection system for judges and prosecutors. Cultivate a group of legal talents and reserve forces that adhere to the socialist legal system. Persist in using Marxist legal thought and the theory of the socialist rule of law with Chinese characteristics to guide legal education and research and strengthen the construction of legal teaching staff. Build a lawyer team with complementary advantages and a reasonable structure, including social lawyers, public service lawyers, and corporate lawyers. Accelerate the integration of the public legal service system and promote the equalization of public legal services. Strengthen public legal services and people's mediation work.

The public's awareness of the rule of law has been significantly strengthened. Legal education has been incorporated into the national education system. In June 2016, the Ministry of Education, the Ministry of Justice, and the National Office for Law Popularization jointly issued the "Outline of Legal Education for Young People," which covers all stages of education, effectively enhancing the legal consciousness and legal awareness of young students. The principle of "who enforces the law, who popularizes the law" is implemented, clarifying that state organs are the main bodies responsible for promoting and educating the rule of law. Constitutional education is carried out throughout society, promoting the spirit of the *Constitution*. The Sixth and Seventh Five-Year Plan for increasing public knowledge of the law are implemented to promote legal awareness and law-abiding behavior among all citizens. The concept of rule of law is strengthened among state officials, focusing on the "key few" of leading cadres and explicitly requiring leaders at all levels to take the lead in acting according to law and obeying the law.

The authority of law stems from the people's inner endorsement and sincere faith. Since the 18th CPC National Congress, with the implementation of the strategy of comprehensively governing the country according to law, the rule of law has become the faith of the Chinese people. The construction of socialism with Chinese characteristics under the rule of law has embarked on a new journey.

Promote the Modernization of the National Governance System and Governance Capabilities

Promoting the modernization of socialism in China has always been the firm goal of the CPC. In the 1950s, the goal of building a modernized powerful country was set, and later, the slogan of advancing toward four modernizations was put forward. Entering the new era of reform and opening-up, the CPC has focused on building socialist modernization for decades.

The third plenary session of the 18th CPC Central Committee held in November 2013 made top-level design for comprehensively deepening reform, clarifying the overall goal of comprehensively deepening reform, including promoting the modernization of the national governance system and governance capabilities. General Secretary Xi Jinping also specifically explained this, emphasizing that this is the first time the CPC has proposed the modernization of governance and that it is a continuation of Deng Xiaoping's important exposition on institutional construction, striving to make China's system more perfect and mature through reform within thirty years after Deng Xiaoping's 1992 conversation. Some people call national governance modernization the fifth modernization.

The fifth plenary session of the 18th CPC Central Committee further emphasized that during the Thirteenth Five-Year Plan period, "various institutional systems will become more mature and more established," and "major progress will be made in the modernization of the national governance system and governance capabilities, and the basic system of basic institutions in various fields will be formed." The 19th CPC National Congress made a strategic plan to build a socialist, modernized, powerful country that is prosperous, democratic, civilized, harmonious, and beautiful by the middle of this century, with the goals of institutional construction and governance capability construction by 2035, "various institutional systems will be perfect, and the modernization of the national governance system and governance capabilities will be basically realized"; by the middle of this century, "realize the modernization of the national governance system and governance capabilities." The second and third plenary sessions of the 19th CPC Central Committee made arrangements for amending the *Constitution* and deepening the reform of Party and state institutions, taking new major steps in institutional construction and governance capability construction. The third plenary session of the 19th CPC Central Committee pointed out: "In order to better lead the people in carrying out great struggles, building great projects, advancing great causes, and realizing great dreams, our Party must accelerate the modernization of the national governance system and governance capabilities, and strive to form a more mature and more established socialist system with Chinese characteristics. This is a major task before us." This highlights the new thinking of the Central Committee of CPC since the 18th National Congress on deepening reform from the perspective of institutional construction and reflects the fundamental and important nature of institutions.

After years of comprehensively deepening reform, significant progress has been made in the modernization of the national governance system and governance capabilities. For example, the "simplification of administrative procedures, decentralization of powers, and improvement of services" reform promoted by the State Council, Zhejiang's "maximum one visit" initiative, and Beijing's street and township whistle-blowing and department reporting governance practices all demonstrate this progress. Among them, the "maximum one visit" reform is an innovative service model that integrates one-window acceptance, integrated services, and one-time completion, realizing the administrative goal of "maximum one visit" for enterprises and the public to deal with government affairs. At the end of 2016, the "maximum one visit" reform was first proposed in Zhejiang. This inward-facing self-revolution targeting the old-style governance model has already shown results. However, the concept and practice of "maximum one visit" are still being rolled out nationwide.

To further improve the various systems of the Party and the country and continue to promote the modernization of the national governance system and governance capabilities, the fourth plenary session of the 19th CPC Central Committee, held from October 28 to 31, 2019, deliberated and passed the "Decision of the Central Committee of CPC on Some Major Issues Concerning Upholding and Perfecting the Socialist System with Chinese Characteristics, and Promoting the Modernization of the National Governance System and Governance Capabilities." This decision is a political declaration and action program for upholding and perfecting the socialist system with Chinese characteristics and promoting the modernization of the national governance system and governance capabilities.

The plenary session summarized the significant advantages of China's national system and national governance system in thirteen aspects and clarified the guiding ideology and major significance of upholding and perfecting the socialist system with Chinese characteristics, and promoting the modernization of the national governance system and governance capabilities. The plenary session also put forward the overall goals: by the centenary of the founding of the CPC, significant achievements will be made in making various systems more mature and more established; by 2035, various systems will be perfect, and the modernization of the national governance system and governance capabilities will be basically achieved; by the centenary of the founding of the People's Republic of China, the modernization of the national governance system and governance capabilities will be fully realized, and the socialist system with Chinese characteristics will be further consolidated, with its superiority fully demonstrated.

The plenary session focused on upholding and perfecting the fundamental, basic, and important systems supporting socialism with Chinese characteristics. It clarified the fundamental points that various systems must adhere to and consolidate and the direction for their improvement and development. The main contents include: upholding and improving the Party's leadership system, enhancing the Party's ability to govern scientifically, democratically, and in accordance with the law; upholding and improving the system of the people being the masters of the country, and developing socialist democratic politics; upholding and improving the socialist legal system with Chinese characteristics, and enhancing the Party's ability to govern and rule the country according to law; the socialist administrative system with Chinese characteristics, building a government governance system with clear responsibilities and administration according to law; the socialist basic economic system, promoting high-quality economic development; the system of flourishing and developing advanced socialist culture, consolidating the common ideological foundation for the unity and struggle of the whole people; the coordinated urban and rural livelihood security system, meeting the people's ever-growing needs for a better life; the system of co-construction, co-governance, and sharing of social governance, maintaining social stability and safeguarding national security; the ecological civilization system, promoting harmony between man and nature; the absolute leadership system of the Party over the people's army, ensuring the people's army faithfully fulfills its missions and tasks in the new era; the "One Country, Two Systems" principle, promoting the peaceful reunification of the motherland; an independent and peaceful foreign policy, promoting the building of a community with a shared future for mankind; the Party and state supervision system, strengthening the restriction and supervision of the exercise of power. Among them, the Party's leadership system is the fundamental leadership system of the country, which guides and runs through other aspects of the system. The plenary session also put forward requirements for strengthening the Party's leadership in upholding and perfecting the socialist system with Chinese characteristics and promoting the modernization of the national governance system and governance capabilities.

Holding a plenary session of the Central Committee to study national institutions and governance issues and make decisions is a first in the history of the CPC and also a first in the history of New China. This plenum is a pioneering and milestone meeting of great significance.

"Whenever a country is to be established, its system must be thoroughly examined." It is precisely because the CPC attaches great importance to institutional construction, making China's system more scientific and effective, that China has created the rare miracles of rapid economic development and long-term social stability that are seldom seen in the world. The socialist system with Chinese characteristics is a great creation in the history of human civilization. We must both adhere to seeking truth from facts and keep up with the times, constantly improving the socialist system with Chinese characteristics.

CHAPTER 21

Prosper Socialist Culture

Excellent culture can continuously provide spiritual energy for a country and a nation to strive forward. When culture thrives, so do the nation and the country. General Secretary Xi Jinping attaches importance to the outstanding traditional Chinese culture and the construction of a socialist culture with Chinese characteristics, emphasizing cultural confidence. In December 2014, former German Chancellor Helmut Schmidt wrote in his book review of *Xi Jinping: The Governance of China*: "President Xi Jinping's interpretation of Confucianism demonstrates China's growing cultural confidence. In a large country like China, national cohesion is crucial... The long-standing and rich Chinese civilization can boost the confidence and self-awareness of the Chinese people." Over the years, the construction of Chinese culture has been persevering, and cultural undertakings have become increasingly prosperous.

Practice the Core Socialist Values

The core values are the spiritual bond that a nation relies on to maintain cohesion and a country's common ideological and moral foundation. Without shared core values, a nation and a country will have no soul and no guidance. The core socialist values were explicitly proposed at the 18th CPC National Congress in November 2012. The report of the 18th National Congress pointed out that it is necessary to strengthen the construction of the core socialist value system, carry out in-depth study and education of the socialist core value system, and guide social trends and consensus with the core socialist value system. "Advocate prosperity, democracy, civilization, and harmony; advocate freedom, equality, justice, and the rule of law; advocate patriotism, dedication, integrity, and friendliness; and actively cultivate and practice the core socialist values." Later, General Secretary Xi Jinping introduced the core values in a speech at a symposium with teachers and students at Peking University, saying, "After repeatedly soliciting opinions and synthesizing various understandings, we propose to advocate prosperity, democracy, civilization, and harmony; advocate freedom, equality, justice, and the rule of law; advocate patriotism, dedication, integrity, and friendliness; and actively cultivate and practice the core socialist values. Prosperity, democracy, civilization, and harmony are the national-level value requirements. Freedom, equality, justice, and the rule of law are the social-level value requirements, and patriotism, dedication, integrity, and friendliness are the citizen-level value requirements."

In accordance with the spirit of the 18th National Congress, in December 2013, the General Office of the Central Committee of CPC issued the "Opinions on Cultivating and Practicing the Core Socialist Values." The "Opinions" consist of six items and twenty-three articles, which put forward specific opinions on the guiding ideology, basic principles, and basic requirements for cultivating and practicing the core socialist values.

General Secretary Xi Jinping attaches great importance to the promotion of core socialist values. On February 24, 2014, when presiding over the 13th Collective Study of the Central Committee of CPC Political Bureau, he proposed, "Efforts should be made to integrate the requirements of the core socialist values into various activities concerning intellectual and cultural progress, so as to attract more people to participate in such activities, upgrade their moral outlook and foster civic virtues in society for family happiness, extending care to others and contributing more to society. We should make use of every opportunity to make this happen, anytime and anywhere. We should give full play to our policies concerning the economy, politics, culture and society to better serve the cultivation of the core socialist values. Laws and regulations should act as a driving force for the spread of the core values. All social administrative agencies should make it their responsibility to advocate the core socialist values and reflect them in their routine work so that all activities conforming with the core values are encouraged and those running counter to the core values are rebuffed." On October 15,

General Secretary Xi Jinping once again raised the requirements at the symposium on literary and artistic work: "We must vigorously promote and practice the core socialist values in the whole society, making them omnipresent like air, becoming the common value pursuit of all people, becoming the unique spiritual pillar of being born Chinese, and becoming the daily behavior norms that people unconsciously follow. We must call on the whole society to take action, internalize the core socialist values as people's spiritual pursuit, and externalize them as people's conscious actions through education, guidance, media publicity, cultural edification, practice, and institutional guarantees."

In response to the spirit of the Central Committee of CPC, various localities nationwide have intensified their publicity and education on core socialist values. Posters have been put up in the streets and alleys of cities, and introductions to the core socialist values can be found in subways, overpasses, and display screens. From primary school to college, students must learn and understand the importance of core socialist values. In order to make the core socialist values truly become people's inherent habits, in December 2016, the General Office of the Central Committee of CPC and the General Office of the State Council issued the "Guiding Opinions on Further Integrating the Core Socialist Values into the Construction of the Rule of Law." This opinion made specific arrangements for integrating the core socialist values into the construction of the rule of law by using laws, regulations, and public policies to convey correct value orientation to society. In March 2018, the "state advocates core socialist values" were written into the *Constitution*, and the core socialist values embodied national will. In May, the "Legislative Amendment Plan for Integrating Core Socialist Values into the Construction of the Rule of Law" issued by the Central Committee of CPC clearly proposed to focus on integrating the core socialist values into the whole process of the enactment, revision, abolishment, and interpretation of laws and regulations, ensuring that legislative guidance is more distinct, requirements are clearer, and measures are more powerful. This demonstrates the core socialist value orientation of laws and regulations and points out the direction and path for further promoting the realization of good laws and good governance.

Setting up role models is an important way to implement the core socialist values, and many advanced examples of practicing the core socialist values have emerged in various industries. On the afternoon of March 4, 2017, General Secretary Xi Jinping emphasized during his visit to the members of the China Association for Promoting Democracy, Chinese Peasants and Workers Democratic Party, and the Jiusan Society participating in the Fifth Session of the 12th National Committee of the CPPCC that he hoped that the vast majority of intellectuals in China would consciously become role models for practicing the core socialist values, adhering to the supremacy of the nation, the people, and the nation, always bearing in mind the overall situation and having a great sense of self, always adhering to the right path and pursuing the truth, starting from oneself, starting from now, and starting from daily life, and leading the whole society to follow the core socialist values through personal actions. In fact, many outstanding intellectuals are exemplary examples of consciously practicing the core socialist values. For example, Huang Danian, who was a famous geophysicist and served as a professor and doctoral supervisor at the College of Earth Exploration Science and Technology, Jilin University. In 2009, Huang Danian resolutely returned to his homeland, giving up favorable conditions abroad, engaging in painstaking research and innovation, and achieving a series of significant scientific and technological achievements, filling many gaps in domestic technology. Unfortunately, he passed away due to illness on January 8, 2017, at the age of 58. General Secretary Xi Jinping made important instructions on the advanced deeds of Huang Danian, pointing out that Comrade Huang Danian adhered to the ideal of serving the country with science and technology, contributing to the prosperity and strength of the motherland, the revitalization of the nation, and the happiness of the people as his lifelong pursuit, and made outstanding contributions to the cause of education and scientific research in our country. His advanced deeds are touching. General Secretary Xi Jinping emphasized that we should take Comrade Huang Danian as an example, learn from his patriotic feelings of having a great self and sincere dedication to the country, learn from his professional spirit of teaching and being willing to be the first, learn from his noble character of indifference to fame and fortune, and willingness to dedicate, integrate the feelings of loving the country and the ambition of serving the country into the great cause of reform and development of the motherland, and into the great struggle of the people to create history, start from ourselves, start from our own posts, and contribute wisdom and strength to the realization of the Two Centenary Goals and the realization of the Chinese dream of the great rejuvenation of the Chinese nation.

The cultivation of core socialist values is not achieved overnight. We must persist in progressing from easy to difficult, from near to far, and strive to transform the requirements of core socialist values into daily behavioral norms, and then form a belief in the concept of consciously following them. For every Chinese person, when things go smoothly, they see mountains as mountains and water as water. When encountering setbacks, they should not become doubtful and shaken, seeing mountains not as mountains and water not as water. At any time, we must adhere to the core socialist values formed and developed on Chinese land, make achievements in the tide of the times, and achieve our precious lives.

Promoting the Construction of a Cyber Superpower

Since officially gaining full access to the Internet in 1994, China's network construction has developed rapidly. The Internet and informatization work have achieved remarkable results, reaching thousands of households, with the number of netizens ranking first in the world, making China a cyber superpower. At the same time, it should be noted that China is still relatively lagging in independent innovation, with significant regional and urban-rural differences, particularly in the gap between per capita bandwidth and the international advanced level. The bottleneck in the development of the domestic Internet remains prominent.

To strengthen network construction, in 2014, the Central Committee of CPC decided to establish the Central Cyber Security and Informatization Leading Group, led by General Secretary Xi Jinping, with Li Keqiang and Liu Yunshan, members of the Political Bureau Standing Committee, serving as deputy leaders. The main responsibility of the Central Cyber Security and Informatization Leading Group is to play a centralized and unified leadership role, coordinate and coordinate major issues in the field of cyber security and informatization, formulate and implement national cyber security and informatization development strategies, macro plans, and major policies, and continuously enhance security guarantee capabilities. The group held its first meeting in February 2014. At the meeting, General Secretary Xi Jinping clearly put forward the goal of building a cyber superpower and made important statements on cyber security, network information, network public opinion, and network economy, especially emphasizing the importance of network security. He said that without network security, there would be no national security, and without informatization, there would be no modernization. To build a cyber superpower, we must have our own technology and solid technology; we must have rich and comprehensive information services and a thriving network culture; we must have good information infrastructure and form a strong information economy; we must have a high-quality network security and informatization talent team; we must actively carry out bilateral and multilateral Internet international exchanges and cooperation. The strategic deployment of building a cyber superpower should be synchronized with the Two

Centenary Goals, and we should continue to advance toward the goals of universal network infrastructure, significantly enhanced independent innovation capabilities, comprehensive development of the information economy, and strong network security guarantees. Since then, the group has held several meetings to deploy and promote the construction of a cyber superpower.

In November 2014, the World Internet Conference initiated by China was held in Wuzhen, Zhejiang. Chinese President Xi Jinping attended and delivered an important speech. According to statistics, this conference held more than 20 forums, meetings, and events, with over 1,000 guests from nearly 100 countries and regions gathering in Wuzhen. This event, the largest and highest-level Internet conference held in China so far, attracted global attention, with high domestic and international media coverage. More than 110 Chinese and foreign media outlets and over 600 journalists attended and reported on the event in Wuzhen. *Forbes* magazine's website reported that hosting the first World Internet Conference gave China certain credibility. Chinese Internet companies such as Alibaba, Tencent, and Baidu have been making rapid progress internationally, which has also given the Chinese government more confidence. Bloomberg reported that China's growing influence in the Internet sector was evident at the first World Internet Conference. One of the conference's goals was to show China was ready to take on greater Internet management and development responsibility. Before the conference's opening, Aleksey Shelyeshev, a reporter from RIA Novosti-TASS, discussed the significance of the World Internet Conference and China's Internet development with Zhejiang Online reporters. Aleksey said, "This Wuzhen Internet Conference provides an opportunity for countries to exchange information and benefit from mutual cooperation." President Xi Jinping's speech also sparked heated discussions. Singapore's *Lianhe Zaobao* reported that Xi Jinping's speech reflected China's desire to strengthen its voice and participate in rule-making in the Internet world, which still lacks international rules, as the country with the largest number of netizens and the largest electronic information product manufacturing base. The BBC's interpretation of the conference was that China set the theme of the Internet Conference as "interconnectivity and shared governance," meaning that Internet governance should not be dominated by American companies. The beautiful town of Wuzhen became the permanent venue for the World Internet Conference, held annually ever since.

The Central Committee of CPC attaches great importance to the construction of a strong cyber power, not only holding symposiums to solicit opinions but also conducting collective learning and research deployment. On April 19, 2016, the Central

Committee of CPC held a symposium on cybersecurity and informatization work. During his speech, General Secretary Xi Jinping said, "I've always wanted to hold this meeting. Since the 18th CPC National Congress, China's Internet industry has developed rapidly, cybersecurity and informatization work has been steadily advancing, and significant progress and achievements have been made. At the same time, there are many shortcomings and problems. The purpose of this symposium is to listen to everyone's opinions and suggestions face-to-face and to discuss some measures and methods together so that we can do our work better." He emphasized the need to focus on core Internet technology and pointed out that the core technology of the Internet is China's biggest "lifeline," and the dependence on foreign technology is China's biggest hidden danger. Even if an Internet company has a large scale and high market value, if it heavily relies on foreign core components, and the "lifeline" of the supply chain is in the hands of others, it is like building a house on someone else's foundation, which may not withstand wind and rain, and may even be vulnerable. To ensure Internet security and national security, we must take control of the development of the Internet. It is necessary to break through the difficult problem of core technology and strive to achieve "overtaking on a curve" in some fields and aspects. What is core technology? It can be grasped from three aspects: 1) basic technology and general technology, 2) asymmetric technology and "trump card" technology, 3) cutting-edge technology and disruptive technology. China is on the same starting line in these areas as foreign countries. If we can deploy and focus on tackling key issues in advance, we will likely achieve a transition from following and running to leading. General Secretary Xi Jinping said, "Entrepreneurs, experts, scholars, and technicians in the field of cybersecurity in China should have this ambition and strive to achieve new major breakthroughs in core technology as soon as possible. As the saying goes, 'Take action every day, and you won't be afraid of millions of miles; do it often, and you won't be afraid of millions of things.'" On October 9, 2016, the 36th Collective Study Session of the Political Bureau of the Central Committee of CPC focused on implementing the cyber power strategy. General Secretary Xi Jinping emphasized during the study session that we must accelerate the promotion of independent innovation in network information technology, speed up the digital economy's driving force for economic development, improve the level of network management, strengthen cybersecurity defense capabilities, promote social governance using network information technology, enhance China's international discourse and rule-making power in cyberspace, and make unremitting efforts toward building a strong cyber power. In 2017, the 19th CPC National Congress once again emphasized the need to strengthen the construction of a strong cyber power.

After the 19th CPC National Congress, the Central Committee of CPC made a series of significant decisions, leading to the rapid and healthy development of cyberspace affairs. The construction of a cyber superpower has been continuously strengthened, the capability of cybersecurity protection has steadily improved, and the important role of the Internet in economic and social development has become even more prominent. The vast majority of people have gained a stronger sense of fulfillment from sharing in the achievements of internet development. *The China Internet Development Statistics Report* released at the end of February 2019 shows that China ranks first in the world in terms of the number of Internet users, Internet penetration rate, and scale of online retail transactions. The Internet is deeply integrating into and profoundly changing every aspect of society.

In terms of core technologies, which are crucial for the country, China's research capabilities in fields such as big data, artificial intelligence, and 5G have been continuously enhanced. Multiple 5G technology solutions have been incorporated into international core standards, leading 40% of standardization projects, and both the speed and quality of progress are among the top in the world. The number of artificial intelligence-related patent applications has exceeded 144,000, ranking first globally.

The development of the cybersecurity industry represents a new form of productivity and direction for growth, with innovation and advancements in information technology constantly giving birth to new industries, business formats, and models. A clothing manufacturing company in Wuhan has reduced the production time of a garment from design to factory delivery from three days to two hours through the automated operation of an intelligent production platform. The number of products developed and designed annually has increased from 500 to 3,000. In 2020, the digital transformation of traditional industries brought a total market size of over 40 trillion yuan to China, and the digital economy has become a new driving force for China's economic growth.

For the continuous development of the Internet to drive social and economic growth, it is essential to ensure the healthy operation of the Internet within the framework of the rule of law. In response to prominent issues such as vulgarity and sensationalism on the Internet, the buying and selling of data on social media, and mobile apps that violate users' personal information, national authorities have joined forces to address these issues, conducting a series of "combined heavy punches," such as interviewing self-media platforms and including violators in a cross-platform blacklist. In 2019 alone, 1,497 websites were interviewed according to law, 6,417 illegal websites had their licenses or records revoked or were shut down, and 1,177 cases were transferred to judicial authorities for investigation.

To strengthen the management of the Internet, relevant national departments have issued normative documents such as the "Regulations on the Administration of Internet News and Information Services" and the "Regulations on the Administration of Internet User Public Account Information Services," as well as laws and regulations such as the *E-Commerce Law*. They have also forcefully carried out special rectification actions such as "Net Clean-up," "Sword Net," and "Child Protection" to effectively rectify online rumors, pornography, and other network disorders. A series of activities, such as the "National Network Integrity Promotion Day" and the "China Good Netizen Project," have been implemented, and the legal governance of the Internet has been further strengthened. China also attaches great importance to inspiring a sense of social responsibility among Internet companies, strengthening the management of Internet celebrities, live streamers, and live-streamed sales while advocating good online mass relations and paying attention to online public opinion. As cyberspace becomes increasingly clear, citizens' online literacy is also significantly improving, and the rapid and healthy development of the cybersecurity industry is increasingly benefiting the people.

Firmly Upholding Cultural Confidence

Firmly upholding cultural confidence is crucial for the rise and fall of a nation, cultural security, and the independence of the national spirit. General Secretary Xi Jinping pointed out that cultural confidence is a more fundamental, more extensive, and more profound confidence and a more foundational, deeper, and enduring power. Without a high degree of cultural confidence and cultural prosperity, there can be no great rejuvenation of the Chinese nation. There was a time when some people believed that "the moon is rounder abroad" and that everything foreign was better. In the final analysis, cultural confidence is about Chinese people's self-confidence.

With firm cultural confidence, the Chinese people have a strong foundation. Chinese culture has survived thousands of years and is universally acknowledged. The fundamental reason for the continuous inheritance and vitality of Chinese civilization is that traditional Chinese culture has a long history, is brilliant, profound, open-minded, and possesses a strong vitality. The Chinese characters, which serve as the carriers of Chinese culture, record the long cultural history of China and contain the vast world of the Chinese people with their simple strokes. Take the characters "正" (righteous) and "直" (straight) as examples: walking without deviating from the path is righteous, and not looking askance is straight. Chinese character creation intends to tell the world to see the road clearly and head toward the goal. This is the thinking of the ancients, and it also perfectly aligns with our spirit today. Chinese characters' unique charm and evolution history have deeply attracted people worldwide who love them. According to a report by CCTV.com, Richard, an American "Chinese Character Uncle," has spent half his life studying Chinese characters. To study Chinese characters, he spent all his savings and almost got deported. He spent 20 years sorting out oracle bone inscriptions, bronze inscriptions, and small seal scripts and put them on the Internet so that more people could understand, recognize, and promote Chinese characters. He said, "I feel that I can change the lives of these young people, even if just a little bit." Although he has blond hair and blue eyes and stumbles in his language expression, the perseverance in his heart, the brightness in his eyes, and the elegance of his manners embody the spirit of Chinese character inheritance and the image of a modest gentleman in the artistic conception of traditional culture walking toward the world.

The profound Chinese culture, with Chinese characters as its carrier, provides powerful spiritual support for the Chinese nation's continuous development and growth. In particular, the ideological concepts contained in the excellent traditional Chinese culture, such as discarding the outdated and bringing in the new as closely as possible with the demands of the times, being practical, taking roots, benefiting the people, enriching the people, following the natural law, and harmonizing man and nature, provide useful enlightenment for people to understand and transform the world, and valuable references for governing the country. The excellent traditional Chinese culture contains a humanistic spirit characterized by principles such as seeking common ground while preserving differences, handling things in a harmonious but distinct manner, educating people about culture, and pursuing the aesthetic integration of form and spirit. This spirit has nourished the unique and rich literature, art, science, technology, and humanities of the Chinese nation, and continues to have a profound impact today. The moral norms contained in the excellent traditional Chinese culture, such as the sense of responsibility embodied in "the rise and fall of the world rests on the shoulders of every individual," the patriotic sentiment of "loyalty to the country and revitalizing China," the social customs of "upholding virtue and emulating the virtuous," and the concepts of honor and disgrace in "filial piety, brotherly respect, loyalty, trustworthiness, propriety, righteousness, integrity, and shame," reflect the value standards for judging right from wrong and subtly influence the behavior of the Chinese people.

China's vast historical and cultural literature contains rich philosophical wisdom, life wisdom, political wisdom, abundant historical experience, governance concepts, and distinctive Chinese spirit, wisdom, concepts, and values. Once understood by people from all countries, these ideas and wisdom with distinct Chinese characteristics will be warmly praised and have a far-reaching impact. For example, "Do things for the good of others, don't do unto others what you don't want others to do unto you" values the life dignity and life value of others. It is a great wisdom for handling interpersonal relationships and a moral principle for dealing with relations between countries, which countries and international organizations worldwide have highly recognized. Furthermore, Chinese culture advocates a culture of harmony, promoting the cultivation of honesty, trustworthiness, generosity, solemnity, humility, and gentleness to achieve that "harmony is most precious." Cultural confidence in China is primarily based on a holistic understanding and grasp of the Chinese spirit, wisdom, concepts, and values contained in the carriers of Chinese culture. It is also based on the grand pattern, grand vision, and broad-mindedness of the excellent traditional Chinese culture, which features "value openness and inclusiveness" and "openness, inclusiveness, and eclectic."

Firm cultural confidence stems not only from the fact that Chinese culture has nurtured a developed agriculture and handicraft industry, produced many great thinkers, scientists, inventors, politicians, military strategists, writers, and artists, and had a wealth of cultural literature. It also comes from the modern history of China. When the Chinese nation was impoverished and weakened, countless benevolent people sought to save the nation and the people and to survive in the difficult struggle, especially when the CPC led the Chinese people in the great struggle for national liberation, national independence, and social progress, forming revolutionary culture, red culture, and fine traditions. Furthermore, it comes from the advanced socialist culture with Chinese characteristics formed, enriched, and developed after choosing the socialist path, including the difficult exploration, setbacks, and mistakes, especially during the more than forty years of reform and opening-up. Both revolutionary culture and advanced socialist culture are extremely rich new chapters and new traditions in Chinese culture.

Cultural confidence also comes from the achievements made in cultural construction since the founding of New China, especially since the 18th CCP National Congress. Let's take a look at some data: in 2016, China's national cultural expenditure was 77.69 billion yuan, an increase of 60.5% compared to 2012; the total collection of public libraries nationwide reached 900 million volumes, with per capita possession of public library collections rising from 0.51 volumes (items) in 2012 to 0.65 volumes (items); nationwide mass cultural institutions carried out 1.84 million activities, serving 579 million people, an increase of 52% and 32% respectively compared to 2012. The allocation of public cultural resources is further tilted toward the grassroots level.

Since 2012, the Central Government has invested 1.6 billion yuan to support the new construction, expansion, and renovation of 214 municipal public libraries, museums, and cultural centers. The Ministry of Culture and other departments jointly issued the "Guiding Opinions on Promoting the Construction of the County-Level Cultural Center and Library Branch System," delivering high-quality resources for county-level cultural centers and libraries to rural areas. At the same time, the efficiency of public cultural services has significantly improved.

Shanghai has created a "Culture Shanghai Cloud," turning a vast amount of public cultural information into a large public cultural data set. Cultural supermarkets in Qingdao, Chengdu, Jiaozuo, and other places have adopted personalized, "order-based" services to meet the diversified needs of the public; Beijing, Tianjin, Hefei, Dalian, Qingdao, Quanzhou, Huizhou, and other places have issued "Culture Benefit Cards," bundling discounted cultural products and giving the public the right to choose. This plays an active role in continuously satisfying the growing high-quality cultural needs of the people.

While China's cultural undertakings are thriving, the cultural industry is also booming, and it will soon become a pillar industry of China's national economy. From 2012 to 2016, the number of feature films in China increased from 745 to 772, with box office revenue rising from 17 billion yuan to 49.3 billion yuan; TV drama production has been ranked first in the world for consecutive years, reaching 334 titles and 15,000 episodes in 2016; book publishing increased from 414,000 titles and 7.93 billion copies in 2012 to 499,000 titles and 9.04 billion copies in 2016. According to the National Bureau of Statistics, in 2016, the added value of culture and related industries nationwide increased from 1,807.1 billion yuan in 2012 to 3,025.4 billion yuan, breaking through 3 trillion yuan for the first time, with the proportion of GDP rising from 3.48% in 2012 to 4.07%. TV documentaries such as *Carrying Reform to the End*, films such as the *Wolf Warrior* series, and other works combining ideological, artistic, and entertaining features have gained popularity and succeeded in viewership, box office, and distribution. During the Spring Festival of 2019, a film directed by a young director, *The Wandering Earth*, ignited the enthusiasm of Chinese audiences, with a domestic box office of more than 4 billion yuan and an overseas box office exceeding 100 million US dollars, setting a record for the highest-grossing domestic film in the history of the North American market. China's movie box office reached new heights during the Spring Festival of 2021.

In the new era, we must continue to uphold cultural confidence, promote the prosperity and development of Chinese culture, continuously improve national cultural soft power, promote the creative transformation and innovative development of excellent traditional Chinese culture, inherit revolutionary culture, develop advanced socialist culture, remember our origins, absorb foreign elements, look to the future, and better build Chinese spirit, Chinese values, and Chinese strength.

Disseminating the Glorious History and Excellent Culture of the Chinese Nation and People

As China increasingly takes center stage, the outside world's views on China show a diverse trend. On the one hand, most people realize that China's rise is unstoppable and see the opportunities that China brings. For many developing countries, in particular, China's successful path is worth pondering, and the help and support provided by China offer them new opportunities to overcome development challenges. China's global governance and public goods proposals have brought fresh air to the increasingly solidified and conservative world, giving the international community hope for a more just and reasonable transformation of the international order. On the other hand, China's rapid development has caused unease in many countries, with theories such as "China collapse," "China threat," and "China responsibility" emerging one after another. Even China's planned scientific research activities are given political implications. Some people worry that China is engaging in "new colonialism," exploiting other countries to nourish its own interests, or even following the path of historical powers toward hegemony. Most notably, the existing world powers and traditional forces have become more vigilant and cautious toward China, attempting to construct a mindset and plan to encircle and hinder China's rise. After solving the problems of "being hit" and "going hungry," the issue of how to deal with "being criticized" is indeed placed before the Chinese people. "We can handle China's affairs well, but can't we tell China's story well? We should have this confidence!" These succinct words from Chinese leader Xi Jinping underscore the importance of telling China's story well.

Telling the China story is an urgent need to respond to international concerns in a timely manner. Public opinion surveys show that after the 18th CPC National Congress in November 2012, the international community generally wanted to know why the CPC has achieved continued success, what impact the new central leadership will have on the world, and where China is headed. Western countries are very concerned about China's foreign policy and performance in global governance. In contrast, developing countries are more concerned about China's experience and practices in economic development, anti-corruption, and party building. In this context, Chinese relevant departments carefully organized the publication of *Xi Jinping: The Governance of China* and seized opportunities such as Chinese leaders' visits, bilateral or multilateral important activities, and participation in significant book fairs to hold a series of events like book launches, seminars, roundtable discussions, and promotional months targeted at different countries and languages. They invited many foreign dignitaries, well-known think tank scholars, and media figures, such as Cambodia's Prime Minister Hun Sen, Pakistan's Prime Minister Sharif, and Nepal's President Bhandari, to participate in relevant activities, effectively enhancing the international recognition and influence of the book. Since its publication in September 2014, the book has been published in 21 languages and 24 versions, with more than 6.25 million copies distributed globally, covering over 160 countries and regions. By 2019, it was available in more than 30 languages.

The overseas success of *Xi Jinping: The Governance of China* is mainly because the book responds well to the international community's concerns. Since the 18th National Congress, the Central Committee of CPC, based on China's current situation and development practice, has proposed a series of new governance ideas, thoughts, and strategies revolving around reform, development, stability, domestic affairs, diplomacy, defense, and party governance, all of which are embodied in this book. Through this book, overseas readers can understand China's development philosophy and path, see China's perspectives and solutions to world problems, and hear China's aspirations and voice for joint development and shared prosperity with the international community. *Xi Jinping: The Governance of China* can be seen as a golden key for the international community to understand contemporary China and its future direction fully.

Telling the China story is a new requirement of the new era. The new era is an era when China is moving from a major country to a powerful one and an era when

China is making greater contributions to the world. The international community is very concerned about where China is heading, so we must take the initiative to tell the stories of the CPC's governance, the Chinese people's struggle for their dreams, and China's adherence to peaceful development and win-win cooperation so that the world can better understand China. In recent years, China has taken the initiative to publish and distribute abroad a series of books such as *Why the Communist Party of China Can*, *Spirit of the Communist Party of China*, *Chinese Dream*, *Belt and Road Initiative*, *China Keywords*, and *Great China Library*, which introduce the CPC, China's basic national conditions, China's contemporary development achievements, and outstanding Chinese cultural themes. In recent years, China has paid more attention to conducting public diplomacy when hosting international events such as APEC Meetings, G20 Summits, and Belt and Road Initiative International Cooperation Summits, actively leveraging its home field advantage, carefully showcasing China's positive image and conveying friendship and cooperation to the world. The 2018 Beijing Summit of the Forum on China-Africa Cooperation welcomed 51 African leaders, including 40 presidents, 10 prime ministers, and one vice president. This indicates the good development of China-Africa relations and shows that China's international influence is gradually increasing. In 2018, China successfully hosted the International Import Expo, which was a first in the world, making more friends and showcasing China's good image of opening-up to the world. In 2020, China overcame difficulties in successfully hosting the third International Import Expo.

To tell the China story well, China's top leader, Xi Jinping, leads by example and sets a precedent. As the "first interpreter" of the China story, he used the method of "telling stories" on many diplomatic occasions to spread Chinese culture, interpret Chinese concepts, convey Chinese friendship, and demonstrate a global perspective, leaving a deep impression on the international community. For example, he talked about the poet Cen Shen's "A Million Households in the City of Chang'an," recounting the glory of Chinese urban civilization during the Tang and Song dynasties, reviewing the brilliant achievements of ancient China, focusing on the humiliation of modern China, analyzing the overtaking of contemporary China, and demonstrating the broad vision of Chinese leaders. This allowed people to appreciate the hard-won "Chinese miracle truly." He told the story of three Chinese expatriates who risked their lives to save 12 Congolese neighbors, expounding on the friendship between the two countries' people. He quoted, "Do not do unto others what you would not have them do unto you," to convey China's diplomatic concept of righteousness and interests; he cleverly refuted the "China Threat Theory." He shared personal experiences and historical stories, discussing traditional friendships and the latest developments. One by one, these vivid stories are told by him with awe-inspiring intellectual power, heart-touching character power, and approachable language power, demonstrating China's charm and captivating audiences worldwide. His storytelling is attractive mainly because he pays attention to finding common ground between different countries and their citizens, using real stories to pass on China's concepts of win-win cooperation and peaceful coexistence.

To tell the China story well, everyone is taking action. The Central Government has issued documents such as "Guiding Opinions on Further Strengthening and Improving the Work of Promoting Chinese Culture Overseas," "Opinions on Accelerating the Development of Foreign Cultural Trade," and "Guiding Opinions on Strengthening the Soft Power Construction of the Belt and Road Initiative," coordinating foreign cultural exchanges, cultural dissemination, and cultural trade to tell the China story and spread China's voice. In conjunction with the Belt and Road Initiative, deepening Sino-foreign cultural exchange and cooperation, the impact of brand activities such as Experience China, China Culture Year, and Happy Chinese New Year has expanded with remarkable results, and projects like Silk Road Film Bridge and Belt & Road Book Program have been promoted. In 2016, the Spring Festival "Chinese Film · Global Screening" global distribution platform was officially launched, successfully connecting with mainstream theaters in many countries in Asia, Europe, and North America. By the end of 2016, China had established 513 Confucius Institutes and 1,073 Confucius Classrooms in 140 countries and regions. Thirty overseas Chinese culture centers have been built. In 2017, the "Happy Chinese New Year" event was held in 140 countries and 500 cities, with over 2,000 activities and 280 million direct viewers. These platforms and brands will become important carriers for disseminating the China story and enhancing China's image, serving as important stages for Chinese thought and Chinese values to resonate globally and benefit humanity.

On the international stage, stories of innovation from China have been met with acclaim from all quarters: Famous Peking Opera artist Zhang Huoding entered New York's Lincoln Center, successfully performing the full Peking Operas of *The Legend of White Snake* and *The Locked Golden Bag*; Shanghai Kunqu Opera Troupe was the first to fully stage Tang Xianzu's *Four Dreams of Linchuan* and launch a world tour, which was unprecedented wherever they went; a group of Chinese writers including Cao Wenxuan, Liu Cixin, and Liu Zhenyun, have taken their place in the spotlight on the international award stages.

To tell the China story well, we need to tell authentic stories. For example, when the Indian President visited the suburbs of Shanghai, the village head introduced the local situation, mentioning the GDP, per capita income, and the number of houses built. When the Indian President visited a new house of a local farmer, he asked the woman of the house why her son and daughter-in-law's house was better, bigger, and brighter than the older couple's. The rural woman said, "The daughter-in-law is the most important guest here, and we must treat guests well." Which is better, the village head's explanation or the woman's story? It is easier to remember stories, and when communicating with foreigners, the stories around you and your own stories matter. In his lecture, Zhao Qizheng, a famous Chinese expert in public diplomacy, mentioned this story.

To tell the China story well, we also need to stand firm and pay attention to skills. During the China-US trade war, China has been trying to explain the situation to the world and the United States. In September 2018, China released a white paper titled "The Facts and China's Position on China-US Trade Friction," which used a large amount of factual information and detailed data to illustrate the harm that US protectionism and trade bullying have done to the world economy and demonstrated China's determination and will to safeguard national interests and uphold the multilateral trading system firmly. Jon Taylor, a professor at the University of St. Thomas in Houston, believes that the white paper clarifies China's position and shows that trade between China and the US is more balanced than the US thinks. Stephen Roach, a senior fellow at Yale University, also believes that the white paper provides a very detailed explanation of China's response to US accusations and clearly points out the US's improper practices. By publishing the white paper at this time, China is taking a constructive approach to avoid further escalation of trade friction, fully demonstrating China's insistence on resolving disputes through dialogue and consultation. To help the American public understand the impact of the China-US trade war, on September 23, 2018, *China Daily* published a four-page advertisement in the *Des Moines Register* in Iowa, stating China's position. Iowa is the "bean farmer base" of the United States, known as the "American granary." The US President also responded to this. Publishing advertisements abroad is an important aspect of telling the China story well, and this is not the first time.

In today's world, the right to speak actually exists in a situation where the West is strong, and we are weak. China sometimes finds itself in an awkward position where it cannot explain its rationale or speak effectively. It is essential to improve the ability to tell the China story vigorously. This requires strengthening the capacity for international communication, carefully constructing a foreign discourse system, enhancing the creativity, appeal, and credibility of foreign discourse, spreading the Chinese voice well and interpreting Chinese characteristics, improving a system for international speech to tell, innovating publicity concepts, and innovating operating mechanisms to gather more resources and strength; establishing the concept that everyone is a spokesperson for the national image, continuously improving the moral cultivation and civilized quality of the people, and promoting the improvement of the civilization level of the whole society; enhancing cultural self-confidence, promoting cultural prosperity and development, and effectively improving the country's cultural soft power.

Following the 18th CPC National Congress's proposal to build a culturally strong country, the 19th National Congress in 2017 laid out new plans to prosper and develop a socialist culture with Chinese characteristics. In August 2018, General Secretary Xi Jinping pointed out that in order to do a good job in publicity, thought, and cultural work under the new situation, we must consciously undertake the mission of raising the banner, gathering the people's hearts, cultivating new people, promoting culture, and displaying the image. All of these have clarified the direction of effort and the goals of the struggle for further strengthening cultural construction, enhancing the soft power of Chinese culture, and increasing the influence of Chinese culture. We believe China will rise as a civilized nation in the not-too-distant future, realizing the glorious dream of national rejuvenation.

— CHAPTER 22 —

Improving People's Livelihood and Innovating Social Governance

From December 29 to 30, 2012, General Secretary Xi Jinping made a special trip to Fuping County, Hebei Province, for research and investigation. He warmly told the villagers, "I have always wanted to find an opportunity to visit the villagers, understand the production and living conditions of the needy masses, and discuss how to escape from poverty through people's hard work with everyone. We must truly understand the situation of the poor and learn about the reality of impoverished areas through typical examples."

General Secretary Xi Jinping mentioned that Marshal Nie Rongzhen cared deeply for Fuping and said that he would not rest in peace if Fuping remained poor. Xi Jinping also said that he had been impressed by Fuping since childhood and had feelings for the revolutionary old district of Fuping. His visit to Fuping marked the beginning of the battle against poverty. Since the 18th CPC National Congress, the Central Committee of CPC, with Comrade Xi Jinping as its core, has focused on poverty alleviation, strengthened social construction in areas such as education, medical care, employment, and distribution, improved the social governance system through deepening social system reforms, and fought the COVID-19 pandemic in the interest of the people. People's sense of gain, happiness, and security have been continuously enhanced, and the miracle of long-term social stability has been sustained.

Winning the Battle against Poverty

After the 18th CPC National Congress, the Central Committee placed poverty alleviation in a prominent position in governance, made poverty eradication among that part of the population who were impoverished a prominent shortcoming, a bottom-line goal, and a landmark indicator of building a moderately prosperous society in all aspects. With the efforts of the whole Party, the whole country, and the whole society, extraordinary measures were taken to launch a comprehensive battle against poverty. By 2020, China had eliminated absolute poverty, and the battle against poverty had achieved a comprehensive victory.

For effective poverty alleviation work, the approach is very important. On November 3, 2013, General Secretary Xi Jinping visited Shibadong Village, Paibi Township, Huayuan County, Xiangxi Tujia and Miao Autonomous Prefecture, Hunan Province, and first proposed the concept of "targeted poverty alleviation," emphasizing the "seeking truth from facts, adapting to local conditions, classified guidance, and targeted poverty alleviation" in sixteen characters. He pointed out that poverty alleviation must be realistic and adapted to local conditions. Precise poverty alleviation should avoid shouting slogans or setting excessively ambitious goals. He further explained the concept of targeted poverty alleviation: targeted poverty alleviation means implementing refined management for the target population, precise allocation of poverty alleviation resources, and precise support for the target population, ensuring that poverty alleviation resources are truly used for the target population and impoverished areas. The proposal of the "targeted poverty alleviation" idea is a major theoretical innovation made by the CPC under new historical conditions to solve the poverty problem in deeply impoverished areas, reflecting a significant transformation in poverty alleviation methods and concepts.

In April and June 2014, the State Council Poverty Alleviation Office successively issued the "Poverty Alleviation and Development Archiving and Registration Work Plan" and the "Poverty Alleviation and Development Archiving and Registration Indicator System," requiring precise identification of impoverished households and villages through archiving and registration. This is the fundamental and primary task for targeted poverty alleviation. A total of 128,000 impoverished villages, 29.48 million impoverished households, and 89.62 million impoverished people were identified that year and a unified national poverty alleviation and development information system was established for the first time. On May 12, 2014, the State Council Poverty Alleviation Office and seven other departments issued the "Implementation Plan for

Establishing a Targeted Poverty Alleviation Work Mechanism," requiring precise identification, assistance, management, and assessment of impoverished households and villages, guiding the optimization of various poverty alleviation resources, realizing poverty alleviation to villages and households, and gradually constructing a long-term targeted poverty alleviation work mechanism. Subsequently, the Organization Department of the Central Committee of CPC and the State Council Poverty Alleviation Office issued the "Opinions on Improving the Assessment of Economic and Social Development Achievements of Party and Government Leading Groups and Leading Cadres in Impoverished Counties," arranging and deploying the improvement of the assessment mechanism for impoverished counties and the political achievements of leading cadres. The introduction of these documents made detailed regulations on the top-level design, overall layout, and working mechanism of targeted poverty alleviation, promoting the comprehensive implementation of targeted poverty alleviation work.

On June 18, 2015, General Secretary Xi Jinping spoke at a symposium with the principal leaders of the Party Committees of some provinces, autonomous regions, and municipalities directly under the Central Government in Guizhou, emphasizing that the success of poverty alleviation and development lies in precision; he put forward the "six precises" requirements for poverty alleviation and development work: all regions should find ways and practical measures to achieve precise results in support of targeted objects, project arrangements, fund usage, measures for households, assigning first secretaries to villages, and poverty alleviation effectiveness. He pointed out that we should adhere to policies tailored to individuals and local conditions, causes of poverty, and types of poverty, distinguish different situations, and achieve targeted treatment and precise irrigation without resorting to flood irrigation, superficial inspections, or generalizations. On October 16, Xi Jinping first proposed the "five batches" of poverty alleviation measures at the High-Level Forum on Poverty Reduction and Development: supporting a batch of production and employment development, relocating a batch of people to more suitable locations for those who cannot escape from poverty locally can be relocated year by year in a planned and organized way, protecting the environment for poverty alleviation and allowing a batch of the local impoverished population with labor capacity to become forest rangers and other ecological protection personnel, educating a batch of people for poverty alleviation, and providing a safety net for a batch of people through low-income assistance policies. The "six precises" and "five batches" proposals profoundly elaborated the basic requirements and main approaches of targeted poverty alleviation, enriched the connotation of targeted poverty alleviation ideas, and had strong practical relevance, laying out the next steps in the battle against poverty.

Various regions and departments resolutely implemented the Central Government's decision-making and deployment, treating poverty alleviation as a major political task and comprehensively advancing key tasks. Focusing on the issue of "who to support," continuous improvements were made to establishing poverty records. Based on the identified impoverished villages and populations in 2014, "look-back" reviews of the record establishment were organized in 2015 and 2016 to enhance the accuracy of identifying impoverished populations. Concerning the issue of "who will provide the support," a responsibility system was established where each takes responsibility in the joint effort, forming a situation where "secretaries at five levels focus on poverty alleviation, and the entire Party mobilizes to push forward the effort." Nationwide, 775,000 cadres were stationed in villages, and 195,000 first secretaries were appointed, achieving full coverage of assistance in impoverished villages. Regarding the issue of "how to support," the investment guarantee and policy support system for poverty alleviation was strengthened. Efforts were made in areas such as poverty alleviation through developing characteristic industries, organizing labor export, asset income, relocation, ecological protection, education development, medical insurance, and medical assistance, ensuring basic living standards and social welfare, and enhancing the effectiveness of poverty alleviation measures.

After arduous efforts in the five years since the 18th CPC National Congress, the intensity, scale, and impact of poverty alleviation have been unprecedented, and decisive progress has been made in targeted poverty alleviation and targeted poverty eradication: the number of rural poor under the current national standard has decreased from 98.99 million at the end of 2012 to 30.46 million at the end of 2017, with a cumulative reduction of 68.53 million people and a poverty reduction rate of about 70%. The poverty incidence rate dropped from 10.2% at the end of 2012 to 3.1% at the end of 2017. The number of impoverished counties has decreased for the first time, with 28 impoverished counties lifted out of poverty in 2016 and 125 impoverished counties applying for poverty removal in 2017, taking solid steps to solve regional overall poverty. The living and production conditions of people in impoverished areas have improved significantly, and the income levels and sense of gain of the poor have increased significantly.

In order to achieve a decisive victory in the fight against poverty, the report of the 19th CPC National Congress in October 2017 called for mobilizing the whole Party, the whole country, and the whole society to adhere to targeted poverty alleviation and targeted poverty eradication, insisting on the Central Government's overall planning, provinces taking overall responsibility, and cities and counties implementing the work mechanism, strengthening the responsibility system of the Party and government's top leader, adhering to the overall pattern of poverty alleviation, focusing on the combination of poverty alleviation with helping people's will and intelligence, deeply implementing the poverty alleviation cooperation between the eastern and western regions, focusing on overcoming the poverty eradication task in deeply impoverished areas, and ensuring that by 2020, rural poor under the current national standard will be lifted out of poverty, all impoverished counties will be removed from poverty, regional overall poverty will be resolved, and real poverty eradication will be achieved. At the end of 2017, General Secretary Xi Jinping pointed out at the Central Rural Work Conference that improving the quality of poverty alleviation should be given top priority, focusing on the combination of poverty alleviation with helping people's will and intelligence, accurately assisting the poor population, focusing on the concentrated efforts in deeply impoverished areas, stimulating the endogenous power of the poor, strengthening responsibility and supervision in poverty alleviation, carrying out special governance on corruption and work style issues in the field of poverty alleviation, adopting more powerful measures, more focused support, and more refined work, and resolutely fighting the decisive battle of targeted poverty alleviation, which is of decisive significance for building a moderately prosperous society in all respects.

In accordance with the spirit of the 19th CPC National Congress, on June 15, 2018, the Central Committee of CPC and the State Council issued the "Guiding Opinions on Winning the Three-Year Action of Poverty Alleviation Campaign." The whole country has been working together to promote various tasks of targeted poverty alleviation and targeted poverty eradication, implementing industry-based poverty alleviation, employment-based poverty alleviation, relocation-based poverty alleviation, and ecological poverty alleviation, strongly promoting poverty alleviation cooperation between the eastern and western regions and targeted poverty alleviation, continuously increasing the supervision of poverty alleviation funds, carrying out special rectification of issues that neglect and infringe on the interests of the masses, and promoting the effective implementation of targeted assistance measures. Overall, the progress of poverty alleviation is in line with expectations and has attracted worldwide attention: the goal of poverty alleviation is nearing completion, the number of impoverished people has decreased from 98.99 million at the end of 2012 to 5.51 million at the end of 2019, the poverty incidence rate has dropped from 10.2% to 0.6%, and more than 10 million people have been lifted out of poverty each year for seven consecutive years; the income level of the poor has increased significantly, from 2013 to 2019, the per capita disposable income of farmers in 832 impoverished counties increased from 6,079 yuan to 11,567 yuan, with an average annual growth rate of 9.7%, 2.2 percentage points higher than the national per capita disposable income growth rate of farmers during the same period; the basic production and living conditions in impoverished areas have improved significantly, all villages with conditions have hardened roads, every village has a health clinic and village doctor, the schooling conditions of 108,000 weak compulsory education schools have been improved, the reliability of agricultural power supply has reached 99%, the proportion of broadband coverage in deeply impoverished villages has reached 98%, and more than 9.6 million impoverished people have escaped poverty through relocation-based poverty alleviation.

As long as there is confidence, the yellow earth can turn into gold. The people of Fuping, Hebei, kept in mind the instructions of General Secretary Xi Jinping, united their efforts, worked hard, and after eight years of arduous struggle, they handed in a satisfactory answer sheet: the per capita disposable income of farmers in the county increased from 3,262 yuan in 2012 to 10,830 yuan in 2020. In early 2020, Hebei announced that Fuping had lifted out of poverty, and the old look of Luotuowan Village, which General Secretary Xi Jinping had visited, was replaced with a new one. On November 24, 2020, all 832 impoverished counties in the country were lifted out of poverty. This means that China has unprecedentedly eradicated absolute poverty.

On December 3, 2020, the Standing Committee of the CPC Political Bureau held a meeting to listen to the summary and evaluation report on poverty alleviation. General Secretary Xi Jinping chaired the meeting and delivered an important speech. He pointed out that since the 18th CPC National Congress, the Central Committee has united and led the people of all ethnic groups across the country, prioritized poverty alleviation in the governance of the country, fully utilized the political advantages of the Party's leadership, and China's socialist system, adopted many major measures with originality and uniqueness, and organized and implemented the largest and strongest poverty alleviation campaign in human history. After eight years of continuous struggle, we have completed the poverty alleviation goal of the new era as scheduled; all rural poor people under the current standards have been lifted out of poverty, all poverty-stricken counties have been delisted, absolute poverty and regional overall poverty have been eliminated, and nearly 100 million poor people have achieved poverty alleviation, achieving a major victory that has attracted worldwide attention.

The significant victory in poverty alleviation has completely changed the face of poor areas, improved production and living conditions, and improved the quality of life of the people. The common people express their heartfelt gratitude to the CPC, saying that they will not forget Chairman Mao for turning over and will not forget President Xi for poverty alleviation. Some people even said to General Secretary Xi Jinping, "You're doing a great job." Of course, it should also be seen that the problem of unbalanced and inadequate development in China is still prominent; the task of consolidating and expanding the achievements of poverty alleviation is still arduous, and we still have to fight a long and hard battle against relative poverty.

Focusing on Education and Healthcare Work

Since the 18th CPC National Congress, the Central Committee of CPC has been committed to a people-centered approach, striving to provide education that satisfies the people, increasing the construction of health and wellness facilities, and introducing a series of measures to benefit the people, which has continuously improved the people's living standards.

Providing education that satisfies the people. Education is the cornerstone of national rejuvenation and social progress and concerns the future of thousands of households and the country. First, by issuing the "Implementation Opinions on Deepening the Reform of the Examination and Enrollment System," the comprehensive reform of the examination and enrollment system was launched. The reform aims to establish a classified examination, comprehensive evaluation, and multi-dimensional admission model, improve a fair and scientific talent selection and supervision system, and build a lifelong learning interchange that connects various levels and types of education and recognizes multiple learning outcomes. Second, crucial steps have been taken to construct a modern school system. Adhering to and improving the principal responsibility system under the leadership of the Party committee of ordinary universities, perfecting the decision-making system, and coordinating operation mechanisms of the Party committee and administration. Strengthening the construction of academic organizations and giving full play to the role of academic committees in academic affairs. Third, the reform of the education management system has been vigorously and orderly advanced, with 21 administrative approval items for education canceled and the number of review and evaluation items reduced by one-third. By implementing the "Opinions on Deepening the Reform of the Professional Title System," comprehensive reform of the professional title system for primary and secondary school teachers has been promoted, establishing senior teacher titles (positions) in primary and secondary schools and broadening the career development channels for primary and secondary school teachers. Fourth, actively and steadily advancing the opening-up of education. In 2015, the State Council promulgated the "Overall Plan for Coordinated Promotion of World-Class Universities and First-Class Disciplines Construction," which determined the major measures for the "double first-class" construction, focusing on supporting a number of universities and disciplines to enter the world-class ranks and several disciplines to enter the forefront of world-class disciplines. These reform measures have promoted significant progress in education.

Continuously improving the level of medical services. Since the 18th CPC National Congress, significant progress has been made in deepening the reform of the medical and health system, forming a series of practical and effective experiences and practices. First, promoting the reform of public hospitals. Successively promulgating documents such as the "Guiding Opinions on the Comprehensive Reform Pilot of Urban Public Hospitals" and the "Opinions on Integrating Urban and Rural Residents' Basic Medical Insurance Systems" by August 2016, 18 provinces had achieved integration of urban and rural residents' medical insurance. Second, strengthening the reform of children's medical and health services. Children's health is related to family happiness and the future of the nation, but there are only 0.49 pediatricians (assistants) per 1,000 children in our country, which is lower than the number in the world's major developed countries (0.85–1.3). In March 2016, the Central Leading Group for Comprehensive Deepening Reform reviewed and approved the "Opinions on Strengthening the Reform and Development of Children's Medical and Health Services." It proposed to focus on strengthening the training and team building of pediatric medical staff, improving the children's medical and health service system, promoting reform in the field of children's medical and health services, and combining prevention with treatment to improve service quality and other key issues. This would systematically design reform paths to effectively alleviate the shortage of resources in children's medical services. Third, promoting the family doctor contracted service system. In April 2016, the Central Leading Group for Comprehensive Deepening of Reforms deliberated and adopted the "Guiding Opinions on Promoting Family Doctor Contracted Services." Fourth, promoting the reform and improvement of the drug production and distribution mechanism. In December 2016, the Central Leading Group for Comprehensive Deepening of Reforms deliberated and adopted the "Several Opinions on Further Reforming and Improving the Policies on Drug Production, Distribution, and Use." In addition, the new *Food Safety Law* and other laws and regulations have been officially implemented, using the strictest supervision system to ensure "safety on the tip of the tongue"; the reform of the drug and medical device review and approval system has been implemented, allowing patients to access life-saving and safe drugs more quickly and at lower prices; the implementation of the "Traditional Chinese Medicine Health Service Development Plan (2015–2020)" has constructed a new pattern of the emerging industry combination development of medical rehabilitation, elderly care, health management, and fitness and wellness. The implementation of a series of measures has promoted the brilliant achievements of China's health and wellness undertakings.

Vigorously implement the household registration system reform. A document of household registration, like a high wall, separates urban and rural people on both sides of the wall. Loosening household registration and solving the identity problem of farmers entering the city, the reform of the household registration system not only concerns the vital interests of hundreds of millions of people but also directly relates to the success or failure of new urbanization construction. The third plenary session of the 18th CPC Central Committee clearly stated: "Accelerate the reform of the household registration system, fully liberalize the settlement restrictions of towns and small cities, orderly liberalize the settlement restrictions of medium-sized cities, reasonably determine the settlement conditions of large cities, and strictly control the population scale of mega-cities." In July 2014, the State Council issued the "Opinions on Further Promoting the Reform of the Household Registration System," proposing the establishment of a unified urban and rural household registration system. Abolishing the distinction between agricultural and non-agricultural household registration and the derived, blue-stamped household registration types, unified registration as resident household registration. Laying a solid foundation for the reform of the household registration system by reflecting the population registration management function of the household registration system. On September 29, 2016, the "National Human Rights Action Plan (2016–2020)" was released, proposing to implement the State Council's household registration system reform plan, abolish the distinction between agricultural and non-agricultural household registration, and establish a unified urban and rural household registration system. Fully implement the interim regulations on residence permits to promote the coverage of the residence permit system for all non-settled urban permanent residents. Many domestic large and medium-sized cities have also canceled the restrictions on settlement and actively attracted talents from all sides.

Fully implement the two-child policy. Adjusting and improving fertility policies and promoting the long-term balanced development of the population is a major decision made by the Central Committee of CPC from the strategic height of the long-term development of the Chinese nation by scientifically grasping the laws of population development. At the end of December 2015, the Central Committee of CPC and the State Council issued the "Decision on Implementing the Comprehensive Two-Child Policy and Reforming and Improving the Family Planning Service Management," followed by the revision of the *Population and Family Planning Law of the People's Republic of China* by the Standing Committee of the National People's Congress. Starting from January 1, 2016, the two-child policy was fully implemented. The first year of the full implementation of the two-child policy was 2016, which was also the third year of the separate two-child policy's implementation, and the effects of the policy gradually became evident. According to a 1‰ sample survey by the National Bureau of Statistics, the estimated total births in the country were 17.86 million, and the fertility rate rose to over 1.7. Decisions regarding fertility policies, which affect the country's long-term development, must be made cautiously and scientifically. Short-sightedness must be avoided at all costs to prevent any adverse effects on the grand cause of the Party and the country.

Deepening Social System Reform

It is essential to deepen social system reform to improve the social governance system. The third plenary session of the 18th CPC Central Committee explicitly proposed social system reform and established a special group for social system reform. In February 2014, the Central Leading Group for Comprehensive Deepening of Reforms reviewed and approved the "Opinions on Deepening Judicial System and Social System Reforms and Implementation Division of Labor Plan."

Since the 18th CPC National Congress, social system reform has involved various aspects of the social system and mechanism, with many highlights mainly reflected in the following areas:

First, deepening employment system reform. Eliminate institutional barriers and employment discrimination affecting equal employment due to urban-rural, industry, identity, gender, etc., promote employment of college graduates as the focus of youth employment, rural migrant workers, urban disadvantaged groups, and retired soldiers, and form a new situation of mass entrepreneurship and innovation. Enhance the unemployment insurance system's functions to prevent unemployment, promote employment, and improve the employment and unemployment monitoring and statistical system.

Second, deepening income distribution system reform. Standardize income distribution order, establish a personal income and property information system, protect legal income, regulate excessively high income, clean up and standardize hidden income, ban illegal income, increase the income of low-income earners, expand the proportion of middle-income earners, and strive to narrow the urban-rural, regional, and industry income distribution gap. With the increasing efforts of various income distribution adjustment policies, the Gini coefficient measuring the income gap in China has gradually declined in recent years.

Third, deepening social security system reform. Promote the realization of a nationwide unified basic pension system and officially launch the reform of the pension system for government agencies and institutions. Establish and improve a reasonable social security benefit determination and regular adjustment mechanism that takes into account various personnel. Establish an open and standardized housing provident fund system and improve the housing provident fund withdrawal, usage, and supervision mechanism. Accelerate the development of enterprise annuities, occupational pensions, and commercial insurance to build a multi-level social security system.

Fourth, deepening social governance system reform. Improve social governance methods, strengthen party committee leadership, give full play to the government's leading role, encourage and support participation from all aspects of society, and realize the benign interaction of government governance, social self-regulation, and resident autonomy. Adhere to governance according to law, strengthen legal guarantees, and use legal thinking and methods to resolve social contradictions. Establish a smooth and orderly mechanism for expressing appeals, psychological intervention, conflict mediation, and rights protection. The upward trend of petitions and mass incidents across the country has been effectively curbed, and overall social order remains stable.

China's employment situation has improved in recent years, with an average annual increase of more than 13 million urban jobs. The income growth rate of urban and rural residents exceeds the economic growth rate, and the middle-income group continues to expand. The social security system covering urban and rural residents has been established, people's health and medical health levels have been significantly improved, and affordable housing has been constructed. By deepening social system reform, China's social governance system has become perfect, the overall social situation remains stable, and it has become one of the countries with the highest sense of security globally.

Combatting the COVID-19 Epidemic

On December 27, 2019, the Jianghan District Center for Disease Control and Prevention in Wuhan City received a report of pneumonia cases of unknown cause. The clinical manifestations of the cases were fever, fatigue, and dry cough, and a few patients had difficulty breathing, with chest radiographs showing bilateral infiltrative lung lesions. Experts analyzed the cases based on the clinical manifestations, treatment outcomes, epidemiological investigations, and preliminary laboratory testing and concluded that the cases were viral pneumonia. On the 30th, the Wuhan Municipal Health Commission issued an "Urgent Notice on Doing a Good Job in the Treatment of Pneumonia of Unknown Cause" to medical institutions in the jurisdiction.

Upon learning of the relevant information, the National Health Commission made arrangements and deployments in the early hours of December 31, dispatching a working group and expert group to Wuhan to guide the epidemic response work. At the same time, an epidemic response and disposal leading group was established, and four research institutions, including the Chinese Center for Disease Control and Prevention, were organized to identify the pathogen from the case samples. After careful study and judgment, the expert group preliminarily determined the pathogen of this unexplained viral pneumonia case as a novel coronavirus and confirmed the occurrence of human-to-human transmission of the virus. Due to the characteristics of strong infectivity, rapid transmission, and difficulty in prevention and control of the novel coronavirus, the epidemic quickly showed a spreading trend. According to the epidemic report, as of 6:00 p.m. on January 20, 2020, a total of 217 cases of COVID-19 have been reported in China, with 198 cases in Wuhan City. In just over 20 days since the initial epidemic report was received, the number of confirmed cases increased nearly tenfold, and the epidemic situation was very severe.

After the outbreak, the Central Committee of CPC and the State Council attached great importance to it. On January 7, 2020, General Secretary Xi Jinping presided over a meeting of the Standing Committee of the Political Bureau of the Central Committee and put forward requirements for epidemic prevention and control work. On the 20th, he issued instructions again, requiring party committees, governments, and relevant departments at all levels to put people's lives and health first, formulate careful plans, organize forces from all sides to carry out prevention and control, take practical and effective measures, and resolutely curb the spread of the epidemic.

The epidemic prevention and control work entered a critical period, and the prevention and control situation was severe and complicated. On January 22, the total number of confirmed cases of COVID-19 in China increased to 571, with 95 severe cases and 17 deaths (all from Hubei Province). From the perspective of the transmission scope, there was a local outbreak in Wuhan and sporadic cases in multiple points across the country. As it coincided with the peak of the Spring Festival travel season, the vast majority of cases found in other parts of the country were imported cases from Wuhan, which posed great difficulties for epidemic prevention and control.

In order to block the transmission of the epidemic as soon as possible, on January 22, the Central Government issued an order to immediately implement strict traffic control and seal off personnel flow and external channels in Hubei Province and Wuhan City. At 10:00 a.m. on the 23rd, according to the No. 1 announcement issued by the Epidemic Prevention and Control Command of Wuhan, the airports and railway stations were temporarily closed for departure.

At the same time, six departments, including the National Health Commission, the Ministry of Public Security, the Ministry of Transport, the General Administration of Customs, the Civil Aviation Administration, and the National Railway Group, issued a notice regarding "Strict Prevention of the Transmission of Novel Coronavirus Infection Pneumonia through Transportation Tools." They required good health management of vehicles, trains, airplanes, and key places such as stations, airports, and docks to prevent the epidemic from spreading to the greatest extent.

The Central Government's decisive decision to close the exit channels from Wuhan and Hubei bought time and space to prevent the spread of the epidemic. This is a key move to block the transmission of the virus and marks the full start of the defense battles in Wuhan and Hubei.

On January 25, the first day of the Lunar New Year, a special meeting of the Standing Committee of the Political Bureau of the CPC was held in Beijing. The meeting studied and deployed epidemic prevention and control work. The meeting clearly put forward the general requirements of "strengthening confidence, working together, scientific prevention and control, and precise implementation," emphasizing the determination to win the battle against the epidemic; it pointed out that Hubei Province should regard epidemic prevention and control work as the current top priority, adopt stricter measures, prevent internal spread and external output; it emphasized that, according to the "four centralizations" principle of centralized patients, experts, resources, and treatment, severe cases should be concentrated in designated medical institutions with strong comprehensive strength for treatment. All confirmed patients should be admitted in time. The meeting decided that the Central Committee of CPC would establish a leading group for epidemic response, working under the leadership of the Standing Committee of the Political Bureau of the Central Committee; the Central Committee of CPC would send guidance groups to Hubei and other severely affected areas to promote the comprehensive strengthening of frontline prevention and control work. On January 27, Li Keqiang, Premier of the State Council and leader of the Central Leading Group for Epidemic Response visited Wuhan to inspect and guide the epidemic prevention and control work. The central guidance group was stationed in Wuhan to comprehensively strengthen guidance and supervision of frontline epidemic prevention and control. The country quickly established a leading system led by the main responsible persons of the local party and government and a joint prevention and control mechanism involving multiple departments. At the critical moment of epidemic prevention and control, establishing a command system with unified command and dispatch by the Central Committee and coordination and cooperation among various localities and aspects provided a strong guarantee for winning the battle against the epidemic.

On January 27, General Secretary Xi Jinping issued instructions, requiring the CPC at all levels and the majority of party members and cadres to bear in mind that the people's interests are above everything else, stay true to our original aspirations and founding mission, unite and lead the people in resolutely implementing the decisions and plans of the Central Committee, and let the Party flag fly high on the front line of epidemic prevention and control. The Central Committee of CPC issued a "Notice on Strengthening the Party's Leadership and Providing a Strong Political Guarantee for Winning the Battle against the Epidemic," requiring Party committees (Party groups) at all levels to regard winning the battle against the epidemic as a major political task, inspiring and guiding the majority of Party members and cadres, especially leading cadres, to stand up bravely, fight courageously, work solidly, and withstand the test in the fight against the epidemic, and effectively fulfill their responsibilities, bear responsibilities, and fulfill their duties.

Under the unified deployment of the Central Committee of CPC, various parts of the country initiated the first-level response to major public health emergencies, achieved joint prevention and control, and various Party, government, military, and mass organizations and enterprises and institutions took emergency actions. Grass-roots communities and villages implemented "grid" management, airports, stations, and highways adopted temperature detection and other prevention and control measures, and cities such as Hubei Wuhan implemented comprehensive and strict control over the flow of people; medical staff fought bravely. Party members and cadres charged ahead, and the people wore masks, strengthened self-protection, and voluntarily reduced outings. A series of correct and effective measures have maximally blocked the transmission channels of the virus.

After arduous efforts, on February 18, the number of newly cured and dis-charged cases across the country exceeded the number of newly confirmed cases, and the number of confirmed cases began to decline. On the 19th, the number of newly cured and discharged cases in Wuhan exceeded the number of newly confirmed cases for the first time. The number of newly confirmed cases and suspected cases across the country showed a downward trend. The number of cured and discharged patients increased rapidly, especially the new cases in provinces other than Hubei decreased significantly. This means that the epidemic prevention and control work has achieved staged results, and the spread of the epidemic has been preliminarily contained.

Although the prevention and control work had achieved positive results, the turning point of the national epidemic development had yet to arrive, and the prevention and control situation in Hubei Province and Wuhan City remained severe and complex. At this time, the prevention and control situation faced challenges in two aspects: first, the epidemic prevention and control work entered the most critical stage, and it was particularly important to strengthen the prevention and control of areas with particularly severe epidemics or higher risks; second, in the face of the considerable impact of the epidemic on the economy and society, how to coordinate the promotion of epidemic prevention and control and economic and social development, and orderly promote the resumption of work and production became an urgent problem to be solved. In response, the Central Committee put forward the requirements of "focusing on key points, balancing various aspects, providing differentiated guidance, and implementing regional policies," emphasizing the need to effectively implement various tasks, refine them, and make them work on the ground, resolutely win the people's war, the overall war, and the defensive war against the epidemic, and strive to achieve the annual economic and social development goals and tasks.

On February 23, the Central Committee held a meeting to coordinate the promotion of epidemic prevention and control of COVID-19 and economic and social development. The meeting, which was the largest teleconference in the Party's history, mobilized and deployed 170,000 cadres across the country via video. The meeting comprehensively summarized the work of epidemic prevention and control, deeply analyzed the epidemic situation and its impact on economic and social development, and put forward the key tasks and major measures for strengthening the Party's leadership and coordinating the promotion of epidemic prevention and control and economic and social development.

In order to coordinate the promotion of epidemic prevention and control and economic and social development, the Joint Prevention and Control Mechanism of the State Council issued the "Guiding Opinions on Doing a Good Job in the Prevention and Control of COVID-19 Epidemic through Scientific Prevention and Control and Precise Implementation of Measures by Regions and Levels," providing guidance for different counties and regions to formulate differentiated prevention and control measures and restore economic and social order. According to the guiding opinions, many provinces across the country conducted scientific assessments of the epidemic and determined the risk levels of different county areas, formulated epidemic prevention and control measures and economic activities for different areas, and made efforts to achieve both solid epidemic prevention and control and the rapid restoration of economic and social order, achieving positive results and forming a good situation.

After the whole nation's hard work, epidemic prevention and control continued to improve, and the order of production and life accelerated its recovery. On March 18, for the first time, no new domestic confirmed cases were reported nationwide. The number of new cases continued to decline, and the overall epidemic remained at a low level. The peak of this round of the epidemic had passed.

Starting from March 25, Hubei Province orderly lifted the control measures for leaving Hubei; from April 8, Wuhan lifted the control measures for leaving Wuhan and Hubei, which had been in place for 76 days.

This indicates that the domestic transmission of the epidemic with Wuhan as the main battlefield had been basically blocked. The defense battles of Wuhan and Hubei achieved decisive results, and major strategic achievements were made in the nationwide epidemic prevention and control battle. Hubei and Wuhan withstood the largest epidemic test in a century, and they are truly lands and peoples of heroes.

As domestic epidemic prevention and control achieved important phased results, the epidemic situation abroad accelerated its spread. On March 25, 23 provinces in China reported imported confirmed cases. In the face of the urgent overseas epidemic situation, China provided assistance to the international community to the best of its ability, even though it faced enormous pressure in its own epidemic prevention and control. By October 2020, China had provided anti-epidemic assistance to more than 150 countries and seven international organizations, exporting over 179 billion masks, 1.73 billion protective suits, and 543 million testing kits. This demonstrates China's great power responsibility and reflects the story of "repaying a peach with a priceless jade" in human relationships.

Cases imported from abroad have caused related case transmission, making the pressure to prevent the spread of the epidemic still significant. On March 27, the Political Bureau of the Central Committee of CPC held a meeting, pointing out that in response to the new situation of domestic and foreign epidemic prevention and control, it was necessary to improve epidemic prevention and control strategies and measures timely, focusing on "preventing external input and internal rebound" to maintain the epidemic prevention and control situation continuing to improve; it emphasized the need to accelerate the restoration of production and living order under the normalization of epidemic prevention and control, striving to minimize the losses caused by the epidemic and making every effort to achieve the annual economic and social development goals. The Central Government's judgment on the "normalization" of epidemic prevention and control marked a gradual transition to a new stage in China's epidemic prevention and control.

In order to accelerate the recovery of production and living order under the normalization of epidemic prevention and control, the Central Leading Group for Epidemic Response issued the "Guidance on Actively and Orderly Promoting the Resumption of Work and Production While Effectively Controlling the Epidemic," and the State Council's Joint Prevention and Control Mechanism issued the "Guidelines for Epidemic Prevention and Control Measures for Enterprises and Institutions in Different Risk Areas Nationwide," guiding localities in resuming work and production-related epidemic prevention and control and restoring production order in a phased and hierarchical manner.

After continuous efforts, the overall national epidemic situation is characterized by sporadic outbreaks, with local areas experiencing cluster outbreaks caused by sporadic cases and imported cases from abroad basically under control. The positive trend of the epidemic situation continues to consolidate. On this basis, various localities coordinate the promotion of epidemic prevention and control and economic and social development and strive to restore production and living order, achieving significant results.

On September 8, 2020, the Central Committee held a national commendation meeting for the fight against the COVID-19 epidemic. The meeting comprehensively reviewed the extraordinary journey of the fight against the epidemic, profoundly expounded the great spirit of fighting the epidemic, systematically summarized the important enlightenment from the fight, and put forward clear requirements for further doing a good job in epidemic prevention and control and economic and social development. The meeting specifically commended outstanding representatives from various fields during the fight against the epidemic, such as Zhong Nanshan, Zhang Boli, Chen Wei, and others.

In particular, Zhang Dingyu, despite suffering from ALS, led the charge, chasing time with uneven steps, leading the staff of Jinyintan Hospital to treat more than 2,800 patients. All of the hospital's over 240 Party members stood firm in critical positions without hesitation or retreat. The holding of the commendation meeting also marked the significant strategic achievements in China's fight against the COVID-19 epidemic.

Difficulties will never just drift away with the wind. The COVID-19 epidemic showed sporadic outbreaks in autumn and winter, and China remained on high alert in the second half of 2020. However, the Central Committee's strong and balanced approach to epidemic prevention, control, and economic and social development ensured that the economy and society progressed steadily. As we bid farewell to the Year of the Rat and welcome the Year of the Ox, President Xi Jinping fondly reflected on the year 2020, acknowledging the arduous journey and remarkable achievements, emphasizing the need to uphold the spirit of serving the people, innovating, and striving through hardship, to always maintain a sober mind that is cautious and humble, to always maintain a determination that fears no hardship and is eager to forge ahead, and to courageously advance in the new journey of building a modern socialist country.

During the Spring Festival in 2021, the country advocated that people stay local for the Spring Festival. People were no longer as tense as they were during the Spring Festival in 2020. Although they were still taking precautions and wearing masks, they appeared more relaxed. With the acceleration of the vaccine rollout and the refinement of local management measures, we have every reason to believe that China will ultimately win the battle against the COVID-19 epidemic.

CHAPTER 23

Building a Beautiful China

uilding a beautiful China and achieving harmony between humans and nature have always been the ideals and pursuits of the CPC. China achieved rapid development for a period, but environmental pollution was once quite serious. In 2008, Kuhn, the head of a renowned US think tank, said that two-thirds of China's energy-producing enterprises used coal as fuel, emitting millions of tons of pollutants into the air every year. China has become one of the world's largest sources of sulfur dioxide emissions. Toxic industrial chemical wastewater pollutes rivers and lakes, with more than half of the water quality in seven major rivers being unfit for direct safe drinking. Half of the world's 20 most polluted cities are in China. Moreover, the number of cars in China is increasing at a rate of tens of millions per year, resulting in unbearable traffic congestion and exhaust pollution. Since the 18th CPC National Congress, General Secretary Xi Jinping has attached great importance to protecting the ecological environment, emphasizing that lucid waters and lush mountains are invaluable assets. He has incorporated the construction of ecological civilization into the the Five-Sphere Integrated Plan,, strengthened top-level design for environmental protection, strengthened environmental supervision, strictly pursued those responsible for ecological damage, and promoted historical changes in ecological civilization construction.

Lucid Waters and Lush Mountains Are Invaluable Assets

In order to protect the ecology, it is essential first to establish the right concept. On August 15, 2005, Xi Jinping, then Secretary of the Zhejiang Provincial Party Committee, put forward the important concept of "lucid waters and lush mountains are invaluable assets" during a research symposium in Yucun, Anji, Zhejiang. This concept addressed the contradictions, confusion, and hesitation among officials and the public regarding how to balance environmental protection and economic growth. It pointed out the direction for Anji County, which was at a critical moment in promoting the "ecological county" policy and provided important theoretical guidance and practical basis for Zhejiang Province, which was experiencing "growing pains," to advance the construction of an ecological province.

The concept of "lucid waters and lush mountains are invaluable assets" has enlightened the majority of officials and the public. Yucun is an important birthplace, practice base, and beneficiary of the "two mountains" theory, which advocates both economic development and environmental protection. Over the past decade, Anji County has been unwaveringly upholding the "two mountains" banner, walking the "two mountains" path, and creating "two mountains" industries. Successive generations of officials have worked together to carry out a blueprint that has led to a scientific development path that has made the ecology beautiful, industries prosperous, and the people wealthy, achieving a virtuous cycle of economic development and ecological protection. Yucun has become a well-known ecological civilization demonstration village and a rightful sacred place for ecological civilization construction. Tourists and visitors from home and abroad come every day to admire the ecologically friendly culture of Anji's rural areas, which is no less impressive than that of the European countryside. Yucun in Anji is an example, a sample, and a banner for China to practice the "two mountains" theory. The theory has been transformed into a vivid practice across China. "Lucid waters and lush mountains are invaluable assets" has become a household phrase and a conscious, voluntary behavior for both the young and old in China.

The "two mountains" theory not only responds to the trend of the relationship between humans and nature but also reflects General Secretary Xi Jinping's profound insights into the construction of ecological civilization. Since the reform and opening-up, with social development and the improvement of people's living standards, Chinese people's demand for clean water, fresh air, safe food, and a beautiful environment has been increasing. The ecological environment's role in people's happiness index has become more prominent, and environmental issues have increasingly become significant livelihood concerns. In the past, people hoped for adequate food and clothing; now, they hope for environmental protection. They used to seek survival, and now they seek ecology. In response to the people's ever-growing demand for a better life, especially the need for an ecological environment, General Secretary Xi Jinping repeatedly emphasized that the environment is people's livelihood, green mountains are beauty, blue sky is happiness, and lucid waters and lush mountains are invaluable assets. He advocated protecting the ecological environment as we protect our eyes and treating it as we treat our lives. We must not sacrifice the ecological environment for temporary economic development, gradually forming Xi Jinping's Ecological Civilization Thought.

Xi Jinping's Ecological Civilization Thought is rich and profound, clarifying the goal and direction for ecological civilization construction in the new era. General Secretary Xi Jinping pointed out that the rise of ecology leads to the rise of civilization, while the decline of ecology leads to the decline of civilization. He regards the construction of ecological civilization as an essential part of the overall layout of socialism with Chinese characteristics, emphasizing that humans and nature are a community of life, and humans must respect, follow, and protect nature. He proposed that socialist modernization is a modernization of harmonious coexistence between humans and nature. We need to create more material and spiritual wealth to meet people's ever-growing demand for a better life and provide more high-quality ecological products to satisfy people's increasing demand for a beautiful ecological environment. We must adhere to conservation, protection, and natural restoration principles as the primary approach, forming a spatial pattern, industrial structure, production method, and lifestyle that saves resources and protects the environment. We should strive to build a beautiful China where we can see mountains, see water, and remember nostalgia.

General Secretary Xi Jinping's discussion on lucid waters and lush mountains being invaluable assets provides fundamental guidance for building an ecological civilization. Lucid waters and lush mountains are essential elements of people's happy lives, which money cannot replace. Lucid waters, lush mountains and invaluable assets are not contradictory; the key lies in people and their ideas. Some areas are rich in ecological resources but relatively impoverished, and they need to explore a new path to ecological poverty alleviation through reform and innovation. They must vitalize elements such as land, labor, assets, and natural scenery in impoverished areas, turn resources into assets, funds into equity, and farmers into shareholders, transforming lucid waters and lush mountains into invaluable assets.

Xi Jinping's Ecological Civilization Thought was first explicitly proposed at the National Ecological and Environmental Protection Conference held in May 2018. The conference recognized that since the 18th CPC National Congress, the Central Committee, with Xi Jinping at its core, has profoundly answered major theoretical and practical questions concerning why to build an ecological civilization, what kind of ecological civilization to build, and how to build it. It has put forward a series of new concepts, ideas, and strategies, forming Xi Jinping's Ecological Civilization Thought. It has become essential to Xi Jinping Thought on Socialism with Chinese Characteristics for a New Era. This thought covers various aspects of the construction of ecological civilization, including its status, principles, and system.

In his speech at the conference, General Secretary Xi Jinping pointed out that the construction of ecological civilization is a fundamental plan for the sustainable development of the Chinese nation. He proposed six important principles for advancing the construction of ecological civilization, namely "pursuing the harmonious coexistence of humanity and nature," "lucid waters and lush mountains are invaluable assets," "a good ecological environment is the most inclusive public welfare," "mountains, waters, forests, farmlands, lakes, and grasslands form a life community," "protecting the ecological environment with the strictest system and the most stringent rule of law," and "jointly pursuing eco-environmental progress." To follow these six principles, General Secretary Xi Jinping also proposed for the first time to accelerate the construction of the "five systems" of ecological civilization, namely the ecological culture system, ecological economic system, target responsibility system, ecological civilization institutional system, and ecological security system.

The "five systems" define the basic framework of the ecological civilization system for the first time. The ecological economic system provides a material basis; the ecological civilization institutional system provides institutional guarantees; the ecological cultural construction provides ideological assurance, spiritual motivation, and intellectual support; the target responsibility system and ecological security system serve as the responsibility and driving force for the construction of ecological civilization, as well as the bottom line and red line. The "five systems" are the specific deployment to implement the "six principles" and also the countermeasure system to fundamentally solve ecological problems.

The convening of the National Environmental Protection Conference not only explicitly proposed Xi Jinping's Ecological Civilization Thought but also made plans for the next step in the construction of ecological civilization, enhancing the sense of direction and drawing up a roadmap. General Secretary Xi Jinping pointed out that the construction of ecological civilization is currently in a critical period of accumulating pressure and moving forward under heavy burdens. It has entered a crucial period of providing more high-quality ecological products to meet the growing needs of the people for a beautiful ecological environment and has reached a window of opportunity to address prominent ecological and environmental issues with the conditions and capabilities in place.

We must actively respond to the people's thoughts, hopes, and urgent needs, vigorously promote the construction of ecological civilization, provide more high-quality ecological products, and continuously meet the growing needs of the people for a beautiful ecological environment. A good ecological environment is the most inclusive of public welfare. Adhering to ecological benefits for the people, ecological interests for the people, and ecology for the people, we must focus on resolving prominent environmental issues that harm people's health and prioritize addressing prominent ecological and environmental issues in the field of people's livelihood. Winning the battle for blue skies is of paramount importance. We must improve air quality significantly as a rigid requirement, strengthen joint prevention and control, and basically eliminate heavy pollution weather, giving the people blue skies, white clouds, and twinkling stars. We must deepen the implementation of the water pollution prevention and control action plan, ensure drinking water's safety, eliminate black and odorous water bodies in cities, and give the people clear water, green shores, and scenes where fish swim shallowly. We must comprehensively implement the soil pollution prevention and control action plan, focusing on key areas, industries, and pollutants, strengthening soil pollution control and remediation, effectively preventing risks, and allowing people to eat confidently and live in peace. We must continue to carry out the rural residential environment remediation actions, create beautiful villages, and preserve the idyllic scenery of birdsong and flowers for the people.

To implement Xi Jinping's Ecological Civilization Thought, we must establish the concept of green development. Green is a necessary condition for sustainable development. Humans are born of nature and exist in a symbiotic relationship with it. Human development activities must respect, comply with, and protect nature. Currently, China's ecological and environmental protection situation is still very severe, and the people's demands for clean air, clean drinking water, safe food, and a beautiful environment are becoming increasingly strong. To establish the concept of green development, we must adhere to the basic national policy of resource conservation and environmental protection, persist in sustainable development, firmly follow the path of civilized development with production growth, prosperous life, and sound ecology, accelerate the construction of a resource-conserving and environmentally friendly society, form a new pattern of modernization construction featuring harmonious development between humans and nature, promote the construction of a beautiful China, and make new contributions to global ecological security.

Winning the Battle against Pollution

To win the battle against pollution, we must take real and effective actions. Since the 18th CPC National Congress, China has made great efforts to eliminate backward production capacities such as cement and flat glass, cutting over 170 million tons of steel and 800 million tons of coal production capacity. Both central and local governments have strengthened the management of scattered coal, promoted energy conservation and emission reduction in key industries, and 71% of coal-fired power units have achieved ultra-low emissions. Fuel quality has been improved, and more than 20 million yellow-label and old vehicles have been eliminated. Prevention and control of water pollution in key rivers and seas have been strengthened, and the use of chemical fertilizers and pesticides has achieved zero growth. Major ecological protection and restoration projects have been continuously promoted, and comprehensive management of desertification, rocky desertification, and soil erosion has been strengthened.

The Central Environmental Protection Inspection System has been established and implemented with strict accountability. Since the launch of the pilot inspection in Hebei Province in December 2015, the Central Environmental Protection Inspection has continued to exert its efforts, triggering a lasting environmental inspection storm across the country. Inspections were carried out in four batches in July and November 2016 and April and August 2017, covering all 31 provinces (autonomous regions and municipalities). In this process, strict law enforcement and serious handling of some localities and units that were not doing enough to protect the environment were implemented.

Qilian Mountains is an important ecological security barrier in western China, a major water source for the Yellow River Basin, and a priority area for biodiversity conservation in China. The Gansu Qilian Mountains National Nature Reserve was established in 1988 with the approval of the state. For a long time, the problem of local ecological damage in Qilian Mountains has been very prominent. In response to this, General Secretary Xi Jinping has repeatedly issued instructions urging prompt rectification. Although Gansu Province has done some work under the supervision of relevant central departments, the situation has mostly stayed the same.

From February 12 to March 3, 2017, a central inspection team composed of relevant departments of the Central Committee of CPC and the State Council conducted a special inspection on this issue. The inspection team believed that in terms of ecological and environmental protection in Qilian Mountains, Gansu Province, from the competent departments to the reserve management departments, from the comprehensive management departments to the specific approval units, due to the lack of responsibility implementation, inadequate performance of duties, inaction, and random actions, the supervision has failed at every level, allowing some illegal and non-compliant projects to proceed unhindered, and the relevant provisions of the natural reserve management are in name only. In July, Meeting of the Standing Committee of the Political Bureau of the Central Committee of CPC listened to the inspection report, deeply analyzed the typical ecological and environmental damage cases in the Gansu Qilian Mountains National Nature Reserve, and held relevant responsible persons accountable. Gansu Provincial Party Committee and Provincial Government were instructed to make a profound self-examination to the Central Committee, and the then main leaders of the Provincial Party Committee and Provincial Government seriously reflected and learned lessons.

On July 20, the General Office of the Central Committee of CPC and the General Office of the State Council issued a circular on the ecological and environmental issues of the Gansu Qilian Mountains National Nature Reserve. The circular pointed out that through investigation and verification, the ecological and environmental damage in the Gansu Qilian Mountains National Nature Reserve is prominent. The main issues are as follows:

First, the illegal and irregular development of mineral resources is severe. Of the 144 exploration and mining rights set up in the reserve, 14 were illegally and irregularly approved and continued after the State Council clearly defined the reserve boundaries in October 2014, involving 3 in the core area and 4 in the buffer zone. Long-term, large-scale exploration and mining activities have caused local vegetation destruction, soil erosion, and surface subsidence in the reserve. Second, some hydropower facilities were illegally constructed and operated irregularly. The local area has intensively developed hydropower projects in the Heihe, Shiyang, and Shule River basins in the Qilian Mountains region, with a total of more than 150 hydropower stations, 42 of which are located in the reserve, with problems such as irregular approval, construction before approval, and incomplete procedures. Due to insufficient consideration of ecological flow in design, construction, and operation, water reduction or even interruption has occurred in downstream river sections, causing serious damage to the aquatic ecosystem. Third, the problem of illegal discharge by surrounding enterprises is prominent. Some enterprises need more investment in environmental protection, lack of pollution control facilities, and repeated illegal discharges. Julong Iron Alloy Company, adjacent to the reserve, has long been unable to meet the emission standards for air pollutants, and local environmental protection departments have repeatedly enforced the law, but it has yet to be implemented. The Shimiao second-level hydropower station dumped waste oil, sludge, and other pollutants into the river, causing pollution to the water environment. Fourth, efforts to rectify prominent ecological and environmental problems could be stronger. In September 2015, the Ministry of Environmental Protection and the State Forestry Administration jointly held an open interview with the Gansu Provincial Forestry Department and Zhangye Municipal Government on the ecological and environmental issues in the reserve. Gansu Province needed to attach more importance to the issue, and the interview and rectification plan concealed and omitted 31 exploration and mining projects, and the progress of ecological restoration and rectification needed to be faster. By the end of 2016, 72 production facilities had not been cleaned up as required.

The emergence of the above problems, although there are reasons such as the system, mechanism, and policies, the root cause is still the deviation of ideological understanding of Gansu Province and relevant cities and counties, inaction, lack of responsibility, and unwillingness to tackle tough issues, and the Central Government's decision-making and deployment have not been truly well-implemented. First, the implementation of the Central Government's decision-making and deployment is not resolute and thorough. Second, legislation has "relaxed" restrictions on behavior that destroys the ecology. Third, inaction and disorderly action lead to supervision failure at all levels. Fourth, there is a lack of responsibility and reluctance to address difficult issues, resulting in weak implementation of rectification. To strictly enforce laws and regulations, in accordance with the relevant provisions of the "Regulations on Accountability of the Communist Party of China," "Regulations on Disciplinary

Actions of the Communist Party of China," and "Measures for Holding Party and Government Leading Cadres Accountable for Ecological and Environmental Damage (Trial)," and in accordance with the principles of Party and government shared responsibility, dual responsibility for one post, lifelong accountability, and consistency of power and responsibility, it was decided, with the approval of the Central Committee, to hold the relevant responsible units and persons accountable.

The report points out that the ecological and environmental problems in the Qilian Mountains National Nature Reserve in Gansu Province are typical, and the lessons are profound. All regions and departments must learn from this and draw inferences from other cases, consciously align their thinking and actions with the Central Government's decision-making and deployment, strictly observe political discipline and rules, resolutely prioritize ecological civilization construction in the overall work, and create a good production and living environment for the people. In this environmental accountability process, more than a hundred people, including three deputy provincial-level cadres in Gansu Province, were held accountable for the ecological damage in the Qilian Mountains. This so-called "strictest in history" environmental accountability storm has also triggered profound reflections among the cadres and masses in the affected areas. It demonstrates the Chinese government's strict enforcement of laws against environmental damage.

In the "look back" action of environmental inspections launched in 2018, it was found that many places had not properly addressed the issues. At 5:00 p.m. on June 6, the second Central Environmental Protection Inspection Group opened a reporting hotline for Inner Mongolia's "look back." By 12:00 a.m. on June 7, in less than a day, two of the 32 valid reports received involved the same enterprise: a wood processing factory in Xigoumen Immigrant New Village, Helingeer County, Hohhot City, with a strong smell of paint and serious noise pollution, and no environmental assessment procedures. As early as 2016, during the environmental inspection group's stay in Inner Mongolia, they received reports about this wood processing factory, which had been banned at the time but resumed operation two months later and gradually expanded its production scale. The informant reported several times to the local relevant departments, but the problem remained unresolved. To evade inspection, the factory temporarily suspended production a week before the second Environmental Protection Inspection Group's "look back" in Inner Mongolia. After the investigation, it turned out that the factory had never ceased production after being reported and shut down in the first round of central environmental inspections. The one-week suspension was also to "welcome" the inspection team. "This is a typical example of perfunctory and superficial rectification," the Central Environmental Protection Inspection Group commented. The relevant responsible persons were later dealt with seriously.

The Central Environmental Protection Inspection has achieved remarkable results, significantly raising awareness of strengthening ecological and environmental protection and promoting green development, effectively addressing a large number of prominent environmental problems that affect the public, promoting the transformation and upgrading of local industrial structures, and effectively promoting the improvement and perfection of local environmental protection and ecological civilization mechanisms. Strengthening environmental protection requires both a decisive battle and a protracted battle. The environmental storm caused by the environmental inspection will not stop, but it will also avoid the "one-size-fits-all" approach, truly achieving mutual promotion of environmental protection and development.

In-depth implementation of the three major action plans for air, water, and soil pollution prevention and control. After arduous efforts, the "Ten Measures on Air" tasks have been successfully completed. Compared with 2013, the average concentration of PM10 in 338 cities at or above the prefecture level nationwide decreased by 22.7% in 2017. The average concentration of PM2.5 in key regions such as Beijing-Tianjin-Hebei, the Yangtze River Delta, and the Pearl River Delta decreased by 39.6%, 34.3%, and 27.7%, respectively, making the sky bluer. A total of 150 million *mu* of desertified land has been treated, 508 million *mu* of afforestation has been completed nationwide, and the forest coverage rate has reached 21.66%, making China the country with the largest growth of forest resources globally during the same period, making the mountains greener. Some Chinese directors went to Shaanxi to shoot films, originally intending to capture the scenery of the Loess Plateau, but unexpectedly, due to good greening efforts, the once bare plateau was now covered in green. Compared with 2012, the proportion of surface water better than Class III water quality increased by 6.3 percentage points in 2017, and the proportion of inferior Class V water bodies decreased by 4.1 percentage points, making the water clearer.

Desertification control has achieved remarkable results, turning deserts into oases. From August 1 to 3, 2013, the Fourth Kubuqi International Desert Forum was held in Inner Mongolia, China, with the theme of "Desert, Ecology, and Technology." UN Secretary-General Ban Ki-moon sent a congratulatory message to the opening of the forum: In the face of the challenge of desertification, we can use advanced technology, market-based solutions, and economic incentives. The Kubuqi International Desert Forum provides a platform for everyone to share excellent experiences in afforestation and desertification control. China has demonstrated extraordinary leadership and achieved many important results in this regard. Kubuqi was chosen as the keyword for the International Desert Forum because China has made miraculous achievements in desertification control, particularly in the Kubuqi Desert, which has amazed the world.

The construction of an ecological civilization not only requires the design and promotion of the Central Government but also depends on the active efforts of local governments. For example, Inner Mongolia's forest area has increased from 373 million *mu* in 2013 to 392 million *mu* in 2018, and the forest coverage rate has increased from 21.03% to 22.10%, according to the Inner Mongolia Autonomous Region Forestry and Grassland Bureau. In recent years, Inner Mongolia has carried out large-scale afforestation, continuously implemented key national ecological construction projects such as natural forest protection, Beijing-Tianjin sandstorm source control, and the construction of the Three-North Shelterbelt, and promoted integrated restoration and management of ecosystems according to the "Three Mountains, Two Sands, and Four Zones" forestry ecological construction framework.

Everyone enjoys the shade, but we must also be good tree planters. In accordance with General Secretary Xi Jinping's requirements to "adapt to local conditions and vigorously advance large-scale greening actions," large-scale afforestation has been fully launched since March 2019 in various places, from the desert of Inner Mongolia in the west to Baopo Ridge in Sanya, the tropics of the South China Sea, from Jincheng, Shanxi in the Taihang Mountains to Wanzhou, Chongqing in the Three Gorges Reservoir area. In the Xiong'an New Area of Hebei, the "Millennium Show Forest" project is progressing vigorously. The first tree was planted here a year ago, and now 110,000 *mu* have been planted. In January 2019, during his inspection of the Xiong'an New Area, General Secretary Xi Jinping emphasized planting greenery before building the city. In 2019, the Xiong'an New Area plans to create a new forest area of 200,000 *mu*. In constructing the "Millennium Show Forest" in the Xiong'an New Area, the principle of choosing the right tree for the right location was followed, and most of the tree species chosen were native species. They achieved greenery throughout the four seasons through the reasonable combination of different tree species.

At the National Ecological Environment Protection Work Conference held in January 2019, the deployment of ecological and environmental protection work was planned, with requirements to actively promote high-quality economic development, strengthen research and formulation of major strategic planning policies, resolutely win the battle for blue skies, go all out to fight the battle for clear water, solidly advance the battle for clean soil, strengthen ecological protection and restoration and supervision, actively respond to climate change, continuously improve nuclear and radiation safety supervision, vigorously promote ecological and environmental protection supervision and law enforcement, and deepen reforms in the ecological and environmental field, focusing on twelve aspects.

Since the 18th CPC National Congress, the pace of land greening has accelerated significantly, and China has now become the country with the largest growth of forest resources in the world. A study published by the US National Aeronautics and Space Administration in February 2019 pointed out that the earth is greener than it was twenty years ago, with global greening increasing by 5%, equivalent to the area of an Amazon rainforest, mainly contributed by China and India. Data shows that a quarter of the world's greening comes from China, with afforestation accounting for 42%.

Improving the Ecological Civilization System

The system has fundamental, stable, and long-term characteristics. To build a beautiful China, we must focus on institutional construction and seek practical results. Since the 18th CPC National Congress, the Central Committee of CPC has insisted on deepening ecological system reforms and accelerating ecological civilization's top-level design and system construction.

From 2013 to 2017, out of the 38 meetings held by the Central Leading Group for Comprehensively Deepening Reforms, 20 were dedicated to ecological civilization system reforms. The "Overall Plan for Ecological Civilization System Reform," reviewed and approved by General Secretary Xi Jinping in 2015, clearly states that by 2020, clear property rights, multi-participation, incentive and constraint-based, and complete ecological civilization system consisting of eight systems, including natural resource property rights, land and space development protection, spatial planning, total resource management and comprehensive conservation, paid resource use and ecological compensation, environmental governance, and ecological protection market systems, ecological civilization performance evaluation and accountability systems, will be established to promote modernization of the national governance system and governance capabilities in the field of ecological civilization and strive for a new era of socialist ecological civilization. Since the 19th CPC National Congress, the Ministry of Ecology and Environment and the Ministry of Natural Resources have been established during the reform of the party and state institutions to better protect "green mountains and clear waters" and control pollution. This is conducive to the better implementation of the overall planning and institutional mechanisms of ecological civilization construction and helps to cure the chronic problems of "nine dragons controlling water" in the field of ecological and environmental protection. This is a profound change in promoting the modernization of governance systems and capabilities in the field of ecological civilization construction in our country.

To clarify rivers and lakes, China has comprehensively implemented the river chief and lake chief systems. In December 2016, the General Office of the Central Committee of CPC and the General Office of the State Council issued the "Opinions on Comprehensively Implementing the River Chief System" and issued a notice requiring all regions and departments to implement it in accordance with actual conditions carefully. The river chief system means that the main leaders of the Party and government at all levels in China serve as "River Chiefs" and are responsible for organizing and leading the management and protection of corresponding rivers and lakes. The Lake Chief system is also being piloted and promoted. In this way, China's rivers and lakes have clear ecological "stewards," and their responsibilities are clarified. Dongting Lake, one of China's five major freshwater lakes located in the middle reaches of the Yangtze River, is known as the "kidney of the Yangtze River." However, the ecological environment of Dongting Lake deteriorated rapidly. Monitoring data show that from 2003 to 2013, the proportion of inferior Grade V water quality in Dongting Lake increased from zero to 5%, and the Grade II and III water quality sections disappeared. Hunan has made a determined effort to fight the battle for the ecological environment of Dongting Lake—stopping sand mining, shutting down polluting enterprises such as paper mills, and dismantling aquaculture cages. The magnificent scene of the 800-*li* Dongting Lake gradually reappears.

From Dongting Lake to Poyang Lake, from Dianchi Lake to Taihu Lake, fish swim in the shallow waters, and the clear waves ripple, witnessing the achievements of China's vigorous promotion of ecological civilization construction over the years.

The "Zhejiang Province River Chief System Regulations" implemented in 2017 clearly define the "river chief system" as "a system and mechanism in which the river chief supervises and coordinates the governance and protection of waters, urges or advises the government and relevant competent departments to perform their statutory duties and solve existing problems in the responsible waters." The river chief system is not a system that replaces the daily supervision and inspection responsibilities of competent departments with newly appointed River Chiefs but serves as a supplement and assistance to daily supervision and inspection, promoting and helping departments to better perform their duties. The river chief system was first piloted in Zhejiang. In Zhejiang, every riverbank has a river chief public notice board with the names, phone numbers, and positions of River Chiefs at all levels clearly written, and the blue signs are eye-catching. Any problems can be contacted immediately. Currently, Zhejiang has equipped more than 57,000 River Chiefs at all levels, including six provincial-level River Chiefs, 272 municipal-level River Chiefs, 2,786 county-level River Chiefs, 19,320 township-level River Chiefs, and 35,091 village-level River Chiefs, forming a "five-level linkage" river chief system and extending the river chief system to small and micro water bodies to achieve full coverage of water bodies. In the "five-level linkage" river chief system, provincial-level River Chiefs mainly manage river basins and are responsible for coordinating and supervising the resolution of major issues in the management and protection of responsible waters; city and county-level River Chiefs are mainly responsible for coordinating and supervising relevant competent departments to formulate and implement responsible water management and protection plans; township and village-level River Chiefs coordinate and supervise the implementation of specific tasks for water management and protection, and carry out daily river patrols. Some River Chiefs say that they need to take photos and upload them to the river chief app every week during river patrols. The River Chief System not only assigns responsibility to specific individuals for each river, solving the issue of unclear responsibilities and roles in the management of river water environments, but it also changes the mindset of every resident living by the river. In the past, people would casually discard waste with no one in charge. Now, with the "River Chiefs" in charge, inspectors patrolling, and cleaners, people are less inclined to litter or dump indiscriminately. Villagers not only start to restrain their own behavior and that of their families, but they will also actively prevent strangers from dumping garbage into the river.

In addition to "official River Chiefs," Zhejiang has various river protection teams and volunteers, such as the police implementing the "River Police Chief," the Communist Youth League organizing "River Patrol Youth," the Women's Federation establishing "Women's River Protection Teams," and village collectives having "Pond Uncles" and "Pond Aunts." Preliminary statistics show that there are 100,000 such civilian River Chiefs. In this way, everyone participates and becomes a guardian of the water environment. Statistics show the public's support for water treatment has been over 96% for many years.

Now, with "River Chiefs" supervising, inspectors patrolling, and sanitation workers cleaning, people are more embarrassed to litter and pollute indiscriminately. Villagers restrain themselves and their family members and actively stop strangers from throwing garbage into rivers. In addition to the "official River Chiefs," Zhejiang also has various river protection teams and volunteers, such as the "River Police Chiefs" implemented by public security agencies, the "River Youth Patrols" organized by the Communist Youth League, the "Women's River Protection Team" established by the Women's Federation, and the "Pond Grandpa" and "Pond Grandma" from village collectives. Preliminary statistics show that there are 100,000 such civilian River Chiefs. In this way, the whole population participates, and everyone becomes guardians of the water environment. Statistics show public support for water treatment in the province has been above 96% for many years.

After implementing the river chief system, Zhejiang's water environment has achieved a historic improvement, comprehensively eliminating 6,500 kilometers of garbage-filled rivers and 5,100 kilometers of black and smelly rivers, and basically eliminating the sensory pollution of "black, smelly, and dirty." Statistical data shows that in 2017, among the province's provincial control sections of surface water, more than 82.4% were of Grade III or better, and the province had eliminated inferior Grade V water quality sections. In the 2016 annual assessment of the implementation of the "Water Pollution Prevention and Control Action Plan" ("Ten Articles on Water") carried out by the Ministry of Environmental Protection, Zhejiang Province ranked first in the country. By the end of 2016, the river chief system had been promoted nationwide. Nowadays, in most parts of the country, whether it's large rivers or small streams, you can almost always see the presence of River Chiefs.

With the advancement of the river chief system, the forest chief system has also been piloted and promoted. Since 2017, Anhui and Jiangxi have taken the lead in exploring the reform of the forest chief system, and by 2020, 23 provinces have carried out pilot reforms of the forest chief system. In early 2021, the General Office of the Central Committee of CPC and the General Office of the State Council jointly issued the "Opinions on Comprehensively Implementing the Forest Chief System," which clearly stated that the forest chief system should be fully established by June 2022.

As we enter a new era, the rule of law has accelerated construction in the ecological and environmental protection field. According to the overall idea of China's ecological civilization construction, the environmental protection law passed in the 1980s was revised after the 18th CPC National Congress. The new *Environmental Protection*

Law adds law enforcement measures such as daily continuous penalties, and it has been praised for "finally growing teeth"; the revision of the *Air Pollution Prevention and Control Law, Water Pollution Prevention and Control Law,* and *Environmental Impact Assessment Law,* among others, has increased the cost of environmental violations; the *Soil Pollution Prevention and Control Law,* which is under formulation, will become a "sharp sword" for preventing and controlling soil pollution.

Becoming an Important Participant, Contributor, and Leader in Global Ecological Civilization Construction

The changes in the world's environment and climate are inseparable from the joint efforts of people from all countries. As the largest developing country, China has always been committed to international environmental protection work. Especially in the new era, China has not only made great progress in domestic ecological governance but has also become more actively involved in global ecological governance, making its own contribution to the improvement of the world's environment.

China has actively promoted the entry into force of the *Paris Agreement* and prepared a "Chinese Plan" for implementing relevant issues, demonstrating the image of a responsible major country. On November 30, 2015, President Xi Jinping said at the Paris Climate Conference that China's "nationally determined contribution" proposes to peak carbon dioxide emissions around 2030 and strive to achieve carbon neutrality as early as possible. On September 22, 2020, President Xi Jinping mentioned at the general debate of the 75th United Nations General Assembly that efforts should be made to achieve carbon neutrality by 2060. This means that from 2020 to 2060, China's carbon emissions will be reduced from 16 billion tons per year to almost zero. The news shocked the world and was reported by major mainstream media headlines. This is the internal need for China's sustainable development and also demonstrates China's responsibility to promote the construction of a community with a shared future for mankind.

China has invested 20 billion yuan to establish the China South-South Climate Cooperation Fund. In September 2014, Zhang Gaoli, Chinese President Xi Jinping's Special Envoy and Vice Premier of the State Council said at the United Nations Climate Summit that China would vigorously promote South-South cooperation on climate change and double its annual financial support on the existing basis starting from 2015 to establish a South-South Climate Cooperation Fund. In September 2015, during President Xi Jinping's visit to the United States, he officially announced that the Chinese government would invest 20 billion yuan to establish the China South-South Climate Cooperation Fund. The fund aims to support other developing countries in coping with climate change and transitioning to green and low-carbon development, including enhancing their ability to use funds from the Green Climate Fund and their climate adaptability and strictly controlling investment in high-pollution and high-emission projects both domestically and abroad. The establishment of the fund is a practical measure for the Chinese government to promote South-South cooperation in climate governance and provide support to less developed countries and regions.

Supporting Pacific Island countries in coping with climate change. On November 22, 2014, President Xi Jinping held a collective meeting with leaders of Pacific Island countries. At the meeting, President Xi Jinping pointed out that although China and the Pacific Island countries are far apart, the people of the two sides have a natural affinity and a long history of friendly exchanges. Since the 1970s, China has successively established diplomatic relations with eight Pacific Island countries, and the friendly and cooperative relations between the two sides have entered the fast lane. Currently, China and the Pacific Island countries have a more solid traditional friendship, constantly expanding common interests, and increasingly broad prospects for cooperation. The relations between the two sides are facing a good opportunity to rise. China's emphasis on developing relations with Pacific Island countries will only strengthen, not weaken, and its investment will only increase, not decrease. On behalf of the Chinese government, President Xi Jinping said that China would provide support for island countries to cope with climate change under the framework of South-South cooperation, provide energy-saving and environmentally friendly materials and renewable energy equipment to island countries, and carry out cooperation in earthquake and tsunami early warning and sea-level monitoring. This has been highly praised by the leaders of the participating countries, demonstrating China's strong commitment to actively participating in global ecological governance.

Cooperating to establish the "Belt and Road" Green Development International Alliance. Promoting green "Belt and Road" construction and sharing green development experiences will positively improve the level of green development in countries and regions along the route. The "Belt and Road" Green Development International Alliance is an important platform for building international cooperation on green development and is jointly initiated by China and the United Nations Environment

Programme. It aims to promote the integration of green construction into the "Belt and Road" as an international consensus and joint action and to implement the United Nations 2030 Agenda for Sustainable Development. In April 2019, the "Belt and Road" Green Development International Alliance was officially established, with more than 120 Chinese and foreign partners joining the alliance. Meanwhile, China took the lead in releasing "China's National Plan for the Implementation of the 2030 Agenda for Sustainable Development" and implementing the "National Plan for Climate Change Response (2014–2020)," which stands in stark contrast to some Western developed countries that tend to withdraw from international agreements for self-interest, demonstrating the demeanor of a major power. Yu Jie, a Senior Research Fellow at the Center for Diplomacy and International Strategy at the London School of Economics and Political Science and Director of the China Project, said that ecological civilization construction is not only necessary for environmental protection but also for China's next economic transformation and is a solemn commitment China makes to the world.

In recent years, China has actively participated in international cooperation on environmental protection, joined the international community in addressing climate change, and voluntarily assumed international responsibilities. It has ratified more than 50 multilateral conventions and protocols related to ecology and the environment and played a constructive role in promoting global climate negotiations and the achievement of new climate agreements. China's efforts in the field of environmental protection have been recognized by the international community. The United Nations Environment Programme, the World Bank, and the Global Environment Facility have successively awarded the "United Nations Environment Programme Sasakawa Environment Prize," "Green Environment Special Prize," "Global Environment Leadership Award," "Earth Guardian Award," and other awards to China's environmental protection departments.

When talking about China's participation in global ecological governance, it is impossible not to mention the Eco-civilization Guiyang International Forum, which began in Guizhou. In 2009, the first Eco-civilization Guiyang Conference was successfully held, and the concept of a "green economy" was first proposed in China. In 2012, the 18th CPC National Congress was held, and the Central Committee of CPC included the construction of ecological civilization in the "Five-Sphere Integrated Plan" overall layout, elevating ecological civilization to the national strategic level. In the same year, the Eco-civilization Guiyang International Forum became the only Chinese forum organization to participate in the United Nations Conference on

Sustainable Development Rio Summit and submit voluntary commitments to the conference, spreading China's determination to build an ecological civilization to the world.

In early 2013, with the approval of the Central Committee of CPC and the State Council, the Eco-civilization Guiyang International Forum was upgraded to a national and international high-end forum. General Secretary Xi Jinping sent a congratulatory letter to the forum, for the first time, proposing that "moving toward a new era of ecological civilization and building a beautiful China is an important part of realizing the Chinese dream of the great rejuvenation of the Chinese nation." In 2015, during his inspection of Guizhou, General Secretary Xi Jinping said that the forum "has conducted in-depth discussions on a series of theoretical and practical issues of ecological civilization construction and has issued the Chinese voice on ecological civilization construction." He also said, "We must continue to hold this forum well and deepen exchanges and cooperation with the international community in the fields of ecological environment protection and climate change response." The forum has been held for more than ten years. Over the past decade, tens of thousands of scholars from nearly a hundred countries, regions, and organizations worldwide have discussed environmental protection and formulated various plans, which have been implemented and achieved good results. Through the Eco-civilization Guiyang International Forum, China has demonstrated its attitude toward ecological governance and is gradually becoming a "stabilizer" in global ecological governance.

In recent years, people have felt that the ecological environment is getting better day by day, with visible mountains and waters during the day and bright moon and twinkling stars at night. However, protecting the ecological environment and building a beautiful China is a long and arduous task. To build an ecological civilization, we need the leadership of the Party and the government, and more importantly, we need every Chinese person to take action, practice green development concepts, advocate green lifestyles, and truly integrate green into life and into the soul.

CHAPTER 24

Promoting National Defense and Military Construction, National Unity, and Major-Country Diplomacy

History, both ancient and modern, Chinese and foreign, has shown that for a country to be strong and stand tall among the nations of the world, it must have a powerful army, wise diplomacy, and national unity while maintaining a constant awareness of potential dangers. Since the 18th CPC National Congress, the Central Committee of CPC, with Comrade Xi Jinping at its core, has not only focused on combat effectiveness to build a strong army, fully implemented the "One Country, Two Systems" policy, but also proposed building a community with a shared future for mankind and opening-up a new landscape for China's major-country diplomacy with distinctive features. It has coordinated development and security and made remarkable achievements in China's national defense construction, national unity, and diplomatic affairs.

Build the People's Army into a World-Class Military

The realization of the Chinese Dream of the great rejuvenation of the Chinese nation depends on the protection and defense of a strong People's Army. From December 8 to 10, 2012, during President Xi Jinping's inspection of the Guangzhou Theater of Operations, he first proposed the "dream of building a powerful military." He said that realizing the great rejuvenation of the Chinese nation is the greatest dream of the Chinese nation since modern times. This dream is a dream of a strong country, and, for the military, it is also a dream of a strong army. To realize the great rejuvenation of the Chinese nation, we must adhere to the unity of a prosperous country and a strong military and strive to build a solid national defense and a powerful army. First, we must keep in mind that resolutely obeying the Party's command is the soul of a strong army, and we must unswervingly adhere to the Party's absolute leadership over the army, resolutely follow the Party's commands and walk with the Party at all times and under all circumstances. Second, we must remember that being able to fight and win battles is the key to a strong army, and we must build and prepare according to the standards of combat, ensuring that our army can always be called upon, fight, and win. Third, we must bear in mind that governing the army according to law and strictly governing the army is the foundation of a strong army, and we must maintain strict style and iron discipline to ensure the high concentration, unity, safety, and stability of the troops. He expressed his firm belief that, in the journey to realize the great rejuvenation of the Chinese nation, the heroic People's Army would surely carry forward its traditions, forge ahead, and effectively fulfill its historical mission. This important speech clarified the thinking of future national defense and military construction and outlined Xi Jinping's strong military thought.

In March 2013, at the first plenary session of the 12th National People's Congress, President Xi Jinping further pointed out that building a People's Army that obeys the Party's command, can fight and win battles, and has an excellent style is the goal of strengthening the army under the new situation. This was the first time that the goal of a strong army was clearly put forward. In order to build a strong People's Army, President Xi Jinping masterminded and deployed the deepening of national defense and military reform in March 2014, followed by a conference on the political work of the whole army in Gutian in October to unify the thoughts of the whole Party and promote military reform. Since the 18th CPC National Congress, the Central Military Commission has been strengthened, five major theater commands have been established, joint combat command institutions of the military commission have been improved, joint combat command institutions of theater commands have been established, and strong anti-corruption measures have been taken, opening up a new situation in political construction, reform and strengthening, technology and talent strengthening, legal governance, and strict discipline enforcement, greatly boosting military morale.

In February 2016, President Xi Jinping first proposed "building a world-class military" at an expanded meeting of the Central Military Commission. In October 2017, the 19th CPC National Congress further clarified that the goal of the Party in the new era is to build a People's Army that listens to the Party's command, can fight and win battles, and has excellent style, and build the People's Army into a world-class military. A new strategic arrangement was also made to basically achieve mechanization by 2020, make significant progress in informatization construction, and greatly enhance strategic capabilities; by 2035, to basically achieve the modernization of national defense and the military; and by midcentury, to build a world-class military. This three-step strategy is highly consistent with the national modernization construction goal, demonstrating the role of the people's army as the steel Great Wall.

"Raise troops for a thousand days; use them for a moment. If you can win, everything works; if you can't win, everything returns to zero." Since the 18th CPC National Congress, a prominent feature of national defense and military construction has been focusing on improving combat effectiveness. Whether it is emphasizing the Party's absolute leadership over the army, implementing the responsibility system of the chairman of the Military Commission, optimizing command institutions, cutting 300,000 personnel, or promoting military-civilian integration, all focus on improving the military's combat effectiveness. Particularly since January 2018, when the Military Commission first organized and mobilized military training for the entire army, President Xi Jinping has issued training mobilization orders to the entire army for four consecutive years at the beginning of the year, setting a clear direction for focusing on military training. On January 4, 2021, President Xi Jinping signed the Central Military Commission's No. 1 Order of 2021, issuing a training mobilization order to the entire army.

In 2021, the entire army must adhere to the guidance of Xi Jinping's Thought on Socialism with Chinese Characteristics for a New Era, implement Xi Jinping's Strong Military Thought, implement the military strategy guidelines for the new era, implement the spirit of the Central Military Commission's military training conference, strengthen the Party's leadership over military training work, focus on preparing for war, deepen the transformation of military training, build a new type of military training system, comprehensively improve the level of training actual combat and the ability to win. Deepen real combat and real training, insist on leading training by war and promoting war by training, strengthen research on war and combat issues, strengthen case-based confrontational training, strengthen emergency and combat special attack drills, strengthen military struggle frontline training, promote deep coupling of war and training, achieve integration of combat and training, and ensure full-time readiness and combat readiness at any time. Deepen joint operations and joint training, adhere to joint training leading military and arms training, and military and arms training supporting joint training, focus on the study and practice of major global issues, focus on joint command training, focus on cross-domain and cross-military joint special training, focus on military and civilian joint training, develop our military's characteristic joint training system, and accelerate the improvement of integrated joint operations capabilities. Deepen technology-based training, strengthen the idea that technology is the core combat capability, strengthen the study of modern technology, especially military high technology knowledge, strengthen the training of new equipment, new forces, and new fields and integrate them into the combat system, strengthen the construction of simulation, network, and confrontation means, explore "technology+" and "network+" training methods, and significantly increase the technological content of training. Deepen training according to the law, promote training management reform, strengthen the overall planning of training programs, improve training regulations and standards, innovate training content and methods, strictly follow the training guidelines, strengthen and improve training supervision, improve training assessment and evaluation, focus on training safety prevention and control, and achieve the unity of strict training, scientific training, and safe training. All military personnel must resolutely implement the decisions and instructions of the Party Central Committee and the Central Military Commission, carry forward the fighting spirit of fearing neither hardship nor death, correct training style, temper the will to fight, hone their skills, resolutely complete the mission and tasks entrusted by the Party and the people in the new era, and greet the 100th anniversary of the founding of the Communist Party of China with outstanding achievements.

Under the strong leadership of the Central Committee of CPC, historical achievements have been made in national defense and military construction. The political ecology, organizational form, force system, and style image have been reshaped, undergoing a phoenix-like rebirth. In November 2020, the Chinese military basically achieved mechanization. The People's Army has taken firm steps on the road to strengthening the army with Chinese characteristics.

Efforts to Promote the Peaceful Reunification of the Motherland

Since the 18th CPC National Congress, the Central Committee of CPC has attached great importance to the work of Hong Kong, Macau, and Taiwan, striving to maintain the prosperity and stability of Hong Kong and Macau, steadily promoting the peaceful development of cross-strait relations, and resolutely opposing "Hong Kong independence" and "Taiwan independence."

In December 2012, General Secretary Xi Jinping solemnly declared "three unchangeable" when listening to the report of the Chief Executive of the Hong Kong Special Administrative Region, which is the Central Government's adherence to the implementation of "One Country, Two Systems" in Hong Kong and Macau and strict adherence to the *Basic Law* will not change; the determination to support the Chief Executive and the SAR government in administering according to the law and fulfilling their duties will not change; and the policy of supporting the development of the economy, improving people's livelihood, promoting democracy, and promoting harmony in the two SARs will not change. At the same time, he emphasized the need to understand and implement the principle of "One Country, Two Systems" and earnestly respect and safeguard the authority of the *Basic Law* fully and accurately. This reassured Hong Kong and Macau society.

With the support of the Central Government, the development of Hong Kong and Macau has been incorporated into the 13th and 14th Five-Year Plans, sharing the benefits of progress with the Chinese mainland. In December 2015, the Central Government clearly defined the 85 square kilometers of Macau's maritime and land boundaries, creating new conditions for the moderately diversified development and long-term prosperity and stability of Macau's economy. In March 2016, the 13th Five-Year Plan outlined the expansion of cooperation between the mainland and Hong Kong and Macau, upgrading the arrangements for establishing closer economic and trade relations between the mainland and Hong Kong and Macau (CEPA). In July 2017, Xi Jinping pointed out at the 20th anniversary of Hong Kong's return to the motherland that "one country" is the root, and deep roots can produce lush leaves; "one country" is the foundation, and only when the foundation is solid can the branches flourish. In specific practice, it is necessary to firmly establish the awareness of "one country" and adhere to the principle of "one country." In 2017, the 19th CPC National Congress emphasized the need to support Hong Kong and Macau's integration into the overall national development strategy, focusing on the construction of the Guangdong-Hong Kong-Macau Greater Bay Area, Guangdong-Hong Kong-Macau cooperation, and Pan-Pearl River Delta regional cooperation to comprehensively promote mutually beneficial cooperation between the mainland and Hong Kong and Macau. In July 2018, the Central Committee of CPC and the State Council jointly issued the "Outline Development Plan for the Guangdong-Hong Kong-Macau Greater Bay Area," proposing to take Hong Kong, Macau, Guangzhou, and Shenzhen as the core engines of regional development and to play a role in radiating and driving development. This highest-level planning marked a new stage in Guangdong-Hong Kong-Macau cooperation. With the support of the Central Government, Hong Kong and Macau's economies have achieved relatively good development in recent years. Hong Kong's GDP has increased from HKD 2,037.1 billion in 2012 to HKD 2,868.2 billion, while Macau's GDP has grown from MOP 342.82 billion to MOP 434.67 billion. After the outbreak of COVID-19, the Central Government also extended a helping hand to Hong Kong and Macao, taking active measures from nucleic acid testing to vaccine supply.

In response to the increasingly chaotic situation in Hong Kong triggered by "the law amendment disturbance," the fourth plenary session of the 19th CPC Central Committee made systematic institutional designs and work arrangements for advancing the practice of "One Country, Two Systems" from the perspective of the Central Government's governance over the Special Administrative Region. In May 2020, the Third Session of the 13th National People's Congress passed the "Decision on Establishing and Improving the Legal System and Enforcement Mechanism for Safeguarding National Security in the Hong Kong Special Administrative Region," authorizing the NPC Standing Committee to formulate relevant laws. By the end of June, the *Law of the People's Republic of China on Safeguarding National Security in the Hong Kong Special Administrative Region* was passed, thereby establishing and improving the system for safeguarding national security in Hong Kong. This law has played a significant role in stabilizing the situation in Hong Kong.

In terms of work related to Taiwan, in February 2014, after consultations between the two sides of the strait, the Taiwan Affairs Office of the State Council and the "Mainland Affairs Council" established a normalized contact and communication mechanism based on the common political foundation of the "1992 Consensus."

The heads of the two departments have visited each other multiple times. Cultural exchanges based on cross-strait economic, trade, and cultural forums have also been carried out vividly. On this basis, the two sides of the Taiwan Strait witnessed a historic moment.

At 3:00 p.m. on November 7, 2015, at the Shangri-La Hotel in Singapore, under the focus of about 600 reporters, the leaders of the two sides of the strait, Xi Jinping and Ma Yingjiu, walked toward each other with smiles and shook hands. This was the first handshake between the leaders of the two sides of the strait in 66 years. The two leaders shook hands for as long as 80 seconds, and upon the suggestion of the on-site reporters, they smiled and waved at the reporters for 25 seconds. During the meeting, Xi Jinping emotionally recalled, "Once upon a time, the Taiwan Strait was shrouded in dark clouds, with military confrontation across the strait, and compatriots on both sides gazed at each other across the sea, with family communication cut off, leaving countless families with deep-seated pain and even irreparable regrets. However, the strait cannot sever the bonds of brotherhood between compatriots, nor can it block the longing for hometown and the desire for family reunion. The power of the affection between compatriots finally broke through the blockade across the strait in the 1980s." He also pointed out, "Compatriots across the strait are brothers connected by blood, thicker than water. We should demonstrate to the world with actions that people on both sides of the strait are fully capable and wise to solve their own problems and jointly make greater contributions to world and regional peace, stability, development, and prosperity." At the same time, Xi Jinping put forward four points, emphasizing the need to adhere to the common political foundation across the strait, consolidate and deepen the peaceful development of cross-strait relations, seek the well-being of compatriots on both sides of the strait, and jointly achieve the great rejuvenation of the Chinese nation. This meeting has historical significance.

After the Democratic Progressive Party took office in 2016, the development of cross-strait relations encountered setbacks. However, Mainland China has been actively promoting economic, cultural, and educational exchanges across the strait, and in 2018, it issued "Several Measures to Promote Economic and Cultural Exchange and Cooperation Across the Strait." In 2019, the mainland introduced "Several Measures to Further Promote Economic and Cultural Exchange and Cooperation Across the Strait." In January 2019, at the Commemoration of the 40th Anniversary of the "Letter to Taiwan Compatriots," General Secretary Xi Jinping articulated the mainland's new proposition for Taiwan relations in his speech, which included jointly promoting the revitalization of the nation and achieving the goal of peaceful unification; exploring the "One Country, Two Systems" plan for Taiwan and enriching the practice of peaceful unification, among others. This important speech has elicited enthusiastic responses from insightful people on the island.

The unification of Taiwan is a matter of course and cannot be delayed indefinitely; "Taiwan independence" does not win the hearts of the people and is bound to fail. In response to the "Taiwan independence" movement, the mainland has adopted measures to resolutely contain it, indicating that "not a single inch of the great motherland's territory can or will be separated from China." In May 2020, a forum was held on the 15th anniversary of the implementation of the *Anti-Secession Law*, clearly conveying the determination to defend the unification of the motherland resolutely.

Implementing Foreign Policy with Chinese Characteristics

Since the 18th CPC National Congress, Chinese diplomacy, while maintaining the continuity of reform and opening-up and the stability of major foreign policy, has achieved innovation on multiple levels, such as the proposal and implementation of the "Belt and Road" initiative, the establishment of the Asian Infrastructure Investment Bank, the proposal of a community with a shared future for mankind, and the creation of the National Security Committee, among others. As an integral part of overall diplomacy, China's peripheral diplomacy has also achieved many results and experiences in facing greater pressures in the peripheral environment. China's diplomacy is increasingly characterized by Chinese characteristics, style, and demeanor, opening up a new situation in major-country diplomacy with Chinese characteristics.

The concept of building a new type of major-country relationship. With China's rise and the narrowing gap in economic strength with the United States, some people, based on the historical experience of conflicts and wars between emerging and established powers, worry that confrontation or even military conflicts may occur between China and the United States. In response to this situation, during his meeting with US President Obama in June 2013, President Xi Jinping proposed the concept of building a new type of major-country relationship between China and the United States based on the principles of "no conflict, no confrontation, mutual respect, and win-win cooperation." This proposition has become the goal and guiding thought for China's development and stabilizing China-US relations. In November 2014, at the Central Conference on Foreign Affairs Work, General Secretary Xi Jinping emphasized the need to promote the establishment of a new type of international relationship with win-win cooperation at its core, adhering to the open strategy of mutual benefit and reflecting the concept of win-win cooperation in various aspects of foreign cooperation in politics, economy, security, and culture, and promoting the establishment of a new type of international relationship with win-win cooperation at its core. This is an innovation and development of the concept of international order, opening up a new vision for international relations. Under this guidance, major-country relations have been healthy and stable. Since 2013, the heads of China and the United States have held multiple meetings, promoting the construction of a new type of major-country relationship between China and the United States and achieving important results. After the inauguration of the new US administration, President Xi Jinping and President Trump successfully held their first meeting in Mar-a-Lago, Florida, in April 2017, clarifying the direction and principles of China-US relations, planning priority areas and mechanisms for bilateral cooperation, and strengthening communication and coordination on international and regional affairs. The meeting ensured a smooth transition in China-US relations and was significant in promoting the development of bilateral relations along the right track.

High-level exchanges between China and Russia have been frequent, with President Xi Jinping and President Putin having met more than 20 times. Strategic mutual trust has deepened, the alignment of the "Belt and Road" initiative with the construction of the Eurasian Economic Union has been promoted in an orderly manner, breakthroughs have been made in major project cooperation, and the comprehensive strategic partnership of coordination between China and Russia in the new era has continuously reached new heights, becoming an important "ballast stone" for maintaining world peace and stability. In June 2018, Putin revisited China, taking a ride on the Chinese high-speed rail and expressing a romantic feeling. The signing of the *China-EU Investment Agreement* in 2020 further deepened China-EU economic and trade relations. In 2020, China replaced the United States as Europe's largest trading partner, which is of historic significance. Important bilateral relations, such as those between China and Japan, have also shown warming and improving trends.

Promoting the construction of a community with a shared future for mankind. In March 2013, during his first foreign visit after being elected as the President of China, Xi Jinping proposed: "In this world, the interconnections and interdependence among countries have deepened to an unprecedented degree ... increasingly becoming a community of shared destiny where you are in me, and I am in you." In September

2015, at the General Debate of the 70th Session of the United Nations General Assembly, President Xi Jinping once again emphasized, "We should inherit and carry forward the purposes and principles of the *United Nations Charter*, build a new type of international relationship with win-win cooperation at its core, and create a community with a shared future for mankind." In January 2017, during his speech at the United Nations headquarters in Geneva, President Xi Jinping stressed, "All countries should control the fate of the world, international rules should be written by all countries, all countries should govern global affairs, and the fruits of development should be shared by all countries." He further pointed out that the key to building a community with a shared future for mankind lies in action. We must adhere to dialogue and consultation, building a world of lasting peace; adhere to joint construction and sharing, building a world of universal security; adhere to win-win cooperation, building a world of common prosperity; adhere to exchange and mutual learning, building an open and inclusive world; and adhere to green and low-carbon development, building a clean and beautiful world.

The idea of a community with a shared future for mankind carries China's lofty ideals and unremitting pursuit of building a better world and reflects the aspirations of people from all countries for a peaceful and just new order, thus receiving widespread welcome and strong support from the international community, especially the vast number of developing countries. On February 10, 2017, the United Nations Commission for Social Development adopted the resolution on "The Social Dimension of the New Partnership for Africa's Development," calling on the international community to strengthen support for Africa's economic and social development "in the spirit of win-win cooperation and building a community with a shared future for mankind." The inclusion of the concept of "building a community with a shared future for mankind" in the United Nations resolution indicates that the international community has widely recognized this concept. What is a community with a shared future for mankind? In his 19th CPC National Congress report, General Secretary Xi Jinping emphasized: "To build a community with a shared future for mankind is to build a world of lasting peace, universal security, common prosperity, openness, inclusiveness, and a clean and beautiful environment." He then systematically elaborated on how to build a community with a shared future for mankind with five "requirements": mutual respect, equal consultation, resolute abandonment of Cold War mentality and power politics, adherence to dialogue to resolve disputes, and consultation to resolve differences; working together to promote trade and investment liberalization and facilitation; respecting the diversity of world civilizations; and protecting the Earth, the home on which humanity depends for survival.

Proposing and practicing the "Belt and Road" initiative. In 2013, President Xi Jinping accurately grasped the new changes in China's domestic and international environment for opening-up and proposed the major initiative of building the "Belt and Road," which is a continuation and upgrade of the ancient Silk Road in line with the requirements of the times. The "Belt and Road" provides an inclusive development platform for countries to consult, build, and share, connecting the Asia-Pacific and European economic circles. The "Belt and Road" aims to achieve policy coordination, infrastructure connectivity, unimpeded trade, financial integration, and people-to-people bonds among the countries along the route. Over the years, the joint construction of the "Belt and Road" has gradually changed from an initiative to action, from a concept to practice, becoming an open and inclusive international cooperation platform and a widely welcomed global public product. Over 100 countries and international organizations actively support and participate, a large number of influential landmark projects have been successfully implemented, China's development strategy has been smoothly aligned with many countries, and the level of infrastructure connectivity has been rapidly improved. From 2014 to 2016, China's total trade with the "Belt and Road" countries exceeded 3 trillion US dollars, and its accumulated investment in these countries exceeded 50 billion US dollars. In May 2017, the "Belt and Road" International Cooperation Summit Forum was attended by more than 1,600 representatives from over 140 countries and 80 international organizations, achieving more than 270 cooperation results in 76 major categories, forming a powerful momentum for the international community to participate in and jointly promote the construction of the "Belt and Road." All parties praised the construction of the "Belt and Road" for providing a Chinese solution for building an open world economy and improving and strengthening global governance. The Second "Belt and Road" International Cooperation Summit Forum was held in 2019, with even more fruitful results.

Building an all-round diplomatic layout with the goal of global partnerships. With his grand vision and strategic thinking as an outstanding politician and strategist, General Secretary Xi Jinping planned and coordinated the overall situation of foreign work and personally visited different types of countries on five continents as well as major international and regional cooperation organizations. He extensively and deeply interacted with leaders, people from all walks of life, and the general public of various countries, telling stories of mutually beneficial cooperation between China and foreign countries and friendly exchanges between peoples and emphasizing the significance of countries and their people working together to create a better future. Since the 18th CPC National Congress, China has focused on its neighbors and major powers, taken developing countries as its foundation, multilateralism as its stage, and deepening pragmatic cooperation, strengthening political mutual trust, consolidating the social foundation, and improving mechanism construction as its channels to develop friendly cooperation with all countries comprehensively. By the end of 2016, China had established different forms of partnerships with 97 countries and international organizations, realizing full coverage of partnerships with major powers, neighboring countries, and developing countries. On November 15, 2020, in the international context of high trade barriers, the global rampage of COVID-19, and the recession of economies worldwide, the Regional Comprehensive Economic Partnership (RCEP) was finally announced after eight years of difficult negotiations. This regional organization was initiated by the ten ASEAN countries (Indonesia, Malaysia, the Philippines, Thailand, Singapore, Brunei, Cambodia, Laos, Myanmar, and Vietnam), inviting China, Japan, South Korea, Australia, New Zealand, and India to participate. It aims to reduce tariff and non-tariff barriers, establish a trade agreement for a unified free market among the sixteen countries, and implement regional economic integration through mutual market openness among member countries. RCEP is currently the world's largest free trade zone, covering nearly 3.5 billion people, with a combined GDP of 23 trillion US dollars, accounting for one-third of the global economy. If RCEP is implemented successfully, the Asia-Pacific region may become the center of world economic development in the future.

Practicing the diplomatic concepts of "amity, sincerity, mutual benefit, and inclusiveness" in neighborhood diplomacy and the principles of "truth, practicality, affinity, and sincerity" in work with Africa. The surrounding areas are where China settles and thrives, and they form the foundation for development and prosperity. In October 2013, the Central Committee held a seminar on neighborhood diplomacy, where General Secretary Xi Jinping emphasized that China should adhere to the principle of amity and partnership with neighboring countries, pursue good neighborliness, stability, and prosperity, and highlight the concepts of "amity, sincerity, mutual benefit, and inclusiveness." China should uphold friendly relations with its neighbors, support each other, emphasize equality and affection, maintain frequent contact and interactions, and do more heartwarming things that people appreciate, making neighboring countries friendlier, closer, more supportive, and more aligned with China, thus enhancing China's affinity, appeal, and influence. During President Xi Jinping's visit to Africa in 2013, he proposed the four-character guideline for working with Africa: "truth, practicality, affinity, and sincerity." These concepts have become the new guiding principles for China's relations with neighboring countries and developing countries in the new era.

Participating in and promoting innovation in global governance. In response to the major practical issues and challenges faced by global governance, General Secretary Xi Jinping put forward a series of new concepts and propositions such as global governance, new security concepts, new development concepts, the right view of justice and interests, and globalization, promoting the establishment of a more just, reasonable, inclusive, and balanced global governance system. Since the 18th CPC National Congress, China has actively participated in and led the reform of the global governance system, presenting a remarkable "trilogy." First, China successfully hosted the APEC Leaders' Meeting in Beijing, initiating the Asia-Pacific Free Trade Area process and determining the relevant roadmap, playing an important leading role in regional cooperation in the Asia-Pacific region. Second, China successfully hosted the G20 Hangzhou Summit, for the first time making innovation a new driving force for global growth recovery, structural reform the main direction for solving world economic problems, developing a prominent position in macro-policy coordination, and forming a global multilateral investment rules framework, effectively promoting the G20's transformation from crisis response to a long-term governance mechanism, achieving a series of groundbreaking, leading, and institutional important results. Third, in early 2017, President Xi Jinping attended the World Economic Forum Annual Meeting and visited the United Nations Headquarters in Geneva, promoting the development of economic globalization in an open, inclusive, universally beneficial, balanced, and win-win direction, declaring China's determination and commitment to building a community of shared future for mankind, and outlining a blueprint and boosting confidence for the development and progress of human society. The international community highly appraised and unanimously praised these efforts, and the Chinese concept gradually became an international consensus. At present, more and more Chinese people are serving as heads of specialized agencies and important international organizations of the United Nations. China's share in the International Monetary Fund has jumped from sixth to third place, and the RMB has been included in the IMF's Special Drawing Rights currency basket. China's international discourse power and influence are significantly improving.

In the new era, China is exploring solutions to hotspots and global issues with Chinese characteristics through diplomacy, striving to make new and greater contributions to the world. General Secretary Xi Jinping emphasizes that China has always been a builder of world peace, committed to seeking peace, safeguarding peace, and sharing peace with all countries. China successfully held commemorative activities for the 70th anniversary of the victory of the Chinese People's War of Resistance against Japanese Aggression and the Second World War, sending a strong message in defense of the achievements of the Second World War and world peace. China is committed to resolving international and regional hotspot issues politically, playing a constructive role in bridging differences and promoting peace talks. China insists on the goal of denuclearization of the Korean Peninsula and resolving the nuclear issue through dialogue and negotiation, proposing the "dual-track" approach and the "double suspension" initiative, making important contributions to easing tensions on the Peninsula, promoting the resumption of contact and dialogue, and maintaining regional peace and stability. In 2018, General Secretary Xi Jinping met with North Korean leader Kim Jong-un twice, laying a solid foundation for the healthy development of China-North Korea relations. China actively participates in the resolution of issues such as Iran's nuclear program, Syria, South Sudan, and Afghanistan, establishing the United Nations Peace and Development Fund, taking the lead in setting up a standing peacekeeping police force and an 8,000-strong peacekeeping standby force, demonstrating China's image as a responsible major power. China also works with countries worldwide to address global challenges such as terrorism, cybersecurity, public health, and refugees, playing an important role in promoting the *Paris Agreement* on climate change and responding to the Ebola epidemic.

In the face of rising trade protectionism, China adheres to the trend of globalization and resolutely abandons zero-sum thinking and divisive thinking. At the Shanghai Cooperation Organization Qingdao Summit, President Xi Jinping pointed out that although unilateralism, trade protectionism, and anti-globalization sentiments continue to manifest, the "global village" world determines that the interests of all countries are increasingly intertwined. Their destinies are shared, and cooperation for mutual benefit is the general trend. This far-sighted diplomatic wisdom has gained increasing recognition from more countries.

China's diplomatic work emphasizes a people-centered approach. Now, about 130 million Chinese people travel abroad each year, millions of Chinese citizens work, live, and study in various places around the world, and more than 30,000 Chinese companies are spread worldwide. In response to new situations and tasks, diplomatic work has been constantly strengthening its consular protection capabilities and actively building overseas people's livelihood projects. In recent years, it has successfully organized nine overseas citizen evacuation operations and handled nearly 300,000 consular assistance cases, including more than 100 major cases of Chinese citizens being kidnapped or attacked abroad. China's Ministry of Foreign Affairs has also launched a new version of the Chinese Consular Service Network, the 12308 hotlines, the "Consular Express" WeChat public account, and other consular information and service platforms, actively providing 24/7, zero-time difference, and barrier-free consular services for overseas compatriots. At present, more than 100 countries and regions have implemented conditional visa-free or visa-on-arrival policies for holders of ordinary Chinese passports, and simplified visa procedures agreements have been signed with China, continuously enhancing the "gold content" of Chinese passports and making it safer and more convenient for compatriots to travel abroad.

Adhering to the Holistic Approach to National Security

National security work is a crucial aspect of ensuring the country's and its people's well-being. Since the 18th CPC National Congress, the Central Committee of CPC has strengthened its centralized and unified leadership over national security work, incorporated the overall national security concept into the basic strategy of adhering to and developing socialism with Chinese characteristics, made a series of major decisions and deployments on national security from a comprehensive and strategic perspective, strengthened the top-level design of national security work, improved national security policies in various important fields, and perfected national security laws and regulations. These efforts have effectively addressed a series of major risks and challenges, maintaining overall national security stability.

On the morning of April 15, 2014, General Secretary Xi Jinping, as Chairman of the Central National Security Commission, presided over the First Meeting of the Central National Security Commission and delivered an important speech. General Secretary Xi Jinping emphasized the need to accurately grasp the new characteristics and trends of changes in the national security situation, adhere to the overall national security concept, and embark on a path of national security with Chinese characteristics. In October 2017, the 19th CPC National Congress confirmed the adherence to the overall national security concept as one of the fourteen basic strategies that must be adhered to in the new era of socialism with Chinese characteristics. General Secretary

Xi Jinping emphasized in his report, "Coordinating development and security, enhancing a sense of crisis, and being prepared for dangers in times of peace are major principles of our Party's governance. We must uphold national interests as paramount, take people's security as our purpose, political security as fundamental, and coordinate external and internal security, territorial security and national security, traditional and non-traditional security, our own security, and common security. We must improve the national security system, strengthen national security capacity building, and resolutely safeguard national sovereignty, security, and development interests." In April 2018, at the First Meeting of the 19th Central National Security Commission, General Secretary Xi Jinping emphasized the need to fully implement the overall national security concept and create a new situation for national security work in the new era.

As a socialist country, in the new era of socialism with Chinese characteristics, the connotation and extension of national security are richer than at any time in history, the spatial and temporal domains are broader than at any time in history, and the internal and external factors are more complex than at any time in history. The task of maintaining national security and social stability is extremely arduous. Based on an accurate understanding of the new characteristics and trends of changes in the national security situation, the Central Committee of CPC, with Comrade Xi Jinping at its core, has innovated the concept of national security, taken an overall view of national security, and creatively put forward the overall national security concept. The overall national security concept emphasizes the systematic thinking and methods of national security work, highlights the concept of "comprehensive security," and covers a wide range of fields, including politics, military, territory, economy, culture, society, science and technology, cyberspace, ecology, resources, nuclear, overseas interests, space, deep sea, polar regions, and biology, and will continue to expand with social development. The overall national security concept has elevated the Party's understanding of national security to a new level and realm, providing basic guidance for solving the difficult problems facing national security and promoting national security work in the new era.

On December 11, 2020, the 19th Political Bureau of the Central Committee held its 26th Collective Study Session, focusing on effectively carrying out national security work. In his speech, General Secretary Xi Jinping put forward ten requirements for implementing the overall national security concept, including adhering to the Party's absolute leadership in national security work and adhering to the centralized and unified leadership of the Party Central Committee in national security work. This is, in fact, a new summary of the overall national security concept.

To ensure security, one must be prepared for dangers. General Secretary Xi Jinping pointed out, "The sense of crisis for us Communists is a concern for the Party, the country, and the people. This is not only a responsibility but also a commitment." "The road ahead will not always be smooth. The brighter the prospects, the more we need to enhance our sense of crisis, be prepared for dangers in times of peace, and fully understand and effectively respond to major risks and challenges." We must prioritize risk prevention and resolve various contradictions and problems, striving to prevent major risks or to withstand and overcome them when they do arise. Preventing and resolving major risks is the political responsibility of Party committees, governments, and leading cadres at all levels. We must be courageous in taking responsibility and daring to struggle and do a solid, detailed, and good job of preventing and resolving major risks. We must not let minor risks evolve into major risks, individual risks into comprehensive risks, local risks into regional or systemic risks, economic risks into social and political risks, or international risks into domestic risks.

CHAPTER 25

Strengthening Overall Party's Leadership and Strict Self-Governance in Every Respect

The CPC is the core of leadership in the Chinese socialist cause. Without the leadership of the Party, it would be impossible to achieve the unity of the "six domains and nine regions." Every majestic mountain must have a main peak, and a great country's advancement relies on its leader's guidance. Entering the new era, the CPC has affirmed General Secretary Xi Jinping's core position in the Party Central Committee and the entire Party. Under the strong leadership of the Central Committee of CPC, the Party's comprehensive leadership has been significantly strengthened, and the in-depth implementation of strict governance has advanced. The Party's self-revolution continues to deepen, and the new great project of Party building has entered a new stage.

Upholding and Strengthening Overall Party Leadership

The leadership of the CPC is the most essential characteristic of socialism with Chinese characteristics and the greatest advantage of the socialist system with Chinese characteristics. General Secretary Xi Jinping has repeatedly emphasized that the Party exercises overall leadership over all areas of endeavor in every part of the country; upholding the Party's leadership means, first and foremost, the whole Party obeys the Central Committee and upholds its authority and centralized, unified leadership. In the grand chessboard of the national governance system, the Central Committee of CPC is the "marshal" who sits in the central military camp, with each piece playing its part and the overall situation clear. The entire Party must enhance the "Four Consciousnesses," strengthen the "Four Matters of Confidence," and achieve the "Two Upholds."

Since the 18th CPC National Congress, General Secretary Xi Jinping has proposed that upholding and strengthening overall Party leadership is an urgent need to consolidate the Party's governing position and promote the development of its cause. This is because, compared with the development and changes in domestic and international situations and the historical tasks undertaken by the Party, there is still a significant gap in the Party's leadership and governance levels. In particular, under the new situation, strengthening and improving the Party's construction faces the "Four Tests" and "Four Dangers," and the task of implementing the Party's self-governance and strict governance is more arduous and urgent than ever before. At the same time, many localities and units have experienced a weakening and hollowing out of the Party's leadership for a period of time.

The Party's leadership conforms to the legal and rule of law principles. The *Constitution of the People's Republic of China* grants the Party's leadership position and provides legal support for the Party's leadership as it keeps pace with the times. On the afternoon of March 11, 2018, the First Session of the 13th National People's Congress passed the *Amendment to the Constitution of the People's Republic of China* at its third plenary session. The statement "Leadership by the Communist Party of China is the defining feature of socialism with Chinese characteristics" was written into the nation's fundamental law, providing constitutional guarantees for upholding the Party's leadership position and better playing the role of the Party's leadership.

Under the strong leadership of the Central Committee of CPC, and in terms of organization, systems, and mechanisms, new steps have been taken to uphold and strengthen the Party's comprehensive leadership. The four central leading teams for "comprehensively deepening reform," cybersecurity and informatization, finance and economics, and foreign affairs have been "upgraded" to committees. The Commission for Law-Based Governance under the CPC has been established, and some party and government institutions have been integrated and restructured to ensure the

Party's overall control and coordination of all aspects of the system and mechanism. The Central Committee of CPC has successively issued a series of major decisions on deepening reform, expanding opening-up, poverty alleviation, and environmental protection, further highlighting its role in setting direction, planning the overall situation, formulating policies, and promoting reform. The National Commission of Supervision of the People's Republic of China has been formally established, and for the first time since the founding of New China, the supervision of public power has been incorporated into the political system, comprehensively strengthening the Party's centralized and unified leadership in anti-corruption work.

In the deepening reforms of the Party and state institutions initiated at the third plenary session of the 19th CPC Central Committee, the important principle of strengthening the comprehensive leadership of the Party was adhered to. At the third plenary session of the 19th CPC Central Commission for Discipline Inspection, General Secretary Xi Jinping summarized the valuable experience of adhering to Party leadership and strictly governing the Party since the reform and opening-up. The first point is, "We must resolutely uphold the authority of the Party Central Committee and its centralized and unified leadership to ensure unity in the Party's steps and actions." When discussing the insights and experiences formed by the disciplinary and supervisory work since the reform and opening-up, the "Communique" took "Always uphold the fundamental principle of strengthening the comprehensive leadership of the Party, resolutely uphold the authority of the Party Central Committee and its centralized and unified leadership, and ensure the implementation of the Party's line, principles, policies, and the Party Central Committee's major decision-making deployments" as the first point.

The fourth plenary session of the 19th CPC Central Committee held in October 2019 not only highlighted the Party's centralized and unified leadership as a prominent advantage of China's system but also specifically made arrangements to adhere to and improve the Party's leadership system, enhance the Party's scientific governance, democratic governance, and governance according to the law. This arrangement includes six systems: establishing a system never to forget the original intention and keep the mission in mind; improving various systems to firmly uphold the authority and centralized unified leadership of the Party Central Committee; perfecting the Party's comprehensive leadership system; perfecting various systems for governing for the people and relying on the people; improving the Party's governance capacity and leadership level system; perfecting the system of comprehensive and strict governance of the Party. The main purpose of establishing and improving these systems is to ensure that the Party leads everything and implements the Party's leadership in all aspects, fields, and links of national governance.

In just a few years, from ideological concepts to institutional mechanisms, from various fields to various aspects, the Party's leadership has been comprehensively strengthened, and the phenomenon of the weakening and virtualization of the Party's leadership has been fundamentally reversed. The CPC is the "stabilizing force" in the development of the Party and the nation's undertakings. Under the strong leadership of the Party, the cause of socialism with Chinese characteristics has made continuous progress.

The Party's Political Building Is of Fundamental Importance to the Party

As a large Party with more than 90 million Party members and as the governing Party of a large country with 9.6 million square kilometers of land area and a population of 1.4 billion, it is impossible not to talk about politics. But how do we talk about politics? The Central Committee of CPC, with Comrade Xi Jinping as the core, not only sets an example in talking about politics but also emphasizes taking the Party's political construction as the guide and putting the Party's political construction in the first place of the Party's construction at the 19th CPC National Congress.

On October 23, 2014, General Secretary Xi Jinping deeply discussed the importance of highlighting politics in his speech at the second plenary meeting of the fourth plenary session of the 18th CPC Central Committee. He said, "Without a strong political guarantee, the unity of the Party is just an empty phrase. Our country has experienced a period of political leadership and 'class struggle as the main focus,' which was wrong. However, we cannot say we should not talk about politics or less about politics. Is the Communist Party still called the Communist Party if it does not talk about politics? 'If the rules are abolished, what will not happen?' I want to clarify that the political discipline and rules cannot be loosened here. Corruption is a corruption issue, and politics is a political issue. We cannot just talk about corruption and not talk about political issues. When officials have political problems, the harm to the Party is no less than corruption. In some cases, it is even more serious than corruption. No one can cross the red line on political issues; if they do, they must be held accountable for their political responsibility.

Some things are absolutely forbidden in politics, and if done, there will be a price to pay. No one can treat political discipline and political rules as a joke." The ambitious and conspiratorial figures investigated and dealt with by the Central Committee since the 18th CPC National Congress are actually typical examples of not talking about politics. Their political problems were the first to emerge, and they failed to maintain their political bottom line.

The primary task of political construction is to resolutely uphold the core position of General Secretary Xi Jinping in the Party Central Committee and the entire Party and to firmly uphold the authority and centralized and unified leadership of the Party Central Committee. Achieving the "Two Upholds" is not abstract but specific, and we must not practice duplicity or go our own ways, and we must not engage in "high-level black" or "low-level red" tactics. Upholding the core refers to upholding General Secretary Xi Jinping as the core, not anyone else. Upholding and supporting the core is key to implementing it into practical actions, implementing the Central Committee's decisions well, and resolving the issues that the people are concerned about.

To further strengthen the Party's political construction, in February 2019, the Central Committee of CPC issued the "Opinions on Strengthening the Party's Political Construction," which deployed the strengthening of the Party's political construction in the new era. First, it aims to strengthen political beliefs. Focusing on consolidating the ideological foundation of the Party's political construction, the "Opinions" emphasize arming the mind with the Party's scientific theory, with the most important task being to arm the whole Party and educate the people with Xi Jinping Thought on Socialism with Chinese Characteristics for a New Era, firmly establish the lofty ideals of communism and the shared ideals of socialism with Chinese characteristics, strengthen the "Four Matters of Confidence," firmly implement the Party's political line, resolutely stand firm in political positions, remember the initial mission, and gather the majestic force to build the Chinese dream together with one heart.

Second, it aims to strengthen political leadership. The "Opinions" grasped the fundamental requirement of the Party's political leadership and put forward clear requirements for adhering to and strengthening the Party's comprehensive leadership, especially in resolutely achieving the "Two Upholds," perfecting the Party's leadership system, and improving the Party's leadership methods.

Third, it aims to improve political capabilities. The "Opinions" focus on improving organizations' political capabilities at all levels, Party members, and cadres, and put requirements for different subjects forward. It emphasizes further enhancing the political functions of Party organizations, highlighting the political attributes of state organs, playing the political role of mass organizations, strengthening the political guidance of state-owned enterprises and institutions, and continuously improving the political capabilities of Party members and cadres, especially leading cadres.

Fourth, it aims to purify the political ecology. The "Opinions" propose to create a clean and upright political ecology as a basic and regular task, focusing on enhancing the political, contemporary, principled, and combative nature of the Party's internal political life, strictly enforcing the Party's political discipline and political rules, developing a positive and healthy Party's internal political culture, highlighting political standards in selecting and employing personnel, maintaining the clean and honest political nature of Communists, and promoting a vibrant and politically clear atmosphere.

Improving political capabilities is essential to strengthening the Party's political construction. The Central Committee of CPC has made arrangements and plans for strengthening political capability construction in the Party's political construction. General Secretary Xi Jinping has also discussed the importance of improving political capabilities on many occasions. On October 10, 2020, General Secretary Xi Jinping pointed out in his first lecture for the training class of middle-aged and young cadres at the Party School of the Central Committee of CPC (National Academy of Governance), "Among the various capabilities required for cadres to perform well in their work, political capability comes first." With solid political capabilities, one can consciously maintain a high degree of consistency with the Party Central Committee in thought, politics, and action and remain calm in any situation.

To improve political capabilities, we must first grasp the correct political direction and adhere to the leadership of the CPC and our country's socialist system. There can be no confusion or wavering on this issue! The fight against the COVID-19 pandemic has once again proven that the CPC is the most reliable backbone for the Chinese people in times of crisis, and our socialist system is the most powerful institutional guarantee to withstand risks and challenges. Young cadres must always stand firm in doing everything that benefits the adherence to the Party's leadership and our country's socialist system and resolutely not engage in anything that undermines them! We should constantly improve our political acumen and discernment, focus on political factors when analyzing the situation, and especially be able to see the essence through the phenomenon with sharp eyes, early detection, and swift action. We must hold the Party's political discipline and political rules in awe to improve political capabilities. We should consciously strengthen political training, enhance political self-discipline, and always be politically "clear-headed" and "honest." It is essential to focus on improving the level of Marxist theoretical understanding, deepen comprehension, integrate and apply the knowledge, master dialectical and historical materialism, grasp the Marxist standpoint, viewpoint, and methodology throughout, and master sinicized Marxism, becoming a firm believer and loyal practitioner of Marxism. If we adhere to the above aspects, our political capabilities will naturally improve.

Strengthening the Construction of Ideology, Organization, and Work Style

To forge iron, one must be strong. The Party must manage and govern itself well. General Secretary Xi Jinping has explicitly proposed and resolutely promoted the comprehensive strict governance of the Party. A strong focus on the Party's workstyle construction has become an entry point for the comprehensive strict governance of the Party.

On December 4, 2012, the Political Bureau of the Central Committee of CPC reviewed and approved the "Eight Regulations of the 18th Political Bureau of the Central Committee of CPC on Improving Work and Maintaining Close Ties with the People." The "Eight Regulations" are simple and easy to remember, convenient to implement, and have produced significant effects in the short term, profoundly changing the Party's internal political ecology and strengthening the Party's work style construction.

In order to further strengthen work style construction, in April 2013, the Central Committee of CPC decided to carry out the Party's mass line education and practice activities in batches from top to bottom throughout the Party. The main content of this activity was to serve the people, be pragmatic, and maintain integrity, resolutely oppose formalism, bureaucracy, hedonism, and extravagance. The overall requirements were to "look in the mirror, dress properly, take a bath, and cure the illness." The main tasks were to educate and guide Party members and cadres to establish a mass perspective, promote good work styles, solve prominent problems, maintain integrity, and further enhance the thinking, work style, and Party-mass and cadre-mass relationships of Party members and cadres, and further establish a good image of the Party. In March 2014, General Secretary Xi Jinping pointed out, "Leaders at all levels should establish and promote good work styles, being strict in self-cultivation, strict in the use of power, and strict in self-discipline, as well as being practical in planning, entrepreneurship, and personal conduct." In April 2015, the Central Committee of CPC issued the "Plan for Carrying out 'Three Stricts and Three Earnests' Thematic Education among County and Division-Level Principal Leading Cadres." The one-year "Three Stricts and Three Earnests" thematic education has sublimated the thinking, work style, and Party spirit of the majority of county and division-level leading cadres and continuously improved the political ecology within the Party.

In February 2016, the Central Committee of CPC decided to carry out the "Two Studies, One Action" learning and education among all Party members, insisting on using the Party constitution and Party regulations to regulate the words and deeds of Party members and cadres, arming the whole Party with the spirit of Xi Jinping's series of important speeches, and guiding all Party members to be qualified Party members. The "Two Studies, One Action" learning and education is an important measure to promote the expansion of Party education from the "key minority" to the majority of Party members and from centralized education to regular education. In March 2017, the Central Committee of CPC decided to promote the normalization and institutionalization of the "Two Studies, One Action" learning and education. In 2019, the "Staying True to Our Founding Mission" thematic education was carried out throughout the Party in accordance with the deployment of the 19th National Congress, deeply educating the entire Party once again.

The work style construction is unremitting. In 2017, the First Meeting of the 19th CPC Central Committee Political Bureau reviewed and approved the "Implementation Rules of the Central Committee of CPC Political Bureau for Implementing the Central Eight Regulations." The Central Committee of CPC, with Comrade Xi Jinping at its core, has set an example from the top down, persistently implementing the spirit of the Central Eight Regulations, resolutely rectifying the "four winds," establishing a "new trend," persisting in opposing formalism and bureaucracy, and continuously polishing the "golden business card" of work style construction.

The Party must manage the Party, starting with the Party's internal political life, and strictly governing the Party must begin with the strictness of the Party's internal political life. In October 2016, the sixth plenary session of the 18th CPC Central Committee deliberated and adopted the "Several Guidelines on Party's Internal Political Life under the New Situation" and the "Regulations on Inner-Party Supervision of the Communist Party of China," providing basic guidance and institutional guarantees for strengthening and standardizing Party's internal political life and purifying the political ecology in the new era. The plenary session emphasized that the focus of strengthening and standardizing the Party's internal political life is on leadership organs and leading cadres at all levels, especially the members of the Central Committee, the Political Bureau, and the Standing Committee of the Political Bureau. Since then, Party organizations at all levels have strictly adhered to the Party's organizational life system, persisted in and improved the Party's internal political life, effectively carried out criticism and self-criticism, effectively solved the problems of irregular, insincere, and unserious party organization life, strengthened and standardized the Party's internal political life, and purified the Party's internal political ecology.

To strictly enforce political discipline and rules, we must insist on putting discipline and rules first. In January 2013, the second plenary session of the 18th CPC Central Commission for Discipline Inspection proposed to enforce the Party's political discipline strictly. General Secretary Xi Jinping pointed out that the primary task of strictly enforcing the Party's discipline is enforcing political discipline. The Party's discipline is multifaceted, but political discipline is the most important, fundamental, and critical discipline, and adherence to the Party's political discipline is an important foundation for adherence to all the Party's disciplines. In January 2014, the third plenary session of the 18th CPC Central Commission for Discipline Inspection proposed strengthening the Party's organizational discipline requirements. In January 2015, the fifth plenary session of the 18th CPC Central Commission for Discipline Inspection emphasized the importance of adhering to discipline and rules. In January 2016, the sixth plenary session of the 18th CPC Central Commission for Discipline Inspection emphasized that discipline is stricter than the law and precedes the law. To strengthen discipline construction, in December 2013, the Central Committee issued the "Regulations on Disciplinary Actions of the Communist Party of China"; in October 2015, it was revised, defining six types of disciplinary violations, such as political discipline, organizational discipline, honesty and discipline, mass discipline, work discipline, and life discipline, drawing a bottom line that party organizations and members cannot touch. The 19th CPC National Congress included discipline construction in the Party's construction layout. In August 2018, the newly revised disciplinary action regulations were announced, incorporating the valuable experience of the Party's construction, especially discipline construction, since the 18th CPC National Congress, emphasizing the "Two Upholds" and the intensity of the Party's discipline construction has been continuously increased. At the same time, the Party's system construction has also achieved remarkable achievements, and the system "cage" is becoming increasingly tight.

Cultivate a high-quality cadre team that is loyal, clean, and responsible. In June 2013, General Secretary Xi Jinping proposed at the National Organizational Work Conference that the standard for good cadres in the new era is "firm in belief, serving the people, diligent in government affairs, daring to take responsibility, and honest and clean." In October 2014, General Secretary Xi Jinping instructed in his work for Yunnan, requiring Party members and cadres to be "loyal to the Party, personally clean, and daring to take responsibility." In January 2015, he proposed the "four haves" requirement for county Party secretaries, which essentially requires all Party cadres to have the Party in mind, the people in mind, responsibility in mind, and caution in mind.

In terms of organizational construction, it is important to strengthen the leadership and gatekeeping role of Party organizations in cadre selection and appointment and prevent the promotion of those with problems. We must seriously rectify unhealthy practices and corruption in personnel employment and severely investigate and deal with issues such as running for office buying and selling official positions. Implement the reporting system and spot-check verification system for personal matters related to leading cadres. Establish a lifelong accountability system and a retrospective responsibility mechanism for major decision-making, and vigorously rectify issues such as "do-nothing officials," "mediocre officials," and "lazy governance." Explore establishing a fault-tolerance and correction mechanism, being tolerant of cadres' mistakes in their work, especially in reform and innovation.

In July 2018, the National Organization Work Conference was held in Beijing. General Secretary Xi Jinping proposed at the conference that the Party's organizational line in the new era is to fully implement socialism with Chinese characteristics thought in the new era, focus on the construction of the organizational system, strive to cultivate high-quality cadres who are loyal, clean, and responsible, strive to gather outstanding talents from various fields who are dedicated to the country, adhere to the principle of virtue and talent, prioritize virtue, and appoint people based on their merits, providing strong organizational guarantees for upholding and strengthening the Party's overall leadership and adhering to and developing socialism with Chinese characteristics. This is the first time that the Party's organizational line in the new era has been clearly summarized. The Central Committee of CPC also issued a series of documents such as the "Opinions on Further Encouraging the New Roles and Responsibilities of the

Majority of Cadres in the New Era" and the "Opinions on Vigorously Discovering, Cultivating, and Selecting Outstanding Young Cadres to Meet the Requirements of the New Era," making systematic plans and comprehensive deployments for the construction of the Party's cadre team at the institutional level.

Strengthening Party supervision in an all-around way and giving full play to the role of inspections as a sharp weapon. First, promote the establishment of a Party supervision system that includes central unified leadership, comprehensive supervision by Party committees (Party groups), specialized supervision by discipline inspection organs, functional supervision by Party work departments, daily supervision by grassroots Party organizations, and democratic supervision by Party members. Second, put into practice the "four forms" of supervision and discipline enforcement, such as regular criticism and self-criticism, and talks and inquiries, making "blushing faces and sweating" the norm; light disciplinary actions and organizational adjustments account for the majority of disciplinary actions; severe disciplinary actions and significant job adjustments are in the minority; and a very small number of cases involve serious disciplinary violations that are suspected of breaking the law and are subject to case investigation and review. Third, clarify that inspection is political inspection rather than business inspection, and give full play to the role of inspection as a sharp weapon. Fourth, achieve full coverage of stationed supervision, comprehensively dispatch discipline inspection teams to central-level Party and state organs, and give full play to the authority of "dispatch" and the advantages of "stationing."

The Central Committee of CPC regards inspection as a strategic institutional arrangement for intra-party supervision, establishes inspection work guidelines, detects problems, forms a deterrent effect, and addresses both the root causes and symptoms of issues. It innovates organizational systems and methods and, for the first time, achieves full coverage of inspections within a single term. The 18th CPC Central Committee conducted 12 rounds of inspections, covering 277 local organizations and units, conducting "look-backs" in 16 provinces and autonomous regions, and carrying out "mobile" inspections in four divisions. The inspections achieved full coverage of provinces, autonomous regions, cities, Xinjiang Production and Construction Corps, central and state organs, major state-owned enterprises, central financial units, and centrally managed universities, fully playing the role of political "microscopes" and political "searchlights." After the 19th CPC National Congress, the intensity of inspections has not diminished, and the strength is increasing. The Central Committee of CPC promulgated the "Central Inspection Work Plan (2018–2022)," determining the roadmap and task book for the 19th Central Inspection Work and continuously highlighting the essential attributes of political inspections. After the 19th CPC National Congress, inspections as a strategic institutional arrangement for intra-party supervision have been deepened, emphasizing the resolute maintenance of General Secretary Xi Jinping's core position in the Party Central Committee and the entire Party and resolutely safeguarding the authority and centralized and unified leadership of the Party Central Committee as the fundamental political task of inspection.

In the process of strictly governing the Party, the Party's ideological construction has also been further strengthened. Organizing the "Staying True to Our Founding Mission" thematic education campaign has made the entire Party's ideals and beliefs firmer. The study of Xi Jinping Thought on Socialism with Chinese Characteristics for a New Era has continuously reached new heights, with the *Outline for Learning Xi Jinping Thought on Socialism with Chinese Characteristics for a New Era* compiled by the Central Publicity Department distributed over 70 million copies. The Party School of the Central Committee of CPC (National School of Administration) meticulously launched the *Basic Questions of Xi Jinping Thought on Socialism with Chinese Characteristics for a New Era*, which received a positive response.

In 2021, the CPC celebrated its centennial anniversary. The Central Committee of CPC decided to carry out Party history learning and education throughout the Party. By summarizing experiences from the 100-year journey and comprehending the founding mission, the entire Party can further strengthen its ideals and beliefs and gain a deeper understanding of innovative theories.

Zero Tolerance for Corruption

The courage to carry out self-revolution is a distinct characteristic of the Party and also the secret to the success of the CPC, from its small beginnings to its growth and strength. The Party must maintain its political character as Communists through continuous self-purification, self-improvement, and self-innovation. General Secretary Xi Jinping repeatedly reminds the entire Party to always maintain a revolutionary spirit and fighting spirit and to rejuvenate the spirit of never slackening and the indomitable struggle in the face of turbulent practices.

The severe punishment of corruption within the Party since the 18th National Congress vividly manifests the Party's self-revolution. With the fearless courage of "offending thousands of people but not failing 1.3 billion," General Secretary Xi Jinping has cracked down on corruption with an iron fist, greatly boosting the Party's and the people's confidence.

On December 6, 2012, the CPC Central Commission for Discipline Inspection announced that Li Chuncheng, former Deputy Secretary of the Sichuan Provincial Party Committee, was under investigation for serious disciplinary violations, marking the beginning of major corruption cases since the 18th National Congress. The Central Committee of CPC, with Comrade Xi Jinping at its core, has insisted on zero tolerance, full coverage, and no forbidden zones in the fight against corruption, resolutely "taking out tigers" and "swatting flies," and carrying out "hunting foxes" and "sky net" actions, deepening the anti-corruption struggle.

Taking out "tigers" without mercy. Between the 18th and 19th National Congresses, the Central Committee of CPC severely investigated and dealt with Zhou Yongkang, Bo Xilai, Guo Boxiong, Xu Caihou, Sun Zhengcai, and Ling Jihua. This shows no "iron-capped kings" in the CPC and no so-called ironclad guarantees. In the process of investigating major cases, the CPC Central Commission for Discipline Inspection strictly grasped policies and emphasized key points, severely investigating Party members who did not converge or stop after the 18th National Congress, those with concentrated reflections of problems and strong public reactions, and those in important positions who might still be promoted and used. By October 2017, 440 provincial and military-level Party members and other centrally managed cadres had been approved for investigation by the CPC Central Committee. Among them were 43 members and alternate members of the 18th Central Committee and nine members of the Central Commission for Discipline Inspection. After the 19th National Congress, the intensity of anti-corruption efforts did not diminish, and some major cases were investigated and prosecuted.

Cracking down on both "tigers" and "flies," the CPC Central Commission for Discipline Inspection insists on highlighting the focus of its investigations and intensifying punishments for "petty officials with large corruption." The Central Commission for Discipline Inspection seriously investigates and punishes embezzlement, private misappropriation, and fraudulent claiming of poverty relief funds and handles corruption issues that occur close to the public, such as "plucking a feather when a goose flies over," accepting bribes, seizure and plundering, favoritism and nepotism, in fields like "three-capital management" (state-owned capital, state-owned assets, and state-owned resources), benefits for the people, land acquisition, and so on. According to statistics, from December 2012 to June 2017, a total of 1.343 million Party officials at the township level and below were punished nationwide, including 648,000 rural Party officials. After the 19th CPC National Congress, the governance of petty corruption has been continuously carried out.

Carrying out the pursuit of fleeing and recovering stolen assets. Treating the pursuit of fugitives and the recovery of stolen assets as an important part of curbing the spread of corruption is included in the overall deployment of anti-corruption work. On June 27, 2014, the CPC Central Committee decided to establish the Office for International Pursuit of Fugitives and Recovery of Stolen Assets of the Central Anti-Corruption Coordination Group. The central and provincial anti-corruption coordination groups have set up a centralized and unified coordination mechanism, strengthened basic work, established databases for fugitives, formulated accountability systems, and implemented the responsibility of the Party organizations where the fugitives are located for pursuing the fugitives. On March 26, 2015, the Office for International Pursuit of Fugitives and Recovery of Stolen Assets of the Central Anti-Corruption Coordination Group launched the "Sky Net" operation targeting corrupt fugitives for the first time. On April 22, the Chinese National Central Bureau of the International Criminal Police Organization (Interpol) collectively announced the red notices for 100 people, including suspects who had fled the country, state employees, and those involved in major corruption cases. According to the information on the website of the Central Commission for Discipline Inspection and the State Supervision Commission on September 12, 2019, 60 of the 100 red notice persons announced on April 22, 2015, have been brought to justice. In addition, international anti-corruption law enforcement cooperation has been deepened, forming a powerful deterrent against fugitives.

Consolidating the overwhelming victory in the fight against corruption. At the third meeting of the 19th CPC Central Commission for Discipline Inspection held in January 2019, the CPC Central Committee believed that an overwhelming victory had been achieved in the fight against corruption and that the overwhelming victory must be consolidated and developed. The anti-corruption struggle is more focused on addressing both the symptoms and root causes, emphasizing systematization and precision in combating corruption, and insisting on the important strategy of strictly governing the Party with a focus on ensuring that officials do not dare to be corrupt, cannot be corrupt, and do not want to be corrupt. The Central Commission for Discipline Inspection meeting held in January 2021 once again emphasized that the fight against corruption cannot be relaxed and must be carried through to the end.

Epilogue

The Communist Party of China (CPC) has been established for a hundred years and is becoming more and more vibrant. Having been in power for more than seventy years, its governing position is becoming increasingly stable. Over the past century, the CPC has greatly changed China and influenced the world. Few political parties in the world can compare with the achievements of the CPC. Why has the CPC been so successful? The best way to understand this question is to comprehend the history of the CPC.

This book divides the hundred-year history of the CPC into four sections: New Democratic Revolution, Socialist Construction Period, Reform and Opening-Up and Socialist Modernization, and New Era of Socialism with Chinese Characteristics, detailing the efforts and achievements of the CPC in realizing the Chinese Dream of the great rejuvenation of the Chinese nation at different stages.

The contributors to this book are comrades from the Party School of the Central Committee of CPC (National Academy School of Governance), who are teachers and researchers of the history of the CPC. The New Democratic Revolution section was written by Lu Yi, Liu Baodong, and Qi Xiaolin; the Socialist Revolution and Construction section was written by Li Qinggang; the Reform and Opening-up and Socialist Modernization section and the New Era of Socialism with Chinese Characteristics section were written by Shen Chuanliang; Xie Chuntao completed the final draft. We would like to express our gratitude to renowned publishers Yang Yuqian, Wang Xiaodong, Zhu Zuolin, and Zhao Hongshi for their significant contributions to the writing and publication of this book.

XIE CHUNTAO

February 2021

About the Editor

Mr. Xie Chuntao, born in 1963 in Linshu, joined the Communist Party of China in July 1988. He graduated from Renmin University of China with a postgraduate degree and holds a doctorate in law. Currently a professor, Xie is a member of the 20th Central Committee, serves as the Deputy Director of the Party School of the Central Committee of CPC (National Academy School of Governance), and is President of the Modern History Society of China.

As editor-in-chief, Xie has published numerous works, including *History of Socialism with Chinese Characteristics, Why Can the Communist Party of China? How Does the Communist Party of China Govern the Country? How Does the Communist Party of China Respond to Challenges? How Does the Communist Party of China Fight Corruption?*, and *How Does the Communist Party of China Govern the Party?* He has been recognized as a National Advanced Worker by the State Council and is included in the "Four Batches" of talents in national publicity and ideological work, as well as the first batch of leading talents in philosophy and social sciences in the National "Ten Thousand People Plan."